Managing Information Services

Managing Information Services

A Sustainable Approach

JO BRYSON

ASHGATE

Published by
Ashgate Publishing Limited
Wey Court East
Union Road
Farnham
Surrey, GU9 7PT
England

Ashgate Publishing Company
Suite 420
101 Cherry Street
Burlington
VT 05401-4405
USA

www.ashgate.com

British Library Cataloguing in Publication Data
Bryson, Jo, 1950-
    Managing information services : a sustainable approach. --
    3rd ed.
    1. Information services--Management.
    I. Title
    025.5'2'068-dc22

Library of Congress Cataloging-in-Publication Data
Bryson, Jo, 1950-
    Managing information services : a sustainable approach / by Jo Bryson. -- Third edition.
        pages cm
    Includes bibliographical references and index.
    ISBN 978-1-4094-0694-5 (hardback) -- ISBN 978-1-4094-0696-9 (paperback) 1. Information resources management--Handbooks, manuals, etc. 2. Corporate libraries--Administration--Handbooks, manuals, etc. 3. Information services--Management--Handbooks, manuals, etc.
    I. Title.

    T58.64.B795 2011
    658.4'038011--dc22

                                                            2010049356

ISBN 978 1 4094 0694 5 (hbk)
ISBN 978 1 4094 0696 9 (pbk)
ISBN 978 1 4094 0695 2 (ebk)

Printed and bound in Great Britain by the
MPG Books Group, UK

Contents

List of Figures

List of Tables

List of Boxes

Preface

There are three kinds of organizations: those who make things happen, those who watch things happen, and those who wonder what's happened.

Anonymous

This opening quotation is equally and even probably more applicable to those individuals who are today's leaders and those who aspire to be in the future than to organizations. It paraphrases the very essence of management and leadership; that is, to position and make things happen in an unpredictable, challenging and changing world. My desire in writing this book is to capture the essence of leadership that makes things happen and infuse these into a management textbook/handbook for people who wish to be the future leaders of information services. These future leaders and their associates may already work in small to medium sized organizations, or be embarking on their first or subsequent career as a student in information services, librarianship, records management and information and communications technology (ICT). The book therefore has a dual purpose: as a management handbook as well as a management textbook.

Organizations, leaders, project managers and individuals take a journey of life, along the path of which they encounter challenges and opportunities that arise from within or through external forces. *Managing Information Services: A Sustainable Approach* has been written to equip them for this journey in an age of uncertainty. A continued theme throughout the book is the need to shift mindsets and strategically position and transform information services so that they are on the pathway to a sustainable and promising future. Continuing with this analogy, organizations and individuals have to map out their future direction and be ready to take up the challenges and potential openings, to adopt new mindsets and create new directions and successfully manage dilemmas and obstacles as tomorrow's opportunities, as well as make the right decisions as to which path to take in rapidly changing business and societal environments. The underlying philosophy is that anything is possible and, if looked for, solutions can be found for even the most exceptional and extraordinary circumstances.

The book is a further edition in the series of *Managing Information Services* by the same author. When I was first approached by my managing editor at Ashgate to write a third edition (which because of a change in title is the fourth book on the topic of managing information services) we discussed how much change was needed from the previous edition. A subsequent visit to several universities in the United Kingdom where the book is set as a text or required reading provided a new perspective. Whilst the pragmatic and passionate approach to *Managing Information Services* has been retained, the book has been substantially revised and rewritten and there is now greater emphasis on the 'why'. This change in emphasis and perspective is immediately evident in the new framework and structure of the book, as well as the different emphasis in chapters, particularly in Part II, *Strategy and Planning*. It also flows through to the focus and content.

Common themes that centre on leadership occur throughout the book and include:

- Instilling a passion for what can be possible in the future through dynamic leadership and innovation that involves vision, personal energy and commitment;
- Encouraging others to succeed beyond their dreams by creating an inspiring environment, sharing enthusiasm and generating the desire to excel;
- Turning challenging environments into opportunities; especially where the information service has been energized from within;
- Rethinking information services in a virtual age so that they are sustainable yet dynamic;
- Instilling flexibility to withstand strategic shocks and cope with unpredictable and changing circumstances;
- Adopting a customer- or citizen-centric approach and using technology to enable self-services that reduce costs and deliver 24x365;
- Integrating services to provide a rich service delivery experience;
- Using vitality, quality and innovation as tools that can be used to enable products and service offerings to exceed customer expectations; and
- Engaging in change and unlocking ideas in order to create the next advantage ahead of others.

This edition continues the theme of integrating the disciplines of librarianship, records management and archives, information systems, computing and telecommunications to promote an integrated approach, as well as the scenario in which institutions such as art galleries and museums that have similar cultural and social capital business drivers to libraries join forces to give a rich integrated customer experience. Rethinking service delivery away from their traditional siloed institutional, professional and media focus towards an integrated multimedia approach can also place services on a more sustainable footing as well as delivering a richer and more efficient citizen centric experience.

Managing Information Services: A Sustainable Approach adopts the reality that information services exist in a market space, rather than the traditional market place. This is a global, connected and always on environment where integrated multi-channel service delivery is required to meet different customer and workplace generational needs and expectations. It is also an unpredictable world where seeking competitive advantage and managing change is not good enough. Successful organizations need continually to invent the next advantage and make themselves financially, environmentally and physically sustainable, using bright ideas, information, knowledge, creativity and innovation to do so. They must also build individual and organizational capability to create, engage and sustain change and protect their corporate reputation in the global media environment.

Ensuring success and sustainability in this environment requires concentration on five critical success factors:

- Understanding the changing environment;
- Strategy and planning;
- Leadership and innovation;
- Governance and social responsibility; and
- Customer and market focus.

The concept of the parent organization is used throughout the book. This refers to the corporate environment in which the information service operates. It may be the local government authority, government department, private sector organization, research centre or academic institution. It is an important concept as the environment of the parent organization often shapes the environment of the information service. Within this environment, the information services manager plays a role in transforming the information service as well as contributing to and working with executive management to transform the parent organization. Many of the topics are scalable in terms of understanding the management issues at different levels within the parent organization. For example, they can be used for reference to assist in the day-to-day management activities of the information service. They can also be used to provide an understanding of the wider organizational management issues that occur in the parent organization.

Orientation

Part I, *Management Influences in a Changing Landscape*, addresses the first critical area that needs to go well. That is, an understanding of the concept of management and its importance in transforming organizations in a world of global and local challenges. It provides context to the challenges of managing for the future and survival in an uncertain and unpredictable environment, where sustainability is critical to success. It identifies different mindsets and approaches required in this environment. It also describes the various managerial roles and responsibilities, skills and mindsets that can be found in organizations. The second chapter provides context to the unpredictable and chaotic environment in which information services operate. It considers the drivers of change and the strategic influences being felt in both the internal and external environment and also explains the internal environmental characteristics that sustain organizations and which are most likely to be found in successful organizations.

Part II, *Strategy and Planning*, acknowledges the importance of planning for the future. It provides an integrated approach to strategic and scenario planning, as well as the specifics of how to plan, attract and retain the best and most talented workforce, ensure value for money and a cost-sustainable future through sound finance practices, strategically manage knowledge and information for competitive advantage and profitable business outcomes, and to take a smarter approach to technology and other strategic assets. Whilst there is a chapter devoted to managing each of the resources in a sustainable manner, the underlying approach is that they are planned as an integral part of the strategic planning process.

Leadership is a further critical factor in ensuring success and sustainability in uncertain environments. It involves engaging change and creating the right innovative corporate environment for environmental and organizational sustainability as well as smoothing conflict situations, motivating and communicating with individuals and groups. *Leadership* is the theme of Part III of the book. There are chapters on:

- Leadership roles and responsibilities, especially those in effectively managing diversity brought about by having different expertise and multiple generations in the workplace and in positioning the organization as an employer of choice;
- Developing and managing a strong, ethical and high-performance values-driven corporate culture, such that it is able to cope with uncertainty through managing in a sustainable way, supported by flexibility, innovation and change from within;

- Creating an innovative environment that is the basis for ensuring that the organization is equipped to think differently, turn risks into opportunities and secure new advantages ahead of others;
- Building and shaping an organizational capacity to think differently, to be innovative, to create and embrace change to sustain the organization in an unpredictable world, as well as developing ownership and commitment to action where change is energized from within;
- Managing group dynamics and leading teams of people to achieve outcomes as a group rather than as individuals and to enable people to effectively work across more than one team;
- Managing and resolving conflict that inevitably occurs through change as well as negotiating win-win outcomes that is a necessary element of good leadership in transforming organizations and managing change;
- The nature of politics and political behaviour from both an individual and organizational perspective;
- Strategies for developing policy to ensure that individual interests are managed for the greater good and that individuals within the organization are moving forward in the same direction;
- Personal communication and networking; and
- Ensuring the well-being of individuals not just from a social responsibility perspective but also as a strategy for workforce sustainability in which Generations X, Y and the Millennials have expectations that their well-being will be considered by the employer.

The theme for Part IV is *Governance and Social Responsibility*; which is a very necessary requirement in times of global uncertainty and need for sustainability. It includes a new chapter on managing for sustainability as well as corporate governance principles, ethics, codes of conduct, and different forms of capital. Power, influence and authority are brought together and considered in a chapter on accountability. Decision making is given a higher priority in ensuring transparency in organizations and a section is included on understanding perceptions and intuition. The chapter on evaluating benefits and performance addresses how to realize benefits, to enhance the return on investment through adding value, price for services, as well as strategies for measuring and evaluating performance.

The competitive global environment is introducing new risks for organizations. Risk factors increasingly involve security, including information security, physical security and the risk of damage to the organization's reputation and image. All of which can have financial, political, competitive, legal, human or technological impacts. With this in mind, risk management and security make up the remaining chapters in Part IV.

The final and most critical success factor is having a customer and market focus in service delivery. Part V, *Customer and Market Focus*, deals with defining and managing the end products and services that result from all of the other activities in the book. It contains chapters on strategic marketing strategies to increase the competitiveness of the information service and its parent organization, managing the corporate image and ensuring service quality. These ensure that services and products are delivered in multi-channel environments that meet the needs of customers.

The final part of the book, *Success and Sustainability*, brings all of the parts of the book together in explaining the sustainable approach.

Acknowledgements

This book builds upon a rich source of ideas that have accumulated from over 30 years of experience that have taken me on a journey from managing large public library systems, lecturing in information service management, setting the strategic direction for ICT as a government chief information officer and now as a global management consultant. This journey has been in the public and private sectors and academic institutions. It has taken place at local, national and international levels. I have learnt a great deal from my interactions with my team members, managers, peers, students, colleagues and friends that have been part of this journey over the years. Some of this has been what not to do, as well as what to do. There are too many people to thank individually, but you know who you are and I am grateful for the opportunity to have shared moments in my working life with you all.

Ideas have also come from discussions and writings in general management and information management. I appreciate the time that others have spent in sharing and documenting their wisdom and knowledge.

Finally, I wish to thank my husband, Dr Vic Fazakerley, for his support and constructive feedback whilst I have been writing this and the previous editions, Emeritus Professor Nick Moore who encouraged me to write the very first edition, the staff from the universities that I visited early in 2010 who provided input and the editorial and other staff at Ashgate Publishing who have provided support and encouragement over the years.

In closing, I have written this edition to continue to share my passion for information services and to give something back to those working in these disciplines, so that they may inspire others and excel in challenging environments.

Jo Bryson, Perth, Western Australia
October 2010

I

Management Influences in a Changing Landscape

The theme for Part I is managing the influences and drivers present in an unpredictable and increasingly complex environment; where survival and success is often founded on sustaining the organization and creating the next advantage from within. This requires an unprecedented measure of cleverness, ingenuity and flexibility on the part of the manager. They need to foresee and make sense of threats in the changing landscape that is typical of the global environment, whilst being highly creative and inventive in seeking out new opportunities. Their role has been likened to dancing on a moving carpet.

To put this in context, Chapter 1 explores a number of challenges facing management in the uncertain world of today. It explains some of the skills, new mindsets and roles of managers that are necessary to meet these challenges.

The environment in which information services operate is undergoing significant and continuous change. Chapter 2 describes different techniques for sustaining and future-proofing organizations by considering concepts of possibilities and probabilities and introducing the reader to some of the drivers of change and strategic influences in the external environment. Chapter 2 also explains the internal environmental characteristics that sustain organizations and which are most likely to be found in successful organizations.

Management Influences in a Changing Landscape
1. Managing in an uncertain world
2. Strategic influences

Strategy and Planning
3. Strategic Planning – positioning for a sustainable future
4. Attracting and retaining the best people in challenging times
5. Ensuring value for money and enabling a cost-sustainable future
6. Knowledge and information management – a key to survival
7. Strategic technology and asset management – a smarter approach

Leadership and Innovation
8. Leadership
9. Utilizing a values driven culture for sustainability
10. Innovation and creativity
11. Engaging change in positioning for the future
12. Group dynamics and team building
13. Effective negotiation and conflict management
14. Managing the political arena
15. Policy-making
16. Personal communications and networking
17. Managing yourself and others in challenging times

Governance and Social Responsibility
18. Ensuring good corporate governance
19. Using authority and influence
20. Encouraging transparency
21. Managing for sustainability
22. Managing risk
23. Sustaining trust and continued operations
24. Evaluating benefits and performance

Customer and Market Focus
25. Competitive strategies
26. Corporate image and communications
27. Ensuring service quality

Success and Sustainability
28. Bringing it all together

Figure P1.1 Management influences in a changing landscape

1 *Managing in an Uncertain World*

The challenges of an uncertain world

In the last two hundred years, Western societies have transitioned through economies and societies first based on agriculture, then on industry and knowledge. Now there is yet another dimension, that of the virtual world. The magnitude of these changes is such that they are called revolutions and each one has challenged the way in which people work, think, live and communicate. The virtual world that is a further development of the knowledge age differs little in its level of impact, its ability to present challenges and the associated requirement to rethink economies, societies and lifestyles from its previous counterparts. However, a key difference between the virtual world and the knowledge age and the first two ages is that the earlier ages were built on knowing how and knowing what. The knowledge age is founded on knowing who and why in an uncertain and now virtual world. We live and work in an era where unpredictable events have an immediate global impact, where corporate reputations can be destroyed through worldwide condemnation about their slowness to react or respond to situations, and where the market environment is no longer solely a physical presence as per the market place; it is increasingly a virtual presence, or market space. It is a learning age where an understanding of trends and possibilities goes hand in hand with identifying the inconceivable and making choices or preferences as to where to position for the future.

Recent developments influencing service delivery in the knowledge age are:

- Virtualization that enables information services to participate in global information-centric collaboration to deliver 24x365 services;
- The proliferation of mobile devices enabling anywhere anytime support and service delivery; and
- Information savvy generations who are using social networking tools in unprecedented ways.

All these are reshaping the organizational landscape and the demand for services.

The abilities to create, share and use knowledge in a virtual environment are key factors in the creation of wealth and high value employment, in stimulating creativity and sustainability, as well as improving the quality of life. Sharing knowledge, learning and creativity goes beyond the workplace and is evidenced in the rise of social networking tools that have become the most important means of communication. Community engagement, collaboration and participation in decision making, being the hallmarks of progressive governments, are also predicated on knowledge, know-how, knowing who and knowing why.

A feature of the current environment is that organizations face major uncertainty about their future and are subject to sudden strategic shocks in a global environment. These sudden, unprecedented shocks may originate from the other side of the world, but their effect is still profound. Their origins can be financial, economic, political, climatic or natural disasters. Examples include the Global Financial Crisis, foreign investment and takeover bids, the 9/11 attacks and the Boxing Day tsunami that caused widespread destruction in South East Asia. Creative and making-the-connections thinking is needed to envisage what these unprecedented risks and extraordinary shocks may be, and how to best prepare organizations to withstand them in the event of their happening.

To manage the challenges of the uncertain world, leaders and organizations have to think and act in new ways to anticipate change and:

* Sustain their impetus and operations;
* Develop new business opportunities and advantage;
* Attract and retain people with the required mindsets, skills and expertise;
* Better utilize their knowledge and information including social networking tools;
* Transform and rejuvenate existing products and services; and
* Prepare for sudden, unprecedented shocks.

Customers have raised expectations in service delivery, requiring organizations to transform the way in which products and services are delivered. However not all customers have the same needs and expectations. Employee, as well as customer, needs and expectations will differ according to their age group or generation, physical locality and personal circumstances. Therefore the information service must be prepared to deliver different solutions for different generations to meet different circumstances and sustain these in an environment of dwindling financial resources. Examples of customers might be:

* A field worker who requires corporate information provided to their laptop or mobile device whilst they are out of the office visiting clients or worksites;
* Senior citizens who are advised that their book reservation is available for collection through a text message sent to a mobile device or an email;
* A primary carer who may work from home and require access to corporate office and business systems;
* Office workers who work with both hard copy information and corporate business systems either at home or in the office;
* Researchers who require 24x365 support regarding the latest global research on complex issues;
* Students for whom the library is the gathering place conducive to study and discussion about issues; and
* Millenials whose preferred choice of communicating is through social networking applications using mobile devices.

Successful information services now focus on the management of relationships and opportunities to use technologies to enhance the customer experience rather than just transactions, as well as making better use of collaborative approaches in servicing customer needs. Mobile and other electronic delivery mechanisms make possible the availability and delivery of financially sustainable services and information 24x365 to anyplace, mobile and global, as well as providing avenues for social networking and input into decisions. Customers expect to see seamless services across multiple channels that are tailored to need; being customer centric rather than organization or discipline centric.

There are also sustainable financial reasons for adopting a customer-centric approach. Moving customers to online self-service anytime, anyplace reduces counter staff and other overhead costs as well as reducing the amount of travel, time and expense for the customer. One-stop integrated services can also lower capital and operational costs as well as adding value by increasing the level of customer convenience. For libraries, information services and other cultural institutions this means taking a multi-institutionalized and multi-disciplined collaborative approach to service delivery. It also means managing a range of flexible and integrated channels for service delivery in order to meet multi-generational preferences that include push services to mobile devices, social networking tools, traditional one-on-one service delivery and web enabled transactions.

To illustrate this, Parker et al. (2005: 176) quote Troll (2002) on the future of libraries, which is still relevant in the 2010s: 'As libraries struggle with the fallout of the digital age, they must find a creative way to remain relevant to the twentieth century user who has the ability and means of finding vast amounts of information without setting foot in a brick and mortar library … The freely accessible information on the web, in conjunction with the escalating costs of library materials, threatens the traditional mission of libraries to create and sustain large, self-sufficient collections for their patrons'.

Alongside these challenges, new advantages and opportunities are arising that draw upon the skills and expertise of information workers. Large companies are developing and implementing sophisticated knowledge management systems to capture, store and disseminate much needed customer-related and other information gathered from their internal and external environment. Chief Executive Officers are improving their understanding of the role of information in the corporate environment. Increasingly they understand that an organization's information is a trusted asset that is essential for business strategy, applications, processes and decisions. An important role for the information service manager is to capitalize on this understanding by:

- Further developing the technical and business expertise and analytical skills of information workers;
- Developing strategies and principles that will guide the organization's efforts to exploit and create trusted information;
- Creating a culture to ensure that information is shared by all parts of the business;
- Instilling a single standard in data quality; and
- Paying attention to information accuracy, its value to the organization and governance.

The increasingly sophisticated expectations and knowledge-based activities described above are some of the drivers for change in libraries and information services. Libraries and information services managers have the unique and dual responsibilities for planning and managing their own corporate intelligence, knowledge and information, as well as facilitating access and disseminating knowledge and information to others that assists them to predict the future, facilitate decision making, create new products and for lifelong learning and personal development.

No matter what their title as Chief Information or Knowledge Officers or Library and Information Services Manager, the occupants of these roles will be strategic change managers. They will need to re-conceptualize their function and reinvent themselves as challenges, needs and opportunities come along. Those supporting business and corporate environments, research and development institutions will be at the forefront of change as their abilities to offer new information and services and exploit new opportunities in ICT will be critical to the sustainability and success of their parent organization. They will need to be versatile, proactive, strategic and willing to be innovative and measured in a complex and challenging world.

Managing for the future and survival

Uncertainty and change present new challenges that need to be managed from new perspectives in order to survive and prosper in the future. Progressive organizations recognized that their imagination, creativity and consequential business advantage are predicated on educated and skilled people who can create, share and use knowledge well. They look for ways to increase the level of innovative by establishing corporate values that encourage openness and originality. Information technology and business applications are also important to connect and harness collective intelligence.

The ability to sustain the funding base for many information services is being challenged. A whole generation of people have retired or are about to retire from the workplace or move to part-time employment, with a commensurate loss of workforce capacity, corporate knowledge and an income-related tax base which is a traditional source of funding for many information services. At the same time there is greater demand for knowledge and information in the corporate environment, fuelled by the use of social networking tools to assist collaboration, as well as by people making lifestyle and other decisions concerning their future. Managing in this environment requires the ability to make smarter decisions; especially in ensuring the sustainability of services in an era of decreasing financial contributions and loss of corporate knowledge.

Sustainability and diversity in lifestyle, the environment and in cultures are dependent on creative and innovative thinking, the sharing of knowledge and collaboration, and breaking down silos of institutions. In these environments, the opportunity exists for information services to be managed as valuable centres for living, learning, growing and connecting people.

There are also growing expectations that organizations will take a responsible attitude to social, energy, environmental and workforce sustainability in their management of capital, resources and the environment, in their family friendly work practices, and in their relationships with the community.

New skills, mindsets and approaches

It is also in this environment that the information services manager assumes a significant leadership and change management role in sustaining the organization whilst at the same time understanding and preparing for the challenges of tomorrow. Not just for the library or information service, but also for the whole organization or community that the library or information service serves. This leadership and change management role requires new skills, mindsets and perspectives, capabilities and aptitudes.

Management today embraces a way of thinking, an attitude and behavioural style that is global and innovative. Whilst strategic thinking, technical, interpersonal, knowledge enabling, conceptual and analytical skills are still used they are applied with a different mindset; for it is personal drive and initiative, a passion and an openness of mind that makes a difference. Those that really transform organizations incite a passion in others, build an organizational capability to view adversity as a challenge, and look for new opportunities in fast changing environments.

Of the skills, mindsets and approaches that follow, not all will be used in equal proportion across the organization. Executive management and team and divisional leaders will draw on different skills and mindsets and may apply them differently. For example, the following skills and mindsets will be used by executive management in a role model capacity as well as strategically in setting the direction for the future; whilst at the team manager level the skills and mindsets will be used with a more operational focus.

CREATING AND SHARING THE VISION

First and foremost, leaders and managers have to inspire others, building and sharing a vision for the future of the information service, predictably in an increasing virtual world. As well as painting a picture that describes what the future services may look like, good managers exhibit leadership and build total commitment, enabling everyone to personally identify with and own the vision, working as a team to achieve it. In inspiring others and in creating the common identity amongst individuals, managers will use communicating, networking, motivating and leadership skills.

The vision cannot be achieved just by focusing upon individuals and the internal or corporate environment. The manager must also focus upon the relativity of the information service to its existing and potential competitors in the external environment. This requires skills in competitive positioning, image building and politics.

Effective managers are able to create a mental picture of different future scenarios and to visualize the library, its organization and community in a preferred future space. Strategic thinking skills are also necessary in order to capitalize on these ideas through opportunity and innovation. Together, these visionary and strategic thinking skills are used to shape the destiny of the organization. Strategic thinking skills are used to bring together and consider the implications, interdependencies and possibilities of a huge range of issues.

Strategic thinking skills also include inspiring a sense of purpose and direction for others, and encouraging people to think beyond their traditional boundaries to a very different future. Management success in this area is heavily reliant on innovative thinking and the ability to enthuse others. Advocacy and championing are also important roles in developing an understanding in others of the organization's vision, purpose, value and usefulness.

Both an external perspective and an entrepreneurial flair are needed to envisage probabilities and opportunities, identify issues and determine trends ahead of others.

In shaping thinking and translating action into activities, managers need to take into account the impact of changing environments, and new technical and service delivery possibilities. Good judgement, intelligence and commonsense are required to make the right call and to manage the many varied and sometimes competing issues.

HAVING A GLOBAL PERSPECTIVE

The increasing global focus on external contexts and stakeholder relationships that is a result of the virtual world is driving the need for an international perspective to service delivery. Whilst information has historically been sourced globally, service delivery tended to be localized. Multi-national corporations, virtual operations, international collaboration in approaches to research and development and universal access now mean that service delivery spans continents with its associated management and technical implications for libraries and information centres.

Having a global perspective or mindset entails the ability to look worldwide for opportunities and threats that will have an impact on service delivery and the organization itself. Examples include being prepared to seek answers from elsewhere, delivering services to portable devices anytime, anyplace in the world, considering best practice in service delivery that have worked in other places, being comfortable in managing multi-cultural environments, being open to ideas and having a global view of the library and information service market.

INSTILLING A PASSION

Instilling passion into organizations is part of the visionary mindset and talent of a good leader. In shaping and driving the strategic directions for the organization, effective leaders demonstrate a passion for what they believe the organization can achieve and instil this in others, whilst having the capacity to remain focused on strategic outcomes in turbulent and changing environments. Passion is also necessary to create enthusiasm. People who have passion demonstrate a natural eagerness for results and dedication to the achievements of the organization that ignites keenness in other team members.

Leaders and managers that instil passion are self-motivated, decisive and have a flair for getting things done in extraordinary circumstances and for stimulating others to achieve individual and corporate success. Demonstrating Type A characteristics, they are highly energetic and enthusiastic people, usually with a strong innovative capacity. They possess a strong commitment to personal achievement and in getting others to achieve, especially in areas where there are competing demands and multiple agendas.

STRIVING FOR EXCELLENCE AND QUALITY

Striving for excellence and service quality in the design and delivery of customer-centric services and products takes a similar drive and commitment to instilling a passion in the workplace. However design and delivery are only part of the equation. Of equal importance is the customer relationship management, service experience and service support that encourages the continual use of the service or product. A holistic approach is necessary that instils excellence and quality into the culture and psyche of the organization; extending through every step of value chain and throughout the complete life cycle of the customer interface.

Ensuring an organizational commitment to excellence and quality is also a strategy that leads to a more sustainable future. Designing and carrying out a task right first time, every time, avoids the need for repetition and duplication of effort. However it requires a mindset and attitude that values and distinguishes perfection and attention to detail, and which is translated into activities, processes and procedures at all levels of the organization.

BUILDING AN ORGANIZATIONAL CAPACITY TO CREATE AND EMBRACE CHANGE

To succeed in rapidly changing environments, libraries and information services must seize opportunities quickly, rapidly redesigning their information products and services to assist the organization and meet changing customer and employee needs. Success will be predicated on finding new ways of doing things cost-effectively that exceed customer expectations and in an environmentally friendly manner and which assist in the attraction and retention of staff.

This involves:

- Creating and leading a productive and dynamic work environment that can face new issues and rapidly changing priorities on an almost daily basis;
- Developing the right organizational and individual capabilities to embrace and endure strategic change and new technologies; and
- Encouraging people to be extremely adaptable and enthusiastic about work, to think innovatively and critically, learn quickly and to be immediately responsive to external influences.

The rise of Web 2.0 or Enterprise 2.0 tools in organizations is a good example of this. When these tools were first introduced they were often considered a technological distraction and not part of 'work'. Today they are recognized as mainstream communications tools and legitimate value-adding business application tools facilitating more direct contact with employees, customers and other stakeholders, engendering greater collaboration, information sharing and communications as well as teamwork. Those organizations that embrace and adapt to embracing Enterprise 2.0 and beyond tools that allow employees with the mindsets, skills and know-how of the future to search, link, author, tag, mashup and subscribe to information in these ways will become preferred employers. Those that fail to do this will find that their ideal employees will:

- Use their chosen software and applications in spite of corporate policy;
- Decide not to join the organization in the first place, preferring to join a more progressive organization; or
- Quickly leave as they realize their technology expectations are not met.

Strategic change management skills also include devising and implementing strategies to reshape and implement the future, and being able to clarify and minimize uncertainties for others. Managers with good change management skills display resilience to pressure, can remain focused on the tasks and outcomes, and demonstrate personal courage and coping skills in times of adversity.

DRIVING ORGANIZATIONAL RENEWAL

Linked to the previous skill is the need to keep reinventing or renewing the organization. This is for two reasons: as organizations grow they follow a path that reaches a peak; this is the point at which the organization must renew itself to achieve even greater outcomes and success, and to avert decline. Second, in a competitive world organizations need to keep inventing the next advantage that puts them ahead.

Renewal can come in many forms; in new ways of thinking or doing things differently to achieve greater productivity, in developing new products or services, or taking a different perspective of risks and turning these into opportunities. The increase in digital and virtual information services delivered to people in the always on, anywhere, anytime environment, the implementation of Web or Enterprise 2.0 and beyond tools to support better organizational communications and outcomes, as well as rethinking and integrating cultural and other services for a one-stop integrated customer service are perfect examples of organizational renewal.

EXPLOITING TECHNOLOGY FOR BUSINESS OUTCOMES

Adapting to using new technology opportunities and new versions of software functionality are fundamental skills required of people at all levels of the organization. These skills are developed on the job or through formal education and training programmes. However, using technology as a tool or catalyst to develop product opportunities and further enhance service delivery requires more.

Keeping in tune with technology advances and exploiting these for customer-centric service delivery in the always on, anywhere, anytime environment is an imperative for service delivery. It is a business not a technology issue. Social networking tools, mobile commerce and other connectivity solutions are redefining service delivery by moving customers to more self-sustaining and cost-efficient self-service as well as providing interactive and customized services to a variety of hand-held devices, anytime, anyplace. Customer relationship management tools, new web enabling technologies and wireless based telephony are also driving change and managers must understand the business implications and opportunities of each emerging technology.

BUILDING TALENT AND INTELLIGENT AND LEARNING ORGANIZATIONS

In order to maintain services in a rapidly changing and uncertain world, successful organizations and communities need to be intelligent or learning organizations. Intelligent organizations value individual talent, intelligence and knowledge and enable people to network, share and exploit their talents, aptitudes and knowledge for personal, organizational and community success. Learning organizations institutionalize training and personal development as an ongoing part of the work process and an essential component of implementing a corporate memory system.

Managers in libraries and information centres can play a significant role in creating, building and sustaining intelligent organizations and communities. This includes working alongside the other managers in creating and leading a knowledge-intensive culture and focusing on strategies that support and nourish organizational learning and knowledge creation.

Whilst some knowledge and information comes from published and unpublished sources in hard copy and digital environments, the more strategic knowledge and information is obtained through intelligence gathering, building personal networks with customers, distributors, suppliers, past and present employees, consultants and business contacts. This means allowing individuals time and space to give more attention to creating, managing and valuing their interpersonal and institutional networks, relationships and norms as well as building cooperation and trust.

MANAGING THE POLITICAL AGENDA

To move ideas forward, managers must know how to get things done within the parent organization, how to lobby and constructively use their persuasive skills and power to drive the change. This requires them to correctly interpret the political environment, to 'open doors', to identify supporters and sponsors, and to quickly build networks, commitment and support. Political skills include demonstrating astuteness in acting on intuition and making judgements on emerging or complex issues of a political nature. It includes anticipating events or being able to deal with matters before they become damaging issues.

In the global virtual world where news travels fast and reputational impacts are felt worldwide, managers must continually identify and take action to minimize the effect that actions and external political influences can have on their organization. Whilst not ignoring political messages, minimizing political intrusions on people helps ensure the smooth running of the organization, allowing people to get on with their job of achieving their required targets and outcomes without being hindered by unconstructive external pressures.

CREATING CREATIVE ENVIRONMENTS

A creative environment is fostered through leadership and management skills and mindsets that support and actively encourage people to think differently and bring their creative talents and ideas to work. It is based on the philosophy that everyone has the capacities to solve problems in unique ways, to conceive bright ideas, and to use entrepreneurial thinking, but many are discouraged to do so. The management role is to unlock or free up know-how, talents, skills and expertise in people so that they can be used for everyone's benefit.

Developing creative and innovative thinking is an activity that should be employed at all levels of management. Senior management need to be innovative in their thinking, whilst building and demonstrating their commitment to a corporate culture that values ideas generation, open communication and entrepreneurial thinking. They also need to sustain this commitment through their actions year after year; championing their cause, motivating and preparing others to readily accept innovation and change.

EFFECTING ETHICS AND INTEGRITY

Much more attention is now being placed on the corporate responsibility to act ethically and with integrity, instil public and social accountability, engender transparency and pursue excellence: all of which includes the concepts of legitimacy, fairness and ethics. Whilst each individual has a personal and professional responsibility to act ethically and with integrity, managers at all levels in the organization have the responsibility to set and ensure compliance with ethical standards and demonstrate by example issues such as honesty, fairness and equity, respect and integrity, and accountability. Such standards should define what is right and wrong in terms of the conduct of individuals and how those in a position to materially influence the operations of the information service should operate.

In addition to ensuring compliance with legal and regulatory regimes, senior executives also have responsibilities for establishing management oversight roles and putting the correct governance systems, practices, procedures and corporate culture in place to support accountability and the capacity to make the right decisions throughout all levels of management.

MANAGING FOR A SUSTAINABLE FUTURE

Linked to corporate and social responsibility is the need to manage for a sustainable future. This is a challenging role for managers and includes:

- Having the foresight and capacity to endure and confront financial, environmental, technological and workforce challenges;
- Anticipating future scenarios;
- Implementing strategies and optimizing resources in an environmentally friendly way, including reducing energy, waste and costs; and
- Making decisions and carrying out programmes and projects in a manner that maximizes benefits to the natural environment and humans, their cultures and communities, while maintaining or enhancing financial viability.

Sustainability is not limited to financial, economic and environmental issues. As the number of people of working age in the developed and developing world rapidly declines, workforce sustainability will increase in its importance. In addition to offering employees flexibility in working conditions, increased remuneration and meaningful corporate values, other creative approaches will also be required to position the organization to become an employer of choice.

BUILDING PRODUCTIVE RELATIONSHIPS

With the greater emphasis on building a better understanding of the external environment and customer-centric services, relationship building skills are becoming increasingly important. Relationship building and interpersonal skills are used by all levels of managers in interacting with people, internal and external to the organization, as well as in understanding and motivating others, both individually and in teams. They are used to maintain a network of contacts and relationships through which the organization's objectives are achieved. Interpersonal skills are also used to communicate the vision both internally and externally, in negotiating, lobbying and in promoting the organization to stakeholders.

Relationship building and interpersonal skills include being able to listen to other viewpoints, to understand and adapt the desired message to meet the needs of different audiences, and to build a rapport with people. They also embrace the abilities to negotiate and put forward viewpoints in a persuasive manner where there are a contest of ideas and disparate views. They are used to cultivate productive working relationships and partnerships with a diverse range of stakeholders, including:

- Networking to obtain information about competitors and other developments in the external environment;
- Building trust and nurturing relationships with others;
- Sourcing finance and supplies;
- Getting people to cooperate and collaborate with each other;
- Creating an environment in which tasks are effectively and happily accomplished;
- Discussing needs and delegating;
- Guiding and mentoring people; and,
- Translating policies into actions.

Levels of management

Blurring boundaries brought on by the introduction of mobile and virtual communications technologies, changing cultures and values of employees and the integration of services are changing organizational structures. The traditional triangle shape has long been flattened, with the mid-level and line management strata replaced with flexible teams and team or divisional leaders in a star or networked arrangement. Now Enterprise or Web 2.0 tools and beyond are influencing and reshaping hierarchies and boundaries within organizations so that it is becoming more difficult to identify where the organizational barriers are, or even if they exist.

Within this scenario of blurred organizational structures there are still special mindsets, functions and activities that distinguish the roles and responsibilities of executive management from team and divisional leaders.

EXECUTIVE MANAGEMENT

The executive management team comprises the most senior members of the organization who, together with the Chief Executive, shape the direction and future of the organization and build the organization's capacity to embrace change. The information services manager or Chief Information Officer may be part of the executive team. To reach and sustain their position, executives must have strong personal drive and initiative, strategic and organizational change management skills, as well as personal passion.

In positioning the organization to survive and succeed in challenging and changing environments, senior executives need sound political, relationship building and interpersonal skills. Theirs is a boundary-spanning role. They are the interface between the organization and major stakeholders, those who have a stake or strategic interest in the organization. They spend time troubleshooting and managing the political environment, lobbying and negotiating on issues that have an impact on the organization's business strategies.

Senior executives spend a considerable amount of time with their executive peers in the industry and strategically building their client base; with stakeholders such as board members, financiers and important suppliers. Most of their work is verbal and is often reactive. They receive short snatches of information that they have to piece together to anticipate the future, grow the organization and chart the way forward; keeping the organization ahead of its competitors and determining the changes that are advantageous to the organization. These intelligence-gathering exercises are not just for their own benefit. Intelligence sharing is paramount in an age where survival and success relies upon knowledge and ideas to create new and innovative offerings and make the right decisions in an uncertain environment. In differentiating the organization from others executive managers also need a sound understanding of how technology can be exploited for successful business outcomes.

Finally, reflecting society's expectation for increased corporate accountability and commensurate regulatory regimes executive managers are renewing their emphasis on leading strong corporate commitments to good governance and accountability, excellence and quality, and ethics and integrity.

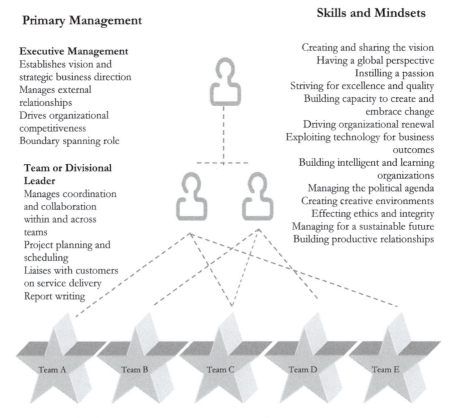

Primary Management

Skills and Mindsets

Executive Management
Establishes vision and
strategic business direction
Manages external
relationships
Drives organizational
competitiveness
Boundary spanning role

**Team or Divisional
Leader**
Manages coordination
and collaboration
within and across
teams
Project planning and
scheduling
Liaises with customers
on service delivery
Report writing

Creating and sharing the vision
Having a global perspective
Instilling a passion
Striving for excellence and quality
Building capacity to create and
embrace change
Driving organizational renewal
Exploiting technology for business
outcomes
Building intelligent and learning
organizations
Managing the political agenda
Creating creative environments
Effecting ethics and integrity
Managing for a sustainable future
Building productive relationships

Team A   Team B   Team C   Team D   Team E

Figure 1.1   Levels of management – roles and mindsets

TEAM AND DIVISIONAL LEADERS

Team and divisional leaders are the product of the merger between line and mid-level management as organizations moved to more streamlined and matrix management structures. In the example in Figure 1.1 mid-level and line management have been totally integrated.

Team and divisional leaders translate the vision, global perspective, and broad overall strategies and policies set by the executive into implementation strategies and specific action programmes. They analyse issues such as the emerging global trends in technology and their impacts on opportunities for innovation in service delivery and future customer requirements and summarize these in reports for the executive. Team and divisional leaders encourage collaboration between the various parts of the organization and a passion for quality service delivery which require excellent interpersonal and relationship building skills. They have good analytical and technical skills which they use to develop an in-depth knowledge of their area and activities, and how these interact with other sections or divisions across the organizational value chain and within the changing organizational environment.

Team leaders are directly responsible for the quality of service delivery within their work units and the administration of resources to meet the parent organization's short-term objectives. They have a supervisory and grievance handling role that requires strong interpersonal and relationship building skills. The grievances can come from staff regarding rosters and other work related issues or from their customers on service delivery issues. Their jobs can be hectic with continued interruptions so a high degree of flexibility is required. They often communicate on a one-to-one basis to solve problems and maintain quality standards.

Team leaders have an oversight role in ensuring compliance to ethical and best practice, integrity in actions of team members, and that good corporate governance is maintained at the operational and service delivery level. Team and divisional leaders have less need for skills in managing the external political agenda, but will use political skills and mindsets in managing internal politics and getting things done in the corporate environment.

Conclusion

In the twenty-first century, the most important business assets are not the tangible assets of the past. Intangible assets such as knowledge, expertise, innovation and branding are the new business enablers and sustainers that require the focus of management. In addition, knowledge and know-how are the key enablers for individual and organizational competitiveness, to manage risk and to service customer needs. This requires managers to shift their thinking, and empower people to invest their time in enabling knowledge, innovation and human capital.

Sophisticated customer expectations and a rapidly changing environment are requiring significant changes in skills, approaches and mindsets in managing and sustaining libraries and information services. New roles and activities are developing and levels of management disappearing in response. Activities are now much more proactive in the attempt to create and shape the future, rather than have the organization succumb to an unwanted future or be passed by.

Managers who focus on the following are more likely to be successful in today's challenging environment:

- Creating and sharing the vision, enabling everyone to personally identify with, own and work as a team to achieve it;
- Having a global perspective and the ability to look worldwide for opportunities and threats that will impact on service delivery and the organization itself;
- Instilling and sharing a passion for what they believe the organization can achieve and motivating others to achieve it;
- Striving for excellence and quality in the design and delivery of customer-centric services and products;
- Building an organizational capacity to create and embrace change, seizing opportunities quickly and rapidly redesigning their information products and services to meet and exceed changing customer and employee needs;
- Driving organizational renewal through new ways of thinking or doing things differently to achieve greater productivity, developing new products or services, and taking a different perspective of risks and turning these into opportunities;
- Exploiting technology for business outcomes in an always on, anywhere, anytime environment;
- Building intelligent and learning organizations that value individuals' talents, intelligence and knowledge and enable people to share and exploit their knowledge for personal, organizational and community success;
- Managing the political agenda by demonstrating astuteness in acting on intuition and making judgements on emerging or complex issues;
- Creating creative environments that support and actively encourage people to think differently and bring their creative ideas to work;
- Effecting ethics and integrity by putting the correct systems, practices, procedures and corporate culture in place to support accountability and the capacity to make the right decisions throughout all levels of management;
- Managing for a sustainable future by having the foresight and capacity to endure and confront financial, environmental, technological and workforce challenges; and
- Building productive relationships with stakeholders, listening to other viewpoints as well as understanding and meeting their needs.

References

Parker, K.R. et al. 2005. Libraries as knowledge management centres. *Library Management*, 26(4/5), 176–189.

Troll, D.A. 2002. How and why libraries are changing: what we know and what we need to know. *Libraries and the Academy*, 2(1), 97–121.

Further Reading

Buckingham, M. 2005. What great managers do. *Harvard Business Review*, March, 70–79.

Corsini, S. 2005. The nine traits of a great manager. *Training and Development*, September, 16–17.

Drucker, P.F. 2004. What makes an effective executive. *Harvard Business Review*, June, 58–63.

Morden, T. 2004. *Principles of Management*, 2nd edn. Aldershot: Ashgate.

2 *Strategic Influences*

The Context of Environments

Consideration of the driving forces and strategic influences on information services over the next decade requires an analysis of the factors that will most likely create the need for change or impact upon people and organizations during this period. Such a consideration is necessary in order to determine the likely management scenarios for the future business direction, to ensure that the delivery of services meet future needs, and ultimately, the information service's and its parent organization's survival. Whilst it is difficult to predict the future accurately, the likelihood of being able to forecast certain scenarios can be increased by analysing trends and strategic influences, and applying 'what if' scenarios to potential change factors.

Information services operate in the context of two environments – internal and external. Both of these affect the way in which information services are planned and managed. Unless management and staff have a clear understanding of these environments and how they impact upon their operations, they will be working in a vacuum.

The external environment comprises the driving forces and surrounding conditions in which the information service and its parent organization operate. These are often complex and unpredictable and continuously create new challenges that must be managed to ensure sustainability and success. The most consistent feature being that once one set of challenges has been mastered, another new set will take its place.

Maintaining an overview or understanding of the internal environment of an organization requires an equal amount of management attention. The internal environment relates to the internal factors that shape the organization and its operating environment. These include knowledge enabling, innovative capacity, leadership style, culture and values, communication, structure and the use of technology. Internal environment factors are influenced by the external environment.

A key management task is to assess continually how the information service is performing and adapting to changes in the internal and external environments. This can be achieved through a number of processes. Information on the external and internal environments must be gathered, assimilated and evaluated for use in the strategic planning processes that are discussed in more detail in the next chapter.

CHANGE IN THE ENVIRONMENT

Change has been a consistent feature of the environment for many years. However, it is both the speed and the complexity of change that most strategically influences the management of organizations and the information services that support their business needs. The successful organizations of the future will be those which are able to create the future, by being in front of their competitors and by being the catalyst for change. They will need to move fast and change fast to keep this position. Even bureaucracies which traditionally consist of unchangeable procedures have become more flexible and adaptable in recognition of this factor.

The effect of rapid change in the business environment, be it public or private sector, is that management must now seize opportunities quickly, rapidly redesigning information products and services to meet changing customer needs and finding new ways of doing things cost-effectively. Speed is a deciding factor and nothing is exempt from change. Whilst being proactive in identifying new end uses for services, resolving problems that enhance quality of output and reduce waste, and in undertaking organizational change, managers will also need to respond continually to turbulent environments.

COMPLEXITY IN THE ENVIRONMENT

The complexity and stability in the external environment dictates the level of responsiveness and therefore impacts upon the required structure, management style and corporate culture of the internal environment. The complexities in the environment relate to the number of drivers that impact or influence the organization. A simple environment is one where only four or five drivers impact upon the organization. A complex environment exists when over 10 drivers readily impact the organization. The stability factor is related to the degree and frequency of change within the drivers. If drivers continually change in the intensity of their impact and, as a result, services change moderately or continually, the environment may be considered to be unstable. Turbulence does not always strike organizations in the same way or at the same time and differs in levels of intensity and predictability.

POSSIBILITIES AND PROBABILITIES

Possibilities and probabilities arise from consideration of different scenarios for the future, ensuring that the organization is as prepared as possible to meet events as they occur. Predicting the inconceivable is one small part of future-proofing the organization. A considerable amount of energy is also spent on identifying the conceivable futures, the possible future and also the probable as part of scenario planning. This is with opportunistic outcomes in mind. By identifying what could conceivably happen, for example in technological advances or lifestyle changes; what is possible given the known changes; and the most probable scenarios, leaders can position their organizations to take advantage of future opportunities successfully.

The further dimension is about positioning and having an impact on the future. This is the consideration of the desirable and the preferable, and is linked to the organization's vision. By establishing the desired and preferred future state for the organization and painting this picture as a vision, leaders are taking the first step in enabling the organization's future. The vision provides a future reference point that sends a single message to which everyone can aspire. It charts the end goal and gives context to all that the organization does and wishes to achieve.

The Drivers of Change in the External Environment

The need to understand the external environment in which information services operate is fundamental to positioning the services to take advantage of technological change, in determining future paths, and to deliver appropriate services to customers. The external environment needs to be constantly scanned to identify new realities, challenges and uncertainties.

The assessment of the drivers of change or strategic influences in the external environment is one of the first inputs into the strategic audit stage of the strategic planning process. It allows managers to identify trends, issues, opportunities and threats that are likely to influence the direction of the organization, and it provides an information base for the conduct of other assessments such as the capability profile.

There are a number of external factors that are driving change and transformation in organizations. The following outline some of these drivers that can lead to strategic surprises and have a consequential impact on people and organizations today.

THE GLOBAL ECONOMY AND SOCIETY

Organizations now operate in a global environment in which national interests compete within a global economy and society. Web-based services enable access to information and services from an increasingly diverse and international source. Markets are now domestic and international, and trade protection has to be rethought in a borderless world. Research and innovation are both dependent upon and products of global cooperation and collaboration. The large proportion of information sources that are in electronic form and available worldwide has implications for sovereignty and the longer-term ability to sustain uniqueness in national cultures.

The Global Financial Crisis illustrated how an economic crisis in one country can rapidly affect the general economic health of another country and the sector in which information services operate. Sooner or later global economic conditions influence both demand and customer usage of services, and the supply and demand of resources. For example the ensuing high levels of unemployment raise the demand for free information services such as those operating out of public libraries, whilst at the same time it can result in a much larger labour market from which staff may be selected.

The changing characteristics of the economy in terms of inflation, money market and exchange rates should be monitored. This is because the information service's purchasing power will be affected by changes in international exchange rates, inflation rates or shortages of supplies in equipment. Information relating to economic conditions can most readily be obtained from the business and financial pages on the Internet or in newspapers, and by scanning other literature for information on economic conditions in the major publishing countries and their effects on information services.

DWINDLING FINANCIAL RESOURCES

Lowered tax bases brought about by large numbers of Baby Boomers ceasing full-time employment and the economic necessities of financial stringency following the Global Financial Crisis have led to the need to reconsider the economic sustainability of services during a time of dwindling financial resources. The most successful organizations will be those that apply innovation and creativity to the use of information and information technologies which enable them to deliver information in new and different cost-effective ways as well as realizing productivity gains and internal efficiencies.

The demand for services may have an inverse relationship to the ability to supply services. For example, constrained budgets (appropriations) and declining purchasing power have lessened the available capital for purchases and services over the past years, whilst customers have demanded more sophisticated services. The answer to this is two-fold: lowering front counter overheads by moving customers to online self-service models which also saves time and energy for the customer and passing costs in service provision directly to the consumer.

In considering how to sustain services in a climate of dwindling financial resources, the clients' maximum thresholds in their willingness to pay for services must be considered. Alternative sources of income to fund discrete services may also be explored. Likely sources are employment-generating schemes, grants or sponsorships, or the provision of certain value-added services that can subsidize other services. Some hard decisions may also be required about the structuring of information service programmes. If external funding and sponsorship is needed for some services, care should be taken to ensure that sponsorship demands do not overly influence or skew the focus and strategic direction of the information service. Strong lobbying, negotiation and marketing skills may be needed in order to ensure that the integrity and impartiality of services are not compromised.

In an effort to curtail expenditure it may not be easy to abandon services or levy charges. There may be enormous exit barriers to some services both socially and economically. There is also a risk of being locked into certain services that are not sustainable and which in the long term consume more resources than can be realistically afforded. A low coverage of too large a client market is inferior to a good quality service for a focused market. The duplication of services offered by other entities should be avoided.

TECHNOLOGY CHANGES

Information and its supporting communications technologies are both the driver and enabler of transformational change. They can create the need for change whilst assisting the organization through the change processes. For example, an organization that uses Web 2.0 and beyond technologies for access to information about their competitors' strategies, clients' and other stakeholders' levels of satisfaction and views on their current performance at any given time is in a much better decision-making position about the future than one that does not.

Social networks, mobile commerce and other connectivity solutions are redefining service delivery by providing customers with multiple sources of specialized services tailored to suit their individual needs. They provide instant communications and customized services to a variety of hand-held devices, anytime, anyplace. Internally, collaborative social networking solutions and 'shared spaces' are now mainstream. They offer new ways of thinking, engaging and working; providing users with the capability of interacting with others on a simultaneous basis.

Technology is increasing productivity by changing the manner in which the workspace operates and services are delivered. Global communications capabilities, collective information gathering and project collaboration are enabling 24x365 service delivery utilizing global alliances. Enterprise collaboration tools support more flexible working conditions; overcoming distance and different time zones by allowing all employees immediate online access to corporate information. The provision of high-quality voice, video and data provides the means for the organization to work with minimal on-site staff; reducing floorspace, overheads and the spread of infection in high-risk periods.

There are other changes in the workspace that are generational in nature. Millennials entering the workplace have spent their lives surrounded by and using computers and other digital devices where instant communications are an integral part of their lives. Fully-featured mobile technologies form part of the 'must have' list for 'digital native' employees who value access to technology tools as an essential component of the employment package. Robinson (2008: 68) cites Prensky as arguing that the absorption of technology into the lives of this generation is so profound that it represents a discontinuity from previous generations, with changes in the way digital natives acquire information, think and learn. They expect immediate responses to information inquiries and have a preference for image over text based content.

The choice in how and what technologies will be adopted by the organization is quite complex as there are many variables to consider:

- The complexity of the technology influences the skills and competences required by the information services' employees and customers. It may also enhance or inhibit the services' ability to adapt to change quickly;
- Different customer age groups have their preferred modes of working and service delivery. For example whilst Baby Boomers are embracing web services, Generation X, Y and Millennials look to social networking applications and the mobile device as the preferred mode of communications and service delivery. For the Silent Generation, those born between the First World War and the Second World War, personal service over the counter remains the preferred choice;
- Competitive advantage can be obtained in either being the first to market or having the ability to maintain the leading edge in a unique application of technology to deliver specialized information services to customers. However, if the complexity of the technology is so great that it inhibits flexibility then the inability to respond to change will itself become a burden for the organization;
- Changes in technology occur in such quantum leaps that what is new technology today is old technology tomorrow. The focus should not just be on keeping up to date with new developments in technology, but also in discovering new business applications for existing technology or new combinations of technologies in order to deliver more appropriate and sustainable services or increased productivity;
- To keep in tune with technology advances, content will also need to be tailored to meet clearly defined and individual customer needs, no matter whether it is in the context of operating in a multinational organization, or in delivering public library services in a small community. Information will need to be customized in format and timing as it is packaged and delivered anytime, anyplace.

DEMAND FOR INTEGRATED SERVICES

Customers who are time-poor are driving the demand for integrated, 'do it once' services. They do not want to spend time visiting multiple websites to obtain relevant information, to provide government and other institutions with the same personal information many times, to deal with stovepipe institutions that look at issues in isolation, or to waste resources travelling from building to building. They want to be able to utilize a single point of contact for the conduct of their business.

The single point of contact philosophy will also drive changes of thinking in the management and location of major cultural institutions. Traditionally institutions such as libraries, archives, telecentres and museums have existed as stovepipes, governed by the materials they housed rather than people's use. Information within organizations, e.g. journals, art pieces, relics, books, specimens, records and databases have been managed according to format rather than content. Indeed whole professions have been created around materials and format. This results in customers having to visit many venues to see the whole picture. The single point of contact philosophy will see libraries along with other information, education, cultural and recreation services converging and transforming into new shapes and forms to deliver seamless service delivery across multiple formats. They will morph into centres for living, learning, growing and connecting people.

Whilst the outcomes are enormous, integrating services is not a straightforward operation. It requires:

- Understanding the bigger whole of service picture and future business needs by all the stakeholders involved in order to make strategic decisions focused on the total integrated service;
- Identifying weak points and considering what needs to change in business process design within and across the partner organizations;
- Rethinking business process responsibilities to take into consideration the wide operational environment;
- Motivating employees to encourage a wider perspective to their service delivery mindset as well as training in the new processes;
- Evolving the idea and looking for further opportunities for integration;
- Ensuring that risk management and mitigation strategies cover all contingencies for all partners in the project;
- Introducing new governance processes that are embraced by all of the partner organizations;
- Instilling corporate values that emphasize collaboration, transparency, partnerships and trust;
- Introducing peer reviews for collaborating partner organizations' investment proposals;
- Designing new ways of measuring performance across the partner organizations; and
- Aligning planning and funding strategies.

INCREASING VALUE OF QUALITY

Whilst traditionally aligned to customer service, quality is not just concerned with product or service outputs. Quality procedures that support the 'do it right first time' concept enable sustainability by eliminating costly time, energy and waste in the production cycle. Information and knowledge are tools that can be used to drive quality and improved performance. Appropriate information enables management and employees to make decisions in order to provide an environment in which quality is embraced and valued in products and services. This type of information underlines the basis upon which performance is measured and strategies for improvement are decided.

FLEXIBILITY IN THE WORKPLACE

The need for greater flexibility in the workplace is being driven by two factors:

- In order to respond to change and dwindling resources, employing organizations require flexibility in the types of services offered and, consequently, the skills and competency profiles and numbers of employees; and
- The retirement of Baby Boomers and movement of Generation X and Y into influencing positions in organizations is changing work attitudes. Baby Boomers are seeking part-time work as a transition to retirement, whilst Generation X and Y are desirous of more life–work balance.

In times of dwindling resources, contract employment and outsourcing of services are two methods by which organizations can achieve flexibility in the type and skills of employees. The impact on the individual is that they may have a series of part-time jobs or contracts, rather than working long-term for a single employer. The lack of job security means that people will need to be motivated so that excellence in customer service and quality products can be achieved in a changing corporate environment where long-term employment may not be guaranteed. This will require the ability to balance the seemingly incongruent goals of encouraging a sense of belonging, self-control over quality, energy and enthusiasm in organizational environments where change and rapid downsizing may occur.

Flexibility in the workplace is increasingly leading to a mobile workforce such that people regularly work from home or another location. This is occurring for several reasons:

- The competitive global business environment demands that employees are available to customers and business partners;
- Individuals are wanting to balance their work and family responsibilities better;
- Environmental considerations and sustainability practices are seeking ways of reducing unnecessary travel; and
- Advanced information and communications technologies are making the virtual workplace of anytime, anywhere possible.

However providing for mobility does not just consist of offering a laptop computer and a remote connection. Organizations that are successful in having mobile workforces purposely design their business processes, operational procedures and reward systems around their people to minimize any sense of detachment, encourage work group interaction, and to ensure that the work/home boundaries do not become blurred.

CROSS-CULTURAL ISSUES

The global information market and the growing diversity in the cultural makeup of the community increase the exposure of information services to cross-cultural issues.

Information content can be obtained and disseminated instantly to most parts of the globe, necessitating the management of issues such as national sovereignty and transborder data flows. Second, greater cultural diversity will be represented in both employees and customers of the information service. Changing religious and racial compositions in the community have implications for management style and service delivery. Cross-cultural issues will also have an increasing influence on organizational behaviour. The differing cultural values and attitudes of individuals to their own individuality, ambition, job satisfaction, authority and time orientation will need to be recognized and respected.

Market research can be used to analyse the demographic makeup of the customer and potential customer base. This can include language, culture, income and purchasing power, age of the population and population distribution and mobility, all of which can influence the provision of information services.

OTHER CONSIDERATIONS

Geographical situation

The geographical environment involves the level and cost of reach in servicing customers as well as the geographical spread of operations of the parent organization. Both of these elements can either facilitate or hinder service levels.

Physical proximity to customers becomes less of an issue where services are delivered electronically. Access to mobile broadband telecommunications is far more important. Special libraries or information centres serving employees may still need a physical proximity to an area of heavy use in which to house the specialized journal and printed material collection, whilst also being able to deliver electronic information services direct to the mobile PDA device or desktop.

Barriers such as highways or territorial boundaries such as political borders or campus sites may also determine the extent of service provision to customers. For public service delivery where physical access is required, the preferred option is a single location, merging or co-locating art galleries, museums, visitors' centres, telecentres, libraries and other public access centres near shopping centres within easy reach of car parks and public transport stops.

Industry strata

The industry may be defined as those competitors or potential competitors that are in the same type of business. Industries may be further grouped according to the characteristics of ownership, services or markets. Within each industry there are leaders and followers. To ensure a common bond and some measure of quality control within various types of information services, minimum standards have often been developed. Standards may applicable at the international, national or organizational level. International standards often set internationally recognized best practice or cover situations where information needs to be transported and shared across countries, an example being standards or protocols for telephony or facsimile transmission. National standards may be set for meta data, which is data that describes the qualities of data so that it may be used and shared between organizations. Increasingly meta data standards are becoming more universal in description. Organizational standards may relate to the use of a standard operating environment or versions of software for office automation across the organization.

Characteristics of Sustainability in the Internal Environment

The following provides a description of the characteristics most likely to be found in organizations that are successful and can sustain their activities in an unpredictable, challenging and changing world. These characteristics can be used as a benchmark upon which to assess or judge the capabilities and capacities of existing organizations.

INTELLIGENT ORGANIZATIONS

An intelligent organization is one that has an empowered workforce though the sharing of knowledge and information. Intelligent organizations recognize that strategic gain comes from releasing the creative know-how, intellectual capacity, talents and experience of their people and in enabling knowledge and organizational learning through a diverse range of social and interactive tools. They have strategies in place to add to and build upon existing corporate intelligence, tacit knowledge and individual insight and aptitudes as a means to position the organization in the future. Knowledge, information and its supporting technologies make possible continuous innovation, productivity improvement and education and skills formation and therefore are fundamental in sustaining the organization. In particular younger employees are building self-organizing networks across traditional boundaries, with the result that their work is becoming more global and immediate.

Whilst information and communications technology (ICT) dramatically increases the usefulness and accessibility of information as well as the overall stock of knowledge, intelligent organizations are not reliant on ICT alone. Intelligent organizations recognize that research and innovation are contributing factors in creating new ideas and turning these into dollars and new business advantages. Intelligent organizations value individual talent, intelligence and knowledge and understand that this will lead to a redistribution of power from those who hoard knowledge and information to those who share this with others.

In this environment, an important task for the information service is to ensure that:

- Information management practices, information systems and information design are synchronized and aligned to creating new business advantage and the future strategic direction of the organization;
- Knowledge and information is of value and is made available when and where it is required in order to make financially and environmentally sustainable decisions, to allocate resources and to provide better services to customers;
- The corporate memory is complete and accessible; and
- Everyone is able to develop high-level skills and proficiencies in knowledge sharing, management and use.

In intelligent organizations that have reached advanced stages in knowledge enablement, knowledge management is considered a core competency. Web 2.0 technologies assist staff to interact and work together, increasing the receptivity and supply of knowledge throughout the organization. Performance appraisals include an assessment of each individual's knowledge-sharing expertise and knowledge-creation abilities. Motivation and reward mechanisms are also in place to encourage and support knowledge sharing and organizational learning. Everyone is responsible for the acquisition, collaboration, documentation and distribution of knowledge and information.

Making knowledge and information available also draws upon skills in information retrieval and navigation, in describing, linking and organizing multiple media formats, as well as the abilities to synthesize and validate the information provided through the global information networks. Such skills may be learnt by the individuals, or they may use the services of information specialists to obtain the information for them.

INNOVATIVE CAPABILITY

Innovation is the ability to predict or achieve the inconceivable: i.e. to invent something that no one else has thought of or done before. In advanced organizations with an innovative capability there is a significant shift from an emphasis on the strategic management of material goods to nurturing the know-how, talents, skills and expertise of people whilst securing and managing intellectual property and corporate branding.

Creativity and innovation are also acknowledged for their role in exploiting change and for providing the organization with the means to deal with the unstructured problems arising out of changing environments. People's capacities to solve problems in new ways, to conceive bright ideas and to use entrepreneurial thinking also become much more important in sustaining the organization in challenging times. The challenge is to generate an environment in which change and challenges are perceived as opportunities rather than threats. This enables people to put forward suggestions without ridicule or judgement, and for risks to be willingly assessed and taken, allowing mistakes to be made as part of the learning process. Systems and processes are in place so that everyone reports regularly on their activities and contributions to the innovative capability of the organization.

VISIONARY LEADERS

In highly successful knowledge age organizations, the leaders are proactive, visionary, entrepreneurial and risk taking. They use these skills to maintain their organization's competitiveness. They share their vision with others and create a collaborative and supportive environment. They also anticipate what could happen, visualizing their preferred future and putting steps in place to ensure a readiness for this. Resistance to change is smoothed by open communication and a participative style where people become used to providing input. Decision making is pushed down to those in the service area through delegation.

Employees also feel more comfortable with change if they have confidence that strategies are in place to manage the future. Sharing a vision of the future as to what the organization will look like in five years' time, the services or information products it will provide, and the types of markets that it will operate in reinforces confidence as well as enabling all employees to work together to achieve the same goal. The shared vision can be supplemented by the manager leading by example with regard to the organizational values that support and sustain the vision.

STRONG CULTURES AND VALUES

Highly successful organizations create a sense of excitement, belonging and commitment. They have strong corporate cultures that are built from the top, with executive management communicating the values personally, by walking the talk. There is mutual respect for people, who are assumed to be interdependent and mature. Individuals are valued and rewarded on performance and innovation rather than on staff functions or length of service. There is public acknowledgement that everyone, regardless of level or position, is capable of providing creative solutions through imaginative thinking. Opportunities for self-development are frequently provided. Importance is attached to expertise, affiliations and ability to network outside the organization. Trust and ethical behaviours are strongly held values.

In sustaining the workforce generational needs, progressive organizations recognize and cater for differences in values and attitudes to work between different generations. For example, whilst Baby Boomers are career oriented, idealistic and consumerists, Gen Y are technology savvy, seeking the latest technology applications and tools and will move elsewhere if they feel that this is being denied.

VALUING PEOPLE

The success of an organization is heavily dependent upon the contribution of its people. This is influenced by their perceptions and feelings of their value to the organization, which in turn influences their level of well-being towards the organization. People have needs and expectations that are either enhanced or frustrated by aspects of the organization. The interaction of people and structures also influence the behavioural processes such as leadership style, planning, communications, conflict management, decision-making processes, problem solving and other interpersonal behaviours. These behaviour processes influence the work output and level of commitment to the organization.

Like other capital resources, people can only grow if they are valued and there is renewal and investment provided through training and support, personal development, encouragement and opportunity. In highly performing organizations, time is spent on increasing expertise, coaching and developing people, and expanding their capabilities. The emphasis is on the provision of advice and relevant information, rather than instructions and decisions. Communication is open and free flowing, vertically and horizontally. Individuals have access to the appropriate information that they require for decision making. Information is readily shared in a trusting environment within the organization and with stakeholders.

Similarly as Cook (2008: 15) indicates, employees will:

- Increasingly expect to be able to use the same 'participatory' tools in the workplace as they do for sharing pictures with relatives or connecting with old colleagues and classmates; and
- Not sit and wait for their employers to evaluate technologies and vendors, and then deploy new technologies on a 12-month schedule. Instead they will use tools that

are already available on the Internet for free. In the future it will be easier and more cost-effective for organizations to let employees organize themselves around social software, not the other way around.

FUTURE-PROOFING FOR TOMORROW

The present and the future are always shaped by the past. In order to predict the future, it is necessary to consider trends of the past. Whilst the future is never certain, the likelihood of recurrent trends of the past being repeated when the same conditions apply tends to make the exercise of predicting the future more successful. It also identifies resulting conditions to avoid. An example of this is the Global Financial Crisis and the impact that this had on the financial sector, jobs and workforce retirement, global politics and all businesses. Governments recognized the need to avoid the collapse of the banking system and other events that occurred during the Great Depression, and so quickly took steps to shore up the banking sector.

The most successful organizations are those that are able to rethink the future so that even the most inconceivable event is possible. Instilling this open frame of mind into the organization is both a risk and an opportunity management strategy. It means that the organization is better placed to manage a catastrophic event if it occurs, than those that are ill-prepared. This mindset is also required for positioning the organization in its preferred future space by capitalizing on ideas about the future through opportunity and innovation.

Conclusion

Today's environment means that organizational readiness to manage continuous and discontinuous change is a required capability. The virtual organization is the reality rather than the exception. By continually analysing the drivers of change and transformation and being aware of the possibilities and probabilities of events occurring in these areas of strategic influence in the external environment, the element of surprise and its associated damage can be lessened. Whilst sudden and unprecedented events will still occur, the organization will have less exposure to the shock element and be more prepared to manage the consequential fallout. The drivers of change that can strategically influence today's environment include:

- The global economy and society;
- Dwindling financial resources;
- Technology changes;
- Demand for integrated services;
- Increasing value of quality;
- Demands for flexibility in the workplace; and
- Cross-cultural issues.

Having an understanding of the strengths and limitations of the internal capabilities of the organization also assists in sustaining the organization to succeed and survive. The following describes those characteristics most likely to be found in organizations that are successful and can sustain their activities in an unpredictable, challenging and changing world:

- Intelligent organizations that empower their workforce though the sharing of knowledge and information;
- Innovative organizations that nurture the know-how, talents, skills and expertise of people whilst securing and managing intellectual property and corporate branding;
- Visionary leaders who are proactive, entrepreneurial and risk taking and use these skills to maintain their organization's competitiveness;
- Strong cultures that create a sense of excitement, belonging and commitment;
- Valuing people with time being spent on increasing their expertise, coaching and developing people, and expanding their capabilities; and
- Future-proofing through instilling an open mind throughout the organization and rethinking the future so that even the most inconceivable event is possible.

References

Cook, N. 2008. *Enterprise 2.0: How Social Software will Change the Future of Work*. Aldershot: Gower.

Robinson, M. 2008. Digital nature and digital nurture: libraries, learning and the digital native. *Library Management*, 29(1/2), 67–76.

Further Reading

Allard, S. 2009. Library managers and information in World 2.0. *Library Management*, 30(1/2), 57–68.

Barnes, N.D. and Barnes, F.R. 2009. Equipping your organization for the social networking game. *Information Management*, November–December.

Castelli, D. 2006. Digital libraries of the future – and the role of libraries. *Library Hi-Tech UK*, 24(4), 496–504.

Charnock, E. 2010. *E-Habits: What You Must Do to Optimize Your Professional Digital Presence*. United States: McGraw-Hill Contemporary.

Chen, L. and Nath, R. 2005. Nomadic culture: Cultural support for working anytime, anywhere. *Information Systems Management*, 22(4), 56–65.

Digital Library Economics: An Academic Perspective. 2009. Oxford: Chandos.

Hamilton, V. 2004. Sustainability for digital libraries. *Library Review (UK)*, 53(8), 392–396.

Libraries in The Twenty-First Century: Charting New Directions in Information Services. 2007. Wagga Wagga: Centre for Information Studies, Charles Sturt University.

McNicol, S. 2008. *Joint-Use Libraries: Libraries for the Future*. Oxford: Chandos.

Mestre, L. 2010. *Librarians Serving Diverse Populations: Challenges and Opportunities*. Chicago: Association of College and Research Libraries.

Parkes, David. 2008. *Web 2.0 and Libraries: Impacts, Technologies and Trends*. Oxford: Chandos.

Sidorko, P.E. and Yang, T.T. 2009. Refocusing for the future: Meeting user expectations in a digital age. *Library Management*, 30(1/2), 6–24.

Tenopir, C. 2009. A new-old role for libraries. *Library Journal*, 134(2), 24.

Venkatraman, A. 2009. Invisible libraries lift veil on content. *Information World Review*, 261, 12.

Winston, M.D. and Quinn, S. 2005. Library leadership in times of crisis and change. *New Library World*, 105(1216/1217), 395–415.

II

Strategy and Planning

The theme of Part II is developing and implementing strategies so that the organization can better predict its future, sustain its financial position by ensuring value for money and enabling a cost-sustainable future, attract and retain a highly skilled workforce, manage its assets in a cost-effective and environmentally friendly manner and utilize its corporate knowledge and information for its greatest business advantage: all of which are important in managing in challenging times. By adopting a systematic approach

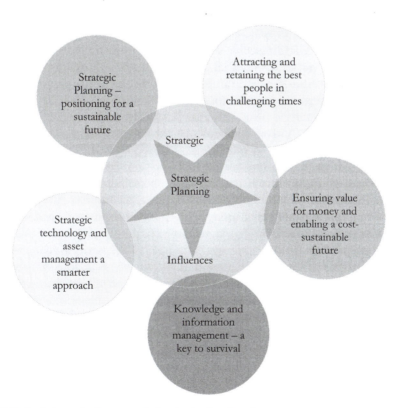

Figure PII.1 An integrated approach to strategic planning

Source: Adapted from Microskills of effective change agents taken from Dunphy, D. et al. *Organizational Change for Corporate Sustainability,* London: Routledge.

to planning for future needs based on possibilities and probabilities and guided by information from the internal and external environment, the organization is better able to survive and flourish. Whilst the activities of strategic planning, human, information, technology and financial resource planning and management are described in separate chapters for convenience, an integrated approach is advocated (see Figure PII.1). Strategic planning sets the overall direction for the organization, within which human, financial, information and technology resources are planned and managed in order to respond to dynamic environments.

Chapter 3 considers how strategy and planning processes can be used to sustain and ensure the survival of the organization in challenging times. It describes how each of the logical steps in the strategic planning process, from defining the mission, conducting the situation audit and needs analysis to developing objectives and programmes can be best used within organizations. A short discussion on the benefits of scenario planning is also included.

Chapter 4 outlines the strategies used to develop and maintain the status of an employer of choice; attracting and retaining the best people in challenging times. It covers the use of environmental analysis to plan for the future with regards to the type of skills, knowledge, competencies, attitudes and mindsets through environmental analysis, how these can be determined through different planning processes, and explores the benefits of skills inventories. The various strategies for attracting and retaining people are discussed, including processes for selecting people and inducing people to the organization. Finally, aspects for developing and getting the best out of people and separation are addressed.

Chapter 5 focuses on strategies that ensure value for money and enable a cost-sustainable future for the organization. It describes the processes of identifying, costing and allocating income and expenditure to resources and activities that can be used in the development of budgets and business cases; as well as exploring the relationships between the budget cycle and the strategic planning cycle. The chapter also distinguishes between cost accounting and activity-based costing. It explains how mechanisms for costing such as fixed and variable costs, unit costs, productivity curves, the law of diminishing returns, variable and total costs per unit are an integral part of ensuring sustainability.

Chapter 6 covers knowledge and information management strategies from the perspective that they are considered a strategic corporate resource. Information is the 'content' of the technology systems. The chapter explains how knowledge and information is used for decision making and advocates a strong consultation process in planning and managing information. The chapter also incorporates strategies for:

- Understanding organizational requirements for knowledge and information;
- Acquiring knowledge and information;
- Making knowledge and information accessible;
- Utilizing knowledge and information for the greatest benefit;
- Ensuring that the desired outcomes are achieved; and
- Deciding what information is no longer required.

Strategies for the optimum management of technology are covered in Chapter 7 along with techniques for managing other strategic assets. As information-related technology is susceptible to radical change, the chapter has not provided detailed descriptions of various technologies. Instead emphasis is placed on strategies for obtaining business rather than technology solutions. The chapter identifies how the technology presents opportunities for the organization to compete in the market place successfully. The technology planning process is described; role and responsibilities for the planning process are defined and the components of the technology architecture are summarized. The management issues associated with developing the technology to support the business strategy and with implementing the technology strategy are discussed.

Management
Influences in a
Changing
Landscape
1. Managing in an
uncertain world
2. Strategic
influences

Strategy and
Planning
3. Strategic
Planning –
positioning for a
sustainable future
4. Attracting and
retaining the best
people in
challenging times
5. Ensuring value
for money and
enabling a cost-
sustainable future
6. Knowledge

Leadership and
Innovation
8. Leadership
9. Utilizing a values
driven culture for
sustainability
10. Innovation and
creativity
11. Engaging
change in
positioning for the
future
12. Group dynamics
and team building
13. Effective
negotiation and
conflict
management
14. Managing the
political arena
15. Policy-making
16. Personal
communications
and networking
17. Managing
yourself and others
in challenging
times

Governance and
Social
Responsibility
18. Ensuring good
corporate
governance
19. Using authority
and influence
20. Encouraging
transparency
21. Managing for
sustainability
22. Managing risk
23. Sustaining trust
and continued
operations
24. Evaluating
benefits and
performance

Customer and
Market Focus
25. Competitive
strategies
26. Corporate
image and
communications
27. Ensuring
service quality

Success and
Sustainability
28. Bringing it all
together

Figure PII.2 Strategy and planning

3 *Strategic Planning: Positioning for a Sustainable Future*

A constant challenge in an unpredictable and changing world is the ability for organizations to be able to deal with and sustain their momentum in an uncertain future. One way of doing this is, as far as possible, to predict and prepare for uncertainty. For example, some trends will remain the same, and in these instances contingency plans can be used to respond to situations that are predictable. Some uncertainties can be eliminated through a variety of means including political lobbying, acquisitions, mergers, divesting and transferring risk to others. A third area for concentration is to build the organization's capacity to respond flexibly and adapt to changes arising from the social, technological, economic, environmental or political environment.

Strategic planning involves the development and implementation of sustainable strategies to position the organization for a successful future and to achieve its vision. Whilst strategic planning processes introduce a systematic approach to managing dynamic environments and enable the information service to respond effectively to new situations, these can blinker or limit the vision to what is known and a single outcome. Scenario planning enables organizations to deal better with uncertainty as it considers a number of possible futures. It identifies patterns and clusters of information from a number of possibilities.

This chapter considers how various strategic and scenario planning processes can be best used within the information service and its parent organization.

The importance of strategy and planning

Planning and implementing strategy are important processes that are used to reduce uncertainty and assist in positioning the organization to take advantage of the global knowledge economy and society. Strategic planning is a continuous technique for use where a systematic approach is appropriate. It takes into account the drivers of change and enables organizations to adapt to meet the challenges of the future and to plan a direction or course of action in a proactive manner. The outcome of which is that the organization is placed on a more sustainable footing and better able to influence external forces in accordance with its chosen strategies. It is also more able to initiate new activities that are conducive to market needs; rather than reactively adjusting or responding to those imposed upon it. Where strategic planning is implemented in a positive manner it will also benefit the communications and decision-making processes within organizations.

The strategic planning process recognizes that organizations cannot achieve everything they would like to do. Instead, it allows for the allocation of resources and planning of strategies on a priority basis best to achieve the organization's vision and mission within the resource constraints and dynamics of the external environment.

Managing the strategy development process

Strategy development and subsequent implementation must not only be valued and wanted, it should be seen to be valued and wanted. As a vehicle for change it is sometimes associated with negative feelings and connotations. Some consider it to be a mechanism for organizational reorganization with the capacity to engender a loss of power, influence or position. Others may view it as a waste of time and resources. The enthusiasm for strategic planning can be enhanced by discussing what could happen without the process being in place, and by explaining how other information services have benefited from strategy planning and implementation.

To be effective, strategic planning requires the commitment and involvement of executive management as it is about the strategic positioning of the organization. There has to be a clear understanding throughout the organization of its purpose and the value of the process. The strategic planning process will fail if inadequate time or resources are spent on it, if there is a lack of commitment to the process, or if there is a lack of good communication about the process and outcomes throughout the organization.

The handling of the management issues arising from the strategy planning and development process will greatly influence the employees' perceptions and their long-term enthusiasm for its implementation. Careful handling of the issues and process that arise from changes to structure, projects, mindsets, attitudes and jobs may pay dividends at the time when the planning process is implemented. If people can participate in the planning process from its inception, especially with reference to their areas of responsibility, they will more readily understand the purpose and objectives of the strategic plan and actively support its implementation.

The strategic planning process for the information service should be integrated with the planning for the parent organization and linked to the planning and management of all of the corporate resources. For example, the manager of the information service should be involved in setting the direction for the parent organization. The strategic plan for the parent organization should also set the strategic direction for the information service.

In order to allocate the necessary priority to strategy planning and development a formalized system should be used that allocates time and resources to the task. Its value and importance should be stressed within teams and throughout the organization, and the process used to strengthen the delivery of services to the total community. Strategic planning will inevitably compete with time to manage the other issues of the day, however it is important that everyone contributes and that this is recognized.

The strategic planning process

The outcome of the strategic planning process is the Strategic Plan, which is objectives-driven and primarily concerned with outcomes within a two- to three-year timeframe. The Strategic Plan should be a simple document and present a clear rationale for the specific objectives; give a clear impression of the relative priorities; and be used as the justification for all projects, activities and resources. It should include the vision, values and key strategies and objectives.

The plan should be flexible, enabling smooth and quick adjustments to meet sudden changes in the environment. However, it should not need extensive modification and should be abandoned if this is the case. When the plan has outlived its usefulness, it should be replaced by another as part of a continuous planning cycle. The replacement plan should not be an extrapolation of the old. It requires the rethinking of the future in the light of the existing environment and prospective changes. The plans should be simple and straightforward as complex plans are difficult to understand, implement and monitor.

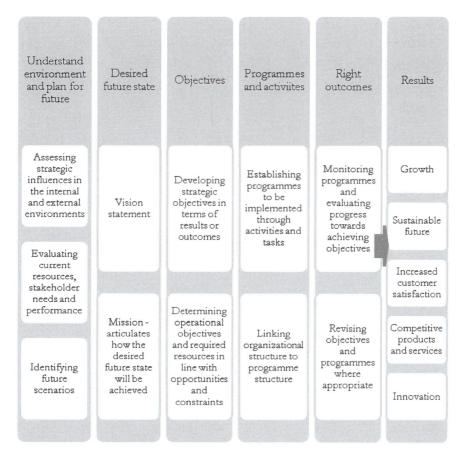

Figure 3.1   The strategic planning process

UNDERSTANDING THE ENVIRONMENT

Understanding the strategic influences in the internal and external environments in which the information service operates is a necessary precursor to any strategic planning exercise. The following tools are useful for this process:

- A strategic audit;
- An analysis of critical success factors;
- A SWOT analysis;
- A PESTLE analysis;
- A capability profile; and
- A needs analysis.

In addition the following internal documents provide useful input in regards to evaluating current resources, stakeholder needs and the current performance of the information service in meeting these needs:

- An outline of the present levels of resources and organizational capability;
- Statements of policy and managerial philosophies;
- The formal and informal mandates imposed on the information service;
- A statement of the desired future in terms of major results and outcomes; and
- A statement of organization-wide objectives that represent the philosophical basis for the information service's operations and articulate the desired future conditions to be achieved.

Different scenarios can also be painted that incorporate the conceivable (what could happen), possibilities (likely) and probabilities (most likely) events. More information on scenario planning processes can be found in the section on scenario planning at the end of this chapter.

Strategic audit

The strategic audit considers the strategic issues from the internal and external environments that have been identified in the previous chapters and which may impact upon the information service and its parent organization. After analysing this important background information the future role of the information service in its environment should be clearer.

The strategic audit should also yield information on existing and potential clients, stakeholders, competitors, the desired image and brand, the appropriateness of services and other important influencing factors. Knowledge of these factors should make the information services manager more aware of the opportunities and threats facing the information service and increase their ability to manage these. If this knowledge is extensive, covering all the relevant factors in the internal and external environments, the element of surprise is reduced. This in turn allows the risk to be managed at the appropriate level. The planning task is also more effective as more of the variables are known. Accident and chance will still play their part in a dynamic environment, bringing with them the need for sudden or unexpected change. However, it is the manager's role to lessen the element of surprise and to respond and adapt to the change as it occurs. Issues to be assessed in the strategic audit include:

- The possible and probable future direction of the information service in the global knowledge economy and society;
- The future direction of the industry sector or business environment in which the information service operates;
- Recent and future events likely to impact on the information service or its parent organization;
- Trends and patterns that could impact on the organization either positively or negatively;
- Current and anticipated future driving forces or strategic external influences on the organization;
- The extent of their impact (positive and negative);
- The vision and preferred future scenario for the organization and the information service;
- The alignment of the current mission, core business objectives, strategies and policies for the information service and its parent organization with the desired future;
- An assessment of their status, for example if they are clearly articulated and acted upon, and consistent with each other and the external and internal environments;
- A stakeholder assessment in terms of their positive or negative influence, knowledge, skills, interests, participation, support and commitment;
- The reputation and standing of the organization amongst its industry peers and competitors; and
- The leadership style and commitment of executive management.

Critical success factors

Critical success factors can be used to identify the most important ingredients for the information service's success. They focus upon the key components or determinants that must be present and correctly managed in the operating environment. Examples of critical success factors are visionary leaders, a motivated and knowledgeable staff, quality and responsive service to customers, and managerial support.

By determining what must go right, priorities can be clarified and understood across the information service. For example, if the ability to respond quickly to any enquiry is a critical success factor then the response time taken to satisfy customer enquiries becomes a priority. Everyone is able to identify with the critical success factor and arrange workloads accordingly so that the customer takes priority. The information service quickly builds up a reputation and customer base because of its responsiveness. Its goals are met and the information service is successful in its achievements. The rate of response can also be used as an indicator to measure the performance of the service.

SWOT analysis

The SWOT (strengths, weaknesses, opportunities and threats) analysis provides an objective assessment as to whether the information service is able to respond to and manage the environmental impacts. The more competent the information service is in dealing with these, the more successful it is likely to be. Strengths and weaknesses deal with factors internal to the organization, whilst opportunities and threats are concerned with its external environment.

Strength is a resource or capability that an organization has to achieve its objectives effectively. In an information service, strength may be its innovative use of technology, or depth and coverage in content. It may also be a particularly helpful and creative member of staff who consistently applies innovative ways to tackle problems.

A weakness is a limitation, fault or defect in the organization that keeps it from achieving its objectives. Limited technology capacity may prevent an information service from meeting all of its customer needs.

It is often difficult to carry out an objective internal assessment upon the information service's strengths and weaknesses. For this reason it is useful to have an external person undertake the assessment as they can remove themselves from the emotional and personal issues involved. Information for the assessment can be gathered through interviews with members of staff, stakeholders, customers and non-users, external evaluations, questionnaires and observations.

An opportunity is any favourable situation in the information service's external environment. It may be a trend or a change that supports the development of an enhanced service, or one that has not previously been identified or filled. An opportunity usually allows the information service to enhance its position, and may be brought about by a technical change. Social networking applications, instant messaging and mobile technologies are examples of technology that create opportunities to deliver new customer services direct to the individual, regardless of time or location.

A threat is an unfavourable situation in the information service's external environment that is potentially damaging to it or its competitive position. It may be a barrier or a constraint, or anything that may inflict problems on the information service.

The SWOT analysis allows strategies to be planned that can realize the strengths and opportunities and overcome the threats and weaknesses. It is also used extensively in marketing.

PESTLE analysis

PESTLE analysis is an environmental analysis tool that examines the political, economic, social, technological, legal and environmental issues that may influence the future direction of the information service.

Capability Profile

The capability profile is the means of assessing the information service's strengths and weaknesses in dealing with the opportunities and threats in the external environment. For example, its capability in the fields of leadership, marketing, technology and finance helps to identify how the organization is placed in comparison with its competitors in its ability to withstand pressures and reposition itself in a changing world.

Leadership capability can be gauged by considering how forward thinking the organization is in repositioning itself in the global knowledge economy and society. It also includes assessing the organization's reputation and image as a trendsetter, its speed of response to changing conditions, the prevailing corporate culture and communication capacity, and its ability to attract and retain highly creative people.

Marketing capability can be demonstrated by its status amongst its competitors, the level of branding, customer loyalty and satisfaction, the percentage of customers versus potential customers, quality of service and ability to maintain growth.

The presence of expertise and advanced technical skills, the level of sophistication in the application of technology, the utilization of resources and personnel to achieve economies of scale, the level of coordination and compatibility, and the integration and effectiveness of service are some of the factors that may determine the information service's technical capability. Financial capability is determined by access to capital, financial strength and the ability to sustain the required financial position.

To complete the capability profile, a bar chart is prepared detailing the degree of strength or weakness in each category. After completing the chart the relativity of the strengths and weaknesses to each other can be determined. Whilst the capability profile is highly subjective, it is still useful. It provides the means for examining the current strategic position of the information service and highlights areas needing attention.

Needs assessment

The needs assessment provides additional environmental information for the development of the plan. It enables the information service to:

- Identify the gap between the current provision and desired level of service;
- Forecast future needs;
- Plan provision to meet such needs in good time; and
- Ensure that the operational policies are effective in meeting real needs.

The needs assessment should not just relate to existing customers of the information service. All stakeholders, including potential customers, should be considered. Many sources of information can be used to provide input to the needs assessment; for example, customer surveys, community analysis, census figures and organizational reports.

The needs analysis should include input in addition to professional judgement or indicators such as (lack of) volume of complaints, comments or suggestions by customers and other stakeholders. To rely just on this information may result in a bias that could lead to an inaccurate assessment of service needs. Underestimation and overestimation are two other pitfalls. Underestimation may arise when the needs of non-vocal sectors of the community have not been brought to attention, or are overlooked. Overestimation of needs can occur by overlooking the fact that a large sector of the customer base is satisfied with the existing provision of service.

The preliminary stage of clarifying what is meant by a need in a particular programme area can be useful in that it forces the examination of real objectives and definition of needs. The concept of need implies a normative judgement: a particular level of need is arbitrary and depends upon attitude. Ideas of what constitutes need can change over time and circumstances in the same way that motivational needs change. 'Wants' and 'needs' should be distinguished; for example, you may want to drive a Mercedes or Porsche to work, yet you may only need a push-bike.

Surveys of both customers and potential customers can be important mechanisms for the collection of information about customer needs. However, they can be comparatively expensive to conduct, arouse or create unrealistic expectations of future service delivery capabilities and require careful planning to provide valid and meaningful results. If such surveys are not properly planned, incorrect information may be obtained that could result in the implementation of a programme totally unsuited to the real needs of the customer base. This could eventually be more costly to the information service in financial, political and social terms than the original costs in conducting the survey.

Implemented correctly, surveys can be a valuable planning tool. However, they should not be relied upon as a 'proven management technique' at the expense of other methods. The gut feeling that arises from a close involvement and working knowledge of the situation should also be considered.

Outline of present levels of resources and organizational capability

The following information can be used in determining the health of the organization and the status of internal resources and organizational capability:

- How closely the information service and its parent organization is aligned to industry standards and profiles of other competing firms in the market place;
- The alignment of information and communication technologies to the strategic objectives and business needs of the organization;
- The consistency between stated or desired corporate culture and the actual prevailing culture;
- The alignment and consistency between the organization's policies and actual practices in the information service;
- The organizational approach to managing and developing expertise;
- The use of power to enhance or detract from organizational success;
- The alignment and fit of decision-making processes and styles to the external and internal environments;
- The rate of turnover of staff in comparison with industry standards;
- The additional skills, competencies and attributes that are needed to transform the organization and enable it to achieve its desired future position;
- The appropriateness of standards and techniques used to evaluate and improve corporate performance;
- The appropriateness, identification and management of risk-mitigation strategies;
- The organizational approach to quality control; and
- The capability of systems to monitor and provide feedback on corporate performance.

Having conducted the situation audit, and made an assessment of the current and desired future state, the desired future state can be better determined.

SETTING THE DESIRED FUTURE STATE

The next task of the strategic planning process is to articulate the vision and define the mission. The vision is the desired future state for the organization. A shared vision across the organization becomes its underlying driving force.

The mission statement articulates how the vision will be achieved. It serves as the focal point for individuals to identify with the organization's vision, purpose and direction. It also provides information about the future direction of the organization and its client base. In order to be readily understood and remembered by all stakeholders, the wording should be simple and explicit. It should be written in such a manner that avoids:

- A narrow perspective of the organization's role;
- The assumption that the organization will be the sole deliverer of specific services;
- Locking the organization into outdated technology or service provision; and
- Consideration of options in service delivery.

If a separate mission statement is to be developed for the information service, it should reflect the mission statement of the parent organization. It should clearly identify the core business and purpose of the information service in contributing to the wider organizational mission statement. The mission statement also identifies those critical factors that distinguish the service from its competitors. It may be a declaration of attitude or value that establishes the organizational climate, or a quality statement about customer service delivery.

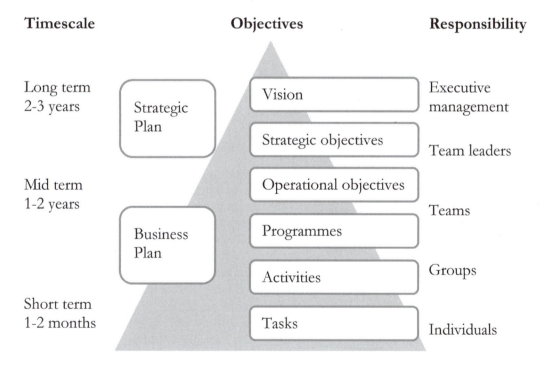

Figure 3.2   The hierarchy of objectives

SETTING OBJECTIVES

Objectives determine the broad strategies for achieving the desired future state. Objectives may be distinguished according to their level in the hierarchy (see Figure 3.2). There is a relationship between level, scope and impact upon the organization and timeframe for implementation. The highest level objectives, the strategic objectives, relate to the organization in its entirety and are usually long term. They are usually articulated in the Strategic Plan. The objectives become more specific and operational at the lower levels in terms of application within the organization. They are also shorter in timeframe. For this reason they are most often found in the information service's Business Plan.

The hierarchy continues in terms of programmes, projects or activities, and tasks. Activities and tasks are directly related to subsets of the objectives and programmes. They are usually short term or repetitive, easily measurable and relate to groups or individuals. The hierarchy is generally shaped like a pyramid. The broader and more future-oriented objectives are fewer in number and appear at the pinnacle of the pyramid. The immediate or short-term objectives are to be found in greater numbers. They are more precise in definition and quantification.

Strategic objectives

The strategic objectives should be long term in nature and allow for improvement and coordination of corporate operations. The strategic objectives should be geared to the desired future state; identifying opportunities whilst increasing the organization's flexibility and ability to adjust to change, and capacity for creativity. They should lead to the definition of corporate or organizational objectives, policies and standards that may be articulated in other documents.

Operational objectives

The strategic objectives are then operationalized into operational plans and objectives. These provide the details of the services to be delivered to meet the strategic objectives and are often found in Business Plans. A set of results and outcomes, qualified by performance measures and a timetable for their achievement, should be provided for each service or project. The Business Plan should also identify how the human, financial, information and technical resources are to be acquired and used to achieve the strategic objectives.

Operational objectives are mid- and short-term focused and are translated in turn into programmes and activities. These are framed with inputs, outputs and constraints in mind. Resources for these are allocated through established functions such as the budget process.

Objectives should be developed within the context of the situation audit and the needs assessment. Opportunities for better service delivery or internal productivity gains should be considered as well as the impact of any known constraints on resources. The parent organization's management philosophies or political ideologies may also shape the development of objectives for the information service.

Effectively formulated objectives should result in concrete outcomes desired by the organization. The formulation of meaningful objectives takes careful thought and analysis. The intention of the objective should be clear and its focus well understood. It should stimulate the action as well as specify it. The objectives must be challenging yet capable of achievement. They should be written so that they can be analysed and reviewed.

Objectives should be defined in terms of results or conditions to be achieved rather than in terms of the activities to be performed, as it is against the objectives that performance will be measured. They should be stated in positive terms, that is, in terms of what is to be achieved rather than avoided. Above all, the objectives should be quantifiable, since the more concrete the information, the more likely will be the achievement of real meaning. An example of a hierarchy of objectives within an information service is shown in Figure 3.3.

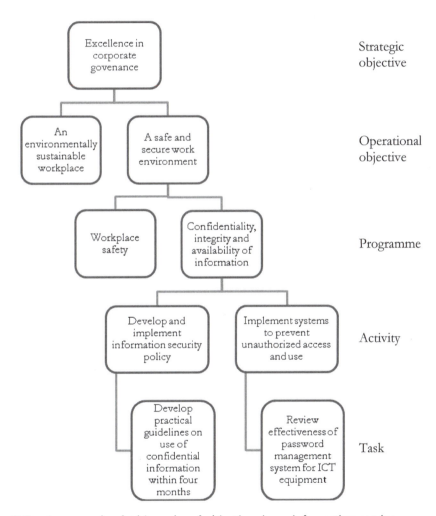

Figure 3.3   An example of a hierarchy of objectives in an information service

The quality of results is just as important as the type or kind of results. Time limits or delays in service provision, percentages, workload volumes and frequency rates are measurable points that can be incorporated into information service objectives. Quantifiable objectives and outcomes define and clarify the expectations and results better than verbal descriptions. They provide a built-in measure of effectiveness.

IMPLEMENTING THE OBJECTIVES THROUGH PROGRAMMES AND ACTIVITIES

Objectives are put into action through a series of programmes and activities which also form part of the Business Plan.

The development of programmes occurs after consideration of the alternative scenarios and strategies whereby the objectives can be achieved. It should be a creative and innovative process, with only the best possible alternatives selected. The selected programmes should represent the best possible use of resources when considered against all other possible uses. They should lead to improved organizational performance or service delivery and derive the greatest possible benefit for the least cost. The evaluation of programme alternatives should assess not only the financial and economic costs and benefits, but also the social and political costs and benefits. Outcomes (quality and quantity) should be measured against inputs.

Programmes are implemented by organizing activities and allocating tasks. Implementation of the plan at this level is often a difficult task as it invariably means organization and personal change because the programmes are often linked to the organizational structure. As major change in programme structure may involve an internal reorganization, strategies for dealing with the required change should be considered prior to the introduction of the new programmes. Responsibilities should be assigned, and monitoring and control processes devised to measure progress towards the attainment of goals.

In addition to linking organizational structure into programme structure, successful planning processes tie implementation strategies into action plans. For example, people should be recruited with skills and mindsets that reinforce the strategic direction of the organization. Performance review systems should be also linked into the achievement of objectives, programmes and activities.

In implementing programmes, the emphasis should be on the outcomes of the decisions rather than the techniques by which the decisions are made. Successful implementations are those that improve the quality of service delivery through employee motivation and an increased commitment to the organization's goals. Positive results should be highlighted and reinforced as short-term improvements can be made permanent through positive reinforcement, monitoring and review.

Information sharing is paramount so that all staff can be fully informed of organizational and personal changes. It is also important that people are able to contribute and be involved in operational decision making. This collaborative approach anticipates that all employees have a commitment to the achievement of organizational goals. It shares the onus of high performance amongst all members of the organization. Mutual discussion regarding the implementation of programmes includes agreement upon resources and assistance necessary to achieve stated objectives. This leads to more effective coordination and collaboration throughout the organization.

Critical to the success of the implementation of the strategic planning process is the need to determine the proper sequencing and relationships of the activities. Appropriate starting and completion dates must be set in order to avoid plans being implemented before the strategies for dealing with the resultant changes are considered. In addition, budgets need to be allocated and people need to be available and supported by information and technical resources before the transition occurs.

ENSURING THE RIGHT OUTCOMES THROUGH REVIEW AND EVALUATION

Often the planning process is considered to be complete upon the implementation of the programme. However this circumvents the need to review and evaluate the performance of the organization continuously against the external and internal environments.

Evaluation through monitoring and review processes is the accountability aspect of planning. It determines whether the objectives are being achieved. It also reduces risk and provides important feedback to fine-tune the delivery of services to meet customer needs. More detail on this issue can be found in Chapter 25.

Managing the future – scenario planning

Uncertainty is a strategic concern for many organizations, which poses specific challenges for managers. It is caused by technological developments and changes in markets with other contributions from environmental, fiscal and political factors. Scenario planning is a proactive way to manage the impact of uncertainty. By using scenarios it is possible to identify key factors that will have serious implications in the future. Taking actions and informed decisions based upon the scenarios, future risks can be avoided and possible opportunities anticipated (Walton 2009: 334).

Scenario planning enables organizations to determine what is of strategic importance and concern to the organization and to explain this in terms of the impact they have on the organization. Participants in the process are required to look at concerns and uncertainties, future directions, pivotal events, decisions both for the short and long terms, constraints and what people would like to be remembered for, and develop a series of possible scenarios or stories of the future. The scenarios are constructed in a workshop environment and are each given a name that can be instantly recognized, based on the storyline or data in the scenario.

Capturing multiple images of the future that together encompass the critical uncertainties facing the organization is one of the two key goals of scenario developers. The other goal is to convince managers at all levels of the organization to consider seriously the strategic and tactical implications of each scenario (Ringland 2003: 22).

The scenarios are not used to predict the future, but highlight options based on what is known and unknown. The advantage is that scenario planning assists organizations to think outside of the box by challenging and stretching conventional thinking in order to map out the future. It is concerned with anticipating the potential future and preparing action plans today that will safeguard organizations tomorrow (Walton 2009: 339 quoting Weiss 2003). Scenario planning can be used in developing the organization's strategic plan, particularly:

- In a business environment of high uncertainty;
- For generating new opportunities;
- For developing a common language throughout the organization; and
- Where there are strong differences of opinion.

The development of a number of scenarios about possible or probable futures enables people to better construct a reality view of the future. Culturally and psychologically they can:

- Promote wider thinking by providing insights into complex situations;
- Challenge and free up peoples' mindsets;
- Overcome availability bias where people undervalue what is difficult to imagine or conceptualize; and
- Shift people's thinking that is embedded in the past.

Other advantages of using scenario planning techniques include:

- The ability to detect early warning signals that a particular future is unfolding;
- An increased capacity to evaluate risk and return options; and
- Being able to generate better strategic options in both favourable and unfavourable futures.

However, Ringland (2003: 23) found that professional scenario developers are seldom totally successful in connecting with line managers or team leaders, who see their role as ensuring day-to-day delivery of a product or service, and who are convinced that scenarios are irrelevant to this task. This can be shortsighted, as Ringland explains:

- Many early warning signs of new scenarios emerging are first seen as peripheral issues in the market place, for example, in the concerns of stakeholders who are not customers, but who can influence them; and
- Good scenarios are insurance that line managers' default assumptions will be identified and modified to fit changing conditions.

Ringland believes that after a scenario exercise, if managers have fully participated and have been sensitized to recognize early warning signs and report them, the initial signals of critical change are less likely to be ignored. She goes on to say that making scenarios accessible to line managers or team leaders requires four stages of preparation before introducing them:

- Creating scenarios clearly grounded in today's events and trends;
- Identifying business options under each scenario;
- Having a clear process for making choices based on the scenarios; and
- Developing a clear set of events that would be early indicators for each scenario.

A typical scenario presentation for each scenario would cover:

- What is happening now that makes the scenario credible;
- A description of the world at the end of the scenario; and
- Early indicators of each scenario, and specific events to watch for.

Most of the strategic management and marketing tools used in information services such as the strength, weakness, opportunity and threat (SWOT) analysis and the Boston

Consulting Group matrix analysis can be used very effectively with scenarios. Generally between four and six scenarios are developed, incorporating the major cause and effect issues identified in the planning process. These are then used as the basis for further research and organizational review from which action plans are developed as part of the strategic planning process.

Conclusion

The planning and development of strategies is essential to managing in times of change in the financial, political, environmental, technical and social environments. Strategy planning and development also leads to other benefits. For example the activities associated with setting and sharing the vision, collectively planning for the future, articulating the organization's objectives and creating an understanding of its purpose and values are useful leadership activities in their own right. They can generate a greater knowledge and understanding of the organization and, ultimately, increase the level of commitment, communication and cohesiveness across the organization. This in turn leads to individual feelings of empowerment and strengthens the common goal of all.

Whilst creating and articulating the vision and future position of the organization is a key leadership role for the Chief Executive, all stakeholders who have the potential to be affected should be involved in strategic planning at various stages. For example, customers and suppliers may be asked to provide their thoughts on future services to meet emerging needs, whilst members of the governing body may set policy direction and funding allocators may provide input into future funding strategies. The planning process should be inclusive.

Whilst executive management will not produce the plan alone, their personal knowledge, commitment and involvement are crucial to its long-term effectiveness. Their leadership roles include initiating the process, encouraging support and an involvement in overseeing the process. An important responsibility of executive management is to create the necessary environment to dispel fears that will inevitably arise out of the potential for change, and to encourage the enthusiasm of others in the strategic planning process.

The strategic planning process has five logical steps:

- Using a series of tools to analyse and understand the external and internal environments;
- Setting and describing the desired future state of the organization through the vision and mission;
- Determining how the vision and mission is to be achieved by identifying a series of objectives;
- Implementing the objectives through programmes and activities; and
- Ensuring the right outcomes through review and evaluation.

As the business environments in which organizations operate become more complex, organizations have had to shift from forecasting to developing a series of possible scenarios or stories of the future to further position the organization for a sustainable future.

References

Ringland, G. 2003. Scenario planning: Persuading operating managers to take ownership. *Strategy and Leadership*, 31(6), 22–28.

Walton, G. 2009. Theory, research, and practice in library management 6: Managing uncertainty through scenario planning. *Library Management*, 30(45), 334–341.

Further Reading

Lindgren, M. and Bandhold, H. 2003. *Scenario Planning: The Link Between Future and Strategy*. Basingstoke: Palgrave Macmillan.

O'Connor, S. 2009. *Scenario Planning for Libraries: Imagining Your Organization's Future*. London: Facet Publishing.

Van der Heijden, K. et al. 2002. *The Sixth Sense: Accelerating Organizational Learning With Scenarios*. Chichester: John Wiley.

4 *Attracting and Retaining Talented People in Challenging Times*

How to become and maintain the status of an employer of choice in order to attract and retain the best and most talented people will be one of the next major challenges facing executive management. This is because most Western countries have reached their peak in the number of people eligible to be in the workforce due to the imminent retirement of the Baby Boomer generation and declining population growth in the 1970s and 1980s. In addition to this decline in the labour force, there are other reasons why attracting and retain employees should be viewed as a strategic management issue. Not least is the fact that individuals' talents and skills are an organization's most valuable resource, both in terms of their contribution to business success and the significant cost of salaries and add-on costs.

Individuals' skills, knowledge talents and innovation capabilities are important elements for two other issues confronting executive management today; these being transformation and change. The rich combination of the people's talents, experiences, know-how, skill sets, imaginations, thoughts, philosophies and capabilities is what sets the organization apart and distinguishes it from its competitors. Their attitudes and perspectives can also reinforce the corporate outcomes and organizational values. Yet attitudes and expectations in the workplace are changing. At a time when information services are moving into virtual 24x365 services, many individuals are looking for greater workplace flexibility in terms of working hours and also workplace. Work is how we describe what we do, rather than the place where we go. This chapter looks at workforce planning models and processes for identifying the required skills and talents for the future and attracting, developing and retaining the best people in a changing work environment.

At a strategic level, the activities of workforce planning, attracting and retaining skilled and talented people include understanding the future of the organization and the changing environment in which it will operate; planning and forecasting the competencies, attitudes, skills and talents to meet the mission, organizational and service delivery objectives; as well as determining what additional or different requirements may be required to sustain the organization in the future. This is where workforce planning and attraction and retention strategies are linked to the organization's strategic plan and the external drivers such as the current labour market that are likely to impact on its future. Examples that need to be considered include projections for growth or diversification, whether a rebuilding programme will result in the merger of cultural services into a one-stop integrated experience for the customer, the impact of moving to 24x365 operations or the need for retraining as a consequence of the introduction of new technology and services.

At an operational level, continuous and proactive activities can be found in specifying required skills and competencies to meet current and future needs as well as organizational objectives; recruiting and selecting the right individuals; developing skills, expertise and knowledge; managing diversity, motivating people and acknowledging different generational needs in the workplace; as well as managing performance with opportunities for review and feedback.

Workforce planning for the future

ENVIRONMENTAL ANALYSIS

The first step in workforce planning is to determine what type of skills, knowledge, competencies, attitudes, talents and mindsets are currently required and will likely be needed in the future. This is a forecasting activity, drawing upon input from the environmental analysis. This stage considers what the organization is trying to achieve, its preferred future position and how well structured it is to do the job. It also takes into account the demand for new services, the forming of strategic alliances with other institutions to facilitate extended hours of operation, diversity of staff being employed, productivity, growth and the developmental stage of the information service and its parent organization, together with any other influencing factors and trends in the external environment that may affect conditions of employment. For example, industrial relations, legislation awards and workplace agreements may affect the ability of the information service to attract key people as employees as well as influence the terms and conditions applying in a downsizing situation. Regulatory conditions can also impact upon budgets, rosters, the makeup and classification of staff. Other legislation requirements such as equal opportunity or affirmative action may also influence the makeup of the organization and human resource selection procedures.

Furthermore the organization's ability to attract and keep appropriately skilled individuals will be affected by economic conditions and changes in academic requirements that influence the level and number of courses in universities and training institutions and the commensurate supply of graduates. Input should be given to the designers of university and training courses so that changes in the market place can be reflected in the requirements of the course outcomes.

Determining requirements for a sustainable future

ORGANIZATIONAL STRUCTURE

The structure of the organization influences how and where people will be deployed. In turn it is influenced by the rate of change in the environment and should emerge from the strategic planning process and reinforce the operational plan. For example where the strategic planning process has identified a critical business advantage in having a strong regional presence, the organization may choose to align its structure to certain geographical areas. This will have an impact on the ability to attract and retain people in certain locations. Alternatively where the planning process has discerned the need to differentiate services to specific client groups the organization may reinforce its customer-driven service delivery by structuring according to different service delivery models and the needs of each client group. In this instance the organizational structure will influence the different types of skills required to meet different aspects of service delivery.

In response to global financial pressures the trend is to smaller organizations that are flatter, with fewer management tiers and more flexible structures. This allows the organization to adapt more quickly to change. The global environment and move to integrated services also influences structures and can make attracting and retaining staff distance independent. Traditional organizational boundaries are disappearing as people work collaboratively with strategic partners to deliver integrated services either at a local, national or global level.

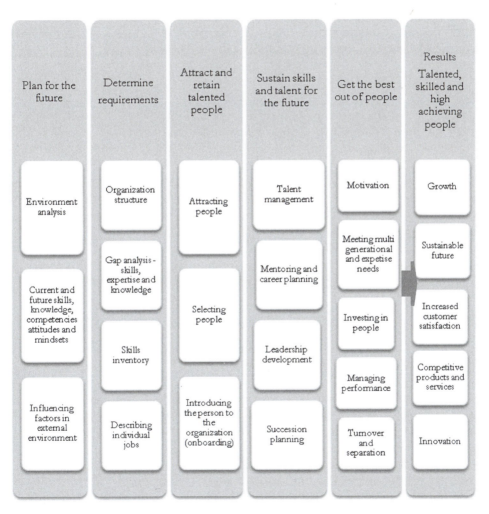

Figure 4.1   An integrated model for attracting and retaining talented and skilled people

GAP ANALYSIS

Having taken into account the impact of the structure of the organization and the projection of the skills, knowledge and expertise required for the future, a gap analysis is undertaken. This compares the projected requirements (needs) with the current status of the existing inventory (availability), and expresses these as a match, excess or deficit of personnel and skills. These may relate to specific skills, expertise and knowledge, occupations or levels of staff and may not be consistent across the organization. Programmes may differ in their types of activities and require different skills and numbers of staff. Levels of growth and attrition, current performance levels, status of the labour market and the reputation of the organization as an employer of choice will also influence the way forward after completion of the gap analysis.

Alternative actions are considered in order to overcome anticipated gaps. These may involve recruitment, retraining, redeployment and/or termination of personnel, automating manual processes through the introduction of technology, redesigning jobs or reorganizing work processes to improve productivity, changing the skill and competency requirements for prospective employees, and developing new skill-training programmes. The impact of changes on existing personnel should also be considered.

SKILLS INVENTORY

A skills inventory is a management information system that describes the skills component of the organization's workforce. This includes details of employees' qualifications, experience, languages spoken, specific knowledge, skills and any other information such as outside interests that may be useful to the business directions of the organization. Skills inventories are useful for several purposes. They can be used to strategically monitor workforce capabilities and performance, and to assist in the identification of employees for promotion, transfer, specific projects and/or training. The usefulness of any skills inventory depends upon the appropriateness, accessibility and current validity of the data. A simple file system may be adequate for a small, relatively stable organization, whilst a computerized data system, updated daily, may be required for a large, more dynamic organization.

DESCRIBING INDIVIDUAL JOBS

An important component of attracting and retaining people is to ensure that everyone is focused on their contribution to the organization and know what is expected of them. This is usually achieved by describing the purpose, responsibilities, activities and duties of a specific job and its potential future direction – the what, who, why and when. In addition the necessary experience, aptitudes and skills to make the required level of contribution and meet other organizational responsibilities should also be described. This serves two purposes: it identifies where further personal development may be needed by the individual doing or being considered for the job as well as ascertaining what is required when attracting people to the organization in the future.

How the job is described very much influences the success in attracting and retaining the right person as it will project the culture, corporate philosophy and uniqueness of the organization as well as the important attributes and characteristics of the position. A creative description will:

- Signal that the organization is most likely forward thinking and innovative and is wanting to attract talented and innovative thinking applicants;
- Set the scene and provide a descriptive and interesting statement of the duties and responsibilities of a specific job;
- Set expectations and provide a measure of performance and outcomes required of the person; and
- Enable prospective applicants to determine whether the job and organization is of interest to them.

Components that can be attractive and useful to prospective candidates include:

- The level of influence and impact that the person is likely to have within the organizational structure, reporting relationships and the people with whom collaborative relationships need to be formed;
- Meaningful information about the desired outcomes and key responsibilities which set the benchmark by which their talents and performance can be judged;
- The what, how and why of the job. Visual guides such as pie charts add contextual meaning as they provide an immediate impact and graphically illustrate the important components and relationships of the job. Other aspects to consider are how much time is devoted to each significant aspect of their work and the degree of supervision received;
- The skills, natural talents, attributes, knowledge and qualifications of the person doing the job;
- Specialized technology, knowledge and equipment used that might require specialized skills or operational understanding; and
- Any other specific working conditions that have an occupational, health and safety aspect or which require pre-selection procedures.

Descriptions of jobs need to be continuously updated to reflect changing technology and other variables such as integrating information services. They also need to leave some scope for initiative and innovative input on how the outcomes can be achieved in an alternative way. An ideal opportunity to review the position is during a formal performance review.

Attracting and retaining people

Survival in the twenty-first century is dependent on the abilities to attract and retain people with the right skill sets, talents, knowledge and expertise to meet future needs as well as having the necessary flexibility to cope with changing circumstances. In turn the attractiveness of the organization as an employer of choice will be dependent on:

- How flexible the organization can be in its capacity to meet workplace demands for family-friendly working hours and mobility;

KnowledgeAge Pty Ltd

Chief Knowledge and Information Enabler

Reporting directly to the Managing Director the Chief Knowledge and Information Enabler's influence will extend throughout the organization. KnowledgeAge is expanding rapidly and as a corporate enabler, advocate and knowledge broker the primary task is to champion the creation and sharing of knowledge within the organization and with clients on a global basis. Critical outcomes from this important leadership role include:

- As an enabler – ensuring that the corporate memory is complete;

- As an advocate – the organization excels in creative thinking, innovation and intellectual capital;

- As a knowledge broker – the commercial investment in the organization's branding, knowledge and intellectual capital is further leveraged yet protected where necessary.

The Chief Knowledge and Information Enabler will have outstanding leadership skills, knowledge of cross-cultural negotiations, highly creative and innovative thinking, the ability to negotiate in an environment where new concepts are being introduced, and an understanding of the commercial value of intangible assets such as branding, intellectual property, knowledge and innovation. The person will be expected to travel internationally on a regular basis, and often at short notice.

Figure 4.2   A sample job description

- The financial position of the organization and its commensurate ability to offer over-award salary payments, personal use of new technology and communications devices and other incentives; and
- The age groups employed and whether the organization recognizes and meets the varying needs and values of different generations it employs.

ATTRACTING PEOPLE TO A JOB

People can be attracted to fill a position by enlisting existing staff that have the required expertise, skills and knowledge, recruiting new people or developing and retraining existing staff. Enlisting existing staff has the advantages of increasing the general level of morale by providing an example of career path development within the organization and stimulating others to greater achievement. The process of recruiting can also be more predictable in its outcome as the applicant's contribution and performance within the organization will be known. However in times of change this may not always be in the organization's best interest. People from outside the organization may bring different talents, perspectives, practices and values than existing staff.

Advertising through electronic job boards, in the local or national media, trade and professional journals, using employment agencies to undertake executive searches and to screen potential applicants, third-party recommendations from existing staff or staff in educational institutions, and considering unsolicited applications are some of the ways by which people can be recruited from outside of the organization.

SELECTING PEOPLE

There are a number of ways to ensure that the right person is selected for the job. These include interviewing and using skills tests, presentations, job trials, psychological and personality testing. The interview is the most widely used method of selecting individuals and is aimed at:

- Assessing an applicant's intelligence, talents, experience, level of motivation, and interpersonal skills;
- Providing information to the applicant about the information service and its parent organization. The includes discussion on matters such as the flexible employment conditions, salary and other incentives to ensure compatibility between the organization's and future employee's expectations;
- Enabling the prospective applicant to evaluate the organization and make decisions as to its suitability as an employing body; and
- Providing the first impression of the organization's culture, values and corporate dynamics.

Ideally the interview or selection committee should include the immediate supervisor and consist of between two and four people who collectively bring knowledge of the job and the organization, diversity of thinking and gender balance as well as an independent view. Their role is to make an objective judgement about which applicant best fits the job and the future direction of the organization.

In addition or as a substitute for the interview, other tests can be used as part of the selection process. Written and skills tests as well as case studies can be used to test intelligence, aptitude, ability and interest. Performance job simulations such as work sampling create a miniature replica of a job. These, and on-the-job trials, provide practical scenarios where applicants are able to demonstrate the degree to which they can do the job. Likewise, the preparation and delivery of a presentation and the provision of portfolios of work also provide tangible evidence in presentation and analytical abilities. Formal assessments such as psychological tests, personality and aptitude tests can also be administered by trained professionals. Referees can also be used to screen or clarify a candidate's suitability for the position.

Leigh (2009: 249) provides an analysis of the accuracy of recruitment tools indicating that assessment or testing centres, structured interviews, giving people sample work to do and ability tests are more reliable than biometric data, personality tests, unstructured interviews and references.

INTRODUCING THE PERSON TO THE ORGANIZATION (ON BOARDING)

Having attracted and appointed the right person to the job, the next stage is to ensure that they remain the right person in the job. Bringing the person on board to the organization through the induction programme is the first stage of a number of activities that enhance the development and performance of both the person and the job in line with the current and future state of the organization. It is a very important facet of management as it establishes what is required of the new employee. Induction orientates and introduces the new employee to the organization and its customer service focus. It allows the employee to become conversant with the job and how this relates to the information service's programmes and activities. If the employee is new to the organization, the induction process can provide them with insight into the organization's culture and values.

The induction process should provide additional background information such as employee benefits; salary schedules; safety; flexibility in working arrangements; probationary period; time recording and absences; leave conditions; organizational code of conduct; grievance procedures; hours of work; lunch and coffee breaks; and use of facilities. It is also helpful to get to know the new person's background and interests, to emphasize the values and culture of the organization and to discuss how their actions and values can reinforce the culture. As they are likely to feel nervous or uneasy at first, it is essential to make them feel that the organization genuinely needs them and to enquire if they have any problems.

The work, goals and objectives of the department, its relationship to the total organization and other departments should also be explained in the first contact as well as informing them of who they report to, and who reports to them. This session can also include information visits to other business units, introductions to all senior officers and a complete overview of special programmes or facilities within the organization. As the new employee begins to be aware of the corporate culture and subcultures they may need some explanation as to why certain things occur and the values that are most prevalent within the organization. With this in mind it is also useful to identify the people to approach to solve work problems as well as providing a policy and procedures manual and making sure they are not left alone to fend for themselves.

During the first week it is helpful to maintain contact and encourage them to talk about problems they have encountered as well as explaining in more detail how their work fits into overall activities now and in the future. Help them to develop a sense of belonging, showing interest in and reviewing their progress. It is also important to be alert for personal problems that could affect their work performance and to clear up any misunderstandings. Discuss the organization's vision, how the service is changing to meet different generational needs and what might further change in the future. Engage them on this and ask for their perspectives and thoughts regarding the future.

Finally, regular contact during the first month should help prevent grievances setting in. Check their progress and correct errors by arranging further instruction. If they have done a job well, tell them so. Let them know that their efforts are appreciated.

Sustaining skills and talent for the future

Having put effort into attracting skilled and talented people to the organization it is appropriate that steps are taken to retain and further develop these talents and skills. Sustaining the right leadership, skills and talent within the organization is set to take on an even greater importance as more organizations realize that their employees' talents and skills drive their business success. Two strategies that can assist organizations in sustaining their human capital in an uncertain future and declining labour force are talent management and succession planning. Supplementing these are the acts of mentoring and career planning and leadership development.

TALENT MANAGEMENT

Talent management involves identifying, managing and developing critical workforce segments and personal traits such as flair and aptitude that can be used for the benefit of the organization, as well as managing 'high value' individuals who excel in these traits. Most people bring a 'talent' to the organization, albeit some may be hidden as the individual prefers not to broadcast their talent or does not recognize the value of the talent. Hidden talents may include artistic abilities, translation skills or ability of a person to use sign language. In information services 'high value' talented people may include those who have entrepreneurial business skills to turn creative ideas into fruition or a flair for identifying political issues at an early stage.

Talent can be nurtured by having a culture of excellence. The role of the information services manager is therefore in:

- Creating a culture for nurturing talent and leadership from within;
- Seeking out and discovering hidden talents;
- Further developing these talents for the benefit of the individual and the organization through coaching and mentoring programmes; and
- Taking a holistic approach that respects, empowers and taps into social capital; building interpersonal relationships, goodwill, cooperation and trust, for the improved well-being of all.

As with workforce planning, talent management should be linked to the business direction in that the critical characteristics and personal traits that are identified as causing outstanding performance should be those that reinforce the values and the preferred future of the organization. For example if the organization has a goal to integrate its cultural services, it will require people who are adept at bringing disparate groups together. In readying the organization for its integrated future and infusing the right mindsets and aptitudes, talents in negotiation, encouragement and big picture thinking will need to be developed in order to bring about the change. Similarly if the information service wishes to move to 24x365 virtual services in collaboration with other services strategically placed around the world it will require talented people who have a global perspective, have a flair for encouraging collaboration and cultural adaptability.

The second part of talent management is the management of 'high value' individuals whose outstanding traits and other particulars may be recorded in either the skills inventory or a specially designed talent database. Information might include details of their individual talent management plan, targeted coaching and accelerated development opportunities, the criticality of their role, the scarcity of their attributes, level of potential, succession opportunities within the organization, cultural adaptability, assessment of their leadership and global-mindedness, length of service intentions and departure risk assessment as well as their readiness to assume higher levels of responsibility.

Responsibility for the attraction, retention, development and recognition of talent across the organization, together with the accelerated development of 'high value' individuals, are both line management and specialized human resource management roles. Recognition is of particular importance as giving prominence to 'high value' people with outstanding talents will create role models for others to emulate. Those with the talented attributes will also act as champions for the desired thinking.

MANAGING CLEVER PEOPLE

Whilst talented people provide special aptitudes, flair and mindsets, clever people provide special skills and knowledge. Clever people have been defined by Goffee and Jones (2010) as being highly talented individuals with the potential to create disproportionate amounts of value from the resources that the organization makes available to them. Whilst a clever person may also be considered a talented person, there is one point of difference. Clever people need an organization to achieve their full potential. Goffee and Jones have defined nine characteristics of clever people:

- Their cleverness is central to their identity – their close identity between what they do and who they are means that they often see themselves as not being dependent upon others;
- Their skills and knowledge are not easily replicated as they are embedded in the individual. Whilst this knowledge may not be able to be captured, it can provide a competitive advantage whilst they are employed by the organization;
- They know their worth. They are confident in their own worth and ability. They have a clear understanding of their value to the organization and that their knowledge and personal networks are hard to replicate;
- They are willing to challenge and ask difficult questions. They also have great passion;

- They are organizationally savvy. Clever people find the organizational context where their interests will be most generously funded. They will often engage in organizational politics to ensure that their projects are indulged;
- They do not want to be led and are indifferent to the corporate hierarchy. Their sphere of influence is their knowledge and skills, not position;
- They expect instant access to senior executives;
- They want to be connected to other clever people to achieve their full potential. Networking is not a social nicety but a source of perpetual improvement and bright ideas. Networking allows them to question assumptions and to make previously unacknowledged links; and
- They won't thank you or acknowledge good leadership.

Clever people need special leadership. They need to be given space and resources, boundaries and a sense of direction within which to focus their efforts, but not close management. Recognition of their achievements is also important, although this is most valued when it comes from prestigious peers and clients outside of the organization.

SUCCESSION PLANNING

Akin to the processes of workforce planning and talent management is succession planning. Succession planning involves identifying talented individuals with the right leadership and communication styles, values, mindsets, attitudes and agility and developing them to play a more significant role in the future. Succession planning involves:

- Determining the critical skills, behaviours and mindsets that will be required by the future business direction of the organization;
- Identifying talented individuals who have the potential to develop these skills, behaviours and mindsets; and then
- Counselling, training, nurturing and providing stretch assignments and other experiences and opportunities for these individuals to develop the required attributes.

Apart from retaining and nurturing talent within the organization, succession planning enables the development of a career path and minimizes the risk of an incongruent fit as the chosen individuals' history and work performance within the organization are known.

Kleinsorge (2010: 67–68) has identified a further valid reason for undertaking succession planning: being better able to support rapid, frequent reorganization in challenging times. He argues that when leaders shift from old to new roles, the tacit knowledge regarding a team's group norms, communication styles, relevant incentives, and other factors moves with the leader transitioning to her new role. This shift creates gaps in the corporate knowledge that develops along with a leader's experience. Following reorganization the new leaders have little time to gain this tacit knowledge and must start from scratch to discover how best to manage larger numbers of employees. Where there are frequent reorganizations succession planning can be successfully used to develop and transition employees into their new leadership roles.

Kleinsorge further advocates the use of Web 2.0 tools to incorporate knowledge management and leadership development into succession planning to make it more responsive. He suggests that executives use information gathered by Web 2.0 tools when preparing for corporate restructures, such as mapping social networks in a company and monitoring blogs and forums for quick identification of new leaders for executing a reorganization. His suggestions for Web 2.0 tools include:

- Identifying potential leaders by:
    - comparing social network diagrams that track where employees go for information with organizational charts;
    - establishing and monitoring a blog that provides the values, ethics, beliefs and expectations of the organization regarding leadership;
    - establishing and monitoring a forum that allows employees to provide input on what managerial qualities work well and should be continued, as well as the characteristics and competencies that successors need in the reorganized structure;
- Expanding leadership readiness by:
    - incorporating an aspiring leader training programme into the succession planning process;
    - delivering a blended learning course that has videos of exiting or retiring leaders providing philosophies on leadership at the company;
    - using multiple delivery modes such as wikis, e-learning courses, and face-to-face sessions to provide employees with continuous access to leadership development training;
    - establishing a leadership community of practice by having employees who participate in the training contribute to wikis etc. with examples of how they practice leadership; and
- Rapidly transitioning new leaders by:
    - requiring the departing leader to have an information-sharing session with the incoming leader through stories and practical tips; capturing these sessions in video and audio formats and adding these to the learning assets of the leadership development programme;
    - using the leadership team to welcome new leaders and holding them accountable for introductions and the passing on of company values and standards for leadership;
    - sending a link to important corporate information and resources in an email for new leaders on day one of their new role; and
    - creating a site within the community of practice intranet that provides knowledge assets for new leaders.

Getting the best out of people

Getting the best out of people involves recognizing individual talents and balancing organizational needs with individual needs in a win-win situation. Most people genuinely want to make a successful contribution to the organization they work in. However their contribution level will further increase if people are recognized and respected for their talents, knowledge, contribution, background and expertise, if the job becomes more meaningful and the individual is given more autonomy and discretion in keeping with their knowledge and expertise in determining how their work will be carried out. This is particularly important in information services where there is a rich diversity in the skills, backgrounds and expertise of employees.

Individual needs are met through two outcomes: the immediate or primary outcomes and secondary outcomes. Immediate positive outcomes can be influenced by generation age groups and professional background and are represented by money, promotion, feelings of achievement, recognition by peers or, negatively, by being shunned by fellow employees. Secondary outcomes arise out of the immediate outcomes. They include the new car that is purchased from the pay rise or the self-esteem that arises out of promotion. At various stages of their careers circumstances will differ and people will be motivated by different needs.

Not every job can be challenging and exciting all the time. In all organizations there are necessary activities to perform that are considered mundane, repetitive or dull. Whilst still respecting those individuals who have a professional standing for their talents, knowledge and expertise, managers may seek to improve the job satisfaction of those undertaking the more operational tasks through providing skill variety and work that challenges people's abilities. Variety can be produced by adding functions through job enlargement. Seeing and understanding how certain 'in between' tasks contribute to the end results and outcomes makes the job more meaningful to the individual and provides a sense of achievement and purpose. This in turn will also increase individual performance and satisfaction. However, the type of work assigned needs consideration. There is no point in enlarging a job merely by adding further onerous duties to an existing list of disagreeable tasks. If anything, this will have a negative effect on motivation.

Flexible work arrangements can also lead to greater output. Arrangements such as flexitime and job sharing can lessen the level of absenteeism and often utilize the individual at the time of their peak of productivity. Flexible work arrangements can increase individual enthusiasm and make it easier for the information service to recruit new people.

PERSONAL DEVELOPMENT AND LEARNING

Investing in organizational and individual learning is important in sustaining and renewing the corporate knowledge of the organization, in motivating and retaining staff as well as keeping the organization ahead of their competitors. Personal learning and development strategies should be designed to balance the individual's personal learning and development needs that have been identified as part of a regular performance appraisal system, and those development strategies that support the organization's and work group's strategic business direction, programmes and activities.

Personal learning is different to training. The former should be viewed as a partnership between the individual and the organization and may include undertaking further study in a career related area. Examples of the latter include training on the features of a new business application or upgrade to an existing ICT system in order to make the most use out of the available functionality. Learning and personal development strategies may also include on-the-job learning delivered face-to-face or electronically, mentoring, attendance at conferences and seminars, management placement programmes, targeted talent management, and opportunities to act in higher level positions.

Personal and professional development and learning is a critical investment for the future of the organization. Without it the organization is in danger of stagnating. Unfortunately during times of economic pressure, the budget for learning and development is often the first to be cut, although this represents a false economy. Gaining support for executive commitment and recognition of the value of development and learning rests on explaining the business value of the development investment. This includes business arguments to the fact that knowledgeable staff project a professional image in customer service delivery as they have an in-depth understanding of the products and services that can be provided, invigorating new ideas that can lead to competitive advantage, meeting generational expectations in the workplace and the ability to retain talented staff through personal development opportunities without whom the organization may struggle.

Designing the programme

An effective professional development or learning programme satisfies both the knowledge and skill requirements of the individual participants and the business direction of the organization. The programme content must be relevant, understandable, easily absorbed, and associated with the work or professional environment. Learning materials should be varied in order to avoid boredom.

If the professional development or learning programme is being designed in-house, a combination of didactic and experiential methods is necessary. Didactic methods include lectures, visual aids, demonstration and panel discussion. Experiential methods of learning can be provided through field trips, structured discussion, brainstorming, case studies, role playing, sensitivity training and encounter training. Adults learn in significantly different ways, testing new concepts and behaviours against what they have previously learnt. Participants should be encouraged to re-examine past experiences in the light of new information and experiences.

Where an attitudinal or behavioural change is required, efforts to change the participants' behaviour should be incorporated into the training programme. Simulation, group and individual participation, role play and case discussion should be incorporated in order to create the desired behaviour and provide immediate feedback on the success or failure of that behaviour to participants.

The potential use of new skills, knowledge or behaviour influences the type of professional development or learning programme to be provided. If the planned outcome is that of increased knowledge, there is generally less need for discovery learning. If the learning is to be applied in an innovative way, then more experience-based learning is needed. If the desired outcome is to have frequent learning-on-the-job applications or it is to be used in an operating mode such as with the introduction of a new technology application there needs to be more experiential learning. Retention is another aspect to consider. The longer the participants need to retain what is learnt in the learning programme, the more experiential the learning programme needs to be.

A good professional development and learning programme provides enthusiasm where individuals will want to demonstrate their newly acquired knowledge, skills or behaviours. This can be assisted through active support and involvement in the workplace. An example is where the immediate supervisor holds meetings with the participant(s) before and after the session to determine the purpose of the programme, to set individual goals and objectives of the session(s), to look at ways in which the newly acquired behaviour can be reinforced back in the workplace, and to evaluate the outcomes of the programme.

The work environment provides the greatest continuing opportunity for professional development and job-related learning. This includes job rotation, secondments and the capacity to act in higher-level positions that can be undertaken in conjunction with other courses, seminars, conferences and other activities to reinforce the individual's effective use of their newly acquired knowledge, skills and competencies on the job.

At the end of any formal professional development or learning programme a review may be held between the organizer, the manager, the presenter (if it is a course) and participants to gather information and evaluate the session. It is preferable for this to be done whilst the programme is still fresh in everyone's mind. Items for review may include the pace of the session, problems with materials, groups, the presenter and general housekeeping issues.

REWARDS AND COMPENSATION

Rewarding or compensating people for their contribution is a further aspect of getting the best out of people. Individuals were traditionally compensated for the time that they spent on the job and years of service rather than to the success or failure of the information service or parent organization. Now value is placed on rewarding people in a meaningful way for their innovative ideas, personal contribution and effectiveness of groups and individuals.

Not all compensation needs to be in the form of a monetary payment. What is important is the acknowledgement of the staff member in a manner that is meaningful to them. Diversity in the workforce means that reward structures need to be flexible to cope with different generational and professional values and recognition factors.

Meaningful rewards can include attendance at a conference or opportunities to further their skills and career opportunities through job enrichment and job enlargement.

Job enrichment is not the allocation of more tasks, but the allocation of increased autonomy and responsibility for work outcomes. Responsibility and autonomy can be increased by:

- Allowing individuals to set their own work schedules;
- Providing skill variety and rotating monotonous tasks between individuals on a regular basis;
- Allowing experienced personnel to train less-experienced workers;
- Enabling individuals to establish direct relationships with the customers and so increase the significance of their tasks and activities; and
- Encouraging staff to make their own quality checks.

Job enrichment will only work when the motivating potential of the job is high. The process has to be instituted selectively and with an acute knowledge of the motivational forces of the individuals. Individuals with high growth needs will eagerly accept the added responsibility. Those people whose growth needs are not so strong may respond less eagerly at first, or react negatively at being 'stretched' or 'pushed' too far. In times of economic constraint, people may also perceive the information service to be increasing duties and responsibilities without the proportionate increases in compensation. The motivational issues will then be lost in a jungle of pay disputes in which the organization will be viewed only as a 'money-saving' entity with no regard for its employees.

Finally, feedback is a necessary part of motivation. This can be measured by the degree to which an individual, in carrying out the work activities required by the job, receives information about the effectiveness of their efforts. Feedback is most powerful when it is received directly from the work itself.

MANAGING PEOPLE'S PERFORMANCE

Performance management is an important part of developing and retaining highly motivated individuals and a corporate environment that is creative, productive and happy. It is a day-to-day management task where continuous monitoring, counselling and feedback on performance take place in a positive environment where the bottom line is success for all. Performance management is often confused or used interchangeably with performance measurement. Fryer et al. (2009: 480) differentiate them as:

> *Performance measurement is quantifying, either quantitatively or qualitatively, the input, output or level of activity of an event or process. Performance management is action, based on performance measures and reporting, which results in improvements in behaviour, motivation and processes and promotes innovation.*

Performance measurement

Fryer et al. (2009) have identified four important areas of performance measurement that need attention when measuring individual and organizational performance:

* Deciding what to measure – with an increasing importance on outcomes rather than outputs;
* How to measure it – ensuring that the indicator and rationale for measuring it are precise and accurate, able to measure results or behaviour and able to deliver the intended results. Tied into this is the 'how' and 'when' to measure;
* Interpreting the data – ensuring that the indicators can be analysed and used to forecast demands, costs and performance; and
* Communicating the results – ensuring that the performance measurement can produce and communicate information that can be used to change behaviours and improve performance.

Performance interview

Supplementing ongoing monitoring and feedback on performance, the performance interview is an opportunity where parties take time to discuss how to improve the organization, and for the employee to map out how their future work programme and personal development desires will contribute to and sustain the organization's success. Opportunities for internal promotion should also be developed and a reward system put in place to encourage productivity and innovation. These opportunities are also important in creating a highly motivated staff and maintaining morale levels.

The words 'appraisal', 'interview' and 'performance review' infer some judgement on an individual's performance. Managed constructively, performance monitoring and appraisal systems can lead to discussions on:

- How the supervisor can make the person's job easier (360 degree feedback);
- What needs to change in the organization to make the job easier (productivity);
- What new ideas the organization could implement to make it more successful (innovation);
- How to make the organization a better place to work (motivation);
- Opportunities that can enhance skills, behaviours, physical and emotional well-being of all employees (corporate development); and
- How to sustain the desired culture and values of the organization (corporate governance).

The discussion should also focus on the personal career ambitions and future personal and professional development needs of the individual concerned. This is because promotion and improvements in performance cannot take place without adequate skills and knowledge development. They can also be used to develop an inventory of human resources that forms the basis for career planning and skills inventory from an organizational point of view. Counselling when negative activities are identified should be balanced with rewards and recognition that reinforce positive ideas and output.

Turnover and separation

Staff turnover can be beneficial or detrimental to the information service, depending on the consequences. On the positive side it allows the opportunity to recruit people with new skills and outlook and can increase the level of flexibility in the type and numbers of employees. This is particularly important in circumstances where the technology, business processes, external environments and customer expectations rapidly change. A controlled turnover of employees can also contain the level of incremental salary creep.

The negatives are associated with the loss of corporate knowledge and employee morale. Financial costs are incurred in severance pay, advertising and the recruitment of new personnel, as well as in their orientation and training. There is often an associated downtime in the use of equipment and lost output and productivity until the new person gains the knowledge and skills of the previous incumbent.

Different jobs will experience different turnover rates and the economic climate will also influence the turnover rate. Notwithstanding this, there is an optimum turnover rate. Too slow a turnover rate will result in a staid organization; too high a turnover rate is unsettling and disruptive for those remaining. It is often a symptom that there is a problem within the organization.

At a personal level there are many reasons why people leave organizations. Some of these are voluntary; such as to relocate, to undertake a different career path, to experience a change in a work environment, or to retire. There are also occasions where the person leaves on an involuntary basis. For example, individuals may also be transferred out of an area to meet operational needs, but may still remain employed in another part of the organization. Redundancy and dismissal, both of which need to be managed sensitively, are other reasons for separation.

Redundancy occurs when employees are released from employment because the organization no longer has a need for their services. Redundancy may be voluntary or involuntary. Redundancy may mean that the individual is placed elsewhere in the workforce, or it may mean total severance. Redundancy can arise through the introduction of new technologies, through business re-engineering, a takeover, or downsizing the organization's operations. Depending upon the reason for the redundancy and the individual's abilities, opportunities for retraining or reskilling may be few. Where a person is made redundant it is important that the process is carried out as quickly as possible, whilst preserving the person's dignity. Placement agencies may be used to assist the person and their family to adapt to their new situation and to search for new employment opportunities.

Dismissal is probably the most distressing method of separation for both the manager and the individual as it may be the culmination of a difficult lead-up time or emotional situation in terms of behaviour, performance or attitude. Depending on circumstances, dismissal should only occur after all attempts to improve or correct the offending aspects have failed. It should be recognized that at some stage, the individual concerned was recruited by the organization for their skills and attributes. Having attracted and employed the individual the organization has an obligation to develop the person according to its needs and values. There is also a responsibility for ensuring that every opportunity is provided for an individual to succeed. This includes the provision of adequate communication, counselling, training and supervision. Managers also have a legal and ethical obligation to ensure that the person's case has been heard objectively and fairly before they are dismissed.

Information services should have formalized grievance procedures that are made known and accessible to management and staff. No employee should be dismissed for a first breach of discipline, and no disciplinary action should be taken unless the case has been carefully investigated. Where dismissal arises from criminal activity, the remaining staff may need counselling as they may vicariously share in the guilt.

THE EXIT INTERVIEW

Many managers overlook the exit interview as an opportunity to review and obtain feedback about their management style and the organization from an employee's viewpoint. Holding an exit interview with employees when they leave allows the manager to actively to seek out suggestions that will enable them to be a better employer.

Whilst open communications should allow employees to bring their concerns to the attention of management at all times, some employees may only feel able to discuss matters that have been of concern to themselves or others when the bond between the employee, the manager and the organization is broken. The highlighting of both the positive and negative aspects of the organization should, if taken notice of, make the organization a better place to work. For example the exit interview might highlight inappropriate policies or procedures or ineffective communication channels that were previously unknown to management.

Performance management systems

Increasingly organizations are employing performance management systems for analysing data and setting targets to report on historical activities and forecast future performance. Some of which are more successful than others. Fryer et al. (2009: 480) outline key features of successful performance management systems as:

- Alignment of the performance management system and the existing systems and strategies of the organization;
- Leadership commitment;
- A culture in which it is seen as a way of improving and identifying good performance and not a burden that is used to chastise poor performers;
- Stakeholder involvement; and
- Continuous monitoring, feedback, dissemination and learning from results.

Conclusion

Attracting and retaining talented people who can achieve personally and corporately is undertaken at a strategic and operational level. The strategic component compromises proper planning that enables the information service to identify its required future talents, skills, expertise and staffing structures and takes into account changes in services and technology. Changing and challenging environments in which organizations now operate make planning and forecasting the competencies, attitudes and skill requirements essential in order to sustain the organization in the future. A continuous review of where the organization is heading can also eliminate problems of oversupply or undersupply of particular skills and expertise within the information service. It also aids in the determining of retraining needs in relation to required skills arising out of change and the introduction of new processes.

At an operational level, continuous and proactive activities can be found in specifying required talents, skills and competencies to meet current and future needs as well as organizational objectives; recruiting and selecting the right individuals; developing skills, expertise and knowledge; motivating people and acknowledging different generational needs in the workplace; as well as managing performance with opportunities for review and feedback. Gap analysis and skills inventories are two tools that can be used in determining whether there is, or is likely to be, a deficit, match or excess of specific skills, expertise and knowledge in the organization.

The emphasis in attracting and retaining the right people includes the need to 'marry' the job, the person and their needs, the organization and the situation. Employees' skills, knowledge, outlook and experience are important in adding value to the organization's objectives and programmes. Development and learning opportunities as well as mentoring add to existing abilities and knowledge, increasing the value of the employee's contribution to the organization as well as providing occasions for individuals to develop their own personal and professional competencies to maximize and sustain their career progression.

It is inevitable that at some stage, an employee will leave the organization. Whether this is for personal or organizational reasons it is important that the process of separation is well managed for both the employee and for those who remain in the organization. Whilst there should be mechanisms in place to provide for continuous feedback and review, the use of an exit interview at the time of separation can provide very useful feedback for the manager and the employee.

References

Fryer, K., Anthony, J. and Ogden, S. 2009. Performance management in the public sector. *International Journal of Public Sector Management*, 22(6), 478–498.

Goffee, R. and Jones, G. 2010. Leading in the clever economy. *Ivey Business Journal Online*, March/April.

Kleinsorge, R. 2010. Expanding the role of succession planning. *T+D Training and Development*, April, 64(4), 66–69.

Leigh, A. 2009. *The Secrets of Success in Management: 20 Ways to Survive and Thrive*. Harlow: Pearson.

Further Reading

Branham, L. 2005. *The 7 Hidden Reasons Employees Leave: How to Recognise the Subtle Signs and Act Before it is Too Late*. New York: Amacom.

Conger, J.A. and Fulmer, R.M. 2003. Developing your leadership pipeline. *Harvard Business Review*, December, 76–84.

Crawford, T. 2005. *Employer Branding*. Aldershot: Ashgate.

Gerolimos, M. and Konsta, R. 2008. Librarians' skills and qualifications in a modern informational environment. *Library Management*, 29(8/9), 691–699.

Munro, A. 2005. *Practical Succession Management: How to Future-proof Your Organisation*. Aldershot: Ashgate.

O'Brien, T. and Hayden, H. 2008. Flexible work practices and the LIS sector: Balancing the needs of work and life? *Library Management*, 29(3), 199–228.

Parry, J. 2008. Librarians do fly: Strategies for staying aloft. *Library Management*, 29(1/2), 41–50.

Pennell, K. 2010. The role of flexible job descriptions in succession management. *Library Management*, 31(4/5), 279.

Smith, I. 2008. People management – be bold. *Library Management*, 29(1/2), 18–28.

Weiss, I. and MacKay, N. 2009. *The Talent Advantage: How to Attract and Retain the Best and the Brightest*. New York: John Wiley.

5 Ensuring Value for Money and Enabling a Cost-Sustainable Future

Ensuring value for money and enabling a cost-sustainable future involves the process of identifying, costing and allocating income and expenditure to resources and activities that can be used in the development of budgets and business cases, to determine which services provide the most value for money or where increased efficiencies should be sought to ensure that the organization can meet its business and financial obligations. Good financial planning and management becomes absolutely essential in ensuring valued investments in times of economic constraint. As well as making certain that the organization can live within its means, the activities of analysing costs, productivity curves and considering alternative options for budgets and in business cases are an integral part of ensuring sustainability, that there is optimum use of these resources and that productivity gains are being achieved.

This chapter provides an integrated approach to planning and implementing sound financial strategies. It considers the relationship between the budget cycle and the strategic planning cycle, the preparation of budgets and business cases as well as methods of calculating expenditure in order to determine where efficiencies are being met or need attention, which services should be continued or retired. It provides examples of financial models and processes which can be used to ensure that programmes or activities are managed in a financially sustainable manner as well as providing inputs into performance management and measurement. These include:

- Developing a business case – provides justification for the approval of a new initiative which might include the introduction of a new technology, service, programme or activity;
- Budgeting – outlines how income and expenditure should be allocated to programmes and activities and managed for a specific period;
- Productivity assessment – identifies differing levels of productivity and efficiencies in programmes or activities in order to determine where attention should be placed in making services more efficient as part of ensuring sustainability in service delivery;
- Accrual accounting – accounts for all expenses and income relating to the programme or activity during the budget period;
- Financing options – considers different ways of financing initiatives to ensure a more sustainable outcome;
- Reporting – enables consistency and transparency in reporting; and
- Auditing – safeguards the integrity in financial reporting.

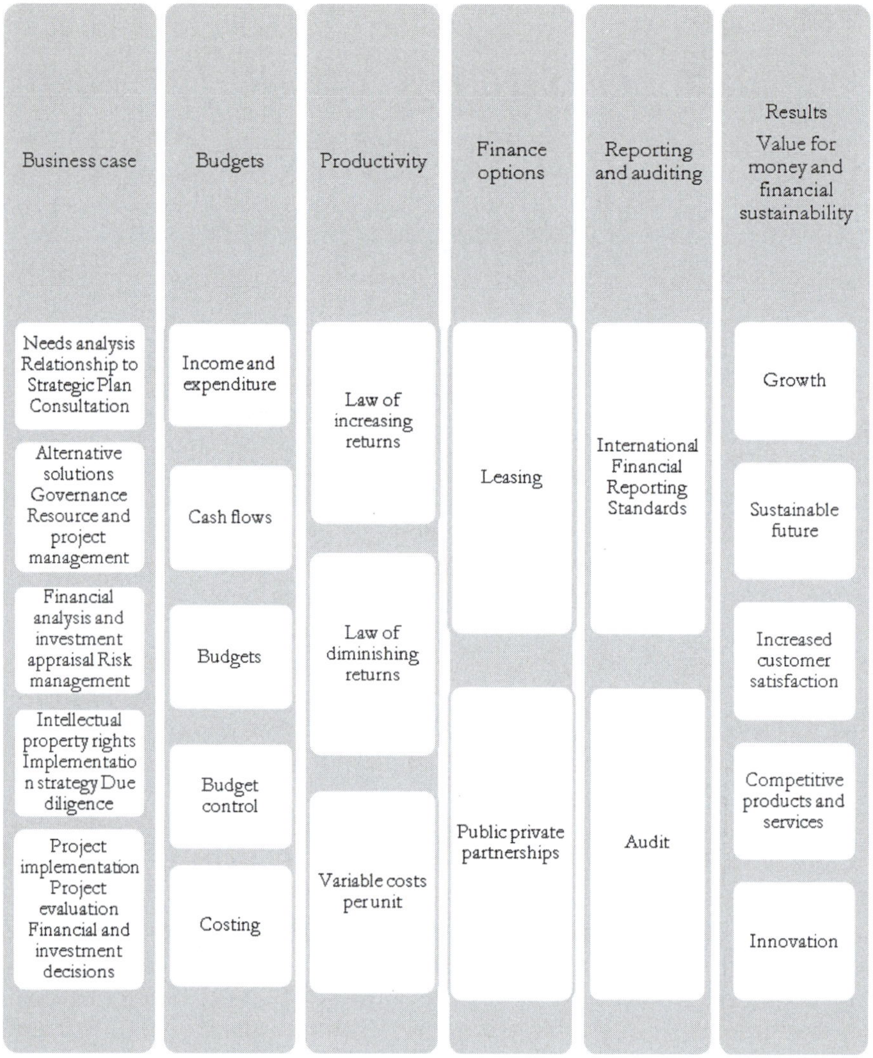

Business case	Budgets	Productivity	Finance options	Reporting and auditing	Results Value for money and financial sustainability
Needs analysis Relationship to Strategic Plan Consultation	Income and expenditure	Law of increasing returns			Growth
Alternative solutions Governance Resource and project management	Cash flows		Leasing	International Financial Reporting Standards	Sustainable future
Financial analysis and investment appraisal Risk management	Budgets	Law of diminishing returns			Increased customer satisfaction
Intellectual property rights Implementation strategy Due diligence	Budget control				Competitive products and services
Project implementation Project evaluation Financial and investment decisions	Costing	Variable costs per unit	Public private partnerships	Audit	Innovation

Figure 5.1   An integrated finance model

Creating a business case for new proposals

When any new major initiative (programme, system, product or service) is proposed it is most likely that a business case will need to be prepared in order to ensure that:

- Correct problem definition has taken place, that alternative solutions have been considered and that the proposed initiative presents the best business solution to the problem at hand;
- The proposed initiative is valid, has been well thought through, properly scoped, has long-term sustainability and can be thoroughly justified;
- The investment has value and importance for the core business and strategic direction of the organization;

- All costs, risks, interdependencies, returns, benefits and change management strategies have been identified;
- The intended objectives, outcomes and benefits have been identified and all parties to the initiative have the capability and capacity to deliver the benefits;
- Proper consultation has been undertaken with stakeholders (customers, suppliers, collaborative partners, etc.) to ensure that the initiative meets their needs;
- A thorough analysis of the market, competitors and environment has taken place;
- There is a project sponsor, sound governance and proven project management process in place at the beginning and for the life of the initiative; and
- Due diligence has been carried out on any business partners to the initiative regarding their capabilities, governance, financial viability and sustainability.

A business case model can be found in Figure 5.2.

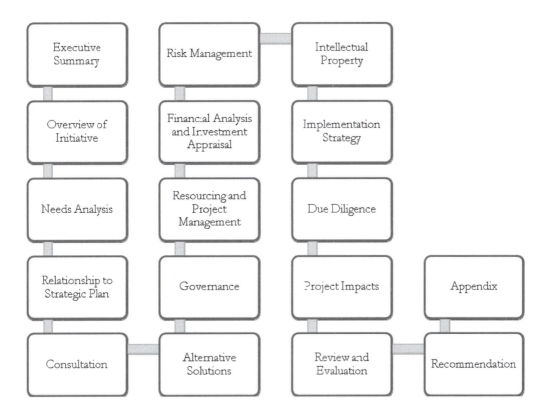

Figure 5.2   Business case model

Generally the project sponsor will complete the business case as they would normally be accountable for the delivery of the outcomes and benefits associated with the initiative. If the initiative proposes the introduction of a new technology the emphasis of the business case should be on the business capabilities and impact rather than on the technology itself.

The business case outlines how the proposed initiative meets the strategic business priorities of the organization and provides the financial justification, market analysis, details of the expected impact, sustainability and value of the initiative in meeting current and future customer needs, as well as addressing alternative means of achieving the goals (including change management strategies), the timing of the initiative, its risks, sponsors, financing sources, change management and project management methodology. Text Box 5.1 provides an outline of the sample contents of a business case that can be used in the preparation of a business case. Business cases should be comprehensive and consider all factors so that a proper and measurable evaluation of the initiative can be made in an environment of scarce resources. They should be clear and concise, addressing all of the factors in a transparent manner so that the initiative can be assessed against the relative merits of alternative proposals concerning;

- Its value for money;
- Its long-term impact and contribution to the strategic business direction of the organization;
- The costs, risks, expected savings and other benefits; and
- Whether the initiative is achievable, sustainable and realistic in terms of financial and human resources allocated, timeframe and technological capability.

Text Box 5.1   Outline of the sample contents of a business case

---

Business Case Framework

1.   Executive Summary

Provides a high level overview of the initiative including:

1.1.   Background to proposal
1.2.   Relationship and contribution to the business strategy and how the initiative links to or supports other organizational projects
1.3.   Project justification and anticipated outcomes
1.4.   Total funding required
1.5.   Critical success factors and timeliness in achieving business benefits
1.6.   How the benefits will be achieved and measured
1.7.   Risks and opportunities – strategic, financial, technical, safety, environmental, operational, compliance, reputational
1.8.   Alternative options considered
1.9.   Impact on business if the initiative did not proceed
1.10.   Specific recommendation as to whether the initiative should be supported

2.   Overview of Initiative

Summarizes the initiative in terms of:

2.1.   Specific objectives of initiative
2.2.   Rationale, timing and priority of initiative
2.3.   Consequences and business impact if initiative is not approved
2.4.   Expected outcomes in terms of tangible products or services
2.5.   Conclusions

3.   Needs Analysis

Provides evidence of business need and demand for outputs of the initiative, including:

3.1. Market analysis – qualitative or quantitative evidence of unmet need, demand for service or product, whether participation in market will strengthen the organization's reputation

3.2. Situation analysis – size of market, state of market e.g. growth, decline, increase or decrease of competition, market structure

3.3. Target audience

3.4. Competitor analysis – size, goal, market share, product or service quality and other information about competitors' intentions, how the initiative compares to similar competitors' products or services

3.5. Explanation of why need or demand is not met by existing programmes, services, products

4.   Relationship to Strategic Plan

Outlines relationships to the business strategy and how the initiative links to or supports other organizational projects including:

4.1. Relationship and alignment to organization's vision, mission, business objectives

4.2. Links with other initiatives, services, current and proposed business activities

4.3. Relationships with other stakeholder offerings

4.4. Impact of initiative on business outcomes and services

4.5. Anticipated benefits

5.   Consultation

Outlines process of consultation undertaken with internal and external stakeholders, including:

5.1. The extent of their agreement to participate in the initiative

5.2. Ability to contribute time and resources to initiative

5.3. Specific responsibilities and whether they are prepared to meet their obligations

6.   Alternative solutions

Outlines alternative solutions that have been considered, including:

6.1. Costs and benefits of each option (including 'do nothing' option)

6.2. Preferred option

7.   Governance

Provides details of how the project will be governed and how any legal requirements that will impact on the initiative will be managed, including:

7.1. Project sponsor

7.2. Legal structure of any proposed joint venture, collaborative agreement etc.

7.3. Membership of governance committee and responsibilities

7.4. Frequency of meetings

7.5. Statutory or regulatory requirements

8.   Resourcing and project management

Provides details of the resources required and how the project will be managed, including:

8.1.   Financial, human, technical resources
8.2.   Timing for resource requirements
8.3.   Project management team – membership, qualifications, level of authority
8.4.   Project management methodology to be used
8.5.   Sourcing strategy e.g. lease, build, buy and rationale for selection
8.6.   Management of supplier relationships
8.7.   Contract management

9.   Financial analysis and investment appraisal

Contains a statement of the estimated total financial costs and benefits that will be incurred and earned over the whole of life for the proposed initiative (and alternative options) including:

9.1.   Amount of investment required and source of funding
9.2.   Key financial parameters and assumptions
9.3.   Total capital and operational costs for the life of the project, including staff costs, insurance, on-costs, physical resources, change management, retraining, data conversion etc.
9.4.   Project income and expenditure for next three years
9.5.   Investment appraisal using Net Present Value (NPV), payback period, breakeven point
9.6.   Discounted cash flow analysis

10.   Risk management

Outlines how and what risks have been identified, and how they will be monitored and mitigated:

10.1.   Identified risks – strategic, financial, technical, safety, environmental, operational, compliance, business reputation
10.2.   Risk management strategies
10.3.   Whether potential opportunities outweigh the risks
10.4.   Whether the risks are insurable
10.5.   Whether everyone accepts the risks

11.   Intellectual property

Outlines how intellectual property is managed and assigned for:

11.1.   New intellectual property
11.2.   Existing intellectual property

12.   Implementation strategy

Outlines how the project will be implemented, including:

12.1.   Project Plan, project milestones and timescale
12.2.   Assumptions and dependencies
12.3.   Change management plan
12.4.   Communications plan

13.   Due Diligence

Outlines formal due diligence process if the initiative includes a third party, including:

13.1.   Description of third parties
13.2.   Location of offices
13.3.   Details of certificate of registration
13.4.   Confirmation that they have resources (staff, funding, other resources) to undertake the initiative and deliver the outcomes
13.5.   Financial viability and sustainability – results of independent credit reference check, summary of most recent financial statements, cash flow analysis, assets, ability to fund start-up costs, absorb operating losses if incurred and fund future capital expansions
13.6.   Procedures to be used to monitor ongoing financial performance
13.7.   Reference checks that provide confirmation that they are able to do the things required
13.8.   Reputation
13.9.   Previous track record
13.10.   Governance – information on directors or officials and whether any director or official has been declared bankrupt, charges with a criminal offence, or is exposed to a conflict of interest
13.11.   Conclusion re status

14.   Project impacts

Outlines the impacts that the initiative might have, including:

14.1.   Economic evaluation on industry and the economy
14.2.   Social impact analysis
14.3.   Environmental impact analysis – broad environmental trends that will impact on the initiative e.g. demographic, technological, political/legal, social-cultural trends, environment
14.4.   Project sustainability

15.   Review and Evaluation

15.1.   Performance measures
15.2.   Strategies for post implementation review

16.   Recommendation

16.1.   Recommendation for project

17.   Appendix

17.1.   Glossary of terms

MAKING FINANCIAL AND INVESTMENT DECISIONS ON NEW PROPOSALS

Any new initiative will require funds that are in effect 'borrowed'. This is true even if the funds are provided as ownership capital by the organization as the selection of the initiative commits funds that could otherwise be invested in some other alternative. Therefore in order to estimate the attractiveness of an investment opportunity it is necessary to know the true cost of the proposed initiative and recognize:

- The cost of using the money (known as interest) over a period of years (compound interest);
- The time value of money i.e. the future value of the money that is invested today (discounted cash flow); and
- How much value or profit the investment makes to the organization (net present value).

Tables and spreadsheets can be used to calculate these costs.

Compound interest

In comparison to simple interest, compound interest arises when interest is added to the principal, so that from that moment on, the interest that has been added also itself earns interest. This addition of interest to the principal is called compounding (for example the interest is compounded). For example a loan with $2,000 initial principal and 5 per cent interest per month would have a balance of $2,100 at the end of the first month, $2,205 at the end of the second month, and so on. Compound interest enables the true cost of using the money to be known by compounding the interest.

Discounted Cash Flows (DCF)

Discounted Cash Flows is a valuation tool that recognizes the time value of money in making investment decisions. That is, a given amount of money invested in one year will attract interest over a given amount of time. For example, $2,000 of today's money invested for one year and earning 5 per cent interest per annum will be worth $2,100 after one year. Likewise, $2,000 paid now or $2,100 paid exactly one year from now will both have the same value to the recipient who assumes 5 per cent interest.

Net Present Value (NPV)

Net Present Value is used to analyse the profitability of a proposed initiative and to indicate how much value the initiative adds to the organization in comparison with other alternatives. It can be used to decide which of two or more proposed initiatives should be implemented by choosing the initiative yielding the higher NPV. NPV is a financial measure based on the present value of cash inflows and present value of cash outflows. That is it compares the value of a dollar today to the value of that same dollar in the future, taking inflation and returns into account.

The use of NPV is purely for financial analysis regarding which initiative will provide the most positive financial return. So that if the NPV of the initiative is positive, it should, all other factors being equal, be accepted. However, if NPV is negative, the initiative should probably be rejected because cash flows will also be negative. As NPV does not take into account other factors such as the initiative's contribution to the strategic positioning of the organization or its alignment to the proposed strategic business direction, it should be regarded as just one input into the final decision about an initiative.

NPV is calculated using table and spreadsheets such as Microsoft Excel. It takes into account:

- Start-up costs – immediate cash outflows (which might include purchase of hardware and software, employee training and change management costs);
- Operational costs – involving other cash outflows for the following years; and
- Incoming cash flows over the period of years.

Planning and managing income and expenditure through budgets

Budgeting is effectively planning for financial resources to support the information service's activities and as such should be integrated and progressed alongside the ongoing activities of the strategic planning process (see Figure 5.3). The overall preparation and coordination of the budget are often the responsibility of the financial services manager or Chief Finance Officer, who is also entrusted with administering the allocation of funds within the organization's overall programmes and activities. However accountability for the overall financial position of the organization rests with the Chief Executive Officer. It is their responsibility to ensure that the organization can meet its financial obligations at all times.

The budget is the financial statement that identifies how all income and expenditure should be allocated and managed for specific period. Usually it is prepared to cover a financial or calendar year, but can cover a longer period of time – for example, a triennium. Occasionally, a half-yearly budget is planned.

As it is prepared in advance the budget serves as the means of control as to how monies are spent and a check on what monies should have been received. It provides a snapshot of the organization and earmarks the amounts of expenditure and anticipated income for items and services delivered by the information service.

Budgets are often broken down by either programmes or activities across an organization. These may be further related to cost centres such as branch libraries, records management office or the geographic information services section. Cost centres may be further broken down to cover specific services.

The process of preparing the budget, ensuring that income and expenditure for the information service's activities stays within the budget and determining the efficiencies of activities and programmes is usually delegated to the team leaders or managers who oversee these activities. Activities and programmes should be continually reviewed to determine how they can be made more efficient or profitable, provide better value for money or made more financially sustainable in challenging times. This may result in services being redesigned to move them to more self-service or lowering overheads by integrating services into a one-stop service.

Timeframe	Strategic planning process	Financial planning process
	Establish strategic objectives	Strategic financial planning
	Identify significant programmes and activities for the next three years	Develop business cases for major initiatives
		Three-year forward estimates (capital and operational) prepared and approved based on major direction set
	Establish projects and activities to meet operational objectives	Establish budget and cash flow for operational year's income and expenditure
	Review progress and performance against operational objectives	Review progress against budget
	Establish priorities for following financial period	Negotiate budget for forward estimates for programmes for the following financial period
	Revise forward work programmes and activities according to budget allocation and costings	Allocate budget for financial period to programmes and activities
		Further economic analysis re costings of activities and services
	Implement programmes and activities	Monitor income and expenditure according to budget and cash flow
	Review and evaluate programmes and activities	Review and evaluate budget

Figure 5.3 Relationship between the activities of the strategic planning process and the financial planning process

The decision on the amount of funds to be allocated to each programme is usually made at the executive or ownership level of the parent organization. Therefore it is most important that managers keep the senior management and stakeholders of the parent organization fully informed of actions they have taken to increase productivity, the costs and benefits of each programme and activity, as well as their progress to meeting the organizational goals and other achievements throughout the year. This is so that when they make hard decisions in times of economic constraint the members of the executive are fully informed.

Similarly, whilst discussions about the value and benefits of continuing with programmes and activities or the merits of individual items in the budget will be part of the budget preparation process, justification should not just be limited to this time period. The review and questioning about the appropriateness of services and levels of funds should be a continuous exercise. The senior management of the parent organization and other relevant stakeholders such as board members should have their views sought on policy directions and matters for the forthcoming budget well before the presentation of the information service's budget. Proposals for new services should be introduced through the formal business case rather than in the budget documentation.

Whilst it is important that the proposed budget is fully supported by documentation linking programmes and activities with approved plans and business outcomes, often this is not enough. The information services manager should take the time and effort to understand the politics of the budget process within the parent organization. They need to win the budget arguments, not just be part of them. Where possible they should be involved in the budget deliberations so that they may learn the rationale behind their bids being accepted or rejected. Networks may be formed with key stakeholders in the treasury or finance department in order to put the information service's point of view forward and gain support for certain proposals.

The lack of a personal opportunity to participate in the final budget deliberations should not prevent the information services manager from obtaining their required budget allocation. Credibility of the budget details and a recognized value of the information service are what matters most. The justification for the information service's budget will already have been made if the arguments for the services have been well presented in detailed and timely reports throughout the year. If the information services manager's personal network has been effective, key members of the budget committee will be supportive of the activities and associated budget.

CALCULATING INCOME AND EXPENDITURE

The preparation of a budget necessitates the calculation of income or revenue and capital and operational expenditure. Capital expenditures are one-off items of significant expenditure such as a new library building or major information technology system.

Operating expenditures are current, ongoing costs associated with the day-to-day operations of the information service. These may be divided further into fixed and variable costs:

- Fixed costs relate to annual overhead charges such as rent, general insurance or energy costs; and
- Variable costs change according to usage and include consultancy fees, use of online information services, postage and courier costs.

A further explanation of fixed and variable costs is given later in this chapter.

Budget breakdowns provide additional information. For example, an item on the budget just labelled 'staff' provides very little management information. It is more meaningful to show a breakdown according to salaries, superannuation on salaries, workers' compensation insurance, training and staff development, conference fees, and advertising staff appointments.

In preparing the budget, some operating expenditure costs will be harder to forecast than others. Some providers may have already announced their rates or increases in charges and so expenditure in these areas can be calculated quite easily. Fixed-price contracts such as for cleaning or maintenance agreements for certain equipment may also be known. Sometimes overheads for buildings are conveniently reduced to a rate per square metre per annum for budget calculations.

Payroll systems can assist the calculation of salaries as the diversity of employees in information services, for example records management, archives, programmers, systems analysis or library services, means that few staff are paid on the same salary scale. Other variations may occur with some staff receiving annual increments in their salaries, whilst others' salaries may be calculated on a ratio associated with profit increases. Annual increments may be adjusted according to age (on birth date) or years of experience (the date they commenced employment in a particular position).

Allowances to cover price increases may need to be built-in to the budget. This is particularly the case with capital expenditure items such as new buildings that are costed in preparation for the budget far in advance of when they are contracted out. Inflation rates and international currency exchange rates will contribute to variations. These changes must also be taken into account when preparing the budget. Assistance in forecasting changes to these rates can often be found in finance areas.

It is important to anticipate correctly revenue patterns and levels. Any income revenue in excess of expenditure at any given time is often invested in the short-term money market to provide additional funds for the organization. Variances in income revenue will disrupt the ability to plan investments wisely. Although some changes in income levels may be unavoidable, any anticipated changes in policies which could affect the income revenue levels should be accounted for in the budget. Examples would be the anticipated increase from the introduction of a new user-pays service or additional income from an increase in the use of a fee service such as a photocopying or scanning machine.

PREPARING CASH FLOWS

As part of the budget processes, the information services manager may also be required to prepare a cash flow for the budget period, highlighting anticipated expenditure and income on a weekly or monthly basis. This is so the overall income and expenditure position of the organization can be managed. Preparing a cash flow requires forecasting when certain expenditure and income falls due. It is usually in the form of a spreadsheet with the time periods (each week or month) across the top or horizontal axis and expenditure and income items on the side or vertical axis. Details of amounts of expenditure for each item are then entered in the relevant time period. Some costs such as rent (weekly or monthly) and energy costs for lighting and air conditioning (quarterly or six weekly) are easy to forecast as to when they fall due, however seasonal variables in energy consumption need to be factored in. Staff costs (including superannuation, work-cover insurance costs, annual leave loadings) in the main can be extrapolated across the whole period, however seasonal fluctuations need to be forecast. The cash flow spreadsheet will also need to identify when items such as software upgrades, new equipment, mobile phones or desktop computers will be purchased, and when travel expenditure and conference attendance will be incurred.

USING DIFFERENT TECHNIQUES FOR PREPARING AND MANAGING BUDGETS

There are several different ways of preparing and managing budgets. Some of these are outlined below.

Line-item budget

This is the most traditional approach to budgeting. It divides expenditures into broad categories such as general administrative expenses, motor vehicles, operating expenses, employment expenses and occupancy costs. There are further subdivisions within these categories. Most line budgets are prepared by projecting current expenditures to next year, taking likely cost increases into account.

Whilst they are easy to prepare, very few organizations use line-item budgets today. This is because it is difficult to relate the line-item budget to the organization's objectives, or to the benefits or outcomes that arise from the allocated monies. Line-item budgets provide few incentives for management to question programmes or activities or look for alternative solutions.

Zero-based budgeting or ZBB

The budgeting technique combines strategic planning and decision making with the budget process. Zero-based budgeting encourages the manager to question priorities and consider alternative methods of service delivery. Activities and programmes are assessed across the whole organization in accordance with the:

- Anticipated benefits from the programme;
- Desired results;
- Advantages of retaining the programme's current activities;
- Consequences of not having the programme;
- Overall efficiency of the programme; and
- Evaluation of the alternative methods of providing the programme.

Budget allocation is based on the priority of the programme in meeting the organization's objectives rather than across the board appropriations. The required resources and associated costs for the programme are calculated. The programmes are grouped and ranked by management according to a hierarchy based on their cost-benefit and ability to achieve the organization's objectives.

The programmes are progressively funded within the priority hierarchy until the budget is exhausted. At some point in the hierarchy there is a cut-off point where some programmes are to be funded and others not. The cut-off point corresponds to the organization's total budget allocation. Those programmes ranked in priority above the funding line are funded; those below it are left unfunded.

Zero-based budgeting does not allow for incremental growth in budgets. It considers efficiency and the relevancy of programmes to organizational objectives. It exposes all information service activities to the same scrutiny as others within the parent organization, preventing programmes from being approved solely on the basis of tradition. More efficient ways of achieving the corporate objectives are sought by examining different methods of service delivery or activities.

To be effective, zero-based budgeting requires decision-makers to have a thorough knowledge of the organization as it can lead to trade-offs among the programmes and objectives. The executive management team decides the level of funding that they are prepared to commit and the programmes and objectives that they are prepared to forgo. Managers and their teams need to know why they want to spend money, where and what to spend it on and the outcomes that can be achieved if funding is available. To do this effectively they must be aware of their service's characteristics and objectives, and major customer groups. Activities and programmes must be well conceived and strengths and weaknesses be known.

There are some disadvantages to zero-based budgeting. It requires commitment of time and effort; it involves a great deal of preparation, planning and organization; and it relies upon all participants being aware of priorities.

Programme budgeting

As its name suggests programme budgeting is based upon the provision of programmes rather than individual items or expenditures. It allocates monies to activities or programmes, having previously explored different means to providing services that have been identified as needed by the customers. Each programme has certain funds allocated for staff, operating expenses, materials and publicity. There are no direct budget allocations to the cost centres, only to the individual programmes. Programmes may run across a number of cost centres, for example a programme that facilitates the provision of information networks to lecturers within a university may cover a number of cost centres at the faculty level.

Performance budgeting

Performance budgeting bases expenditure on the performance of activities and services. It is similar to programme budgeting in format but is concerned with efficiency. It uses cost-benefit analysis techniques to measure performance and requires large amounts of data. Performance budgeting has been criticized as it emphasizes economics rather than quality of service.

Planning-programming budgeting systems (PPBS)

Planning-programming budgeting systems combine the best of programme budgeting and performance budgeting. It combines the functions of planning, programming and budgeting into one. The information service's objectives are established and short-term objectives are stated in a quantifiable manner. Alternative means (activities) of achieving the objectives are considered and selected on the basis of cost-benefit. These activities are grouped into programmes and funded.

Once the programmes are established they are controlled by comparing them with the stated objectives to see if these are being achieved. The results are evaluated so that corrective actions can be taken. PPBS allows costs to be assigned to programmes so that the benefits can be measured in relation to cost.

Whilst the approach appears to be simple, it is complex in practice and can be time consuming. It does not provide an operating tool for line managers or provide the mechanism to evaluate the impact of various funding levels on each programme. Finally, it does not force the continued evaluation of existing programmes and activities.

CONTROLLING BUDGETS

The budget control process is a continuing one. Generally, expenditures and income must be made within the framework of the amount allocated against each item. This is part of an accountability process.

Income and expenditure are usually documented in either weekly or monthly budget reports. These reports show the total income and expenditure amounts budgeted at the beginning of the financial year, the actual expenditure or income received to date, and the committed expenditure to date. Actual expenditure refers to the amounts already paid (expended) for goods or services received. Committed expenditure refers to the outstanding expenditures for goods or services which have been ordered but not yet paid for. The goods or services may or may not have been received by the cost centres in the information service. In calculating total expenditure costs to date, both the actual and committed expenditure amounts should be added together.

Statements of committed and expended funds should be regularly monitored and reviewed in order to control the budget and meet accountability requirements. Appropriate budget adjustment mechanisms should be available to allow for unexpected events or changes in priorities that could not be foreseen when the budget was framed. Any anticipated increase in expenditure above that provided by the budget must often be offset by either an increase in income to offset the expenditure, or a decrease in expenditure in another activity in that area. Unexpected expenditures such as costly emergency repairs to buildings may incur a reallocation of funds from elsewhere. These readjustments of funds need to be authorized by senior management and endorsed by a board if it exists.

UNDERSTANDING EXPENSES AND INCOME THROUGH COSTING

Costing is important in understanding the expenses and income that make up the budget. It is also an important activity in determining where more attention should be paid in increasing efficiencies or productivity to make service delivery more sustainable. In times of change and constraint it provides the opportunity to drill down and be conscious of the expenses that make up the budget. These can be analysed to determine:

- Expenses that cannot be deferred without some impact on service provision (operating costs);
- Expenses that could be deferred with a somewhat lesser impact (capital costs);
- Alternative uses for expenditure (opportunity costs);
- Costs that may or may not alter according to demand (variable and fixed costs);
- Costs that may or may not continue if an activity or programme is withdrawn (direct and indirect costs);
- The true cost of an activity or programme (cost accounting);
- The comparison between inputs and outputs in order to compare and measure performance of different activities and programmes (unit costs);
- The minimum cost that should be charged for a product or service (unit costs); and
- A better picture of the total cost of the service, including the cost of downtime of equipment or the cost of reworking a piece of programming (activity-based costing).

Capital and operating costs

Capital costs represent long-term investments. They are associated with the upfront development and acquisition expenditures associated with an asset. These include the acquisition of real property or equipment, construction costs, furniture and fittings as well as intangible assets. As capital costs often incur large sums of money, their payback is usually funded over a number of years (see financing options later in this chapter). Capital expenditures can recur over time, but they are not ongoing costs.

Operating costs or expenses are associated with recurring or ongoing activities, such as salaries, electricity, telecommunications and training, and are funded through the annual budget provision.

Opportunity cost of capital

The opportunity cost of capital recognizes that funds invested in assets could have alternative uses and that an allowance should be made for a rate of return on the asset.

Fixed and variable costs

Fixed costs are those that do not vary with output. Costs which vary with output are called variable costs. Knowledge of both fixed and variable costs is necessary in order to budget effectively.

Staffing costs are variable costs as an increase or decrease in the number of staff employed will result in a corresponding increase or decrease in the budget for salary, superannuation, training and work-cover insurance.

Energy costs for lighting and air conditioning are examples of fixed costs as they remain unchanged unless the number of staff increases considerably. Energy costs will only increase if longer opening hours are required or additional physical space is necessary that requires lighting, increasing the energy consumption.

Direct and indirect costs

Direct costs are those that can be attributed directly to an output or activity. These are usually easy to determine, for example printing, office equipment and salaries, superannuation and workers' compensation insurance costs of those members of the team associated with the activity.

Indirect costs can be harder to quantify and calculate. These are overheads and other costs that are not directly attributed to a definite activity or output, but which contribute to the cost of the service or product. An example of an indirect cost might be rent on a building from which a number of activities or outputs operate. Indirect costs are usually apportioned to individual activities or outputs on:

- A usage or benefit approach; or
- A pro rata approach.

Cost accounting

Cost accounting measures what it costs to complete an activity. It is a tool that can be used as input to a performance measure and to determine the anticipated value of certain activities, to calculate a minimum charge for a product or service, for comparative purposes to measure efficiency and productivity and, in financially impaired times, to determine which services are more financially sustainable than others. For example;

analysing and comparing the costs of programmes or activities is an important means through which the organization can determine which programmes and activities can be sustained in times of financial constraint.

Cost accounting is the simple process of breaking down resources to the activity being carried out and then collating the monetary cost to show the cost of the activity. An example of this follows under the section relating to unit costs. In addition, special costing exercises can provide a comparison of costs of current operations with the estimated costs of alternative methods. These can then be used along with benefits realization models to determine the best possible outcomes.

Unit costs

Unit costs are used to measure output and can also be used as a performance measure. As it is not always easy to compare the rising curve of total costs, economists convert the total cost figures into unit costs. They do this by dividing the total cost of the activity by the number of units, for example, the number of incoming and outgoing pieces of correspondence that are processed by the records management office. This results in a figure for the average cost per unit of output. Unit costs can also be used in time terms. They may be used to measure performance by comparing inputs to outputs and therefore to determine value for money and financial sustainability of services.

Unit costs concepts may also be used to allocate a cost to an information product or service, to determine a minimum selling price or to compare costs between different information products or services. They can also be used to develop a standard cost for a job in either time or cost terms. The following example outlines how unit costing can be used to determine the price to be charged for four services: a helpdesk call out to a remote user desktop, a premium research service, a report, and a disc of data.

The first stage in the exercise is to calculate the total fixed and variable costs (operating expenses) of the information service of the year (see Table 5.1). In the case of the example these are $7,210,300 per annum. Next the variable costs that are associated with the specific product or service are calculated on a unit basis. In the example given in Table 5.2 for the disc of data, these costs total $33.00.

Once the total fixed and variable costs (operating expenses) and the variable cost per unit are known, a percentage of the operating expenses has to be allocated to the unit as a fixed cost per unit. This is calculated by:

- Determining the percentage contribution of the product or service to the overall business operations of the information service; and
- The likely number of units to be sold per annum for the product or service.

In the case of the disc of data, it is deemed that it contributes 1 per cent of the overall business operations expense ($7,210,300) and that 3,000 discs of data are likely to be sold in the calendar year. Therefore the proportion of the operating expense that can be attributed to each disc of data as a fixed cost is calculated as:

$$\frac{1\% \text{ of } \$7,210,300}{3,000} = \$24.03$$

Table 5.1   Table of expenses for input into costing model

Operating expenses	
General and administrative expenses	
Accounting	20,000
Advertising	45,000
Bank charges	1,000
Borrowing fees	1,000
Consultants	930,000
Courier	8,000
Depreciation	40,000
Donations	5,000
Fines and penalties	1,000
Hire – plant and equipment	12,000
Freight paid	4,000
Insurance	26,000
Licenses and registration fees	30,000
Lease - equipment	90,000
Legal fees	70,000
Postage	4,500
Repairs and maintenance	25,000
Stationery / office supplies	70,000
Subscriptions	190,000
Travel and accommodation	122,000
Motor vehicles	
MV - fuel	33,000
MV – repairs and maintenance	15,000
MV - registration	9,000
MV - parking	800
MV – taxi	3,000
Operating expenses	
Cleaning	25,000
Employment expenses	
Employment tax	30,000
Staff amenities	10,000
Staff training and development	60,000
Wages and salaries	4,500,000
Workers compensation insurance	100,000
Superannuation payable	450,000
Medical expenses	5,000
Uniforms	60,000
Occupancy costs	
Electricity	55,000
Gas	6,000
Property insurance	5,000
Rates	12,000
Rent	120,000
Water rates and consumption	12,000
Waste removal	5,000
TOTAL	7,210,300

Table 5.2   Identifying variable costs and selling costs per unit

Identifying variable cost per unit

Variable costs	Help desk call out	Research service	Report	Data Disc	Annotation
Product raw materials	0.00	0.00	3.00	2.00	Unit cost of any raw materials e.g. Disc
Product value add presentation post sale	0.00	5.00	5.00	1.00	Unit cost of packaging or presentation for sale
Product development pre sale	0.00	0.00	4.00	4.00	Unit cost of any research and development to assist in product development
Printing	0.00	5.00	5.00	5.00	Unit cost of printing
Mastering	0.00	0.00	0.00	1.00	Unit cost of production
Communications expenses	5.00	20.00	3.00	1.00	Average cost of telephone, Internet downloads and other communications charges associated with product or service
Casual wages	0.00	0.00	5.00	5.00	Average cost of causal wages per unit – assistance in supply, after sales service etc.
Marketing attached to volume	1.00	1.00	1.00	1.00	Cost of marketing product or service per unit
Commission	5.00	5.00	5.00	5.00	Commission costs per unit
Travel	75.00	0.00	0.00	0.00	Travel costs associated with delivery of product or service
Consultancy	0.00	0.00	10.00	0.00	Unit cost of special consultancy services or advice associated with product
ICT	1.00	1.00	1.00	1.00	Unit costs associated with provision of specialized ICT services
Distribution	0.00	0.00	5.00	5.00	Unit cost of distributing the product or service

Table 5.2 (continued)

Postage/courier	0.00	0.00	2.00	2.00	Unit cost for postage or courier services
Total variable cost per unit	87.00	37.00	49.00	33.00	Total variable cost per unit of the specialized service or product
Identifying selling price per unit					
% Fixed costs	10/100/15000	2/100/250	1/100/1000	1/100/3000	Percentage of overall budget expenses allocated to product or service/total/ average number of units
Fixed Costs % of $7,210,300 operating expense	48.07	576.82	72.10	24.03	Unit cost based on percentage contribution to the overall budget expense as per above (see expense table showing total expenses of $7,210,300
Profit	4.81	57.68	7.21	2.40	Profit required per unit product or service (based on 10% of fixed costs per unit)
Fixed and profit	52.88	634.50	79.31	26.43	Total of percentage of fixed costs and profit
Total variable costs per unit	87.00	37.00	49.00	33.00	Total variable cost per unit of the specialized service or product
Total variable cost plus fixed and profit	139.88	671.50	128.31	59.43	Total cost per unit (variable cost + percentage of fixed cost + profit)
Minimum selling price rounded up or down	140.00	670.00	130.00	60.00	Minimum selling price rounded up or down to nearest $10

As in the example, a profit margin of 10 per cent has been included, the total unit cost of a disc of data (the variable cost + fixed costs of the unit + 10 per cent profit) is:

$33.00 + $24.03 + $2.40 = $59.43

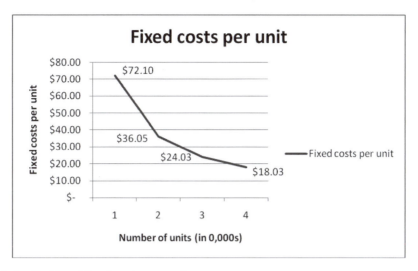

Figure 5.4   Profile of fixed costs per unit

Rounded up, the minimum selling price for a disc of data would be calculated as $60.00

Changing the contribution percentage of the business operating expense, or the number of services or products being sold, will change the final unit cost figure. For example, if it is anticipated that the information service will only sell 1,000 discs of data, then the fixed cost associated with the annual operating expenses will be allocated across fewer units and will therefore increase ($72.10) and so the final unit cost figure will be higher ($33.00 + $72.10 + $7.21 = $112.31). In decreasing the number of sales for the discs of data, the information service must make a minimum charge of $112.40 to break even; an additional amount of $52.40 to the cost where 3,000 discs of data are sold.

Generally fixed costs per unit decline as outputs rise, and rise as outputs fall. Figure 5.4 illustrates this for the production of 1,000, 2,000, 3,000 and 4,000 discs of data. Where variable costs per unit are involved the situation is more complex. It depends upon marginal productivity and the productivity curve (law of variable proportions).

In the example above, the term minimum price is used as pricing does not always relate directly to cost. Pricing is associated with the amount someone is willing to pay for a product or service. Some products and service will attract a premium price; for example where services are fast-tracked ahead of others, where added analysis or features are provided, where the product or service is new or has an element of innovation.

Activity-based costing

Activity-based costing costs the whole process, including those indirect costs involved in supply, process, installation and service delivery. It links all costs to the activity or output and gives a better picture of the total cost and performance of the service. For example, it also takes account of the costs associated with lost opportunities, namely:

- Downtime of equipment, such as when the equipment is sitting idle out of hours or is inoperable whilst waiting for a spare part;
- The cost of goods sitting in a warehouse; or

- The cost of reworking a piece of programming.

Activity-based costing can be used in competitive markets to highlight those activities that are unexpectedly unproductive and those that are yielding the greatest return on investment.

Assessing productivity

In times of economic constraint it is important to design activities so that they are sustainable long term and yield the highest levels of productivity, or make inefficient services more efficient as an alternative to disbanding them. As the ratio of inputs to outputs does not always correlate, productivity curves can be used to determine the point of maximum efficiency and the optimum levels of inputs to effect the greatest levels of sustainability and efficiency in information services.

USING THE LAW OF INCREASING RETURNS

Physical productivity changes when different amounts of one factor are combined with fixed amounts of others. For example, in an information centre with a physical stock of 2,000 items and most information being available online to the desktop, there may only be a need for a librarian or information specialist. If the organization diversifies and expands, then another person may be required to meet the demand. The capacity increases again when a third person is hired and so on.

The appointment of the second librarian or information specialist will have value as the two can begin to specialize and divide the work. Each will perform the jobs they are better at and save time formerly wasted by moving from one job to the next. As a consequence this division of labour may allow the information centre to analyse, index, catalogue and process 5,000 items per year to meet the diverse interests and improve services to more customers. Since the difference in output is 3,000 items, the marginal productivity of the two librarians or information specialists is 3,000 items.

The marginal productivity of labour is not to be spoken of in terms of the second person as, by themselves, their efforts are no more productive than those of the first staff member. If the first staff member left, the second person would still analyse, index, catalogue and process only 2,000 items. What makes the difference is the jump in the combined production of the two librarians once specialization can be introduced. It is regarded as the changing marginal productivity of labour, not the individual.

Increased specialization takes place with the third, fourth, fifth librarian or information specialist so that the addition of another unit of labour as an input in each case brings about an output larger than was realized by the average of all the previous librarians. This does not necessarily mean that each successive person is more efficient and productive. It means that, as units of one factor [librarians or information specialists] are added, the total mix of these units plus the fixed amounts of the other factors form an increasingly efficient technical combination.

The range of factor inputs, over which average productivity rises, is called a range of increasing average returns.

Every time a factor is added efficiency rises. The rate of increased efficiency will not be the same, for the initial large marginal leaps in productivity will give way to smaller ones.

However, the overall trend, whether measured by looking at total output or at average output per person, will still be increased. This continues until a point of maximum technical efficiency is reached.

USING THE LAW OF DIMINISHING RETURNS

The law of diminishing returns is used to detect the point of maximum efficiency. Using the previous example, there is a certain point where the marginal output no longer rises when another person is added to the staff. This is the point of maximum technical efficiency. Total output will still be increasing, but the last person to be employed will have added less output than their colleagues. Labour is now beginning to 'crowd' equipment or the premises. Opportunities for further specialization have become non-existent.

This condition of falling marginal performance is called a condition of decreasing or diminishing returns. The information centre is getting back less and less not only from the 'marginal' librarian or information specialist but from the combined labour of all the staff members.

If labour goes on being added, a point will be reached at which the contribution of the 'marginal' librarian or information specialist will be so small that the average output per person will also fall. Eventually, if even more librarians or information specialists were added, the factor mix would be so disrupted that the total output would actually fall, resulting in a condition of negative gains.

Number of librarians or information specialists	Total output (items analysed, indexed, catalogued, processed)	Marginal productivity (change in output)		Average productivity (total output – number of librarians or information specialists	
1	2,000	2,000	Increasing	2,000	
2	5,000	3,000	marginal	2,500	Increasing
3	8,500	3,500	productivity	2,853	average
4	11,800	3,300		2,950	productivity
5	14,800	3,000	Decreasing	2,960	
6	17,300	2,500	marginal	2,883	Decreasing
7	19,500	2,200	productivity	2,785	average productivity

Figure 5.5   Law of diminishing returns

In the example of Figure 5.5, the marginal productivity begins to diminish with the fourth librarian or information specialist who will analyse, index, catalogue and process only 3,300 items rather than the 3,500 processed by the third person. Average productivity continues to rise until the addition of the sixth person, because the fifth librarian or information specialist, although producing less than the fourth, is still more productive than the average output of all four colleagues. Therefore marginal productivity can be falling while average productivity is still rising.

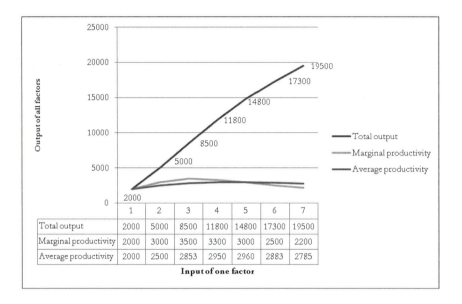

	1	2	3	4	5	6	7
Total output	2000	5000	8500	11800	14800	17300	19500
Marginal productivity	2000	3000	3500	3300	3000	2500	2200
Average productivity	2000	2500	2853	2950	2960	2883	2785

Input of one factor

Figure 5.6   Law of variable proportions

In summary, as successive units of one factor are added to fixed amounts of others, the marginal output of the units of the variable factor will at first rise and then decline. This is called the law of variable proportions or the law of diminishing returns, or, the physical productivity curve (see Figure 5.6)

VARIABLE COSTS PER UNIT

Variable costs per unit can be used to cost increased efficiency in information services in order to make them more sustainable. As in the case of the previous example of librarians or information specialists analysing, processing, indexing and cataloguing the items, the total number of items processed (units produced) will rise at first rapidly, then more slowly with the addition of more librarians. To convert the schedule of physical productivity into a unit cost figure, the total variable cost for each level of output should be calculated. This should then be divided by the number of units to obtain an average variable cost per unit of output.

In the example, the average variable cost per unit (items analysed, indexed, catalogued and processed) declines at first and then rises. This is because the variable cost increases by a set amount ($60,000 per librarian or information specialist). Output, however, obeys the law of diminishing returns. The variable cost per unit of output will therefore fall as long as output is growing faster than costs. It will begin to rise as soon as additions to output start to get smaller.

Table 5.3   Calculating the average variable cost per unit output

Number of librarians or information specialists	Total variable costs at $60,000 per librarian or information specialist	Total output (units)	Average variable cost per unit or output (cost-output)
1	$60,000	2,000	$30.00
2	$120,000	5,000	$24.00
3	$180,000	8,500	$21.17
4	$240,000	11,800	$20.33
5	$300,000	14,800	$20.27
6	$360,000	17,300	$20.80
7	$420,000	19,500	$21.54

Obtaining a true picture of finances through accrual accounting

To obtain a true picture of the cost of the information service, provision for the purchase and replacement of items that are sourced on an irregular basis, such as the expense of a new business system, need to be factored in over the life of the system as well as other expenses such as interest. In accrual accounting all expenses and income are recognized that relate to the budget period. This 'total cost' approach includes provision for depreciation on tangible and intangible assets, interest and loan repayments.

DEPRECIATING COSTS

Asset depreciation allows the cost of an asset to be written off over a period of time. Two common methods of determining the depreciation costs are:

- The prime cost or straight line method; and
- The diminishing value method.

The prime cost method allocates the cost of an asset over the number of years of useful life. For example, personal computers are generally written off over a period of three years. The difference between the personal computer's original cost and the expected proceeds from the sale of the asset at the end of the three years is calculated, and then spread uniformly over each of the three years of its useful life. The diminishing value method allocates a higher proportion of the cost of the asset to the earlier years of its life. For example, a motor vehicle may be written off at a higher rate in the first year, and then at a lower rate in the following two years.

Examining financing options

Once a programme has been proven to deliver a combination of financial, economic and social benefits, the financing alternatives need to be considered. Financing capital assets in-house either via raising capital or using the organization's own source of capital is not always the best option for the organization. For example, there may be a more attractive alternate use of the finance capital (opportunity cost) or the cost of borrowing may be very high. Other financing options can also allow the organization to share its risks and innovation with another party.

LEASING

Leasing offers a number of benefits including the transfer of risk to the financing party, a competitive pricing arrangement, taxation incentives and improved budget management. Leasing can also facilitate a significant investment such as new premises or equipment without the need for a major upfront capital outlay, or free up capital that may be used in the purchase of the property or equipment for other purposes.

Leasing is a viable alternative where there might be uncertainty about the timeframe over which the asset may be used, or where the asset is only required for a short period of time in relation to its economic life. An example may be the leasing of specialized or additional equipment to support a special project that has a limited timeframe. Quantity discounts might also apply to lessors above those available to the information service, which may make it an attractive proposition if the purchase price is significant.

Under the leasing arrangements the asset user (the lessee) has the right to possess and use the asset in return for lease payments to the financier (the lessor) who is the legal owner of the leased asset.

The most common lease arrangements are:

- Operating leases – such as rental agreements for equipment. In this instance the lessor is responsible for all insurance, repairs, maintenance and taxes associated with the equipment. Operating leases can generally be cancelled at little or no cost;
- Financial leases – a non-cancellable lease in which the benefits and risks are transferred to the lessee; and
- Sale and lease-back – where an asset owner sells the asset to another party for the market value and leases the asset back. The title to the property is relinquished and the lessee then makes lease payments. This type of arrangement is often used to provide cash flow to leverage further investment.

PUBLIC–PRIVATE PARTNERSHIPS

Public–private partnerships involve the procurement of public infrastructure and ancillary services through a joint arrangement of public and private sector organizations.

Reporting on finances

INTERNATIONAL FINANCIAL REPORTING STANDARDS (IFRS)

Global financial and investment markets have led to expectations of consistency and transparency in accounting standards and their interpretations regardless of the country of origin. The IFRS have been developed by the International Accounting Standards Board to meet this need. They have been designed to provide a single high-quality, understandable and enforceable international accounting standard for use by participants in global capital markets.

The IFRS offer many more benefits than traditional financial reporting mechanisms. They provide better financial information for shareholders and regulators, enhanced comparability, improved transparency of results, and increased capacity to secure cross-border listings and funding.

Verifying finances through auditing

The audit is one means of safeguarding the integrity in financial reporting. This is a process by which the accounts and finances are independently verified. Usually these are carried out annually at the end of the financial year where the accounts and financial statements are analysed to ensure conformance and integrity. Specific projects may also be subject to an audit; this is often the case where grant funding is used. Finally, spot audits may be carried out as a risk management measure as part of the accountability and governance process.

Audit practices allow the independent review and judgement of internal compliance and control systems, performance and objectivity, significant decisions, records and reporting, risk management and finances. Independence in auditing is important; the parties should be impartial and unconnected with any activity being audited. They should also be provided with the necessary resources, power, access to management and information to meet their needs.

Hamilton (1998: 227–229) provides examples where audits can identify problem areas where decisions need to be made:

- Gaps in existing provision;
- Duplication in existing provision;
- Under-use of resources;
- Incompatibility of IT systems;
- Use of outdated, slow and cumbersome systems;
- 'Jams' in information flow;
- Need for extra staff;
- Need for extra resources; and
- Training needs.

Conclusion

Financial planning and management is integral to the strategic planning and performance management, ensuring that the true costs are known and to placing the service on a sustainable financial footing. Financial practices available to the manager include:

- Business case – provides justification for the approval of a new initiative which might include the introduction of a new technology, service, programme or activity;
- Budgeting – outlines how income and expenditure should be allocated to programmes and activities, measured and managed for a specific period;
- Productivity assessment – identifies and measures differing levels of productivity and efficiencies in programmes or activities in order to determine performance, where attention should be placed in making services more efficient as part of ensuring sustainability in service delivery;
- Accrual accounting – accounts for all expenses and income relating to the programme or activity during the budget period;
- Financing options – considers different ways of financing initiatives;
- Reporting – enables consistency and transparency in reporting; and
- Auditing – safeguards the integrity in financial reporting.

References

Hamilton, F. 1998. Information auditing. *Handbook of Library and Information Management*, ed. Ray Prytherch. Aldershot: Gower.

Further Reading

Digital Library Economics: An Academic Perspective. 2009. Oxford: Chandos.

Gambles, I. 2009. *Making the Business Case: Proposals That Succeed For Projects That Work.* Aldershot: Gower.

Rowley, J. 1997. Principles of price and pricing policy for the information marketplace. *Library Review*, 46(3/4), 179–189.

Snyder, H. and Davenport, E. 1997. *Costing and Pricing in the Digital Age: A Practical Guide For Information Services.* London: Library Association Publishing.

Woodsworth, A. and Williams, J.F. 1993. *Managing the Economics of Owning, Leasing and Contracting Out Information Services.* Aldershot: Gower.

6 *Knowledge and Information Management – A Key to Survival*

Knowledge and information are important corporate assets that, when managed strategically, can sustain the organization to withstand financial and other crises and assist in creating competitive advantage and profitable business outcomes. They are often referred to as intangible assets, assets that are not physical or touchable. However, this is not to imply that they are insubstantial. In fact they are fundamental to intelligent organizations.

Knowledge and information concern content rather than the technology itself. Amongst others, they comprise the tacit knowledge in people's heads, data that can be modelled to forecast probable futures, information in publicly available documents or shared through social networks, mashups and websites, commercial-in-confidence information and other corporate intelligence in hard copy and electronic forms and other content that is held or transported in storage and communication devices. In the global knowledge economy and society, a lot of this content now resides electronically that can be across companies, governments, national and sectoral boundaries.

The increased availability of information and knowledge, largely brought about through the proliferation of information and communications technology (ICT), has driven economic productivity, structural change and the emergence of more open societies. It presents both opportunities and dilemmas as information can now be more readily transferred, stored and manipulated faster and easier than before. In this environment, libraries and information services have the dual responsibilities of planning and managing their own corporate intelligence and knowledge and information, as well as facilitating access and disseminating knowledge and information to assist people and organizations in predicting the future, facilitating decision making, for lifelong learning and personal development.

Knowledge and information management will become increasingly critical for blending business processes and social networks to enhance individual capabilities, maximize productivity and drive competitive advantage. Managers in libraries and information centres can play a significant role in creating and building intelligent organizations and communities in this environment. Their knowledge and skill sets provide them with the capacity to continuously:

- Manage and improve information design, knowledge and information sharing processes and networks;

- Drive and properly apply the benefits of new technologies to increase customer satisfaction;
- Deliver economic and social value;
- Differentiate the brand of the information service or library;
- Foster more productive uses of information;
- Unlock corporate or community knowledge, expertise and innovation; and
- Manage these as valuable intangible assets.

This chapter predominantly focuses on planning and implementing strategies for managing corporate intelligence, knowledge and information to support knowledge enabling and learning organizations. With this in mind the management focus is on maximizing the use of information and knowledge through sharing and enabling corporate and individual knowledge and information, as well as reuse and collaborative techniques. This is increasingly a complex task as more digital and virtual services are offered.

The essential objectives of the knowledge and information management are to ensure that:

- Knowledge and information are recognized and managed as valued and valuable strategic business or community assets that enable good decision making and advantageous outcomes;
- An appropriate range of knowledge and information is provided to meet the core business strategy and objectives of the organization;
- Critical information and corporate knowledge is identified, documented, accessible, shared and secured;
- The culture supports people sharing their knowledge with others and opportunities are provided for people to increase their learning;
- Succession planning allows for the passing on of critical knowledge before people move on;
- Corporate intelligence and information are managed, maintained and available in an integrated manner regardless of their source and format; and
- Information content, knowledge and information flows and delivery mechanisms are compatible with the business and decision-making processes.

Supporting these are operational processes that result in the information being consistent, relevant, accessible, concise and accurate.

Creating knowledge enabled and learning organizations and communities

The rapid evolution of the intensely connected global knowledge economy and society means that developing knowledge capabilities is a business and social imperative. The economic and social imperative can be best demonstrated by the fact that knowledge and information enabled communities and societies are often better able to develop economic relationships through productivity improvements, trade and investment and in the exchange of information, knowledge and skills. As an example, developing content itself provides business opportunities, especially where it is delivered for information and entertainment to mobile devices. Innovation through knowledge is also a key driver of wealth creation.

From a societal viewpoint, individual access to information, skills and knowledge is an important component of lifelong learning, day-to-day living and democracy. The public collections of cultural and heritage materials can lead to a more enriched life and an understanding of the past, the present and the future. Community learning and information services also play an important role in increasing knowledge and skills, greater community cohesiveness and enhanced community development. The rise of social networking tools is further connecting people and enabling open debate on social and other issues.

Corporately, knowledge and information management is enabled through technology, leadership, culture, measurement and process. In the presence of these five enablers knowledge, information and business intelligence is used to:

- Plan strategically and make sense of the external environment;
- Facilitate consistent and rapid decision making;
- Support and improve policy making;
- Enable effective and efficient utilization of resources;
- Identify and manage risk;
- Encourage and capitalize on research and development;
- Utilize resources better and identify waste or inappropriate use;
- Monitor quality and performance;
- Meet legislative and regulatory requirements;
- Know what competitors are doing;
- Understand the mix of products and services their customers need;
- Protect the interests of the organization and the rights of employees and customers;
- Provide evidence of business transactions and activities in the case of litigation; and
- Evaluate and deliver increased productivity.

Parker et al. (2005) summarize other organizational benefits that can be attributed to well-planned knowledge management (KM) that include:

- KM encourages the free flow of ideas, which fosters insight and innovation and creates new value through new products or services;
- KM improves customer service and efficiency by streamlining response time;
- KM enhances employee retention rates by recognizing the value of employees' knowledge and rewarding them for it;
- KM streamlines operations and reduces costs by eliminating redundant or unnecessary processes and promoting reuse;
- KM facilitates better, more informed decisions by reducing uncertainty;
- KM contributes to the intellectual capital of the organization;
- KM boosts revenues and enhances the current value of existing products by getting products and services to market faster; and
- KM leads to greater productivity by increasing speed of response.

Information and knowledge management is not an inexpensive exercise so the issues and opportunities that knowledge enabling and information sharing present for the organization must be well understood and supported by executive management. In particular they need to understand how people's knowledge, intelligence and information can add business value and maintain competitive advantage; whether this is for better decision making, in building social capital and customer relationships, supporting research and development, or for more time-critical risk management. This is because they have an essential role in:

- Assisting the organization anticipate its future knowledge and information requirements;
- Ensuring that the process is given the required impetus, status and commitment within the organization; and
- Guaranteeing that others contribute their time and resources to ensure its success.

Ongoing patronage and oversight of the information planning and management strategies may be delegated to the information services manager or another senior manager. However, it is imperative that executive management continues to be seen to be supportive and involved in the process.

In often being the primary sponsor, the information service manager plays an intrinsic part in the knowledge enabling and information management process. They need to be able to talk the talk of executive management in selling the importance of knowledge and information to the organization; helping them understand the issues and opportunities by using examples that they can relate to and using terminology and language that they can understand. It is also important for them to be given sufficient authority to override differences and resolve conflicting requirements that may arise from different parts of the organization.

Coupled with this, the trend to integrated service delivery as well as virtual service delivery can extend organizational-wide interactions to inter-organizational and global ones. This requires cross-functional collaboration in continuously monitoring and improving processes and determining information requirements.

As communication, knowledge enabling, learning and information sharing are very personal issues, individuals are the bastion of the knowledge and information space. People need to be given opportunities to increase the knowledge, learn more skills and share their ideas and intelligence. Basic information skills and ICT skill proficiencies have been embraced as an essential third set of skills alongside literacy and numeracy for everyone. However different generations of clients as well as employees may have preferred choices in technology and service delivery.

Knowledge management workers also need special skills to identify and share their knowledge sources as well as unlock the key to ensure that knowledge and information is shared amongst others. This is no mean feat and Skyrme (1998) has identified the knowledge and skills required of knowledge management workers as follows:

- Technical skills – information (resources) management, information technology skills;
- Business knowledge – industry, markets, customers, competitors, and general business context;

- Interpersonal skills – networking, listening, interpreting, challenging, teamwork, communication;
- Management skills – motivating, coaching, facilitating, influencing;
- Company/organization knowledge – knowledge of procedures and culture; and
- Personnel characteristics – integrity, confidence, openness, trust, supportive, honesty, willingness to learn.

As competitive tools, knowledge, business intelligence and information should be recognized and managed as a corporate rather than an individual or work unit good or resource. The corporate good philosophy lessens duplication, empowers individuals and opens up the flow of knowledge, information and business intelligence rather than being the privilege of any group or individual.

Using the corporate good philosophy, information and its supporting technologies should be designed and managed so that:

- Relevant knowledge, information and business intelligence can be easily identified and retrieved by those who need it, when they need it, whilst preserving privacy and commercial confidentiality;
- Quality information is available in real time throughout the organization;
- Appropriate security measures are in place;
- People's knowledge and the diverse range of information resources and systems within the organization are accessible in a seamless and consistent way 24x365; and
- Being mindful of the changing environment, the knowledge and information architecture is flexible to withstand organizational restructures and changes to business direction.

USING KNOWLEDGE AND INFORMATION FOR DECISION-MAKING ACTIVITIES

Different levels of management in the organization and external stakeholders require and contribute discrete knowledge and information. This is because the knowledge and information required to make corporate decisions differs in the degree of detail and comprehensiveness at different levels in the organization.

Executive management

Executive management focus on issues related to positioning the organization within the external environment. Most of their knowledge and information comes from external sources such as information and business intelligence about new markets, competitors, business trends, new technologies, or new or impending changes to legislation that may affect the business strategy.

Whilst some management information relates to internal performance and strategic planning and is sourced internally, a large proportion of knowledge, information and business intelligence is obtained verbally from external sources, either in meetings, presentations or during conversations with their peers. Executives often travel and, due to constraints on their time, they are only interested in a highly summarized view, frequently presented on a single page delivered electronically to wherever they are.

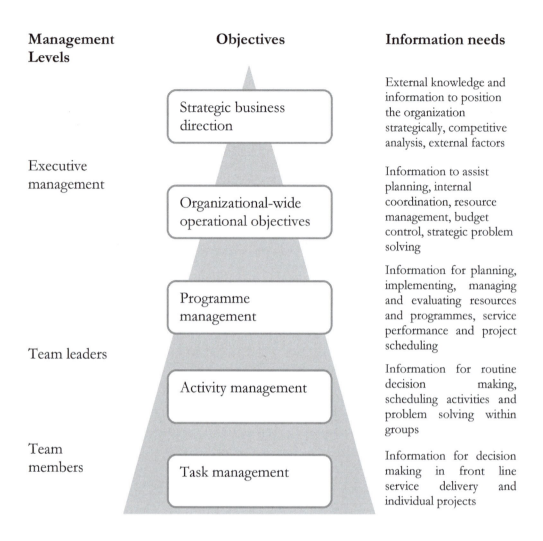

Figure 6.1 Information needs and decision-making activities in organizations

They often employ research or executive assistants to provide these summaries for them.

Team leaders

Team leaders need information from both external and internal sources. They require knowledge and information for decision making on organizational-wide resource utilization and budget control, as well as the coordination of service delivery programmes and work unit outputs.

Team leaders are usually interested in evaluating the performance of the work units and assessing the progress of major projects. Data is gathered from in-house sources relating to the allocation of human, financial and technological resources, budgeting and performance measures. It is combined with other knowledge and information from external sources. This is used for evaluative and comparative purposes to measure performance, to solve problems and to prepare reports for executive management. This information may be used to influence strategic planning and policy-setting processes at the executive level. Team leaders also require knowledge and information for routine decisions relating to the scheduling of activities, accounting for the use of resources, as well as for problem solving.

Team leaders also have an important role in creating learning opportunities for their team members and in encouraging a culture of knowledge sharing across the organization.

At this level of management, external information is significantly different in source and character from internal information or that received by executive management. It often comprises telephone conversations, hearsay and overheard snatches of conversations; the reliability and relevance of which should be determined before using it for important decisions.

Service delivery teams

People working in service delivery require knowledge and information about the customers, the customers' history and their specific service requirements. They also need access to knowledge and information about the parent organization, the services and products that it offers, customer service policies and procedures. This is so that they can inform customers of the products or services offered by the organization, answer the customers' questions quickly and provide a better customer service.

Access to this information will differ in terms of presentation depending on circumstance, location and personal preference. Information may need to be tailored to a small-screen mobile device such as a BlackBerry or iPod, a larger screen device such as a laptop, a large-screen desktop or a mix of both. Location wise information might be accessed in the field, the home or the office.

Customers

The information needs of the parent organization's employees (the internal customers) should be distinguished from the information needs of the parent organization's clients. For example, the information services of a police service will need to support the police officers and civilian staff (the internal customers) in their operational roles in tracking and minimizing crime, maintaining security and presenting evidence relating to alleged offenders. The information needs of the clients of the police service itself (e.g. victims of crime, alleged offenders and other members of the community) will be very different. Their information needs will relate more to their rights and responsibilities or short messages advising of adverse conditions such as a bushfire or seeking the community's assistance in locating a missing child. The police service may also have other clients such as insurance companies, universities or crime research bureaux who may want to purchase or have access to statistical information relating to incidences such as break-ins or robbery in the form of information products.

Customers need information to help them make a decision about their choice of brand, service or product. They may already have knowledge and information about the competitors' products and services and require information to allow for comparisons in making their choice. In a similar manner to employees, customers' personal circumstances, location and personal preference for a device type will also influence how information needs to be presented. Customers and other stakeholders will also have legal access to any personal information that is held by the organization under privacy or data protection and freedom of information legislation.

Other stakeholders

Stakeholders such as suppliers have information requirements for ordering and logistical purposes. Most will utilize electronic systems for the ordering, supply and payment of goods and services. Finance and insurance companies also require information returns. There are also legislative and regulatory requirements for information to be lodged with government agencies. These include industrial relations agencies, corporate and securities commissions, revenue collection and taxation agencies. Increasingly, this information is provided or lodged electronically.

Planning for the future

The information service has a responsibility for ensuring that all information, regardless of source or format, is subject to a managed life cycle. Information is planned with current and future information needs in mind, knowledge and information is acquired, steps are taken to ensure the accessibility and availability of existing knowledge and information and that these are utilized in a manner that reaps the greatest benefit. Finally steps need to be taken to ensure the relevancy and accuracy of the information, to decide what information is no longer required and how out of date, irrelevant information can be retired.

These processes are supported by ICT applications which capture, store, organize, secure, process, track, retrieve, present, transmit or distribute information in a variety of formats and media. Whilst the processes to be outlined will concentrate on the knowledge and information as content, they should not take place in isolation from these ICT applications and infrastructures that support face-to-face, remote access and online services.

Knowledge and information planning is used to:

- Guide the acquisition and redundancy of information;
- Support the knowledge and information flows;
- Facilitate the integration and sharing of knowledge and information; and
- Provide a proactive basis for the meeting of the organization's business and information needs as well as those of its clients and other stakeholders.

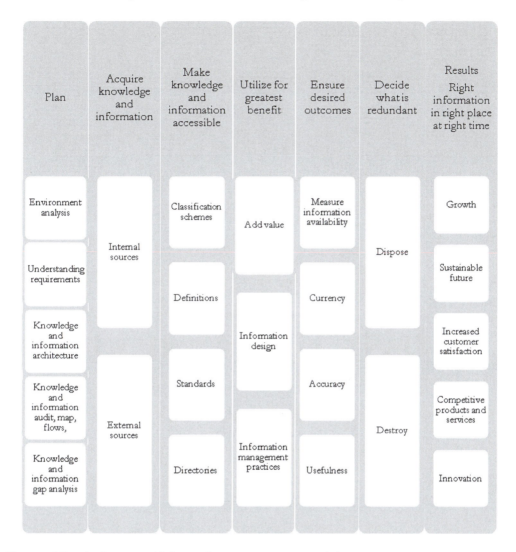

Figure 6.2 An integrated information management model

ENVIRONMENTAL ANALYSIS

The first step in ensuring that knowledge and information are on hand in the future is the environmental analysis. This identifies drivers in the external environment that will influence the type of information and knowledge that is required by the organization and how it will be used, as well as how the organization's business processes, corporate culture and future direction will define information and knowledge flows. The culture has a potent influence on how knowledge and information is used and valued within organizations. For example, the level and abundance of knowledge and information and the extent to which knowledge and information is shared influence and are influenced by the effectiveness of team work, as well as the levels of trust and confidence between team members.

Understanding organizational requirements for knowledge and information

KNOWLEDGE AND INFORMATION ARCHITECTURE

The knowledge and information architecture is the vehicle for determining organizational knowledge and information needs. It shows how the business processes and activities and the knowledge and information that the activities require can be grouped and sequenced, allowing the information service to plan the knowledge and information and its supporting technology architecture around the business objectives of the parent organization.

The knowledge and information architecture defines the different components of the organization's knowledge resources, including a description of its value, its attributes, where it is located, who manages and has responsibility for it, and how to access it. The knowledge and information architecture and its supporting technology architecture, classification scheme, language control and index should be designed to be used across work units and be flexible enough to withstand organizational restructures and changes to business direction. For accountability purposes, it should also be capable of tracking ownership of business decisions and records over time.

In supporting the mission and objectives of the organization, and underlying knowledge and information needed for the organization to carry out its business, the knowledge and information architecture:

- Models how knowledge and information is acquired, managed and stored within the organization or through virtual services (knowledge and information audit);
- Graphically displays the relationships between sources, suppliers and users of the knowledge and information (knowledge and information map);
- Analyses how knowledge and information is used internally by the employees of the parent organization, its clients and other stakeholders (knowledge and information use);
- Looks at communications, interrelationships and movement of knowledge and information throughout the organization, and with clients and other stakeholders (knowledge and information flows); and
- Brings these together with the needs of the organization, customers and other stakeholders to analyse shortfalls in the knowledge and information architecture (knowledge and information needs and gap analysis).

KNOWLEDGE AND INFORMATION AUDIT

The knowledge and information audit provides information on all the current knowledge and information resources and how these are acquired, created and used. This includes the formal and informal records of the organization; information in databases and internal and external business systems; electronic document records management systems; office management systems; the printed and electronic holdings in the library, divisional and individual collections; web services and social media tools; information that can be accessed through external databases; objects, multimedia and information in other formats; and, finally, knowledge critical to the business of the organization that is stored in the minds of individuals.

The knowledge and information audit also identifies how people or systems store, manage or add value to the information, as well as:

- The cost of the management overheads (including maintenance and storage);
- The knowledge and information's value and use within the organization;
- The appropriateness of the format and storage devices;
- The technical and other means of accessing the information;
- The availability of knowledge and information throughout the organization, to clients and to other external parties who may wish to access and make use of the knowledge and information;
- Whether the management of the technology is appropriate and linked to the management of the knowledge and information;
- Statements of policy or objectives for acquiring, using and discarding information; and
- The appropriateness of procedural manuals or instructions for processing or distributing information.

KNOWLEDGE AND INFORMATION MAP

The knowledge and information map identifies those who use the knowledge and information, mapping the users against those who manage, input, process and store it.

The knowledge and information map is scalable. That is, it can be applied or developed:

- With details of just the major customer groups; or
- By identifying individuals as customers.

It can be used to map different levels of knowledge and information use with key personnel (the internal customers), clients and other external stakeholders. The level of detail should be chosen according to the organization's objectives and business needs.

KNOWLEDGE AND INFORMATION USE

The next stage is to analyse how knowledge and information is used within the organization, by its clients and the other external stakeholders within the boundary chosen. It should consider what and how knowledge and information is used, for example:

- Customer profiles to enhance service delivery or sell new products or services to existing customers;
- Financial records to monitor the level of financial expenditure;
- Scientific or technical knowledge and information for research and product development;
- Existing information held in libraries or in databases that is combined or made available in a different format to create a value-added information product; or
- Statistics and other management information to measure productivity or efficiency.

KNOWLEDGE AND INFORMATION FLOWS

The knowledge and information flow analysis traces the flow of knowledge and information between people and groups within the organization (the internal customers), and between the organization, its clients and other external stakeholders. The objective is to determine that the correct knowledge and information is flowing to the right areas and that those who need access to knowledge and information are able to receive it. The knowledge and information flow analysis may also highlight opportunities for improved knowledge and information performance. For example it can expose:

- Systems that do not add value to the business strategy;
- Business processes and activities that are not linked with others in electronic information chains necessitating the re-keying of information;
- Activities that create information that is not useful;
- Knowledge and information that could also be used elsewhere for better decision-making or to support others' activities and processes within the organization;
- Undocumented decision processes; or
- Ill-defined or inconsistent business processes.

KNOWLEDGE AND INFORMATION GAP ANALYSIS

This exercise identifies the weak points or shortfalls between the available knowledge and information and the critical knowledge and information that are required. It can also determine where information design and information processes can be improved. The critical knowledge and information needs of the internal customers, the organization's clients and other external stakeholders should also be matched against knowledge and information availability. The knowledge and information gap analysis should consider both current and future needs.

Business systems planning can be used for the knowledge and information gap analysis. This is a two-phase process, the first phase requiring the identification of the business processes, defining information classes, the analysis of systems and getting the executive's, employees', clients' and external stakeholders' perspectives. It should be focused on business processes and customer needs. The second phase involves setting priorities for the organization in terms of its future development and identifying the knowledge and information requirements that will arise from this.

A second methodology that can be used to identify shortfalls in knowledge and information is critical success factors. This methodology identifies the critical things within an organization that must be done and the knowledge and information required to do them. These can be defined through a series of interviews within the organization and with stakeholders.

Once this has been determined, the findings should also be related to how the knowledge and information can be better used to achieve the organization's objectives, customers' and stakeholders' needs, together with the knowledge and information needed to monitor performance in the critical areas. The findings can also be used to determine new business system requirements or where existing systems require modification.

Acquiring knowledge and information

There are many mechanisms through which knowledge and information are acquired; for example:

- Created internally;
- Captured from an external source such as in electronic messaging services or social networking tools;
- Purchasing or subscribing to information, databases, journals and electronic information services;
- Recruiting a person with specific knowledge or providing them with opportunities to increase their knowledge;
- Received unsolicited such as external correspondence;
- A legal requirement to deposit certain material;
- Commissioning reports; or
- Collected as part of case management such as medical records.

Information may be acquired in a variety of formats such as SMS text, electronic mail, published and unpublished reports, spatial information in geographic information systems, video and satellite imagery.

To ensure its accuracy and reliability, information needs to be captured as close as possible to the original source of the information. The capture and use of some information types and formats of information may need specialized technology. For example, moving imagery and large volumes of spatial information require high broadband capacity to manage the transfer and use of the information.

For accountability purposes, the information may need to be registered on receipt or creation. Examples of formal registration processes are:

- Entering details of the item in an asset or acquisition register;
- Scanning or saving a file or document upon its creation or receipt into an electronic document records management system; or
- Logging the transaction in a system.

Copyright and sometimes moral rights may also need to be cleared for the use and reproduction of the information. The information service may have to identify the copyright owner and obtain their permission for a specific use of the information. In some cases, payment to the copyright holder may be required in return for the right to use the information or copyright work.

Acquiring virtual and digital services also changes the business model for the acquisition of materials that has consequences in cash flow, budgets and finances, for example:

- The move to pay for use rather than upfront costs of purchasing information;
- Changes from generic static collections to distributed and digital collections that support specialization on a global basis;
- The transformation of a visible physical collection into a virtual wall-less invisible entity with continuously updated information;

- Instead of restricted local access there can now be shared global access to expertise, subject coverage, collections, services, programmes and events; and
- Changes to the copyright regime to a creative commons environment.

Making knowledge and information accessible

To be totally effective, knowledge and information should be managed, maintained and secured as a shared corporate resource for the benefit of the entire organization or integrated service. To maintain its accuracy and currency, information should be collected once according to an agreed standard, and then reused to meet all information requirements. The collection or capture point should be as close to the source as possible. Consistency (enabled through classification schemes, standards and definitions) and connectivity (enabled through directories) are important; the underlying principle is that it can be cost-effectively shared and used by others for a variety of purposes.

Unless the information is confidential, the artificial boundaries that occur by reason of media or format, location or work unit ownership should be removed. All information should be managed and made accessible in a consistent way, with standard forms of identification and retrieval procedures.

Vital or valuable information that is to be retained within the organization not only needs to be secured, it also needs to be preserved. In the case of electronic information, this includes additional responsibility for managing different electronic versions of the same information, for example by managing the version control of information contained in reports and by ensuring that all information is kept in a form that can be read by the software and hardware in current use. As new technology or versions of software are introduced, the storage devices and software versions must be upgraded so that the information can be used at a later date. This particularly applies to significant documents or reports that have been produced on word processing or desktop publishing systems and that require continuous use.

Corporate knowledge in people's heads may also be secured through contractual agreements that protect the passing on of competitive information during and after the time of employment of the individual.

Storage requirements in electronic and physical forms may be assessed according to the:

- Physical characteristics of the information;
- Business objectives and client needs of the parent organization;
- Source and level of risk; and
- Required level of security.

Security classifications may need to be assigned to different types of information or its content in order to ensure that only authorized persons have access.

The use of classification schemes, standards, definitions and directories assist in enabling the information to be consistently defined, maintained and accessible by those authorized to use it, whilst being protected from unauthorized use or misuse. Information can be accurately described in information directories and indexes so that its source, relationships and other attributes are known. Standards can be employed that encourage the sharing and integration of the information. Data dictionaries and data models can also be used to provide a clear picture of the information that is available.

KNOWLEDGE AND INFORMATION CLASSIFICATION

The classification of knowledge and information is an important activity in that it defines the parameters of access and use of the organization's knowledge and information. For example, knowledge and information may be classified according to its:

- Strategic or commercial value to the organization – the extent to which the knowledge, information and business intelligence is of a commercial-in-confidence nature or critical to the organization's strategic business advantage;
- Level of privacy – the extent to which it contains personal information about individuals;
- Value in the information market – the extent to which the knowledge and information can be used to develop value-added information products for sale;
- Level of security type and use – the extent to which it can be used in the various activities or levels within the organization or externally;
- Subject area – the extent to which a descriptive title can be assigned using an existing records management index or library classification scheme; or
- Format or source – the extent to which it is sourced externally or internally, and its format.

Where possible, knowledge and information classification schemes should be consistent across the organization, regardless of format.

INFORMATION STANDARDS

In order to ensure that the information can be reused, transferred or integrated with other knowledge and information, the capture and management of the information should be according to predetermined standards. The standards should be set by the organization. The choice of standard should be based on a business case and will depend upon:

- The extent to which the information is to be integrated with external information or used by external stakeholders; and
- Efficiency and effectiveness.

The use of standards must be cost-effective. Information should not be maintained at a higher level standard that is necessary. However, future needs and environments must also be considered when deciding on standards. Standards should be chosen to add value to the use and management of information rather than create an unnecessary level of workload or bureaucracy. Information should not be over-processed for the sake of conforming to national or international standards if this is not warranted by the business case or customers' needs. The purpose of adopting information standards is to maintain the degree of consistency and connectivity that enables information to be shared. For example:

- Information used externally by clients or external stakeholders will need to be captured, maintained and transferred according to a national or international standard;
- Information used internally across the organization should be captured, maintained and transferred according to an agreed standard within the organization; and
- Specific information that is captured and maintained to support a single programme or activity should also conform to organizational standards.

Globalization, increasingly integrated service delivery and the use of inter-organizational systems means that national or international standards will more and more be used; what is more likely to vary is the level of adoption of the standards.

INFORMATION DEFINITIONS

Information definitions provide information, or meta data, about the information itself. Their purpose is to increase the understanding about the information and its relevance to a particular use. They may provide information about the quality, rules of use, source, accuracy, currency, projection type or scale, format, coverage in terms of geographical area or timescale etc. Information definitions may be created as part of a data dictionary in a database administration system.

KNOWLEDGE AND INFORMATION DIRECTORIES

Knowledge and information directories identify what knowledge and information exists and where it may be found. Library catalogues and other tools that identify sources of information are examples of information directories. As a location tool, they contain information about source, access and use constraints, purpose, availability, point of contact for further information, cross-references and other appropriate information found in the information definition. Skills inventories may also yield information about the specific skills, knowledge and expertise of people in the organization.

Data or information definitions make up a large proportion of an entry in an information directory. Initially, the knowledge and information directory can be produced through the knowledge and information audit and mapping processes as these identify what knowledge and information is available and its source. To be of long-term use the meta data must be continually updated.

To assist users, the knowledge and information directory should be designed so that it is searchable on a number of fields. It should be easy to use, convenient to access and available in an appropriate format.

Utilizing the knowledge and information for the greatest benefit

ADDING VALUE

The return on investment for the efforts already in place through planning, understanding the requirements and structuring corporate knowledge and information resource is built on by utilizing these resources for their greatest benefit and to their fullest extent.

This involves being proactive about doing more with the organization's knowledge and information resource, particularly at the touch points where value can be added. It entails looking at strategies and activities for designing and adding value to the original knowledge and information to meet new market needs or in identifying new uses for the existing information. This may include the combining or overlaying of information in a system, considering different delivery media mechanisms and formats, creating mashups where a website or application combines content from more than one source into an integrated experience, or in presenting the information in a different way. All of this needs to be in the context of protecting copyright, privacy and confidentiality.

Value is further added through the choice of delivery mechanisms. The background, skills, knowledge, location and perspective of the customers will influence their ability to use the information and how they would like it presented. The customer may also have a particular preference for information in a certain format or language, or may wish to use a particular distribution method such as mobile phone alert or electronic mail. Further information on channel management and customer needs can also be found in later chapters.

Increasingly, and indicating the way of the future, it is the customer who is adding value through social bookmarking services; posting links to web pages that they find useful or interesting either for their private reference or to share with others. Blogs, discussion forums and wikis are some of the tools being used for collaboration and the distributed creation of documents and information.

Information and its supporting technologies should be designed so that relevant information can be identified, retrieved, manipulated and made available to appropriate individuals when and where they require it. This is where value can be added and the strategic business advantage lies. As Bertrot et al. (2004) identify: 'network-based services and resources offered by libraries today, including digital references, digital collections, online databases, e-journals, and e-books, enable libraries to operate in an anytime/anywhere mode, allowing patrons with internet access to access content, services, and resources 365 days a year, 24 hours a day'.

Information design

Designing information and its supporting technologies to complement communication flows and information needs is another way to add value and ensure that information is utilized for its greatest benefit and to its fullest extent. In most traditional organizations, information flows upwards and commands are passed downwards. The information is prone to distortion and manipulation. Decentralized, highly integrated informal and increasingly global operations require technology architectures that enhance information flows and extend across work group, organizational and national boundaries visibly and simultaneously.

Teams and groups require networks, tools, electronic mail, social media and instant messaging facilities in order that they all receive the same information at the same time. They also make greater use of collaborative processing and shared workspace applications that support more flexible work patterns and teamwork. Not only is hard information required, teams and groups rely upon more qualitative information in both external information and internal information such as members' knowledge experiences, views, successes and problems. Knowledge repositories, expertise access tools, discussion technologies, knowledge representation, expert systems, e-learning applications, synchronous interaction tools, and data warehouse and data mining tools are quoted by Parker et al. (2005: 181) as being sources of qualitative information for decision making.

Information and its supporting technologies can also be designed to overcome distance and time barriers. People from diverse geographic locations, mobile workers and those who work during non-traditional hours can work together in the same team to create a boundary-less organization with the use of the right technology and human resource management policies. Information and its supporting technologies should be designed to be:

- Accessible – information should be able to be accessed easily and quickly at the right time and in the right place by the appropriate people. Access should be seamless, regardless of source or format, with a choice of delivery channels. It should take into consideration any necessary security and privacy considerations;
- Comprehensive – information should be useful, related to need and appropriate to the level of the decision-maker. There is a difference between providing information that is comprehensive enough to satisfy information needs and information overload. Too much information can be as problematic as too little information;
- Accurate – information should be accurate, complete, reliable and current;
- Appropriate – information content, information flows and delivery mechanisms should be appropriate to the business processes, decision making and information needs of management, employees, customers and other stakeholders. Irrelevant information is costly in terms of capture, storage and use. Information should also be presented in a manner that is meaningful and best fits the skills and competencies of the user;
- Timely – the information should be continually kept up to date; although in some cases, historical data is required;
- Clear – information should be free from ambiguity. The source and purpose for use should be immediately obvious to the individual so that they can make informed choices as to the usefulness of the information;
- Flexible – the systems and information content should be designed to be flexible to allow for growth and change within the parent organizations and tailored to suit different service delivery channels. It should also allow a variety of users to navigate through the system(s) to locate the required information;
- Verifiable – the information content should be capable of being verified in terms of source, accuracy and authenticity;
- Free from bias – the information content should not be entered, modified or displayed in such a way as to influence the user's course of action;
- Consistent – data definitions and terminology should be consistent across the organization regardless of format, storage device or location; and
- Compliant – where international or national information or technology standards are used to support the parent organization's objectives and business strategy, all information and its supporting technologies within the organization should be according to the chosen standard.

Inefficient information management practices should be avoided as they can be costly in terms of time, money and lost business opportunities. Inefficient practices include:

- Collecting and storing information when it is no longer used;
- Disseminating information too widely (information overload);
- Not making information accessible to potential users; or
- Duplicating information across the organization.

Ensuring that the desired outcomes are achieved

The desired outcomes in managing knowledge and information are that:

- Appropriate knowledge and information is available to meet the business needs of the organization and the information needs of clients and stakeholders;
- Information flows and delivery mechanisms ensure that knowledge and information is made available when and where users need it;
- The knowledge and information needs are understood, with the result that information is available to users in a relevant and meaningful form;
- Information is appropriately secured in terms of accessibility, integrity and confidentiality;
- Information is consistently defined across the organization;
- Information is accurate and complete, including there being a complete, reliable and accurate documentation of the organization's business activities and transactions (including accounting and finance);
- All legal, evidential and accountability requirements are met; and
- Information is constantly reviewed to avoid redundancy and to evaluate its appropriateness to the organization's business needs.

Efficiency and effectiveness measures should be developed to measure the above and ensure that the planning and management processes are meeting the organization's objectives and the information needs of the internal customers, the organization's clients and stakeholders.

Deciding what information is no longer required

In order to ensure relevancy, accuracy and integrity of information, decisions need to be made about what information should be considered as redundant. Information becomes redundant when it is superfluous to requirements, outdated or inactive. Not all information reaches an outdated stage. A significant proportion of information that exists in live information systems is continually updated, although the information systems can become redundant if they no longer fit the purpose, objectives or business needs of the organization.

Information should not be kept beyond its useful life as this leads to unnecessary and inefficient use of storage space, equipment, staff and resources. However not all information can be destroyed. In deciding if, how and when the information may be disposed of, consideration should be given to legislative and regulatory requirements that require certain corporate information to be kept for a minimum period of time. Some information may also be of archival value. Vital or valuable information may be identified and be made subject to corporate retention and disposal schedules. Succession planning will also assist in retaining corporate knowledge and information when people leave.

Information should be retained, removed or destroyed in accordance with authorized processes. If the information is to be removed off-site or offline, such as to an archive facility, the security and ease of retrievability should be considered. Information should be deleted from hard and floppy disks before either the computer or disk is disposed of. Disks should also be physically destroyed to avoid information being retrieved. If printed information is to be destroyed, it should be burnt, pulped or shredded. It ought to not be disposed of through normal refuse disposal facilities.

Conclusion

Knowledge and information management is now gaining the prominence and awareness that it deserves. Organizations are recognizing the true corporate value of knowledge and information as a resource critical to survival and success in the global knowledge economy and society. Similarly the increased availability of information and knowledge through the proliferation of information and communications technology (ICT) is creating new information and content based industries, driving economic productivity, structural change and the emergence of more open societies.

Managers in libraries and information centres have a significant role in creating and building intelligent organizations and communities in this environment and in planning and managing information and organizational knowledge in a manner that creates the greatest benefit and return on investment. This includes managing the information according to an information life cycle which comprises:

*   Planning for current and future information needs;
*   Understanding organizational requirements for knowledge and information;
*   Acquiring knowledge and information;
*   Making knowledge and information accessible;
*   Utilizing knowledge and information for the greatest benefit;
*   Ensuring that the desired outcomes are achieved; and
*   Deciding what information is no longer required.

By systematically managing each stage of the life cycle in a manner that enables knowledge and information to be shared, valuable and essential knowledge and information will be available when and where required.

The virtual environment also presents new dilemmas and opportunities. As services become more integrated and global in nature, the business process boundaries will extend across organizations and national boundaries requiring different governance models for managing the information life cycle and assets in these circumstances.

References

Bertrot, J.C. et al. 2004. Capture usage with e-metrics. *Library Journal*, available at www.libraryjournal.com/article/CA411564?display=FeaturesNews&industry.

Parker, Kevin R. et al. 2005. Libraries as knowledge management centres. *Library Management*, 26(4/5), 176–189.

Skyrme, D. 1998. *Knowledge Management – A Fad or a Ticket to Ride*, available at www.skyrme.com.

Further Reading

Broadbent, M. and Kitzis, E.S. 2005. *The New CIO Leader: Setting the Agenda and Delivering Results*. Boston: Harvard Business School.

Cross-Cultural Perspectives on Knowledge Management. 2007. Westport: Libraries Unlimited.

Davenport, T.H. 2005. *Thinking for Living: How to Get Better Performance and Results from Knowledge Workers*. Boston: Harvard Business School.

Digital Library Economics: An Academic Perspective. 2009. Oxford: Chandos.

Girard, J.P. and McIntyre, S. 2010. Knowledge management modelling in public sector organizations: A case study. *International Journal of Public Sector Management*, 23(1), 71–77.

Leveraging Corporate Knowledge. 2004. ed. Edward Truch. Aldershot: Ashgate.

Orna, E. 2004. *Information Strategy in Practice*. Aldershot: Gower.

Orna, E. 2005. *Making Knowledge Visible: Communicating Knowledge Through Information Products*. Aldershot: Gower.

Senge, P.M. 1990. *The Fifth Discipline: The Art and Practice of The Learning Organization*. New York: Century Business.

Vincere, A.A. 2000. Ten observations on e-learning and leadership development. *Human Resource Planning*, 23(4), 34–46.

Wiggins, B. 2000. *Effective Document Management: Unlocking Corporate Knowledge*. Aldershot: Ashgate.

7 Strategic Technology and Asset Management – A Smarter Approach

Strategic assets comprise tangible belongings such as plant, machinery and equipment, including information and communications technology (ICT) infrastructure, software and equipment, real estate and buildings, motor vehicles and cultural assets, as well as intangible assets such as branding, intellectual property and know-how, knowledge and information. This chapter concentrates on planning and implementing ICT strategies with consideration for the other tangible assets described above. As ICT is subject to rapid change the operational management of specific technologies has not been addressed. There are three components to ICT, these being business applications, infrastructure and equipment.

ICT business applications are the cornerstone for virtual and digital service delivery. In the corporate world ICT applications support and sustain business growth, lower costs and increase the quality and personalization of customer quality services. ICT applications in a consumer world enable the customer to receive their choice of information in a combination of formats, voice, image and data through the multiple delivery channels and access channels. Groupware, social networking, shared project management are examples of community and business applications providing substantial productivity gains and increased communication on an enterprise, national and international basis.

ICT infrastructure enables the transport of knowledge, data and information in many different formats and media to support strategic corporate intelligence capability and the sharing of knowledge, intelligence and information between internal and external systems and stakeholders. These activities may be global, enterprise-wide and/or local in nature. ICT infrastructure includes mobile and wireless technologies, networks, e-commerce systems, artificial intelligence, intranets, extranets, the Internet, Web 2.0 services, portals, back-end, office, client and supplier systems and their subsequent replacement infrastructure. The Internet and Web have also provided the basis for the development of collaboration tools supporting joint service delivery initiatives across regions and internationally.

ICT equipment includes desktop, portable devices such as mobile phones and e-book readers, as well as servers and other programme and storage devices and is the end device for the delivery of ICT applications. Supporting the ICT infrastructure and equipment are security features to ensure accessibility, confidentiality and integrity, and methods, protocols and standards that enable rather than enforce the business strategy.

Making the Most Out of Technology and Other Assets

ICT is a critical business asset, the application of which offers both considerable opportunities and immense challenges in further developing business capacity and capability as well as supporting strategic alliances. The importance of its application is such that it is a driving force in which senior and executive management need to take a leadership role and be actively engaged: leading by example in their use of mobile and desktop technologies, providing clear direction for the business outcomes required in applying technological solutions, ensuring that business practices are aligned to the technology, championing the business opportunities and advantages of using ICT, understanding market and customer needs and preferences and focusing on the sustainable achievement of goals.

This does not require a strong technical background; rather it is a leadership and strategic direction-setting role. It entails a business-focused understanding of the opportunities presented by ICT, and a readiness to accept ownership, responsibility and accountability for the technology-based assets and outcomes that can be delivered: outcomes that will result in business value and transformation; increasing customer satisfaction by delivering quality customer services, enabling global competitiveness and supporting enterprise-wide connectiveness in internal operations. Furthermore, it requires the understanding and development of business-focused metrics that should be used to articulate the value derived from using any new technology. These metrics must also be able to withstand comparisons between times when the market is buoyant as well as when economic conditions are difficult.

A common point of failure in perceptions of ICT is that it is the panacea for all ills. ICT can only be an enabler of leading-edge customer service delivery, internal efficiencies and connectivity with global business partners where there has been commensurate change to processes, communications and work flows across the length of the value chain. In short, it has to be accompanied by a strategic change management programme including embedding corporate change and sometimes culture, revised business processes and, often, new mindsets.

As with knowledge and information strategy and planning, information services have the dual responsibility of adding value to business policy and strategy, planning and managing all corporate ICT, providing an efficient and flexible infrastructure, and finding competitive opportunities for technical innovation for the whole organization on an enterprise-wide and sometimes global basis, as well as for their own internal operations.

As a leader of business strategy and fusion, the information services manager must chart the way forward for ICT applications, infrastructure and equipment in a manner that delivers value to all, enhances the business capability and capacity, and customer service proposition to a degree that puts the organization's credibility and competitive position ahead of others.

In addition to the above, they have the responsibility for clearly understanding and promoting ways in which ICT as a strategic business asset can add agility and business value to the whole enterprise. This includes using:

- Business intelligence regarding markets and customer needs and preferences to drive technology design, strategy, products and services;
- Technology to sustain the financial situation by lowering costs;

- Technology as a focus for continually improving and refining business processes throughout the business value chain; and
- Change management skills to prepare the organization for changes in mindsets, processes and practices in line with the new business opportunities.

As a corporate enabler the information services manager also has a role in developing people's capacities to better use the available technology, improving performance and decision making through enabling access to quality data, information and knowledge, assisting in the achievement of corporate and environmental responsibilities in acquiring, using and disposing of ICT equipment in an environmentally friendly way, and in protecting commercial, confidential and private information by ensuring appropriate security.

Whilst the information services manager has a focus on the business application of technology, they also need strong people management skills for their immediate operations and for future positioning. New technologies will bring the requirement for new skills and know-how in their own staff and users. In having a holistic view of the organization, the information services manager is in the unique position of blending the skills, knowledge, processes, capabilities and relationships of people in their use and application of ICT across the whole organization. They should also continually evaluate the capabilities and use of ICT by their own staff as well as users, in terms of meeting the business requirements including business intelligence applications and process integration, as well as training requirements and supporting customer relationships.

With the move to integrated service delivery, Web 2.0 applications and mobile technologies, the role of the information services manager is becoming increasingly wider and complex. As the business boundaries extend and become more integrated different governance, management and finance models may be required.

All of this means that the information services manager will need to build alliances with ICT vendors and other stakeholder institutions to take advantage of new developments in products and applications. With this in mind they will spend increased time on building relationships with people outside of the organization in order to influence wider stakeholder relationships and organizational effectiveness in its external environment.

Effective planning and implementation of ICT requires both users and information services managers having a clear vision and objectives of when and what is to be achieved. Many projects fail because of unrealistic expectations or inadequately scoped requirements and specifications. Users should look for integrated service offerings that have a holistic approach to business needs, and also be objective in determining the need for additional training and business process re-engineering to take full advantage of the technology implementation. There should be a clear and concise statement of requirements that is mutually agreed by all parties and strongly aligned to the business requirements and outcomes of the strategic plan.

Increasing the value of information and communications technology

The value of information and communications technology is found in how it sustains core business processes and outcomes. By themselves ICT and other assets do not provide a competitive advantage; they have a value that is in accordance with what the last bidder is prepared to pay. Competitive advantage is realized when ICT and other assets are planned, managed and put to use in a manner that creates real value and gain for the organization.

Managed in a clever way, ICT can reduce inventory levels and make other resources more efficient, free up capital for use on other activities, provide real-time visibility and control, and improve internal operational efficiencies. Further value can be contributed when ICT is a source of accomplishment and innovation; offering differentiation and improvements in customer relationships and service, meeting individual client needs, reducing time to market and increasing the return on investment.

With up to 50 per cent of organizational capital being spent on ICT, it can either be a smart investment or an expensive headache. Properly planned and designed ICT enables knowledge and innovation to be central to the organization's capacities to model future scenarios, add value, discover new opportunities and act quickly on intelligence from internal and external systems.

Technology today is cheaper, more accessible and ubiquitous, but this should not lead to complacency. Besides the substantial financial investment, there is often a short pay-back period before the next business-led application is needed. There is an art to keeping the ICT investment finely balanced between seeking business opportunities at the leading edge of technology where the risk may be high, and maintaining cost-effective solutions without being technology led.

The choice of the ICT platform can commit the organization to a technology direction that will be built upon over a number of years. The information services manager and senior management must have sufficient confidence in the chosen strategy that it will not only bring competitive advantage through the delivery of information and services, but that it is flexible enough to cope with changes in the environment, mergers and acquisitions, with integrated services and to sustain the competitive advantage in the long term.

The ICT industry accounts for 2 per cent of global carbon dioxide (CO_2) emissions, a figure equivalent to that of the aviation sector. Sensible and practical changes to the way in which ICT is used in organizations can help reduce this impact. This includes introducing energy efficient computing, recycling hardware and consumables, power management and reducing paper usage.

As with knowledge and information, ICT and other strategic assets are best managed according to a life cycle that includes planning for the future, understanding how technology is being used in the organization, acquiring technology, managing and utilizing the technology for the greatest benefit in service delivery and information provision, ensuring that the desired outcomes are achieved and disposing of the asset. To assist in the management of ICT through these life cycles, best-practice methodologies have been developed. Two of the most common are the IT Infrastructure Library (ITIL)[1] which identifies best practice in regards to managing IT service levels, the how you do it, and the Control Objectives for Information and related Technology (COBIT)[2] that covers what to do.

---

1   ITIL was developed by the Central Computer and Telecommunications Agency of the UK Government (CCTA), in accordance with the British Standard BS15000 for IT Services Management.

2   COBIT is issued by IT Governance Institute.

In focusing on identifying best practice, ITIL focuses on planning to implement service management, service support, service delivery, security management, application management, ICT infrastructure management and the business perspective. In comparison, COBIT is strong on controls and metrics, breaking ICT down into a set of 34 processes in four domains: planning and organization, acquisition and implementation, delivery and support, and monitoring.

Planning for the future

The introduction of any new technology must serve a specific business purpose or be part of a strategic decision where it can add real business value. Therefore planning and management of strategic assets, including ICT, should be undertaken with the view to:

- Maximize the return on investment for the asset;
- Utilize the asset as a business tool to create the advantageous edge;
- Enhance competitiveness and improve customer relationships and service delivery;
- Improve processes to continually deliver positive, tangible results and outcomes;
- Provide choice for staff and customers in the manner in which they wish to access services;
- Reduce the carbon footprint and support environmentally friendly ICT and workplace practices;
- Provide a point of differentiation in the market place; and
- Reduce future resource requirements by prolonging the asset's life or strengthening its disposal value.

To gain maximum benefit from the investment decisions, planning for strategic assets, including ICT, entails:

- Understanding internal business processes and level of process integration as well as their weak points;
- Understanding the current and desired degree of technology integration and innovation;
- Aligning and integrating the use of the assets with the business strategy and business processes to ensure a value focus and connectedness with the business enterprise;
- Knowing the availability of financial resources as well as the skills and knowledge of users and implementers;
- Understanding the assets' usable lives, performance, capacities and applications;
- Employing the most cost-effective and environmentally sustainable use of the asset;
- Considering future trends in the global industry and the readiness of client markets to embrace and incorporate technology change;
- Determining whether existing asset and ICT management policies support new initiatives or need to be revised;
- Determining sourcing strategies and relationships; and
- Incorporating an element of innovation or surprise in the application to distinguish the organization from others.

Strategic asset and ICT planning also involves:

- Identifying the extent of the long-term contribution of the asset to the organizational direction;
- Identifying the business opportunities presented by new directions in the market place, and the threats that may come from any competitor's use of similar assets;
- Prioritizing areas where ICT and other assets can add the most value to the success of the organization;
- Identifying where the processes and business practices within the organization require re-engineering to maximize the total benefit; and
- Measuring and evaluating the potential value and contribution of the asset to organizational success.

Without these considerations, the exercise can be extremely costly with ill-fitting and overpriced solutions that will deliver little or no business advantage. The historical path of ICT is littered with examples where new technology has failed to reap the benefits because existing and out-of-date processes have been automated with the result that inefficient or bad processes just run faster.

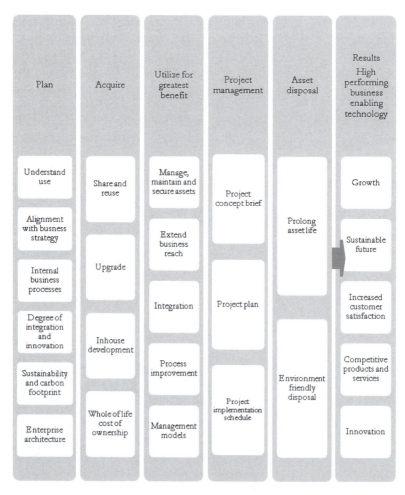

Figure 7.1   Integrated technology management model

Understanding how technology is being used in the organization

The next step is to analyse how ICT and other assets are used within the organization and by its clients and other external stakeholders. The enterprise architecture can be used as the vehicle to align ICT availability and use to the business of the organization.

ENTERPRISE ARCHITECTURE

The enterprise architecture underpins the business drivers of the organization and enables ICT to be used strategically to support the business of the organization. It:

- Integrates business strategy planning and ICT strategy;
- Moves the organization from reactive planning to a proactive planning focus;
- Takes an holistic approach to planning, managing and governance of all ICT across the whole organization;
- Provides the governance framework and context for aligning and integrating ICT with the organization's mission, objectives and processes;
- Defines the principles by which decisions are made and ICT managed;
- Guides ICT investment, acquisition, development and maintenance; and
- Maximizes efficiency through ensuring collaboration and the interoperability and portability of systems, applications and networks.

The enterprise architecture is designed to be flexible to reflect changing business needs and opportunities. It takes into consideration environmental trends, business strategy and the current architecture to determine the future architecture. It typically comprises:

- High-level objectives, high-level business requirements and principles that define and govern the use and application of ICT. High-level principles may include systems being designed to be business driven, protection of confidentiality and privacy in information, use of proven standards and technologies, and consideration for total cost of ownership;
- A restatement of the business drivers that govern the use of ICT;
- A business process taxonomy that describes key business processes and their objectives to assist in determining business proposals, funding and procurement, application development and improvement, evaluation and review;
- A framework for the ICT application, systems and network architectures;
- Governance structures for the overall goals, directions, investments, use and outcomes of ICT within the organization;
- Security architecture to ensure accessibility, confidentiality and integrity;
- Standards, technologies and toolsets in use; and
- Services available.

The enterprise architecture is an enabler not an enforcer of the organization's business strategies. Whilst it can be used as a driver for change in business and process re-engineering, it should not overtake the business strategy. The enterprise architecture is strongly linked to the knowledge and information architecture. It is the business information needs, objectives and business strategy that determine its future direction, not the other way round.

Acquiring technology

After satisfying the planning requirements, new ICT business applications can be acquired through:

- Sharing and reusing an existing system (either internally or externally owned);
- Upgrading to a newer version;
- In-house development;
- Purchasing new hardware, devices and off-the-shelf or shrink-wrap software products; or
- Commissioning an external agent to create the ICT business application.

The manner in which the ICT application is acquired will require consideration as to whether it is to be managed in-house or outsourced to a third party. Outsourcing is often used to acquire services where there is a desire to reduce overhead costs, improve service levels, gain access to know-how, or take advantage of new technology directions.

Whilst the provision of services can be outsourced, accountability for the service levels and strategic decisions relating to service provisions cannot. The fundamental responsibility and accountability for the outcomes and quality of the end product and service still resides with management.

DETERMINING THE TOTAL WHOLE-OF-LIFE COSTS OF OWNERSHIP

ICT acquisition should take into account not just the cost of the hardware, software, peripherals, devices and associated infrastructure, but also the costs of implementation, re-engineering and disposal of the assets. This includes the full costs of integration, maintenance and support, data capture and conversion as well as the cost of disposal and recycling. Intangible assets, data capture and conversion are often overlooked, yet they form a significant proportion of the full acquisition costs. Likewise the costs of business and process re-engineering and retraining also need to be considered in order to provide a total cost of both the capital investment and implementation expenditure.

In selecting the most appropriate asset to fit the business purpose it is often useful to employ a total cost of ownership approach. This means that all financial costs are considered, not just the capital acquisition costs. What might initially be considered a cheaper option may over the course of its life cycle cost considerably more than its alternative. For example a motor vehicle may initially have an attractive purchase price, but prove to have higher fuel consumption, maintenance overheads and insurance costs than its competitor over time. Significant ICT projects may also attract variances in the time to deploy and manage, employee and end-user productivity, and effort required to customize or enhance application usage.

Managing and utilizing technology for the greatest benefit

Extending business reach in a global market, the need for workforce flexibility, integrating service delivery, growing inter-organizational research and development and pressures to reduce travel are some of the drivers influencing how the ICT infrastructure should be structured and managed to gain the greatest organizational benefit in an often virtual world. In addition, increasingly sophisticated client needs, the push for process improvement, shifts in services to more self-service delivery, increased user productivity and reduced costs also influence how technology and assets are managed for profit and business gain.

The bottom line for introducing new ICT projects and managing the infrastructure is to increase the speed, quality, choice and flexibility of services to users and clients at lower costs, and to provide an aspect of uniqueness that makes it difficult for competitors to replicate the exact nature of the business services. However, the introduction of a new ICT initiative will not drive these business benefits alone. It has to be accompanied by a strategic change management programme including embedding corporate change, revised business processes and, often, new mindsets. For example, the introduction of mobile devices and social networking and other Web 2.0 and beyond to enable and support virtual teamwork and collaboration across geographical or organizational boundaries will require new ways of communicating, changes to processes and responsibilities, new corporate policies, protocols and standards and a different perspective on risk.

A further change management factor is the people factor. In commencing any technology project, the impact of change upon individuals will need to be taken into consideration as the people factor can make or break the introduction of new technology. Introduced with thought, ICT can deliver major benefits to individuals in their ability to access and use information, and to the organization in terms of increased productivity, broadening the business base and improving the delivery of products and services. However, it should be properly planned and implemented to take into account the information and business needs, the corporate culture, the need to change or re-engineer business processes, education and retraining of users and technical staff, and the financial and resource capacity of the organization. Those with the potential to be adversely affected should be kept informed of any changes and given training and retraining opportunities.

MANAGEMENT MODELS

An important decision to be made for managing, maintaining and securing assets is whether to undertake this in-house or to move to a managed service in the form of outsourcing or shared computing environment. This decision is a governance issue and frequently focuses on:

- Whether the organization wishes to concentrate solely on its core business;
- Organizational size;
- Availability of expertise;
- Variance in demand utilization;
- Overhead costs; and
- Financial capacity to fund asset investment.

Common areas where managed services are employed include security services, financial accounting, human resource recruitment and office support services, storage and retrieval of records and archives, transportation services, telecommunications network maintenance and facilities management, end-user desktop support, infrastructure development, systems maintenance, systems integration and systems development and design, training and service delivery such as the delivery of value-added information products. In the case of ICT and transportation this obviates the need to invest in ICT and specialized vehicle assets.

Managing the move to managed services involves:

- Determining the right objectives and strategy – the objective rationale determines the nature of the strategy, contract and management mechanisms. For example, a business objective to enable the organization to focus on its core business will require a different partnership arrangement than one that is focused on a shift in technology or the sharing of risks;
- Determining what needs to be moved to a managed service – this is influenced by the key business objectives for outsourcing and the risks associated with outsourcing or another type of managed service;
- Assessing the benefits – these may be derived from increased sustainability, competitive advantage or other value-added factors. These may include financial benefits through the ability to spread the costs over a number of years, shared risks or jointly developing capabilities on a commercial basis. Other benefits to consider include skills and knowledge transfer; flexibility in the technology development and acquisition to support continued innovation; the migration to new ICT platforms and infrastructure at significant lesser cost than outright purchase; the divestment of legacy systems and other underperforming assets; lessening of overheads associated with storage; and access to new markets and services;
- Determining the risks – these include loss of expertise, key competencies and skills of staff within the information service which may have long-term corporate knowledge and financial implications, costs being deferred rather than being reduced, lack of contract negotiation and continued contract management skills within the organization, incorrectly and under-specified service delivery outcomes that lead to business functions not being performed, poor vendor selection, inadequate or unclear contracts leading to costly litigation, integration problems or problems in getting different contractors and/or vendors to work together or find technically sound interoperable solutions, lack of flexibility and responsiveness to the needs of the information service, continually changing service provider staff such that there is little or no understanding of the business by those delivering the service, and delays in project execution or completion;
- Selecting the vendor – this should be based upon the vendor's credibility and capability to provide the services being outsourced, financial strength and viability of the vendor to remain in business for the life of the partnership (and longer), proven technical and service capability and performance in similar information related environments, the variety of platforms offered to support the requirements of the information service and its clients, the level of control in terms of future direction, security and risk management issues, tender conformance, whole of life costs of the proposal, congruency with the vendor's vision, strategic business direction and

client relationship perspective, the vendor's adaptability, understanding and ability to contribute to the organization's business in a timely manner, and the vendor's compatibility with the organization's corporate culture;

- Structuring the relationship – this should result in a partnership of goodwill, understanding and good communication with a high level of trust between the partners and a cultural fit between the organization and the service provider;
- Governance framework – this should outline communication and escalation mechanisms, defined contact points, the business objectives and requirements, each parties' expectations, roles and obligations in the partnership agreement, the organization's business and corporate culture, the distribution of risk between the parties, the ownership of the assets, the required outcomes and outputs and the terms and conditions of the agreement itself;
- Negotiating the contract – the contract should meet the organization's business needs and objectives rather than the vendor's and should specify the areas to be outsourced, the service levels required and the penalties, the level of service and contribution required of the organization and its management staff, all costs, including those for maintenance and support, billing and asset management issues, intellectual property rights and copyright, including ownership of systems and developments, data and indemnities against the intellectual property rights of third parties, integration procedures for systems that may now be managed across multiple parties, for example telecommunications, office and email systems and business systems, risk management, including data redundancy, procedures and responsibilities, distribution of risk between the parties, security, confidentiality and backup, privacy protection, date and value of the transfer of assets, disposal of surplus assets, outstanding liabilities on assets, conditions relating to staff development, transfer of staff and transfer conditions, outstanding liabilities in terms of accrued leave payments, superannuation or other contractual obligations, use of contractors, availability and costs of additional staff, backup arrangements for key or critical staff, minimum proficiencies, poaching of staff, disputes and damages settlements, termination clauses, back out and change requirements for both parties, performance measures, review and monitoring, indemnities and liabilities, contract variation procedures, waivers, publicity and governing law;
- Managing the risks – includes ongoing monitoring of performance levels, ensuring change management strategies are in place and managing the transition period at the end of the contract;
- Being an exceptional client – obligations include acting professionally and with respect for each other, understanding the other's business drivers as a legitimate interest, ensuring that reporting and other obligations are met in a timely manner, using agreed processes, procedures and engagement models, particularly in handling differences, knowing and accepting responsibilities and delivering on them, agreeing that when things are not working as they should, that both parties will strive to fix them, and systematically reviewing progress.

Outsourcing

Outsourcing is the contracting out of services to a third party (the vendor or service provider or partner) to manage on the organization's behalf. It is a means through which the market can be tested under competition policy; or where the organization can divest itself of underperforming corporate assets, increase its flexibility, offer difficult to deliver services, or concentrate its activities on its core business. Outsourcing is also used to overcome continuing capital and operational budget restrictions and reduce overhead costs, to focus on customers and improve service levels, to gain access to changing expertise and know-how, improve security and manage the complexities of continuously developing technology directions.

In most instances it involves the transfer of ownership and responsibility for assets (including the people) from the organization (the client) to the vendor. In all instances accountability is paramount. Ball (2003) also includes difficult to deliver services as contenders for outsourcing. He cites examples such as:

- Sudden unpredictable peaks of activity or demand, where maintaining in-house staffing levels to cope with peaks may be impossible;
- The impracticability or expense of opening service points outside core hours;
- Lack of in-house expertise for specialist work, such as design or health and safety; or
- Poor or declining performance.

In an outsourced or market testing environment, the manager's role changes from managing a workforce to one of contract management, purchasing services and putting processes in place in which the organization and the outsource provider can work cooperatively and productively together in order to get the best out of the relationship. This involves a role in contract administration and performance review to ensure that the outsourced or contracted out service meets the specified service levels and customer needs. For whilst functions and activities can be outsourced, business responsibility for the functions and activities cannot. If the outsourcer is unable to perform, for whatever reasons, it is the organization that bears the consequences and the resulting regulatory, customer or brand damage.

Cloud computing

A further model for consideration is that of sharing computing environments where the business model is on a metered service similar to a traditional public utility for energy and water supplies. Sometimes known as cloud computing, the model obviates the need to invest in costly and complex hardware and software applications. Customers no longer own hardware and software; rather they share these with others, paying only for what they consume. The advantage is that customers have a low or no initial cost to acquire hardware and applications as these resources are essentially rented. The resource requirements of clients are bundled together by the service provider so that peak loads and troughs are ironed out because demand utilization is shared with others in the 'cloud'. A further advantage for the customer is that it avoids the need to invest in hardware and applications requirements to cope with highest peak loads or unexpected demand surges that may occur infrequently.

In a similar manner to outsourcing, a large component of the manager's role is in contract management and putting processes in place to get the best out of the relationship. The decisions to move to and manage services in a shared or cloud computing environment should be based on those already outlined for managed services above.

Managing projects on time and on budget

As project initiatives become more costly and complex in their scope, scale, locations and interdependencies, often involving more than one organization, it is important that there is a project plan to ensure that the project stays tightly focused on the desired outcomes and under control. This includes bringing the project in on time, on budget and in an integrated manner so that it meets the set objectives and diverse expectations of customers and stakeholders involved in the project.

A project plan provides the framework under which the project will be managed, resource requirements identified and sourced, other considerations such as risks and communications managed and the project aligned to the organization's business strategy. A lot of information for the project plan can be sourced and updated from the initiative's original business plan. Where possible, large projects extending over long periods of time should be broken down into more manageable sub-projects.

Projects inevitably mean change. This may be organizational change, changed policies, practices, procedures and/or processes, changes to jobs and the manner in which activities are progressed, legislative changes or changed relationships with customers, suppliers and other stakeholders. Therefore it is important that change management and communication plans are put in place.

Increasingly in the global and virtual world information-based initiatives will be multi-national. International projects add additional levels of complexity and require consideration of culture and style, language barriers, legal and regulatory conditions, currency markets, taxation regimes, time zones and distance.

Project plans are often divided into three distinct parts:

- Project concept brief which defines the project, its scope, key deliverables, business case and governance and organizational structure;
- Project plan which provides details of project activities to date, stakeholder management, project approach, risk management strategies, legal considerations, communications, resources, quality controls, reporting, change management, monitoring and evaluation requirements; and
- Project implementation schedule that outlines key tasks and activities for the execution of the project.

Figure 7.2. (below) illustrates a model framework for project management.

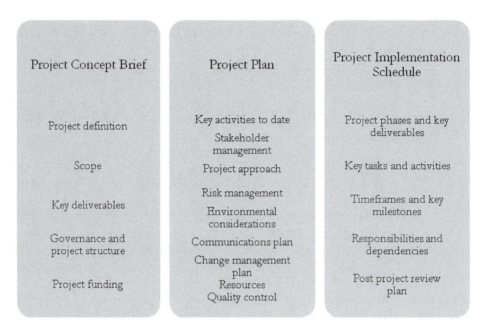

Figure 7.2 Project management model

Text Box 7.1 provides the details of the sample contents of a project plan that can be used in developing a project management plan.

Text Box 7.1 Sample contents of a Project Plan

Project Plan

1.   Project Concept Brief

1.1.   Project definition
1.1.1.   Project description including time, cost, quality
1.1.2.   Project objectives
1.1.3.   Terms of reference
1.1.4.   Background and rationale
1.1.5.   Assumptions

1.2.   Scope
1.2.1.   Definition of terms
1.2.2.   Brief scope and exclusions
1.2.3.   Constraints

1.3.   Key deliverables
1.3.1.   Preliminary business case
1.3.2.   Cost-benefit analysis
1.3.3.   Alignment with corporate direction

1.4.   Governance and project structure
1.4.1. Roles and responsibilities
1.4.2. Project sponsor, membership of project board, leader, manager and team
1.4.3. Project structure
1.4.4. Key accountabilities

1.5.   Project funding
1.5.1. Refine budget in terms of total cost of project
1.5.2. Funding source

2.   Project Plan

2.1.   Project activities to date
2.1.1. Consultation

2.2.   Stakeholder management
2.2.1. Stakeholder risks
2.2.2. Stakeholder management strategy
2.2.3. Stakeholder expectations

2.3.   Project approach
2.3.1. High level project plan
2.3.2. Key milestones
2.3.3. Project tolerances
2.3.4. Impact on stakeholders

2.4.   Risk management
2.4.1. Risks
2.4.2. Risk management and mitigation strategies

2.5.   Environmental considerations
2.5.1. Legal and regulatory
2.5.2. Political
2.5.3. Competition

2.6.   Communications plan

2.7.   Change management plan

2.8.   Resources
2.8.1. Human resources including skill requirements and availability
2.8.2. Financial resources
2.8.3. Technology resources
2.8.4. Procurement requirements

2.9.   Quality control

2.10.   Reporting, monitoring and evaluation

3.   **Project Implementation Schedule**

3.1.   Project phases and key deliverables

3.2.   Key tasks and activities

3.3.   Timeframes and key milestones

3.4.   Responsibilities and dependencies

3.5.   Post project review plan

Complex projects involve a number of activities, some of which have dependencies on others. Project software based on the concept of a GANTT chart is often used to understand and manage the relationships, timeframes and status of the activities. See Figure 7.3.

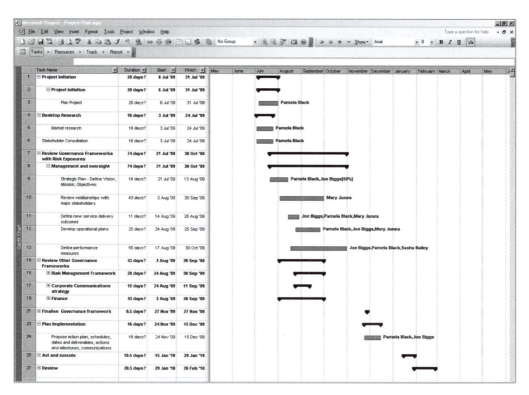

Figure 7.3   Example of project software GANTT chart

Inevitably there will be occasions when something goes wrong and decisions will be needed as to whether to change the focus, timescale or outcomes of the project or to stop or kill the project. Changing the focus of the project can mean minor changes to the timescale, substantial change to scope, timeframe and outcomes, major upheavals within the resources and project itself, or mothballing the project. The decision to terminate a project is a complex one as large projects are difficult to stop without political and interdependency ramifications. Once the decision has been made it is important for the well-being of staff and interdependent projects that the project is terminated quickly. Where a project is stopped in order to cut losses and redirect energies and resources elsewhere it is important to analyse the mistakes and look for what can be learnt for the future.

Ensuring that the desired outcomes are achieved

The desired outcomes in managing ICT and other assets are that:

- They are deployed in the most cost-effective and advantageous way to maximize the return on investment;
- Customer requirements and expectations are met at all times;
- ICT services operate without loss of utilization and functionality for 99 per cent of the time;
- Workplace practices and asset selection and management processes reduce the carbon footprint;
- The health and safety of users are guaranteed;
- Security, confidentiality and legal obligations are met;
- ICT services add measurable value to the business processes at every stage; and
- ICT services are aligned with and support the corporate culture.

Efficiency and effectiveness measures should be developed to assess and evaluate these outcomes.

Disposing of the asset

Assets are disposed of when they become obsolete, underperform or have specific elements that underperform. Obsolescence can occur where:

- A change in business strategy requires the use of new types of assets or new technology applications;
- Significant changes in clients' or suppliers' technology architectures occur to the extent that inter-organizational systems are no longer compatible; and
- The maintenance of the technology is no longer supported in the market place.

The effective management of an asset during its life cycle should result in the asset's life being prolonged and its disposal value being at the optimal level. This might involve refurbishing and reusing old computers and properly recycling unwanted computers and other electronic equipment so that old equipment does not unnecessarily add to landfill. In disposing of assets, especially those where there may be residual toxic matter, it is important to ensure that they are disposed of in an environmentally friendly manner.

Conclusion

Making the most out of technology and other strategic assets involves strategic decision-making in which senior and executive management must take a leadership role. The information services manager also has a responsible and responsive leadership role in enhancing business agility, capability and capacity for the future through astute technology planning and management, promoting and helping others understand how technology can best be used as a strategic business asset now and in the future, selecting and acquiring the right technology for competitive advantage, managing and utilizing the technology for the greatest benefit in service delivery and information provision, ensuring that the desired outcomes are achieved and that assets are disposed of in a financially and environmentally sustainable manner.

Developing the right planning and business processes for the management and utilization of ICT and other assets is critical to the organization's use of knowledge and information, service delivery, productivity, customer retention and return on investment. The correct choice of strategy aligned to the business drivers will deliver considerable return on this investment. An incorrect choice of strategy or no strategy will make the business risks and impact even more expensive.

Accompanying this is the need for a strategic change management programme that includes embedding corporate and culture change, revising business processes, creating new mindsets, and making commensurate changes to processes, communications and work flows across the length of the value chain.

To maintain competitive advantage in a global and virtual world, the ICT infrastructure must enable and support virtual teamwork and collaboration irrespective of geographical or organizational boundaries, using both fixed and mobile devices and social networking and other Web 2.0 and beyond tools. Other planning considerations include:

- Future trends in the global industry and the readiness of client markets to embrace and incorporate technology change;
- Whether, in aligning and integrating technology with the business strategy and business processes, planning for integrated 24x365 services needs to include others beyond the organization;
- Knowing the availability of financial resources as well as the skills and knowledge of users and implementers;
- Understanding the assets' usable lives, performance, capacities and applications;
- Employing the most cost-effective and environmentally sustainable use of the asset;
- Determining sourcing strategies, management models and relationships;
- Incorporating an element of innovation or surprise in the application to distinguish the organization from others; and
- Knowing the total cost of ownership including the initial capital investment, the ongoing operational and development costs, costs of implementation and re-engineering, and costs associated with the retirement and disposal of the assets.

Finally, integrated projects inevitably bring increases in costs and complexity in scope, scale, locations and interdependencies. It is important that there is a project plan to ensure that the project stays tightly focused on the desired outcomes and that it is delivered on time, on budget and in an integrated manner.

References

Ball, D. 2003. A weighted decision matrix for outsourcing library services. *The Bottom Line*, 16(1), 25–31.

COBIT: www.isaca.org/cobit.

ITIL: www.itil.co.uk.

Further reading

Chen, L. and Nath, R. 2005. Nomadic culture: Cultural support for working anytime, anywhere. *Information Systems Management*, 22(4), 56–65.

Cleden, D. 2009. *Managing Project Uncertainty*. Aldershot: Gower.

Dearstyne, B.W. 2010. Groundbreaking trends: The foundation for meeting information challenges and opportunities. *Information Management*, March/April, 27–32.

Geddes, M. 2005. *Making Public Private Partnerships Work: Building Relationships and Understanding Cultures*. Aldershot: Ashgate.

Harrington, K. 2003. Contracting out of a public library service: Business to be, or not to be? *Library Management*, 24(4/5), 187–192.

Hillson, D. 2009. *Managing Risk in Projects*. Aldershot: Gower.

Lafferty, S. 2004. Disruptive technologies: What future universities and their libraries? *Library Management*, 25(6/7), 252–264.

Linder, J.C. 2004. Transformational outsourcing. *MIT Sloan Management Review*, winter, 45–51.

Lock, D. 2007. *Project Management*. Aldershot: Gower.

Miller, M. 2008. *Cloud Computing: Web-based Applications that Change the Way You Work and Collaborate Online*. Indianapolis: Que.

Muller, R. 2009. *Project Governance*. Aldershot: Gower.

Newman, A. 2009. *Enterprise 2.0 Implementation*. New York: McGraw-Hill.

Palmer, M. 2009. *Making the most of RFID in Libraries*. London: Facet.

Sweetland, J.H. 2001. Outsourcing library technical services: What we think we know, and don't know. *The Bottom Line*, 14(3), 164–177.

Turner, J.R. 2008. *The Handbook of Project-based Management: Leading Strategic Change in Organizations*, 3rd edn. New York: McGraw-Hill.

III

Leadership and Innovation

The theme for Part III is how to use leadership and innovation as change agents to future-proof information services so that they can embrace an organizational philosophy and culture in keeping with the demands of the digital and virtual world. It focuses on all aspects of leadership, change management, interpersonal and people management roles needed to drive innovation and change and reposition information services in the global and digital economy and society. Strong leadership, interpersonal and change management skills are also needed to:

- Sustain the impetus of organizations in times of global financial constraint as well as manage the impact of other sudden and strategic changes that emanate from the volatile external environment;
- Provide the required amount of flexibility, innovation and transformational change for the organization to prosper and survive in challenging times; and
- Understand and lead across different cultures and sub-cultures during the process of integrating services.

Putting Part III into perspective regarding the importance of leadership and communication in managing change is best illustrated by Figure PIII.1 which provides context for this part of the book.

In addition to the other leadership roles of creating a values-driven culture, managing group dynamics and building teams, effectively negotiating conflict, managing the political arena, ensuring effective policy making, communications and networking, managing and sustaining the well-being of individuals who work in the information service is another further important function of the leader and change agent. Managing and sustaining the well-being of people is also important from a duty of care perspective as well as being strongly connected to motivation and productivity factors. This also includes managing one's personal well-being. For in a busy and competitive environment it is sometimes tempting to focus on the demands of the job and overlook personal life needs and those of others.

Chapter 8 addresses the issue of leadership. It describes the roles, responsibilities and attributes of leaders who have passion, drive and vigour that are needed to drive the organization and revolutionize its services. Chapter 8 also discusses the need to motivate people, manage workplace diversity and meet multi-generational expectations and needs; considering in detail the leadership implications of attitudes that occur from differentiation

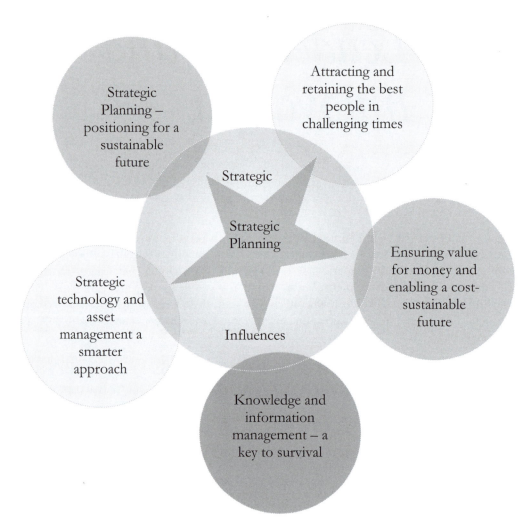

Figure PIII.1 Leadership skills

Source: Adapted from Micro-skills of effective change agents taken from Dunphy, D. et al. *Organizational Change for Corporate Sustainability,* London: Routledge.

and diversity in the workplace which can arise out of generational work styles and professional specialization. Finally, the chapter provides some advice on succession planning for leadership as well as tangible mechanisms for measuring the effectiveness of a leader.

Values-driven corporate cultures are intricate to enabling the success of organizations. They can be considered the glue that holds the organization together. Chapter 9 considers how leadership can influence the values, beliefs, norms and behaviours that create an organization's culture. It explains how corporate cultures develop and evolve and how there can be more than one culture within an organization. This chapter also describes the activities that take place within organizations as corporate rituals. It provides advice on developing and maintaining a corporate culture within the information service, reconciling cultures when integrating services or planning inter-organizational services and addresses the question of ethics and values in information services.

Chapter 10 considers innovation and creativity. The chapter provides leadership strategies to create an innovative environment. It identifies the different roles and functions within organizations that foster a creative environment through which sustainability and a continuous business advantage over others can be achieved.

Chapter 11 introduces the concept of change and how it can be initiated and managed in a positive manner through good leadership. Information services managers are currently leading major change in moving to 24x365 virtual services, implementing self-service delivery mechanisms and integrating cultural services. In addition to this a rapidly changing complex external environment means that information services have to adjust rapidly and radically to sustain their position in the digitally connected and intelligent world.

Change can be planned, arising from organizational life cycles and other proactive forces, or it can be sudden and discontinuous. The strategies for creating and managing change differ according to whether the change is continuous or discontinuous. This chapter includes strategies for creating and engaging change from within as well as strategies for managing strategic shocks. It considers resistance to change at both the organizational and individual levels. The chapter also introduces the concepts of business and process re-engineering that are being used by organizations to rethink their mechanisms of operating in complex and competitive environments.

Chapter 12 provides an understanding of how high-quality leadership can influence group and team dynamics at the organizational and individual levels. Most organizational structures now comprise groups and teams as these are a more effective means of handling diversity and continually changing environments. Increasingly individuals are required to work across teams and organizations so a manager's understanding of group or team behaviour is as important as understanding individual behaviour. This is because people act differently when they are in a group. In order to achieve outcomes, managers have to recognize and manage different group roles and stages of group development.

Both informal and formal groups can be found in organizations. The presence and leadership of informal groups will often provide an insight into the power, politics and authority within the information service and its parent organization. As groups develop they assume certain characteristics that are associated with group norms, member roles and group cohesiveness. As members of groups, individuals play different roles. These roles can change the way in which people behave in certain situations; they can also create a situation of personal conflict. Chapter 12 explains this and why conflict occurs at the personal level, between members of the group during the development stage and between groups.

A further aspect of group development is team building. The major difference between a group and a team is that groups generally have one leader. In a team, all the members are leaders. Chapter 12 explains why team building involves all the leadership and facilitation skills that are required to accomplish individual performance.

In changing, integrating and subsequently transforming environments conflict is inevitable and is a healthy sign of organizational growth and competition. It can also be destructive and inhibit things being done within the information service. Chapter 13 looks at sources of conflict at both the organizational and individual levels and how negotiation can be used to effectively resolve conflicting issues.

A significant focus for leaders is to make sense of the political arena in which they and the information service operate. Chapter 14 covers the nature of politics and political behaviour from both an individual and organizational perspective. Not all organizations are equally political, and likewise differ in individuals and their political gamesmanship. Politics is a natural phenomenon arising out of differentiation, competition and the use of power and influence. The chapter describes a number of political tactics that are commonly used in organizations, and it characterizes these as ethical and unethical. Advice is given on the presentation of political arguments on paper and the use of lobby groups.

Policy making is addressed in Chapter 15. This chapter provides strategies for developing policy and identifies the type of issues for which policies are appropriate. It emphasizes the need to identify and consult with stakeholders whilst developing the policy. The chapter discusses the policy framework and provides examples of general and specific policy issues that can be found in information services.

Chapter 16 considers the human side of communication that is used to lead, support, manage and sustain people in uncertain and changing times. It identifies the interpersonal communication skills required of information service managers and their staff, particularly in simplifying messages and communicating the abstract concepts and ideas that information services managers need to do in influencing senior executives and championing the information service. It also describes the issues associated with interpersonal communication that may affect the communication process. These issues include self-image and attitude to others, listening, stereotyping and the halo effect. Barriers to personal communication are also explored in this chapter.

As part of interpersonal communication, networks allow managers to function successfully. They can be used to seek and provide information, to sustain and support others and to influence outcomes. Chapter 16 explains the value of networks for getting things done, how a network acts as a group, and provides advice on how to establish networks.

Chapter 17 considers three important aspects in planning and sustaining yourself in challenging times: career planning, work–life balance and stress management. These aspects can easily be overlooked in busy and demanding times. People's personal satisfaction with themselves, their lifestyle and their work, and their sense of self-worth and purpose in their career and life goals can be supported and sustained through the activities of career planning and personal development. The chapter looks at the relevant responsibilities for the organization, the information services manager and the individual in career planning. It considers a holistic approach to lifestyle planning using a mind map exercise. The aspect of managing oneself and personal image is also covered.

Chapter 17 also explores why some individuals are vulnerable to stress at certain stages in life. It identifies factors in the workplace that can be stressors and different personality types that cause some people to handle certain types of pressure better than others. Finally, the chapter considers personal and workplace strategies for the management of stress.

Figure PIII.2 Leadership and innovation

Management Influences in a Changing Landscape
1. Managing in an uncertain world
2. Strategic influences

Strategy and Planning
3. Strategic Planning – positioning for a sustainable future
4. Attracting and retaining the best people in challenging times
5. Ensuring value for money and enabling a cost-sustainable future
6. Knowledge and information management – a key to survival
7. Strategic technology and asset management – a smarter approach

Leadership and Innovation
8. Leadership
9. Utilizing a values driven culture for sustainability
10. Innovation and creativity
11. Engaging change in positioning for the future
12. Group dynamics and team building
13. Effective negotiation and conflict management
14. Managing the political arena
15. Policy-making
16. Personal communications and networking
17. Managing yourself and others in challenging times

Governance and Social Responsibility
18. Ensuring good corporate governance
19. Using authority and influence
20. Encouraging transparency
21. Managing for sustainability
22. Managing risk
23. Sustaining trust and continued operations
24. Evaluating benefits and performance

Customer and Market Focus
25. Competitive strategies
26. Corporate image and communications
27. Ensuring service quality

Success and Sustainability
28. Bringing it all together

8 *Leadership*

Leadership was once considered to be an influencing role that used motivation techniques to persuade others to undertake certain tasks to achieve an outcome. Today the expectation of a leader is much larger and more complex. Professional service, staying close to clients, cultivating talent and crisp strategic focus on the critical few priorities are strengths identified by Reid (2010: 1) in speaking to leaders in eight Canadian and American organizations.

The digitally connected and intelligent world requires a far-sighted approach that creates a sense of passion, energy and excitement about the information service and its future role in a virtual world, shifts in thinking about how services might be delivered and a readiness to make quick and effective decisions in a time of crisis. Increasingly the leader is required to guide and motivate highly skilled and multi-talented people who are employed in quite different roles and circumstances to create a creative, flexible, inclusive workplace. Frequently work will take place across distances in time and space, often through electronic communication. Developing future leaders as well as building rapport with and managing the group dynamics of people who have varied backgrounds, cultures, values and sources of professional expertise requires good communication, people management and negotiation skills.

Leadership and corporate culture are very much entwined in their influence on the dynamism and sustainability of the organization. Successful leaders in today's complex, global environment are proactive, visionary, entrepreneurial and risk-taking individuals who can build rapport and encourage others to think differently about the role, culture and purpose of information services in the virtual world. Examples might include:

- Employing people from different backgrounds to give the organization an edge;
- Managing diversity when bringing together and reconciling the functions, cultures and professional expertise in public libraries, art galleries, museums and archives to provide a richer one-stop cultural experience for the customer and reduce overhead costs;
- Ensuring the correct cultural fit when implementing more customer self-service programmes; and
- Adopting new ways of collaboration and communication using social media tools to enhance the organization's competitive advantage and sharing of knowledge and information.

Leadership roles and responsibilities

Effective leaders have a wider perspective on issues, seeing the whole and making connections. They are comfortable working across different domains and meeting multi-generational views and needs in both the workplace and when designing customer services. They have strong talent for advocacy and are skilled in promoting the brand of the information services, both of which are necessary to sustain the position of the information service in challenging and changing times.

The principal role of a leader is to be the creator of the future and of corporate environments and personal capacities. These types of leaders visualize their preferred future for the organization in the virtual world and then make it happen. Whilst they remain in touch with reality they also share their vision with others, so that they can join with them in creating this future. They instil a sense of excitement and passion about future challenges, opportunities and possibilities. Being entrepreneurial, they are concerned with ensuring that the organization is well positioned for the future, that it keeps inventing new business advantages by which it can remain out in front of its competitors.

International business drivers and risk exposures mean that leaders must easily work and collaborate across geographic and organizational boundaries. McCallum and O'Connell (2009: 155) quote Hitt and Ireland (2002) in suggesting that leaders need to develop meta-capabilities for coordinating and integrating relationships between firms. Amongst the leadership competencies they describe are:

- Building and maintaining internal trust;
- Establishment of external relationships; and
- Capitalizing on resources from external relationships.

These competencies are necessary in a virtual and digital world where the organization may team with others around the globe to deliver 24x365 services and where competition and customer markets are global.

Whilst good leaders are adept at anticipating and managing the driving forces that shape the external environment, they must also exhibit a grounded approach when needed. In problem solving they take a strategic view. They also have a strong and analytical focus on planning. By nature of their position, they must have a whole picture perspective and a thorough understanding of the interdependence of various parts of the organization when making decisions for the future.

Leaders both create and make sense of change. To take full advantage of the virtual and digital environment and keep the organization ahead of its competitors they must create and manage a changing environment. In addition, they must also make sense of the environment that is changing around them including emerging customer needs, making connections and applying intuition. Uncertain times can lead to highly distracted or stressed people who don't and can't innovate and change. Good leaders help people to make sense of and to see the imperative for change, as well as helping people innovate and take risks, all without threatening their personal circumstance. In facilitating change, they initiate coping strategies that enable people to let go of the old ideas and practices in order to instil new ways and thinking in service delivery and internal practices.

Successful leaders strive for excellence and deliver on results. However, they recognize that there will also be hard times and catastrophic occurrences, when they have to share bad news and show courage. They ready the organization to deal with these occurrences by identifying and planning actions to overcome potential adverse scenarios, and in building organizational responsiveness and trust in its capability to do this. In challenging and turbulent environments successful leaders also demonstrate agility, being able to identify and capture game-changing opportunities or reallocate resources more quickly than their competitors.

Today's leaders create an achieving atmosphere in which others are encouraged to exceed their expectations of themselves. They have passion, commitment and a willingness to make a personal investment in people and their talents, the organization and its outcomes. They recognize that they do not have a monopoly on all the ideas, that people together with their mindsets and skills are the most precious commodity, who need to be inspired and motivated. They foster an open culture and open communication, where there is respect for differing opinions, generational needs and cultural backgrounds.

To do this, good leaders build rapport, collaboration and personal connections with people in the organization, with those around them and with key stakeholders. Good leaders must collaborate with employees, customers, suppliers and all other stakeholders, and at the same time manage their conflicting interests so that no one set of stakeholders has been paid more than enough to secure their willing and active participation (Allio 2009: 7).

In growing the skills and competencies of their people, they:

- Demonstrate high expectations for others and drive people to do their best;
- Give people important activities and sufficient autonomy to exercise their own judgement in undertaking the tasks;
- Manage diversity and understand differences in values that arise from different generational work styles, backgrounds and people with specialist skills and expertise;
- Enable and empower people to share knowledge and information which are considered key roles in creating an innovative environment; and
- Monitor their results and provide continuous feedback on how they perceive their performance and if they have met their needs and expectations.

In their enabling role, transformational leaders give consideration for different environments, aligning structures and systems and reconciling cultures to support the future business direction of the organization. They also ensure that individual and team roles are aligned with corporate goals and that everyone knows and understands how they contribute to the overall success and direction of the organization. Realizing the importance of being an employer of choice in order to attract and retain the very best, today's leaders promote flexibility in the workplace and continually seek opportunities and solutions to improve workplace conditions.

Successful leaders set high expectations of themselves as well as others, especially in the area of ethical behaviours. As the moral guardians of corporate ethics, integrity and professional conduct, their role is to set and lead by example in their behaviours and in communicating these core values. Synonymous with this, trust is also important. These leaders create a high-trust and highly cooperative environment where there is consistency in messages and a confidence in people acting with integrity.

Being open with employees and stakeholders is part of the integrity of leadership. It reassures people and builds credibility and confidence in the quality of leadership. Honesty and openness builds respect and trust which in turn builds morale and helps employees to remain focused on the desired outcomes. Honesty and openness includes:

- Creating an understanding and dependable relationship between consumers and the information service and the requirement to tell the truth at all times;
- Focusing on people's relationships with the product or service where there is an expectation of quality and consistency of product or service at all times: this focus is as important for the people delivering the product or service as it is for those receiving it;
- Senior management communicating with employees in an honest and open manner about the organization and its place in the changing world;
- Readily explaining the background to issues, reasons for hard decisions and actions taken;
- Developing a corporate culture that values openness, knowledge and information sharing; and
- Nurturing collaborative, open and trusted relationships with stakeholders.

Effective leaders display the following personal merits and traits. Whilst these personal traits may not naturally occur, they can be practised so that they become normal conduct and behaviour:

- Strong commitment and eagerness to enable the organization to survive and excel, often to the point of being a zealot;
- Able to engage with a diverse workforce with a passion to inspire, energize and excite others;
- Able to deal with complexity and view roadblocks and adversity as a challenge;
- Foresight to see future opportunities and threats together with strong intuitive and critical thinking skills;
- Energy, drive and capacity to engage and keep others enthusiastic, even in difficult circumstances; and
- Strong personal commitment to ethics, truth and integrity.

Real leaders are risk-takers. They are willing to take measured risks and consider new and untested approaches themselves. They also help people overcome their fear of risk taking by creating a corporate environment in which it is acknowledged that mistakes are part of the path to innovation.

Motivating individuals

Understanding the nature of human motivation and using this knowledge to motivate people to excel beyond their expectations is a critical leadership role in sustaining and transforming organizations in challenging times. Diversity in the workplace means that not everyone is motivated by the same thing. Differences will occur because of generational age groups, cultural background and expertise and personal circumstances. The key is to understand what motivates each individual and to be flexible enough to satisfy these diverse needs.

Today's diverse workforce no longer fits the traditional stereotype of managing a workplace. The concept that 'work is a thing we do, rather than a place we go to' is relevant here. The availability of technology has moved the point of service to being a remote device such as a wireless-enabled portable device rather than within a fixed service point, so people may not always need to travel to a single place of work to do their job. In this scenario, access to portable devices and flexible work arrangements can allow the organization to meet differences in individual needs and circumstances. Technology change and flexible working hours also offer conveniences that allow individuals to pursue differing lifestyles whilst increasing their commitment and contribution to the organization. This requires a different leadership style incorporating flexibility, trust, communication and collaboration. The reward factor is that individuals can choose the benefits and work arrangements that best suit their personal needs, whilst the leadership factor is ensuring that remote management isn't 'hands off' management.

Similarly the moves to integrating cultural services and virtual work environments also offer leadership challenges in motivating individuals. The lower-order needs such as physiological and safety needs, relatedness needs such as interpersonal relationships and the intrinsic needs for personal development are still relevant to some degree. However, differing time horizons, workplace practices and personal and professional values need to be recognized as these will colour employee perspectives.

Letting people know that they are valued and helping to increase confidence in their personal capacities to excel in challenging and changing circumstances are two ways of motivating people. Individuals who are given personal and professional development opportunities and are allowed to take risks will often have a higher self-esteem and estimation of their abilities than those who have not had their personal comfort zones stretched or been allowed to experiment with their ideas.

Understanding differences in the workplace

Service integration brings together differentiations in backgrounds, qualifications and expertise. In addition, most information services already experience differentiations of task and perspective arising from the subject specialization, media and the technology involved. An important consideration in leading workplaces of this nature is the ability to recognize the individual needs and values of each specialist function in order to guide and motivate them. Differences can occur through the nature of work, professional outlook, how success is judged, career development needs and rewards systems.

THE NATURE AND LOCATION OF WORK

Information services staff work in teams such as archivists, librarians, telecommunications providers or web-based specialists who often develop a strong identity and special expertise with the work unit. This is the result of differentiation in tasks and, often, the physical separation of each component of the service. For example, computing centres, libraries and records management functions are often housed in purpose-built accommodation and may be separate from each other and from the rest of the organization. A similar situation occurs when providing flexible work-from-home opportunities or for people working in a mobile business environment. A key leadership role is to identify 'inclusion' strategies and lessen the perception of information service staff being 'different' by administrators who have different values again.

PROFESSIONAL OUTLOOK

By their nature, most people working in information services are cosmopolitan people. Their strong sense of expertise and specialization in their areas results in the view that they are specialists working for an organization and that their career development lies within their area of expertise.

The various specialists that are found in information services often use particular terminologies linked to their specialist areas, display symbols such as their diplomas and degrees, and often hold the norms and values of their professional association. The use of certain terms or phrases can be threatening to others if they are uncertain of their meaning and can also lead to a misunderstanding of the situation. In these instances leaders can assist by clarifying areas of misunderstanding and explaining the bases for the differences whilst acknowledging the reasons behind them.

PERFORMANCE

The standard of training for specialists in information services and their subsequent expertise and competence is often set by the various professional associations. Their professional peers will also judge their ongoing performance by the number and quality of papers at conferences, publishing on the Internet or in professional journals, which may not be valued to the same degree by the employing organization. As an employee, information service personnel must also conform to internal organizational standards and usually their annual performance appraisal will be based on the achievement of the organizational objectives and standards rather than their professional ones. Leaders can assist in managing these role conflict situations by using performance measures that both balance and recognize the internal and external contribution of the individual.

CAREER DEVELOPMENT AND REWARDS

The difference in outlook between the various specialists in information services has implications for their career development, training and reward systems. Specialists may not always want managerial positions, preferring a career path that enables them to continue working in their area of expertise but which offers flexibility and provides recognition and rewards for their achievements. This might include opportunities for further learning opportunities or a professional secondment to another organization, rather than the money or status that is associated with promotion.

Table 8.1   Generational differences in the workplace

Silent Generation (Born WWI and WWII)	Baby Boomers (Born 1945-1965)	Gen X (Born 1965-1980)	Gen Y (Born 1980s and 1990s)	Millenials (Born late 1990s to 2010s)
Traditionalists, high respect for position power	Idealistic	Realistic	Self-reliant and independent	Not yet in workforce
Uncomfortable with change	Consumer driven	Independent and resourceful	Desire for freedom and flexibility	Digital natives
Strong loyalty and 'job for life' expectation	Process oriented	Free agent approach to careers	Entrepreneurial thinkers	Technology advanced
Historically focussed	Values company commitment and loyalty	Accepting of change and comfortable with diversity	Comfortable with change and diversity	Prefer use of mobile and Web2.0 and beyond
Experience guides decision making	Will sacrifice to achieve success Achievement comes after 'paying dues'	High expectations of work/life balance	Technology and media savvy	
Disciplined and modest approach to life	Seeks long term employment but not 'job for life'	'Want it now' culture	Rely on short, unfiltered communications	
Slow adopters of technology	Ambitious at work, in personal life and status oriented	Technology literate	Place high value on education and skill development	
	Learnt to use technology in the workplace	Early adopters of mobile, internet and technology in workplace	Relish responsibility and want to play meaningful roles	
	Moves between hard copy and digital in work	Value life long learning	Believe social responsibility is a business imperative	
			Desirous of collaboration Multi tasking	

Source: Adapted from Levy, Lester et al. (2005), *The generation mirage? A pilot study into the perceptions of leadership by Generation X and Y,* Auckland, NZ: Hudson.

Leading and leveraging different generations in the workplace

Up to four generations of people can be found working together at any one time; each having distinct values, priorities, views on leadership, demands for technology in addition to expectations and attitudes in life and the workplace. Although there are minor differences in interpretations of the dates, the generations comprise the:

- Silent Generation – born between the First World War and the Second World War;
- Baby Boomers – born between 1945 and 1965;
- Generation X – born between 1965 and 1980;
- Generation Y – born in the 1980s and 1990s; and
- Millennials – born in the late 1990s and 2000s.

A key role for the values based leader is to recognize and manage the differences and preferences of the various generations in the workplace and create an environment in which these differences can co-exist. Importantly for the information service, each generation has a different attitude to technology. As Simons (2010: 32) observes:

> *All three generations embrace technology to increase workplace efficiency. However, employers must be aware that Gen Y digital natives may grow impatient with the applications that are the lifeblood of many corporations: applications they might consider 'tired'. Finding ways for these systems to provide the value these workers anticipate and expect within their terms – unified, electronic and mobile – will enable and encourage them to participate more fully in the organization.*

A summary of the work attitudes, values and preferences can be found in Figure 8.1.

The following outlines how leaders can best leverage the strengths and expertise of the different generations in the workplace for the benefit of the individuals and the information service.

SILENT GENERATION

Most of the members of this generation have retired from the workforce. This generation experienced the austerity years of the depression and war that disrupted family life and career paths. Predominantly the workforce was comprised of males and there was lifelong allegiance to the organization. Recognizing their experience and contribution to the organization is important to this generational group.

BABY BOOMERS

About to retire, Baby Boomers grew up in a post-war era of expansion and prosperity. They have a strong sense of generational identity and are characterized as being materialistic and interested in physical objects such as home ownership and consumer goods. The Baby Boomer workforce witnessed an era where an unprecedented number of women entered the paid workforce; there was movement towards equality in wages and opportunity, and increasingly flexible and varied gender roles for women.

They are the first generation where access to a tertiary education was inexpensive and widespread. In the workplace they have witnessed major transformations, including the transition from a pre-technology world to a digital era, although not all have successfully made this transition.

GENERATION X

Unlike their stereotype definition portrayed in the media, Generation Xers are not lazy and have had to overcome an era of downsizing in organizations where mid-level management career opportunities vanished. Offsetting this, the spread of the Internet created new industries and new technology-related job opportunities.

Generation Xers are less concerned with the trappings of success and more environmentally, economically and socially conscious than previous generations. They care about the quality of their future and that of the earth and environment. In caring about their future, exercise and having a healthy body and mind is important, therefore they look for balance in lifestyle and leisure time. Financial and emotional security is important. They have good work ethics and company loyalty, as long as it is reciprocal. Generation X is not afraid to challenge authority in a changing world of diminishing resources.

Levy et al. (2005: 16) found that Generation X individuals believe high performance in their organization is directly linked to the quality of the organization's leadership. On a personal level, they are convinced that their career progress will be directly affected by the quality of the leadership they demonstrate and consequently development of leadership skills is critical to them. Levy goes on to say that they want to be challenged in a meaningful way and they need a sense of ownership and engagement if they are to perform to their potential. They need to be inspired to lift their performance above the ordinary. They also believe that the more opportunity they have to learn and develop, the more they will achieve for the organization.

On their views on management and leadership, Levy et al. (2005: 16) found that Generation X individuals identify a difference between management (which they see as technical and task focused) and leadership (which they see as creating a sense of purpose, inspiration and alignment). They are convinced that those in management positions need leadership skills and the greater leadership capacity they have, the more effective they will be as a manager. They look to managers for leadership skills such as strategic thinking, motivation, effective communication, constructive conflict management and team building. They appreciate managers with strong coaching and mentoring capability. They do not see the manager and the leader as separate; they see them as integrated in one person.

GENERATION Y

As children of the Baby Boomers, this generation holds political and social values closer to the Baby Boomers than Generation X. While some were born in a pre-digital era, most Generation Y members take the widespread use of digital technology for granted. They are a techno-savvy generation, being the first to grow up immersed in a digital and Internet-driven world. Globalization in the economy and communications has also assisted this generation to be much more tolerant towards multi-culturalism and internationalism than previous generations.

Generation Y exhibits strong people skills and a desire to influence and change the world for others and themselves. Whilst they have mostly been fairly sheltered in their upbringing, they have experienced early pressures for success in their education and work. Their appreciation of their skills can lead to them being considered self-centred.

They tend to be ambivalent towards authority, seeing it as something to work around rather than against.

Levy et al. (2005: 16) found that for Generation Y, ownership, engagement and learning were important leadership factors. They strongly held the view that personalized leadership made the difference in encouraging them to go the 'extra mile' for the organization. Generation Y saw leadership in those that gave them scope, autonomy and opportunity, rather than those who would give them direction, regulation and commands.

MILLENNIALS

Millennials are expected to be the most technologically advanced generation yet. Whilst about to start entering the workforce, they are predicted to spend longer living with their parents and to marry much later than previous generations.

Succession planning

Leadership skills are best developed in a corporate climate that fosters encouragement, cooperation, admiration, trust and loyalty and where there are role models to provide examples of effective leadership.

Often overlooked is the need to proactively identify and then begin cultivating the leaders of the future. This is achieved by:

* Determining the critical leadership skills, behaviours and mindsets that will be required by the future business direction of the organization;
* Identifying individuals who have the potential to develop these skills, behaviours and mindsets; and then
* Counselling, training, nurturing and providing stretch assignments and other experiences and opportunities for these individuals to develop the required leadership attributes.

In seeking future leaders past track records and job experiences are not necessarily the best indicators for the fit of the individual with the organization in the future. This is because the organization will be continually moving forward and will require different leadership skills to those that have been successful in the past. Taking a holistic approach to leadership and communication styles, values, mindsets, attitudes and agility will assist in identifying potential leaders to fit the desired future state.

Measuring leadership effectiveness in challenging times

Leadership effectiveness can be judged by how well the organization is positioned for its changing role in the future as effective leaders create and share a vision for the future and instil a sense of excitement about the challenges, opportunities and possibilities faced by the information service in the global and virtual environment. However, the end game is not to be judged on always being the 'best of all breeds' in showcasing the latest and best in technology at the expense of other things. Rather, it is on focusing on being 'best of breed' on the components that the service identifies as being critical to its success. For example, a reputation for high-quality service delivery that meets the differing generational expectations, in being an employer of choice, and professional recognition of the organization's preparedness to be innovative are worthy indicators of effective leadership.

Ulrich et al. (2008) identify the following five roles for leaders that can be used to measure leadership effectiveness:

- Strategist role – shaping the future by focusing on long-term, strategic direction and the organizational capabilities required to realize strategic possibilities;
- Executor role – making things happen by translating strategy into actions, making change happen and holding people accountable to ensure the right work gets done;
- Talent manager role – attracting, engaging and developing individual capability to be today's talent for the benefit of the organization;
- Human capital developer – identifying and developing future talent and building the next generation to assist the organization realize its longer-term goals and strategies and to assist performance over the longer term; and
- Personal investor role – always learning from successes, failures and people with whom they work.

In addition to the above, effective leaders display a passion for their own work and instil a sense of excitement and enthusiasm that leads to a highly motivated staff within the information service. Where there is strong leadership, and an alignment of structure, roles, systems and corporate culture with the business direction of the organization, motivation will be higher. In contrast, an inappropriate leadership style and a lack of clarity in goals will lead to individual dissatisfaction and lowered morale. In this regard, effective leadership is demonstrated when people:

- Clearly understand and focus on what the information service is trying to achieve and why;
- Know how their tasks fit with their team's and the information service's goals;
- Are willing to foster a dependable relationship between consumers and the information service with the ability to tell the truth at all times without retribution;
- Have a focus on quality and consistency of product or service at all times;
- Communicate with each other in an honest and open manner;
- Work collaboratively with all stakeholders whilst acknowledging and reconciling differences in culture, age groups, expertise and backgrounds;
- Look for opportunities and engage in change from within; and
- Come to work enthusiastic about their work and organization.

Individuals rely upon the leadership skills of their managers to allow them to achieve their need for motivation, rewards and ability to perform their allocated tasks. Consequently, the leader's ability to reduce the roadblocks and increase the opportunities for personal satisfaction can be tested through satisfaction levels with the work that people have accomplished at the end of the day.

Conclusion

Leadership in the virtual age is an enabling act of transforming people and organizations so that they are better prepared to capitalize on opportunities and minimize threats. It involves creating an inspiring vision and shared values, providing clarity of direction, ensuring commitment and creating synergies in a trusted environment where values of ethics, integrity and honesty are honoured during times of upheaval and change. In an era when financial and workplace sustainability is uppermost and where the future lies in the integration of different types of services, the abilities to demonstrate confidence and show respect for differing opinions and professional expertise are paramount to leading change and innovation as well as finding new solutions to problems.

Good leaders communicate openly, listen, support and help others make sense of the changing world. They also involve everyone in times of change, encouraging where possible group decisions. Being open with employees and stakeholders about the organization and its place in the changing world is part of the integrity of leadership. Honesty and openness builds respect and trust, which in turn builds morale and helps employees to remain focused on the desired outcomes. Being open about issues, reasons for hard decisions and actions taken reassures people and builds credibility and confidence in the quality of leadership.

Leadership is about who you are, which then influences what you do. The leadership role of surviving, thriving, innovating and excelling in a dynamic environment calls for qualities of resilience in adversity and passion to energize, empower and enthuse others and for the cause. These leadership qualities are based on skills and natural gifts and strengths, most of which can be learnt.

Successful leaders can look to the future for opportunities in an age of high uncertainty and fast-changing environments, yet provide a clear understanding of what their organization is trying to achieve and why. Leaders lead by example and change people's awareness of issues by helping them to look at issues in new ways. In adverse scenarios, leaders are those who find the exit strategy or the way out when others consider that the situation is lost.

Effective leaders inspire and excite people through their passion and build loyalty and respect for themselves and the organization. They demonstrate courage and persistence, coaching and bringing out the best in people by tapping into their dreams and ideals. They also concentrate on what the organization needs to have in place to outperform others in a globally competitive environment. They do this by creating a corporate capacity to exploit knowledge and innovation in preparing for the future, to think globally, plan for the unthinkable and outwit the competitors. Whilst they are optimistic about the future they understand that undesirable events happen and ready the organization to overcome adverse scenarios and find solutions to negative situations. Trust and ethical behaviour in the corporate environment are also important indicators of leadership effectiveness in information services. These can be measured by considering:

- The extent to which there is open communication and people trust the organization they work for;
- The level of high-trust, highly cooperative working relationships between teams and collaboration with other organizations;

- The level and extent of focus on the purpose of the organization, its products and services; and
- The extent to which people perceive the information service to be a high-trust environment delivering quality and consistency in their products and services.

References

Allio, R.J. 2009. Leadership – the big five ideas. *Strategy and Leadership*, 37(2), 4–12.

Levy, L. et al. 2005. *The Generation Mirage? A Pilot Study into the Perceptions of Leadership by Generation X and Y*. Auckland: Hudson.

McCallum, S. and O'Connell, D. 2009. Social capital and leadership development: Building stronger leadership through enhanced relational skills. *Leadership and Organization Development Journal*, 30(2), 152–166.

Reid, J. 2010. Leading in uncertain times. *Ivey Business Journal Online*, March/April, 1.

Simons, N. 2010. Leveraging generational work styles to meet business objectives. *Information Management*, January/February, 28–33.

Ulrich, D., Smallwood, N. and Sweetman, K. 2008. *The Leadership Code: Five Rules to Lead by*. Boston: Harvard Business Press.

Further reading

Allard, S. 2009. Library managers and information in World 2.0. *Library Management*, 30(1/2), 57–68.

Belasen, A. and Frank, N. 2008. Competing values leadership: Quadrant roles and personality traits. *Leadership and Organization Development Journal*, 29(2), 127–143.

Broadbent, M. and Kitzis, E.S. 2005. *The New CIO Leader: Setting the Agenda and Delivering Results*. Boston: Harvard Business School.

Byham, W.C. 2002. 14 leadership traps. *Training and Development*, 56(3), March, 56–63.

Castiglione, J. 2006. Managing the library labour gap: The role of bridge employment for the older library professional. *Library Management*, 27(8), 575–587.

Chernin, P. 2002. Creative leadership. *Executive Excellence*, 19(5), May, 3–4.

Coupland, D. 1991. *Generation X: Tales for an Accelerated Culture*. New York: St Martin's Press.

Covey, S.R. 2004. *The 8th Habit: From Effectiveness to Greatness*. New York: Free Press.

Crawford, T. 2005. *Employer Branding*. Aldershot: Ashgate.

Forster, N. 2005. *Maximum Performance: A Practical Guide to Leading and Managing People at Work*. Cheltenham: Edward Elgar.

Goldsmith, M., Baldoni, J. and McArthur, S. 2010. *The AMA Handbook of Leadership*. New York: American Management Association.

Hernez-Broome, G. and Hughes, R.L. 2004. Leadership development. *Human Resource Planning*, 27(1), 24–32.

Johnson, M. and Johnson, L. 2010. *Generations, Inc: From Boomers to Linksters – Managing the Friction Between Generations at Work*. New York: AMACOM.

Joiner, B. 2009. Creating a culture of agile leaders: A developmental approach. *People and Strategy*, 32(4), 28–35.

Kahan, S. 2010. *Getting Change Right: How Leaders Transform Organizations from Inside Out*. San Francisco: Jossey-Bass.

Kakabadse, A. et al. 2004. *Working in Organisations*. Aldershot: Ashgate.

Lieberman, S., Simons, G.F. and Berardo, K. 2004. *Putting Diversity to Work: How to Lead a Diverse Workforce*. Boston: Thomson/Netg.

McGurk, P. 2009. Developing 'middle leaders' in the public services? The realities of management and leadership development for public managers. *International Journal of Public Sector Management*, 22(6), 464–477.

Mant, A. 1997. *Intelligent Leadership*. London: Allen & Unwin.

Priestland, A. and Hanig, R. 2005. Developing first level leaders. *Harvard Business Review*, June, 112–120.

Quinn, R.E. 2005. Moments of greatness. *Harvard Business Review*, July–August, 74–83.

Rooke, D. and Torbet, W.R. 2005. Transformations of leadership. *Harvard Business Review*, April, 67–76.

Schulte, A. 2010. Leading bold change. *Leadership Excellence*, April, 4.

Sorcher, M. and Brant, J. 2002. Are you picking the right leaders? *Harvard Business Review*, 80(2), February, 78–85.

Vicere, A.A. 2002. Leadership and the networked economy. *Human Resource Planning*, 25(2), 26–33.

Wilson, K. and Corrall, S. 2008. Developing public library managers as leaders: Evaluation of a national leadership development programme. *Library Management*, 29(6/7), 473–488.

9 *Utilizing a Values-Driven Culture for Sustainability*

All organizations have a corporate culture. Some are more noticeable or stronger than others. A corporate culture is the system of values, beliefs, norms and behaviours that creates a certain organizational climate. Tangible factors such as the external environment, technologies, organization size and structure, generation makeup, corporate environment, leadership and management styles also influence the corporate culture. Creating a values-driven culture is an essential leadership role. It underpins trust and confidence that can sustain the reputation of the information service as an employer of choice, a quality service provider and entity demonstrating ethics, good governance, accountability and social responsibility in challenging times.

Corporate culture is the product or outcome of behaviour patterns and standards that have been built up by individuals and groups over a number of years. High performing organizations are frequently found to be adaptable and values driven, having a strong corporate culture that guides beliefs and values upon which all policies, decisions and actions take place. Their values define and drive the culture and help ensure that all in the organization know and understand what is expected of them. By sharing and ingraining a set of forward thinking values that guides actions, decision making and behaviours, organizations can be less bureaucratic, less hierarchical and more flexible. Employees not only share the same values, they also share the same vision, exhibit trust and collaboratively strengthen the competitive edge as both an employer of choice and leader in the field.

Continuing this theme, it is not surprising that values based leadership is also grounded in corporate culture. Strong corporate cultures have strong leaders who are clear on and keep people focused on the vision. They are also effective in using organizational values as the basis for decision making and translating cultural values at the organizational level into behaviours at the individual level. As a result, getting to know the corporate culture is one of the first tasks that a manager should do when joining an organization, as without this knowledge the manager will be less than effective.

Service integration, the global digital or virtual nature of organizations and the presence of different generations in the workplace are contributing to a cultural revolution caused by a prevalence of different corporate culture types and sub-cultures in organizations that need to be expertly managed in order to achieve the right balance of local values and behaviours with the overall corporate culture. Examples being:

- Reconciling the functional differences between traditional work units such as software development, libraries and records management, or cultural services such as art galleries, museums and historical organizations;

- Recognizing changing values and attitudes to the workplace between age groups in the workforce; and
- Helping others understand the use of languages, meanings and contexts that can vary on a geographic or national basis.

What lies behind values-driven corporate cultures

Leadership plays an important role in how effectively values-driven corporate cultures are developed, nurtured and communicated, and consequently on the ultimate success or demise of the organization. The influence of senior executives in maintaining a positive and forward thinking corporate culture during chaotic and challenging times cannot be underestimated. The activities and behaviours of senior executives and managers that are reflected in the basis upon which they make decisions, their desire for organizational clarity, and their attitude towards the future, innovation and creative thinking, their staff and customers all shape the corporate culture. They determine whether the culture is progressive, outward looking, values driven, innovative and service oriented, or traditional and inward looking.

Sitting alongside today's influence of the leader is the historical perspective. In information services where traditions and values can be deeply rooted, certain behaviours and customs become deeply ingrained. New employees quickly have to learn how the organization operates in order to 'fit in'. Many of these behaviours are tangible issues, such as whether appointments have to be made to meet with senior executives, or whether employees are encouraged to make suggestions to better the organization. Others are more intangible, such as an acceptable topic of conversation in the lunchroom (there may be taboos on certain subjects), who goes to lunch first or whether superiors are addressed formally by title, or informally by first name. A values-driven culture will simplify traditions and historically-based values as the culture will instil a sense of unity in how employees undertake their duties, discharge their responsibilities, make decisions and conduct themselves individually.

A corporate culture is the system of values, beliefs, norms and behaviours that create a certain organizational climate. The person who establishes the service creates the initial, and usually the strongest, corporate culture. This is achieved through both conscious and unconscious acts. For example, their values and beliefs will be translated into policies and procedures. They will tend to recruit staff who share the same ideas and values. These values will then be unconsciously manifested into norms and behaviours over a period of time. If the culture is strong and effective, it will remain long after the founding person has left the service. In the case where a culture has 'served its usefulness' and is no longer relevant to today's challenging and changing world, a new leader is required to nurture and recruit the right people for the next step in the organization's life cycle.

The managers' styles and behaviours must be congruent with the organization's corporate values and behaviours whilst balancing changes that might arise from growth opportunities and the need to transform the organization. Employees will look to their managers to shape shared meanings, define and create values and demonstrate corporate beliefs in times of change. Managers will often find themselves having to deal with changing circumstances and impacts on their own personal position whilst supporting and empowering their people to manage change.

To add to these dilemmas, differences between corporate and professional beliefs and values will often surface during times of change and can result in personal inner conflict and conflict between groups. For example an organization may have a political philosophy or belief that certain services should be delivered on a user pays basis: a belief that is most likely to be reinforced in order to sustain services in a time of financial constraint. However this corporate belief may be at odds with long held individual and professional beliefs that services should be delivered without charge. This situation may result in individuals having an inner conflict between their personal belief that the services should be available free of charge whilst at the same time having to ensure that they and fellow team members implement the policy. In this situation group conflict might also arise between the finance personnel who have led the policy shift and the professional personnel who need to implement it against their professional beliefs.

Similarly, differences in professional beliefs will also be emphasized when entities such as libraries, art galleries and museums are integrated. In these situations the information services manager will not only have an important role in assisting their staff to come to terms with differing or conflicting professional beliefs or values, they will also need to promote a single unifying culture and reconcile the underlying sub-cultures of the different entities over time. Likewise, where 24x365 virtual services may be offered through a global alliance the different languages, cultures and styles will need to be taken into consideration.

The cultural context of knowledge and information sharing that is the bread and butter of the information services assumes a greater level of importance in knowledge-intensive organizations than it has in the past. This is because in traditional cultures knowledge and information were sources of power and jealously guarded by those who had access. Today the emphasis has shifted to knowledge enabling and information sharing as being critical leadership traits in developing strong relationships with staff and stakeholders and making sense of change and complexity in the environment. These are in turn supported by values of openness and collaboration.

Strong values-driven cultures are created, sustained, transmitted and changed through social interaction. This can be through modelling and imitation, instruction, correction, negotiation, storytelling, gossip and observation. They are communicated and reinforced by organization-wide action. High-performing information services ensure that they have well-conceived human resource programmes that reinforce the culture.

Values and a strong culture sustain individual behaviour and provide meaning, direction and motivation for members' efforts. Everyone knows the information service's objectives; people feel better about what they do as values such as excellence, fairness and integrity prevail; there is transparency and accountability about the organization and, as a consequence, people are likely to be more committed and motivated. No matter how distant the work units are from the organization's head office, all sites are treated equally. This is important in information services, where work unit sites may be geographically dispersed over wide areas.

Conversely, poorly performing information services may still have a strong culture, although this may not necessarily be an effective or healthy one. In these cases the pervading culture is often dysfunctional, focusing upon internal politics rather than external commitments such as clients' needs.

Organizational sub-cultures

Organizational sub-cultures arise out of the functional differences between departments in information services. These include the use of different technologies; the identification of different values and interests; the use of different terminologies or languages; the employment of different approaches to problem-solving techniques; and the different aspects of the interactive external environment. Sub-cultures are natural, healthy phenomena unless they interfere with or detract from the overall corporate culture.

Sub-cultures can also be based on gender, occupation, status, task, tenure, age group or ethnic origin of the work group. Socio-economic and educational backgrounds can also lead to sub-cultures being formed. In strong cultures sub-cultures do not cause problems as the overall values and beliefs are clear. However, in weak cultural environments they can be very destructive as they may obscure overriding values and result in cultural drifts.

Corporate culture types

Information services can have many different corporate culture types. In small operations there should only be one culture. This should reflect the corporate culture of the parent organization. In larger information services, where extensive differentiation occurs, more than one culture may exist.

Table 9.1   Differences between traditional cultures and values-driven cultures

Organizational influences	Traditional cultures	Values-driven cultures
Vision	In the present, bettering the status quo	Global, futuristic
Leadership	Enhancing current performance	Entrepreneurial, anticipating and positioning for the future
Corporate values	Technical perfection and efficiency	Trust, excellence, fairness, integrity, creativity
External environment	Static	Turbulent, complex, challenging, changing
Corporate environment	Bureaucratic	Innovative, risk taking, fast moving, intuitive
Relationships	Competitive	Collaborative
Change	Viewed as a threat	Viewed as an opportunity
Heroes	Those with technical knowledge	Those with new thoughts and ideas
Behaviours	Self-preservation, anxiety, confusion, blaming	Belonging, openness, learning, trust, pride, respect for others' ideas and mutual support
Attitude to mistakes	Not tolerated	Considered part of the learning experience and innovation process

Source: KnowledgeAge Pty Ltd 2010 – reprinted with permission all rights reserved.

Differences in corporate culture types arise out of organizational influences such as organization structure, the amount of risk associated with decision making and feedback received from the environment. It is important to understand the culture type in order to minimize those aspects that might be harmful to the future of the organization as well as being able to work effectively within and with it. There is no universally correct culture. The culture of the organization should be appropriate for the circumstances and the people involved.

Table 9.1 illustrates the differences between traditional cultures and those that have a values-driven culture.

Values

Values are core to a values-driven organizational culture and the basis of human activities. In challenging, chaotic and complex times they provide the anchor upon which difficult decisions can be made about the organization's and individuals' future. Values:

- Have a moral dimension and influence the beliefs and attitudes of individuals and groups in that they comprise those matters most important to an individual, group or organization. Examples of such values are honesty, openness and loyalty;
- Contribute to the corporate climate by reflecting desired behaviours or states of affairs and influencing people's perceptions of situations and problems, choices, preferences and decisions. Consequently the corporate values should be shared between management and their people. Examples of such values are respect for others, their professional expertise and backgrounds;
- Transcend both contexts and experiences and can be used in tough decisions in complex situations that have not been experienced before; and
- Can be the preferred mode of decision making as they can be used to create the future that people want to experience.

Corporate values espouse clear, explicit philosophies about the information service's or its parent organization's objectives. Information services and their parent organizations may not necessarily share common values. People with different roles, expertise and functions who are employed in different work areas can place different emphases and value on work processes, timeframes, behaviours and priorities. Likewise, different generations in the workplace may hold different values about the nature of work and work–life balance.

Whilst all might have a customer focus and are of equal value to the organization, their own values pertaining to their roles and expertise within the organization will differ. For example differences in values often occur between people with a specialist and administrative background, or between people with a strategic focus and those providing technical support. This may cause each to view the other with suspicion. Consequently the reasons for these differences need to be acknowledged and understood.

Sometimes differences occur because people in one work group do not fully understand the roles and functions of the other work groups. They are not aware of each other's contribution to the organization. They only see the others' roles in the areas of work that immediately affect them or where the work unit boundaries overlap. Often people with different role functions will be physically separated from each other, which will further reinforce their differences. Despite the advantages of email, geographic isolation means that there is a lack of spontaneous face-to-face communication where personal alliances and understanding can be established. Motives for actions will also differ. For example, finance or administrative staff may value their ability to make savings in expenditure for the organization, whilst the front line or service delivery personnel may wish for more money to increase their opportunities for customer service delivery.

As a service organization in an innovative environment, the information service's highest order values may be used to reconcile these differences and minimize the effect of differentiation. All groups should be able to adopt generic values such as innovative thinking, excellence in service delivery, a commitment to quality and continuous improvement, respect for individuals and their privacy, ethics and integrity, and openness and accountability. These values are in turn reinforced through the values statement (see Figure 9.1).

Information Service

Values Statement

As an organization with a strong customer focus we value:

- Excellence – quality products and solutions

- Respect – for others, their backgrounds, ideas and opinions

- Innovation – creativity and inspiration

- Ethics – integrity and openness

- Achieving – performance and results

- Flexibility – being responsive to customers and change

- Equity – in service and the workplace

Figure 9.1   Values statement

Corporate values also provide the opportunity to develop trust and an ethical philosophy within the information service. Appropriate and workable ethical principles, values and behaviours can be developed and reinforced through the corporate culture. Johannsen (2004) emphasizes personal integrity, professional drive, social skills, new thinking and ethical conscience as the most desirable characteristics of staff. Personal integrity is reflected in empowerment, pride, recognition and self-respect. Professional drive, or 'new thinking', is related to change and quality management oriented values such as care, creativity, entrepreneurship, flexibility, innovation and quality consciousness. Social skills are emphasized through values of recognition and team spirit.

How beliefs, norms, shared meanings and behaviours contribute to a values-driven culture

BELIEFS

Beliefs are the acceptance or convictions about values. They are to a great extent shaped by the consistencies or inconsistencies between values statements and actions or behaviours of senior executives within the information service or parent organization. If there is consistency then their actions will influence the beliefs that would be expected to evolve from the stated values. Inconsistencies between values statements and actions will result in different beliefs and weaken the organizational culture.

To be successful, corporate beliefs should be visible, known and acted upon by all members of the organization. This can only be the case if they are communicated throughout the organization and reinforced through human resource management processes, recognition and rewards. They then become permanently infused and accepted as the norms by which the organization exists.

Rites and ceremonies are efficient and effective methods of communicating and instilling beliefs into an organization. In performing these, people make use of language, gestures, ritualized behaviours, artefacts and settings that heighten the expression of beliefs and shared meanings appropriate to the occasion. Logos also represent organizational symbols with which people identify.

NORMS

Norms are standards or patterns of meaningful behaviour that are passed on to others through modelling, instruction, correction and a desire to comply with others. When people interact they exchange words, tones and pitches and non-verbal behaviours such as gestures, appearances, postures and special relationships. This interaction forms patterns that, after repeated use, become accepted as the rules and systems that determine everyday behaviours and are transmitted unconsciously within organizations.

SHARED MEANINGS AND BEHAVIOURS

Shared meanings are different to social norms as they focus upon message exchange, interpretation and interaction sequencing. Shared meaning assumes that people have similar attitudes, values, views of the world and feelings about situations. Most positive actions take place on the basis of shared meaning or on an assumption that people in the same situation share common experiences and viewpoints. Shared meaning is consequently the system that allows actions, events, behaviours and emotions to take place.

Shared behaviours guide values driven work practices, decision making and dealings with customers, clients and people in the workplace. They set the standard of interaction and service that builds the image of the information service. Examples of shared behaviours that may be emphasized by the information service include listening to and having a mutual respect for customers and other people, solving problems as they occur, or behaving in an ethical manner.

Shared behaviours influence the operational environment of organizations. For example they often determine how:

- Issues are identified and addressed;
- Decisions are made and communicated and who is involved in decision making;
- Work is organized and delegated;
- Actions are taken;
- Flexible the organization is regarding work practices; and
- Technology is viewed.

Corporate rituals

Many activities in organizations are expressions of corporate rituals, the consequences of which go beyond the technical details. Examples include induction, training, organizational development activities, high-profile sackings, and end-of-year celebrations or other festive occasions. Trice and Beyer (1984: 653–669) have identified some organizational rites or activities that have social consequences in organizations and these are described below.

RITES OF PASSAGE

Rites of passage begin with the induction and basic training processes. These allow employees to part with their past identities and status and take on new roles. They minimize the changes that occur in the transition from old to new and re-establish the equilibrium in ongoing social relations. The induction interview with the Chief Executive Officer or the refurbishment of an office for a new manager is part of the incorporation rite. Retirement ceremonies and farewell parties are part of the rites of passage when employees retire or resign.

RITES OF DEGRADATION

Rites of degradation take place when the Chief Executive or person of high authority is fired and replaced, dissolving his or her social identity and power. Such an action may be interpreted as the organization's public acknowledgement that problems exist. As a consequence, group boundaries may be redefined around the previous close supporters of the executive. These supporters may or may not be incorporated into the newly formed groups. The social importance and value of the role are reaffirmed if the executive is replaced. If the position is not filled, it is an indication that it had no importance in the organization.

RITES OF ENGAGEMENT

Enhanced personal status and the social identification of individuals who have been successful within the corporate or professional environment are provided for by 'rites of enhancement'. Examples of such are the granting of membership to an elite group, or the granting of a fellowship or life membership to a member of a professional association. Such a membership is usually jealously guarded by those who have attained such status. Rites of enhancement spread good news about the organization and by association enable others to share some of the credit for these accomplishments.

RITES OF RENEWAL

Rites of renewal are provided in organizational development activities such as strategic-planning processes, job redesign and team-building programmes. These are rites that are intended to refurbish or strengthen the existing social structure and improve its functioning. The latent consequences of rites of renewal are that members are reassured that something is being done to correct organizational problems. However, they can be used to focus attention away from one problem to another.

CONFLICT REDUCTION RITES

Conflict reduction rites involve collective bargaining or feigned fights of negotiation where parties may become hostile, threaten to boycott or walk out of the negotiating process whilst the other parties speak of compromise, point to areas of cooperation and attempt to overcome the anger in a ritualistic way. These actions may deflect attention away from solving problems.

Other forms of conflict reduction rites are the formation of committees, advisory groups or task forces. Most of these groups serve to re-establish equilibrium in disturbed social relations. Confidence is often renewed when it is known that a committee or advisory group has been formed to investigate or advise on an issue.

RITES OF INTEGRATION

Rites of integration encourage and revive common feelings that bind members together and commit them to a social system. Such rites are found in the corporate end-of-year functions. They permit emotions to be vented and allow the temporary loosening of various norms.

Communicating corporate values

Communication is both a consequence and an enabler of a values-driven corporate culture. A values-driven corporate culture is learnt and maintained through interactions between people in the organization. It is also expressed through language, symbols, myths, stories and rituals. Specialized terminology, corporate logos, myths and stories of heroes and their successes, receptions for important visitors and ceremonies to launch new services are examples of these. They are symbolic devices that serve to identify and reinforce the guiding beliefs and values upon which all policies and actions take place.

Cultural values are communicated and reinforced through the various human resource management processes. The selection interview, induction process, training and development practices, performance appraisal, career development and reward systems all provide opportunities for the cultural values to be communicated.

The induction process provides the ideal situation to communicate the information service's philosophies and values and the associated management practices. Here the reasons why certain norms and behaviours are acceptable and others are not can be explained. Training and development programmes can reinforce the foundation values and philosophies.

The performance appraisal interview provides the opportunity for discussion, feedback and reinforcement of the required values and philosophies. Underlying sub-cultures may be detected and corrected if they contradict the overall culture. Incentives and rewards can be used to reinforce the important values and to initiate behaviours leading to good organizational performance.

Corporate stories, legends, slogans, anecdotes, myths and fairytales are also important as they convey the information service's shared values. Anecdotes and stories provide the opportunity for people to share their experiences. The significant stories are those told by many people. These are the ones that are active in the cultural network and provide evidence of the corporate culture. Newsletters and emails are other examples where the corporate culture is communicated.

Stories of 'heroes and villains' provide an insight into corporate values and the personal qualities of employees who are likely to be successful or unsuccessful. The attributes of those heroes who are in high esteem emulate those qualities likely to be found in successful employees. 'Villains and outlaws' are those whose values or attributes were opposed to those of the organization. They provide the corporate guidance of 'what not to do'. Villains are remembered long after they have left the organization for their 'sins'. They are the outlaws.

The rules of communication are themselves part of the corporate culture. These are tacit understandings about appropriate ways to interact with others in given roles and situations. They are generally unwritten and unspoken. As prescriptions for behaviour, they function to coordinate, interpret and justify interactive behaviour and act as self-monitoring devices. They provide guidelines as to what is acceptable interactive behaviour within the organization.

Conclusion

The corporate culture is one of the most significant influences on an organization and the behaviours of the people who work there. In fact an information service's culture may be more influential on employee behaviour than the organization structure because of its subtlety and pervasiveness. A values-driven corporate culture helps instil a sense of unity and underpins trust and confidence in the organization through times of turbulence and change. It can also uphold the reputation of the information service as an employer of choice, a quality service provider and entity demonstrating ethics, good governance, accountability and social responsibility in challenging times.

Leadership is the most important influencing factor on the values-driven corporate culture. Strong values-driven cultures come from within and are built by the founders and by individual leaders, not consultants. These are people who care about their employees and the organization. The corporate values and beliefs can also be reinforced by the selection interview, induction process, training and development processes, performance appraisal interview and reward systems. Cultures are sustained and transmitted through the communication processes of languages, storytelling about the heroes and villains of the past, and through rituals and ceremonies.

Strong cultural values are important to information services as they provide employees with a sense of what they ought to be doing, and knowledge of how they should behave consistent with organizational objectives. Strong cultures represent an emotional feeling of being part of the information service and its parent organization, and lead to greater employee commitment and motivation.

Differences in values occur between specialists and other staff in the organization through varying work emphases, codes of ethics, tasks, work orientations, training standards, identities and sources of motivation. These affect the way individuals view each other and have implications for the management of expertise.

How corporate values and beliefs are managed during the process of integrating services will play an important part in determining the success of the venture. In these situations the information services manager will have an important role in assisting staff in coming to terms with differing or conflicting professional beliefs or values, and in promoting a single unifying values-driven culture. Likewise, where 24x365 virtual services may be offered through a global alliance the different languages, cultures and styles will need to be taken into consideration.

Successful organizations also have strong innovative cultures that tolerate mistakes as part of the learning experience and which champion new ideas. The values statement is an important tool through which the organization can communicate its expectations regarding the behaviours of individuals towards each other. Values need to be reinforced as part of the corporate culture through management actions, practices and procedures.

References

Johannsen, C.G. 2004. Managing fee-based public library services: Values and practices. *Library Management*, 25(6/7), 307–315.

Trice, H.M. and Beyer, J.M. 1984. Studying organizational cultures through rites and ceremonials. *Academy of Management Review*, 9(October), 653–659.

Further reading

Chen, L. and Nath, R. 2005. Nomadic culture: Cultural support for working anytime, anywhere. *Information Systems Management*, 22(4), 56–65.

Semler, R. 2003. *The Seven-Day Weekend: A Better Way to Work in the 21st Century*. London: Century.

10 *Innovation and Creativity*

Innovation is the ability to turn knowledge and bright ideas into an opportunity or to use these ideas to solve a problem. Which according to Walton (2008: 125), citing the European Union, is to do with:

- Renewal and enlargement of the range of products and services and the associated markets;
- Establishment of new methods of production, supply and distribution; and
- Introduction of changes in management, work organization and the working conditions and skills of the workforce.

Innovation is an effective competitive weapon in challenging economic times as it allows organizations to redefine the market place and market space in their favour. This can be achieved by developing new mindsets and business re-engineering, by bringing in new ideas through recruiting talented and clever people, or through engaging in strategic alliances.

Creativity is the process of human thought that can lead to new ideas and innovation. It occurs when people are inspired to show ingenuity, have originality in thought and are willing and able to demonstrate inventiveness. Encouraging creativity (the generation of new ideas) and innovation (the implementation of new ideas) within an organization is an essential leadership role.

Today, senior executives are under constant pressure to withstand financial and other pressures and find new sources of growth in a time of constrained resources, yet within an increasingly demanding and competitive business environment. Innovation and creativity are the new business enablers and sources of growth. They are necessary ingredients to future-proof and sustain organizations by providing:

- Imaginative insight and out-of-the-box thinking when identifying possible risks and opportunities and in forewarning of major changes in the environment;
- The means to deal with the unstructured problems arising out of competitive and rapidly changing environments, rapidly evolving technologies and changing user behaviours;
- Alternative and new solutions to manage and overcome complex and seemingly unresolvable issues; and
- Vision, imagination and inventiveness to create new product and service offerings ahead of competitors.

Progressive organizations acknowledge the need to strategically manage their intellectual property and branding in addition to the strategic management of material goods.

Reflecting the importance of these intangible assets systems are put in place to identify and properly manage all the intellectual property that arise from creative thoughts and bright ideas as well as the organization's brand reputation.

Sustaining this shift in thinking is the recognition that productivity alone is no longer as significant a contributor to success as it was in the past. Brand recognition and reputation as well as people's capacities to solve problems in unique ways, to conceive bright ideas, and use entrepreneurial thinking have equal importance. Employees' know-how, talents, skills and expertise need to be recognized as an important corporate asset and their further development encouraged. To meet this challenge, Leavy (2005) says that 'CEOs must learn to inspire their organizations to new levels of inventiveness in everything that they do, not just in marketing or new product development'.

A creative environment requires excellent leadership to drive a culture that taps into the creative potential of all employees and allows champions of change to set standards, promote ideas, to build support and to implement new ideas. It requires a corporate culture and leadership style that values trust, flexibility and adaptability; one that is risk-taking and supportive of open communication as well as being open to new ideas. A creative environment is fostered through leadership and management practices, as well as making itself attractive to more diverse and unconventional talent. Rewards systems and performance reviews that support and actively encourage ideas generation and divergent thoughts in problem solving also assist in maintaining and reinforcing the creative culture.

Supporting these ideas, Leavy (2005) identifies four climate-setting factors that help create an innovative culture:

- Placing of people and ideas at the heart of the management philosophy;
- Giving people room to grow, to try things and learn from their mistakes;
- Building a strong sense of openness, trust and community across the organization; and
- Facilitating the internal mobility of talent.

Critical sources of creativity

Innovation and creativity have need for a balanced mix of leaders, ideas generation, champions, intraprenuers, upholders, gatekeepers and coaches. These key functions call for people with specific skills and personal attributes who can contribute to and sustain the organization through challenging and complex times.

In traditional thinking organizations, leaders often viewed themselves as having sole responsibility for the new ideas that contributed to the success of the organization. Today most leaders acknowledge that everyone in the organization contributes their ideas in different ways. Consequently a leader's most significant role is in inspiring new ideas and concepts, being open to challenge and in fostering a creative corporate environment where there is:

- Interaction between individuals to bounce ideas off each other;
- A substantial body of knowledge and a learning environment from which new ideas can be drawn;

- A customary thought process that enables new combinations of ideas; and
- Time allocated where people are encouraged to participate in new thinking.

There are several roles within organizations that equally contribute to innovation and creativity. The first of which are the idea generators, those with expertise in the field and who enjoy conceptualization. Idea generators are also good at problem solving and seeing new and different ways of doing things, which are important in discovering new business opportunities in the integrated, virtual and global world. Idea generators need sponsors who are sufficiently high up in the organization to marshal the required resources to support the proposed activity. Executive management has a sponsorship role in ensuring organizational commitment and that the necessary resources in people, knowledge, time and money are available.

Another set of people who perform critical functions are champions. Champions are energetic and determined; they demonstrate a commitment and push ahead with the idea no matter what the roadblocks. Champions take risks in getting things done, sometimes at a personal cost. Whilst they might not have a strong knowledge of the discipline, they are visionary in that they can see how the idea can be applied and sell the idea and its application to others.

Intrapreneurs are the entrepreneurs who champion creativity and change within an organization. They have the cross-specialized talents of entrepreneurship, risk taking, ideas generation and gatekeeping and the attributes to lead and manage natural love–hate relationships, confrontation and conflict.

Their work is often managing the inter-departmental rivalries and conflicts that need to be resolved with care to ensure that creativity is not stifled, that ineffective compromises are not made and that inter-departmental communication and cooperation are not adversely affected during the period of change.

Every innovative idea will need an upholder. Upholders plan, support and organize the innovation as it moves from being an idea into a project or production mode. Upholders focus on the administrative tasks of finance, marketing and coordinating, and know how to progress things within the organization. They also ensure that the legal requirements are met, which might include registration of a trademark, design or complying with copyright. In successfully moving the project forward, they also know and acknowledge where there may be sensitivities in coordinating groups and people involved in the project.

Gatekeepers span the boundary of the organization and the discipline. They possess a high level of technical competence and keep themselves informed of future trends and developments in their field of expertise, which they readily share with others in the organization. They have strong networks and are seen as an authoritative and credible source of knowledge in a particular subject. Gatekeepers are good communicators and are often aware of competitor moves through their connections. They are usually approachable and enjoy the contact with others.

Coaches help develop others' talents and provide encouragement and a sounding board for new ideas. As a source of objectivity, they provide legitimacy and organizational confidence in the innovative project. They also have credibility and can play both a protective role by buffering the project from unnecessary constraints as well as a linking role to other significant stakeholders.

Creating an innovative environment

Creating an innovative environment requires both strong leadership and skills in change management. This is because creativity has both positive and negative forces within organizations. It is both a producer and manager or minimizer of conflict. Creativity produces change that further creates conflict. Creativity can also be used to manage resistance to change and conflict.

MANAGING CHANGE

The conversion of conventional work practices and values into ones that are entrepreneurial and risk taking takes considerable leadership skill and foresight. A values-driven culture needs to be created that not only values knowledge sharing, ideas generation, open communication and entrepreneurial thinking, but also sustains that commitment year after year. This means a major shift in the values for some people, not just a slight increase in awareness of entrepreneurship or the establishment of one or two new programmes or activities for the year. The people leading the change will have to champion their cause, motivate and prepare others to readily accept change.

People must be receptive to innovation and willing to perceive change as an opportunity rather than a threat. Most people are creatures of habit and resist change, seeing it as threatening their existence. It takes leadership skills to create an environment in which change is encouraged and accepted as the norm.

SUPPORTING RISK TAKING

Creating an innovative and creative corporate environment as described above requires a culture that supports risk taking without penalty when mistakes occur. Management must be willing to take risks and allow their people to make mistakes as part of the learning process. If failure means the loss of a job or not being given the opportunity to try something new again either on a group or individual basis, creativity and innovation will be discouraged. Furthermore, the corporate culture will hold the belief that if you value your job, it is not worthwhile to attempt anything difficult or challenging.

Risk taking is a balancing act. It does not mean proceeding with an action prior to considering all its possible consequences, and it is important not to create an impression that only winners get promoted. It is about creating an environment where everyone is valued for bringing their bright ideas to work rather than leaving them at home, where there is a culture of asking 'how' rather than 'why', and people are comfortable with offering ideas that have been thought through.

COMMUNICATING OPENLY

Creativity and innovation are dependent upon open communication channels to share knowledge and new ideas. Unnecessary bureaucratic procedures and lines of authority can stifle the exchange of ideas and experiences between people. Whilst everyone should be encouraged to be creative, divergent thinkers should be particularly motivated and encouraged to share their ideas with others. Individuals with talent should be recognized and persuaded to champion their ideas.

STRUCTURING THE ORGANIZATION

Successful organizations are designed to encourage creativity and change. Organizations that consist of small teams or groups are more likely to foster creativity as new ideas and fast action can flourish without bureaucratic overheads. Strong lines of authority often prevent initiative and creativity. Organizational structures also influence the behaviours, communication and interactions of people. A structure that facilitates the sharing and testing of ideas is a prerequisite for creativity and innovation.

ENCOURAGING PEOPLE TO THINK CREATIVELY

An innovative climate is reinforced through policies and practices that encourage opportunistic practices. Whilst some people will be more creative than others, everyone has the capacity to contribute new knowledge and use their ingenuity regardless of their background and experience. Even the most unusual idea should be given consideration by management. People should be given the freedom to try new ways of performing tasks and their successes celebrated. Challenging, yet realistic, goals should be set and immediate and timely feedback on performance given. Participative decision making and problem solving should be encouraged. Responsibility should be delegated to allow staff to be self-guiding in their work.

Personal development strategies allow for creative pastimes. The balance of right and left brain activities is necessary to assist personal growth and achievement. Creativity can also play a part in making personal career decisions in times of contracting employment opportunities. Individuals who are creative in setting their career goals and who proactively seek opportunities to achieve these will be more likely to succeed than those who do not.

INSTILLING PRIDE AND COMMITMENT

Innovative organizations generally have a culture where acceptance of responsibility and a commitment to the organization goes beyond the individual's functional role. The organization exhibits pride and there is positive reinforcement of it being an employer of choice and a role model for others. Success breeds success and this in turn reinforces the commitment and dedication to the organization.

ATTRACTING AND RETAINING CREATIVE TALENT

Innovative organizations go out of their way to recruit and keep talent. Leavy (2005) says that innovative companies thrive on a diversity of talent and outlook. Accordingly, they put much thought and effort into the recruitment process and Leavy identifies three ways of recruiting creative talent:

- Hire individuals with a range of abilities and interests;
- Hire people with a variety of backgrounds and personalities; and
- Involve peers heavily in the selection process.

Conclusion

Innovation and creativity are critical to sustaining organizational success in times of constraint. Innovation requires a strong corporate culture and leadership style that are flexible and open. Innovative organizations are highly skilled in measuring, managing and improving their intellectual capital, knowledge and know-how. People are inspired to show ingenuity and creativity by senior management and are judged on their contribution, which can come from many roles. The corporate culture encourages originality and resourcefulness, celebrates success and views mistakes as a learning process. These beliefs are communicated formally and informally.

There are several critical roles that support innovation and creativity in organizations, these being:

- Ideas generators;
- Champions;
- Intrapreneurs;
- Upholders;
- Gatekeepers; and
- Coaches.

Critical success factors in creating an innovative environment include having:

- The ability to manage change;
- Support for risk-taking activities;
- Open communications;
- Flexible organization structures to support the sharing of ideas;
- A culture that encourages people to think creatively;
- Leaders and managers who can instil pride and commitment into the organization; and
- The ability to attract and retain creative talent.

Although conflict is inevitable during the change that innovative processes bring, successfully innovative organizations manage this to ensure that creativity is not stifled.

References

Leavy, B. 2005. A leader's guide to creating an innovation culture. *Strategy and Leadership*, 33(4), 38–46.

Walton, G. 2008. Theory, research, and practice in library management 4: Creativity. *Library Management*, 29(1/2), 125–131.

Further reading

Brown, J.S. and Duguid, P. 2001. Creativity versus structure: A useful tension. *Sloan Management Review*, 42(4), 93–94.

Davenport, T.H. et al. 2003. Who's bringing you hot ideas and how are you responding? *Harvard Business Review*, 81(2), 58–64.

Drucker, P.F. 2002. The discipline of innovation. *Harvard Business Review*, 80(8), 95–98, 100, 102–103.

Dundon, E. and Pattakos, A. 2002. Cultivating innovation. *Executive Excellence*, 19(11), 6–17.

Hamel, G. 1998. Strategy innovation. *Executive Excellence*, 15(8), 7–8.

Higdon, L.I. Jnr. 2000. Leading innovation. *Executive Excellence*, 17(8), 15–16.

Kanter, R.M. 2000. A culture of innovation. *Executive Excellence*, 17(8), 10–11.

Rothaermel, F. and Hess, A.M. 2010. Innovative strategies combined. *MT Sloan Management Review*, spring, 13–15.

11 *Engaging Change in Positioning for the Future*

Change, innovation and leadership are inextricably linked. Change in organizations arises out of the need to be innovative, to proactively engage change from within and position for the future or as a reaction to sudden strategic shocks in the external environment that arrive unannounced and unanticipated. Internal catalysts for change include the natural transition that occurs as organizations grow and mature, a desire for performance improvement, business re-engineering and business process change. All require strong leadership skills to energize change in mindsets and, frequently, the corporate culture.

Organizational change inevitably leads to changes in circumstances for individuals, or the human side of organizations, which also need to be managed and supported. With this in mind this chapter concentrates on many of the people management issues associated with sustaining workforce performance through difficult challenges and change.

Change can be defined as an alteration in relationships or the environment. By their nature, information services can be catalysts for change as information and communications technology (ICT) is in itself an agent of disruptive change as well as often being used as a tool for innovation and transforming organizations. Transformational change is also part of the process of building a better organizational future by making it more agile, innovative, flexible and engaged.

External forces that are causing information services to rethink their processes and operations and engage with change are:

- The need for informational services to be more sustainable with regards to the environment, workforce, finances and service delivery;
- New developments in technology that are changing both employees' and customers' expectations and attitudes to service delivery;
- Innovation in service delivery and the merging services to provide a rich customer-centric one-stop integrated experience;
- Changes in the outlook and behaviour of organizations as a result of financial constraints in globalization and global markets; and
- A renewed interest in governance and accountability, community engagement in decision making and diversity in lifestyle and in cultures.

Incremental and internally shaped change occurs as a result of leadership driving the organization forward and responding to the need for innovation and revitalization in a changing business environment. Incremental change is usually planned, allowing some control over outcomes whilst still needing to be quickly implemented in order to make the most out of the opportunity. Amongst other factors, change from within can be initiated through new leadership styles, exposure to new products and customer service, ideas and values, making a commitment to social and environmental responsibility, business strategy and a desire for business growth, or the requirement to place the organization in a more financially sustainable position. Examples include:

- A greater strategic focus on agility and the modification of processes to achieve operational excellence, new levels of cost performance and greater choice in 24x365 customer services;
- Shifts in employees' socio-cultural values that expose new ways of doing things and fresh thinking as well as changes in work practices and attitudes such as work being organized for life, rather than life being organized for work; or
- Grasping the opportunity to incorporate Web 2.0 social media applications as business tools with the ensuing need to proactively redesign internal communications, service delivery offerings and records management practices and processes.

Engaging change from within uses leadership skills in:

- Having and imparting a sound strategic vision and a belief in their strategy and short-term goals;
- Building new mindsets with energy and shaping an organizational capacity to think differently about future opportunities;
- Instilling a culture that is innovative and supportive of the need to create and embrace change;
- Working constantly to attract, retain and engage talent; and
- Developing ownership and commitment to action throughout the organization.

In contrast, radical or disruptive change occurs in response to an abrupt event in the environment. It can be described as a strategic shock that transforms everyday life, alters cultures and values, or disrupts institutions. Examples are a corporate takeover that changes the entire corporate culture and environment, a biological or technical discovery that renders previous achievements obsolete, or a global phenomenon such as a tidal wave or terrorist attack.

Leadership qualities come to the forefront in these situations in both a proactive and reactive capacity. Those organizations best able to survive these situations are ones that have already been proactively readied to withstand unprecedented circumstances and have a resilience and capacity to think innovatively, act and adapt quickly, and find the single survival path to the future. The reactive capacity occurs at the moment of shock or crisis in that strong and directive leadership skills are needed to assess and take charge of the situation, make quick decisions and provide direction.

Reid (2010: 1) has identified 10 common themes or lessons for leading change in turbulent times:

- Strong, emotionally intelligent and resilient leaders who articulate strategic intent, clarify roles, align goals and empower people to act;
- Highly talented, cohesive teams with well-managed talents and tasks;
- Supportive, values-based cultures which engage and energize employees, customers and stakeholders;

- Intense client focus where we listen, collaborate with partners and deliver;
- Reshaped organizational processes, practices and structures that clear obstacles and create customer value;
- Leading edge technology that enables business goals;
- Proactive decision making and intelligent risk taking based on factual, well-tracked data and EQ-IQ partnership;
- Strong implementation focus, project management and sustainment;
- Recognition, reward and celebration of the changes; and
- Lots of fun.

Organizational life cycle and change

A further internal force for change is growth within an organization. It occurs naturally as part of the organizational life cycle and is an essential means for survival. As the information service and its parent organization grow, they progress through an organization life cycle where changes in managerial structure, processes and style occur. These bring significant changes and challenges that need to be managed from one stage to the next.

When an information service is first established it has a youthful and energetic presence. The emphasis is on creativity and management styles are flexible, informal and non-bureaucratic. Services and information products are created and introduced in order to prove its worth. Most decisions are based upon professional knowledge and there is often less differentiation with people performing a variety of tasks. This first stage requires boundless energy and creativity on behalf of the leader in establishing services, thinking of new ways of doing things, and letting people know about the information services and products offered.

As the service grows, people are promoted from within. It is an exciting place to work. However, the increased numbers of people compound the complexity, nature and number of relationships, ideas and ways of doing things. Without formal policies and procedures confusion and duplication of effort can occur. Strong leadership and direction are needed to guide the information service and to keep the creativity and energy going whilst establishing systems that assist rather than hinder service delivery.

If the leadership is strong, clear goals and direction are provided. Differentiation occurs, specialization takes place, teams are established to perform different tasks, and authority is created. This marks the beginning of the division of labour with new positions and levels within the information service being created. The result being that some people will feel they have lost their sphere of influence with the leader. Rapid growth will bring new people with different perspectives, fresh insights and ideas that are in themselves sources for change.

Management systems and formal governance processes become more evident. Communication becomes more formal, and elements of bureaucracy may become apparent. The challenge at this stage is to ensure that formalized processes do not stifle creative thinking, energy and enthusiasm. There is a need to keep momentum, ensuring that energy and vitality continue, and that new service delivery opportunities and business advantages are sought to avoid the organization becoming stale or obsolete.

As growth continues, restrictive practices that could begin to impede the service should be resisted. Taskforces, project and matrix groups are formed to improve collaboration and cooperation, ensuring that new thinking and ideas are continually considered and that energy and momentum are sustained. The organization transforms into a more open and reactive environment.

Throughout the different growth stages it is important for managers to recognize the stage at which their information service is in so that they can help others understand and manage the change, prepare for the future and avoid the pitfalls.

Performance improvement

Performance improvement programmes designed to place the organization on a more sustainable footing can also induce change. Eaton (2010: 49) outlines five improvement framework elements that need to be owned and implemented:

- Understand the context – being clear about the where and why an organization needs to improve based on an analysis of market forces, needs of stakeholders and current issues (such as new technology, regulation, etc.);
- Manage the gap – understand the actual performance and the required performance and then actively managing the gap;
- Maintain stakeholder commitment – gaining and maintaining stakeholder involvement in the process of change;
- Monitor, evaluate, support and improve – making improvement and progress a regular board matter, evaluating what has happened, support front-line teams, and continuously improving the way the improvement process is working; and
- Three-step improvement cycle – for each area that needs to improve, it is important to be clear about what needs to be done, implement it and then vigorously follow up and improve what has been done.

Eaton's five improvement framework elements can also be supported through strategies to assess and address the current state of change readiness, the impact of change on stakeholders and organizational culture, communications and feedback mechanisms, change risk, and the post implementation review of the change process and its outcome.

Business re-engineering

Business re-engineering is the ability to rethink fundamentally the mindset or way in which organizations deliver their products and services in line with their business strategy. It is an important necessity in ensuring the viability of an organization in challenging and changing environments. Business re-engineering is more than the need to continually review and continuously improve organizational processes which is known as business process change.

Business re-engineering is a business strategy that takes a radical approach, completely rethinking and transforming processes and delivery mechanisms to enable better service delivery and increased productivity rather than cost cutting. It is the mechanism through which significant first-to-market competitive initiatives that rewrite the rule books in product and service offerings are achieved. Shifting the delivery model for information services from a localized access point that is open weekdays and part of the weekend to an online global 24x365 operating model utilizing institutions around the world is an example of business re-engineering. In this example, the traditional functional and organizational boundaries are changed to a global business context. Cross-functional and cross-organizational processes have to be radically revised and implemented. This necessitates reshaping job designs, information flows and technology applications, sourcing material differently, as well as changes to organizational structures and management systems. The focus will also shift to managing the cultural dimension of the participating organizations including values and workplace norms.

Business process change

Business process change is a subset of business re-engineering. It is a continuous improvement practice that moves on an incremental basis in terms of cost, time, risk and complexity from business process optimization to business process redesign and finally to business process re-engineering.

Business process optimization involves improving and fine-tuning existing systems and processes for efficiency. It has an operational perspective and is usually low risk, being confined to discrete functions, albeit it should be designed within the context of the value chain in which these functions operate. Process optimization is typically less costly and faster to implement than the other business improvement practices.

Business process redesign is often used to enable more enhanced customer service by streamlining processes as well as reducing productivity bottlenecks in high impact areas. Process redesign involves extensive or comprehensive change to systems and processes or the introduction of new systems and processes that can cut across functional or organizational boundaries. However, it does not involve radical change arising out of rethinking the business. Business process redesign needs to be well planned and have strong executive commitment as it can involve a high level of complexity and risk as well as being costly to implement.

Business process re-engineering concentrates upon rethinking work practices and processes within an organization to achieve dramatically better outcomes either in terms of higher levels of efficiency or productivity or to deliver new value to the customer. Instead of concentrating on functions, process re-engineering looks holistically at all the steps that contribute to the process of creating the outcomes to achieve radical improvements to the organization's bottom line.

Business process re-engineering is often technology-led. An example is where airlines have re-engineered their check-in procedures, dispensing with full check-in counters where hard copy boarding cards were issued and replacing those with the check-in and boarding card information being transmitted to a mobile phone which is scanned at the flight gate. In shifting service delivery in this manner they have:

- Saved check-in staff labour and paper card costs;
- Delivered a more environmentally sustainable solution; and
- Eliminated check-in queues providing greater efficiencies and convenience to the customer.

Michael Hammer (1990: 104–112) was one of the first advocates of business process re-engineering thinking. He argued that organizations should use the power of ICT to redesign business processes radically in order to achieve dramatic improvements in their performance. He argued that organizations could not achieve major breakthroughs in their performance just by trimming the fat or automating existing processes. Organizations needed to recognize and break away from outdated rules and fundamental assumptions that underlie operations in order to avoid simply speeding up inappropriate processes.

Strategic organizational change management

Strategic organizational change brought on by the need to rethink fundamentally the mindset or way in which organizations deliver their products and services must be planned and managed in a formal manner. The four stages of strategic organizational change and likely emotions, behaviours and reactions are summarized in Figure 11.1.

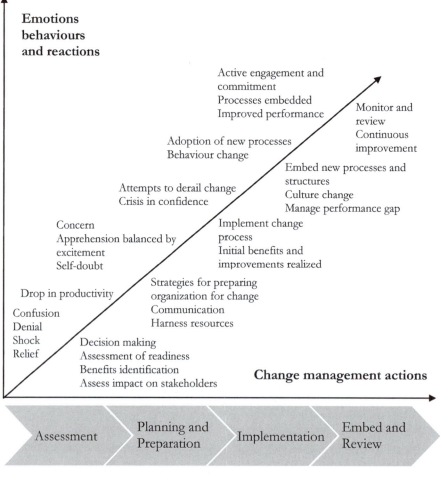

Figure 11.1 The four stages of strategic organizational change management

The first stage involves assessing the environment in order to make an informed decision to improve and embark on change. It has similarities to the strategic planning audit process in that it assesses:

- The current state of readiness, commitment, involvement and leadership capabilities of executive management to lead the change;
- The current state of the culture and organizational readiness to embrace the change;
- Stakeholders' understandings of the purpose and the value of the process;
- The availability of people, technology readiness, finances, assets and infrastructure to undertake and complete the change process;
- The impact of the change on stakeholders and their business practices; and
- The benefits of the change.

This assessment is needed as a lack of resources and commitment can severely impact the ability to change.

The second stage is the preparation or planning stage. Here strategies are developed for getting the organization ready for change and improvement and putting in place the resources to manage and implement the change process, including:

- People – training, leadership, rewards;
- Organization – structure and roles, culture, policies and processes;
- Information – data take-up and data conversion;
- Technology and infrastructure – integration and implementation of systems;
- Finances and benefits management – sources of finance, benefits identification and quantification;
- Risk management; and
- Communications and feedback – creating awareness and understanding, commitment and ownership.

The third stage comprises the physical processes of implementing the change and obtaining the initial benefits and improvements. This includes implementing new business processes, organizational structures and behaviours. Eaton (2010: 47) indicates that at this stage some things will go well and others not so well. The 'naysayers' will focus on the failures and managers will often have a crisis of confidence that may lead to early termination of the change programme.

Embedding the change and post-implementation review is the fourth stage. This stage is where the full benefits of the change are realized. The stage includes monitoring and managing any performance gap between actual and desired performance. Eaton (2010: 49) indicates that recognizing that things are getting better will help reinforce new ways of doing things and encourage further improvement.

Once the change has been implemented and embedded the post-implementation review of the change process and outcome can be undertaken. This allows for feedback about the process, where improvements could be made and where further changes may be required in order to complete the change process and derive the full benefits.

Enabling the capacity to engage in change

Fundamental to the success of any part of change is the management of people. Different stages and types of change call for different leadership roles. The following describe leadership roles that can be used in these circumstances.

CREATING AND ENGAGING CHANGE FROM WITHIN

Like all organizations, libraries and information services now operate in continuously changing environments such that the need for leadership, innovation and building individual and organizational energy and engagement in strategic change is an everyday requirement. True engagement in change is demonstrated where people themselves identify and suggest where change is necessary in order to enhance the quality of services or do things more productively.

Building an agile and flexible organization with the mindsets, culture, capacity and commitment to embrace and engage in change is an important leadership function. A spirit of support, cooperation, collaboration and enthusiasm needs to be created, in which people feel comfortable with the status quo being uncertainty. People need to see and understand the big picture; a total view of the environment where turbulence is the norm and transformational change is necessary either in anticipation of, or in response to, sudden strategic shocks.

The right people need to be engaged, especially those who have access to important information, those who can either make an impact or will be significantly impacted, those who have an authority to effect change and make critical decisions in the area of change, those with responsibility for the areas affected, and those who may oppose the change. Richard Axelrod (2002: 41) has identified several questions for the leader of change to ask when engaging the right people in change. He comments that it is not the leader's role to provide all the answers to the questions, but to ensure that the answers are developed:

- What needs to change and why?
- What needs to be different in the organization?
- What are the boundary conditions?
- Whose voice needs to be heard?
- Who else needs to be here?
- How do we build the necessary connection between people and ideas?
- How will we create a community of people who are ready and willing to act? and
- How will we embrace democracy throughout the process?

Inevitably new workplace behaviours will be needed to propel the organization faster and more effectively to its newly aligned business goals. A sense of urgency should be created to overcome indifference, apathy and the sentiment 'that things aren't really going to be any different'. A free flow of information incorporating both the good and bad news is a fundamental requisite so that people can discuss and make sense of change. Reid (2010) has also identified that organizational barriers like unclear roles, structures with excessive approval levels, lack of staff and customer engagement, and risk aversion dampen the urge to change. Reid also observed that highly distracted or stressed people don't and can't innovate and change. Mental clarity, focus and creativity are needed to change and envision successful business strategies. In times of economic constraint these attributes are often drained.

Different stakeholders will be impacted in separate ways so all views of the world need to be canvassed in order for everyone to gain a complete picture of the environment in which the change is or will take place. These include perspectives of the environment by:

- Stakeholders, especially on how the change may impact on their own environment and relationships with the organization;
- Executives, particularly on their view of the external environment issues and impacts;
- Teams, particularly on their view on the internal operational environment issues that might be affected; and
- Individuals who are likely to be most affected in order to canvass their options for the future.

The involvement and contribution of ideas and concepts, emotions and values, knowledge and experience by people from all parts of the system or value chain is necessary in order that the different parts of the organization or processes are connected, and the whole system and impact is visible to those involved. It is also a necessary process to focus on creating a culture of change by building shared meaning and engaging participants in discussion and developing their vision of what the change means for them so that better and more coordinated outcomes can be developed. Identifying short-term wins and enabling teams to think about planning for change and creating a common language around change are also valuable change management strategies.

In building a common purpose, shared meaning and mindsets, the reason for the change and its implications should be clarified to all stakeholders in order to develop a universal understanding and commitment to the new environment. This should include exploring what needs to go right and what needs to be done differently in the new environment by both the organization as the collective entity and each individual. Past and present achievements and successes also need to be recognized and honoured, as these will form the basis upon which the future is built. People also need to be reassured that their efforts in the past have not been wasted.

Individuals will react to change in one of three ways:

- Accept and support the change (active engagement);
- Comply with the change in action but not in spirit (passive engagement); or
- Actively resist the change (anti-engagement).

In explaining the implications of the change, some of the anticipated reactions and concerns of individuals should be addressed. Change sparks powerful emotions in people, yet at the same time people are required to make changes in their behaviours. The changes in behaviour cannot be learnt if individuals are distracted by fear, anger or uncertainty. These feelings need to be openly acknowledged and dealt with as a natural course of events arising out of the change. The need to empower individuals to manage their emotional response is as important as providing them with the necessary skills and training for the new situation. People also need to be given opportunities in which it is seen that their voice counts.

Building a critical mass of engaged and committed individuals at all levels throughout the organization is vital in setting the example, for relationship building, in sustaining the right corporate culture and mindsets, and in creating the impetus and momentum to champion the change. The faster the momentum for change can occur, whilst allowing for consultation and involvement, the more successful it is likely to be. Urgency and energy in the change processes avoid people holding on to old ways and operating in a destructive twilight zone where confusion and the part implementation of new processes serve no one well. Obstacles that prevent people from operating and thinking in new ways should be identified and removed or overcome.

Collaboration, relationship building, information sharing are all critical functions in developing a will and willingness to work together to effect change and for engaging people in change. Change agents have a critical role in communicating and sharing information, ideas and feelings when empowering others to embrace the change. Instilling self-confidence and liberating people from old ways and old thinking are powerful mechanisms for enabling people to start making their own decisions in the new environment. Visible proof that the new environment is working by having people take action and embrace new thinking or having some 'quick wins' will provide credibility, energy and impetus for the change process.

The timing and frequency of the planned change need to be considered. Ideally, changes should be implemented at a time when the information service is least pressured and has been made ready for the change. However, this is not always possible, particularly in the case of reactive change.

The turning point in change, which occurs between the second or resistance stage and the third or exploring stage, is the most critical. This is the stage where emotions are high, push back occurs from those who are resisting the change and some find ways to undermine the change process. Energy, persistence, drive and self-confidence are required to continue the momentum and make the changes sustainable with those who have already embraced the change, to build on the quick wins and consolidate the new change culture. Guidance, monitoring progress and mentoring will also be needed to sustain the change.

STRATEGIES FOR MANAGING STRATEGIC SHOCKS

Despite having built an organizational capacity to engage readily in change, organizations will still be subject to unprecedented and sudden significant strategic shocks that result in fundamental shifts in the organization's circumstances. 9/11 is an example of an unprecedented sudden and strategic shock. It not only had an immediate global impact, it disrupted the entire airline industry and for the institutions housed in the Twin Towers, it meant that many of their people and organizations did not survive. Other organizational examples may be where a rapid downsize occurs as the result of a merger between two organizations, or where a totally different political philosophy is introduced overnight as a result of a change of government.

The difficulty in managing in these environments is that, as the often-radical decisions are made to counter the situation, the shock waves travel through the organization. The hard task is to identify where the shock wave will be felt most and what the impact will be. Crisis conditions frequently prevail. The resulting chaos and time factors may not allow measured consideration of the impact of all decisions.

The uncertainty brought about by the magnitude and suddenness of the change needs to be managed through strong and direct leadership. Trust, consistency, the ability to make connections and make the right decision quickly and in an unwavering manner are all leadership qualities required in this reactive situation.

New roles, tasks and interim structures should be quickly put in place for the transition period. Strategic areas that are working well should be quickly identified and if possible quarantined in order to preserve and build upon their success. Areas within the information service that do not support the new direction should be dealt with immediately.

Communication and actions are central to effecting successful change, as people interpret the messages about the change according to what they hear and how they see others being treated. Even where individuals are not immediately affected by the change, they will watch with interest and interpret its effect on others. People will view the changes through their own eyes, not those of the leaders of change. So the way in which managers treat any one individual will send signals to the rest of the people in the organization. These signals can be very powerful in determining the people's expectations as to how they may be treated, valued, rewarded or penalized by the organization in the future.

The messages that people hear of changes through the grapevine and through what they are officially told by their managers may not always be consistent or correctly interpreted. It is therefore important to ensure that any actions or signals send the correctly framed message. If the message is distorted because of other political agendas, or if mixed messages are received, people will quickly become despondent and confused. The message should be simple and clearly identify what needs to be achieved by the information service through the change process. Strong internal communications and access to counselling may help individuals deal with their personal anxieties about their own and the organization's future.

MANAGING THE CHANGE CYCLE

In responding to the opportunities of the digital or virtual world, information services are undergoing profound change in the manner in which they are organized and deliver services. This has a considerable impact on the people who are involved. As change occurs, individuals and groups progress through four stages: denial, resistance, exploring and commitment. Each of the four stages has quite distinct behavioural reactions and needs to be managed in different ways. As change occurs, it is unlikely that all individuals will progress through the four stages at the same time. Figure 11.2 illustrates the four stages of change.

Stage one (denial) is characterized by individuals ignoring any signals of change or being frozen in traditional ways. They may be silent observers who neither oppose the change nor actively support it. Others may experience shock if they could not see that change was required, or relief that the inevitable had actually happened. Individuals in this stage of change require information about what the change will mean to them and to the organization, a sense of urgency and pressure to move forward with the change, and mechanisms to unfreeze their thinking and traditional ways of doing things.

Emotions and behaviours

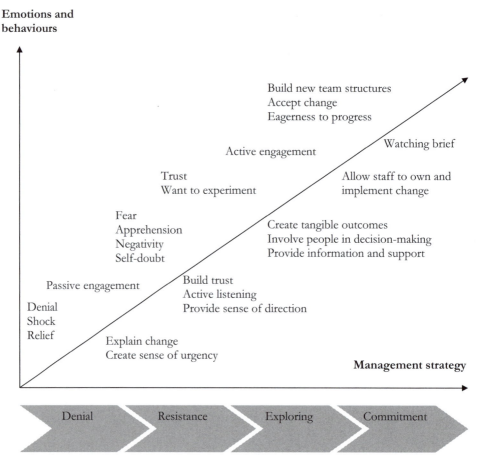

Figure 11.2 The four stages of the change cycle

The second stage of change (resistance) is characterized by fear, apprehension, negativity and self-doubt. This is often expressed in terms of sabotage, absenteeism, anger, anxiety, suspicion and cynicism. During this stage, the information services manager will need to deal with illogical arguments and hostility. The important management process at this stage is to listen with empathy and understanding, rather than to reason or argue. Active listening will help to build trust in people.

The manager may also need strong conviction for the vision and change outcome as they may be subject to personal attacks from those who are feeling vulnerable. They should empathize with staff whilst trying to reconnect them to reality and giving them a sense of direction. Staff will feel a sense of loss and require support whilst still keeping the pressure to move forward.

The third stage (exploring) is the most critical stage as it is the point of transformation. Some people have begun to buy into the change, becoming active participants and exhibiting new behaviours. The change process at this stage relies upon people being given tangible things to do and decisions to make that reinforce their new roles and new thinking. Staff should be encouraged to acknowledge what has happened, reinforcing the positive things of the past whilst exploring the future. Individuals will still feel insecure but their hostility will be diminished.

This stage marks the formation of the new team; with new behaviours, new trusted relationships, new shared experiences and new freedoms. The information services manager should provide information and support through discussion and problem solving. People should be involved in all discussions and provided with opportunities to succeed in the new environment. To mark the transition there should be a launch of something new that signifies a change within the corporate culture. This may be a new logo, new stationery or refurbishing the existing premises.

The final stage is commitment. New behaviours are in place, diluting the power of traditional ones. Those that remain in old thinking are in the minority and have little influence. The information services manager should have a watching brief at this point, being available for consultation and concentrating where needed on making the change complete in the new changed culture. Staff should be allowed to get on with their work and own it.

OVERCOMING RESISTANCE TO CHANGE

The most desirable change situation is where there is such organizational readiness to create and embrace change that the impetus for change is built from within. However, there will be times when this cannot or does not happen and resistance will be encountered. Resistance to change is a natural process and will occur at both the organizational and individual levels. Organizations have inbuilt mechanisms that produce stability and resist change. The selection process and culture of the organization create a persona that is difficult to change. Group norms may also act as a constraint to change.

External factors such as uncertain times also act as obstacles to change. For example Reid (2010: 1) identifies that in 'uncertain times the mental clarity, focus and the creativity needed to change and envision successful business strategies are being drained'. She adds 'In this environment team and interpersonal conflicts impede the kind of exploration and dialogue needed for innovative learning, performance and partnerships'.

However, resistance to change is not necessarily a bad thing. It can serve a useful purpose in which individual and team concerns can be aired and taken into account in bringing about a better solution.

There are a variety of reasons why individuals resist or choose not to actively engage in change. Often the uncertainty of impending change leads to anxiety, particularly in relation to people's ability to cope with a new situation. Familiarity with existing procedures and lack of psychological energy to acquire new skills or change direction add to this resistance. People often fear the thought of having to master something new and the possibility that they may not be able to do this immediately. They may argue that they are too old to learn new systems. Resistance to change can also provoke feelings of loss and uncertainty which in turn lead to insecurity.

Resistance can also occur because of an individual's previous experience in life. If the change is coloured by a previous negative encounter with a similar life experience, there will often be resistance. Change may also produce a threat to an individual's or group's self-interest or status. Their position of authority or power source may be threatened if they are placed in a situation of being dependent upon others whilst they are in a learning situation. The different perceptions of the employee's and management's assessment of the situation also add to the resistance.

Changes in organizational structure or workplace may cause the severance of old relationships with feelings of loss and disruption to existing social networks. The promotion of an internal candidate to a more senior position may sever the close relationships that existed beforehand between the successful candidate and their peers.

Encouraging participation in the decision making, problem solving and planning processes can be effective techniques for overcoming resistance as it allows the affected individuals to understand better the reasons behind the change and provides an element of self-determination. Uncertainty is reduced and self-interest neutralized through the opportunity to express their ideas.

If open channels of communication are established and maintained, there can be a better understanding of all parties' viewpoints and perspectives, uncertainty can be minimized and new options may be found. Even if the final solution is not the most preferable for some, the feeling of being asked for an opinion and that unenthusiastic reactions and emotions are understood will minimize resistance and negative outcomes.

Training, open communication and evidence of clear, tangible benefits as an outcome of change also facilitate the change process. This includes providing opportunities for adult learning so that those affected can learn from others' experiences, become skilled at the new work practices, know more about what needs to be done differently and witness firsthand the anticipated benefits. Experiencing firsthand where and how the change can lead to positive and relative advantages for the individual being asked to change is an important factor in their readiness to accept change. The sooner the benefits are clearly apparent to those affected, the quicker and more likely people are to accept and continue the newly introduced practices.

From a corporate culture perspective, the changes being advocated must be compatible with the existing values and experiences of the individuals otherwise they will be discarded as threatening or inappropriate. Change agents can also be used to facilitate and support individuals through the change.

If resistance to change continues it may be the symptom of one of two causes. Either the correct 'fit' between the change situation, change agent and persons involved has not been found, or the proposed change is a poor strategy and is not in the organization's best interest.

Unsuccessful change can be recognized by the absence of feedback, even though a feedback mechanism is available, or by strong feedback in the form of protests or complaints. A drop in productivity below that anticipated by the learning curve also indicates a problem. Likewise, withdrawal symptoms characterized by lack of cooperation, absenteeism, resignations or transfers indicate that something is wrong. When any one of these symptoms appears, it should be immediately investigated in order to isolate and correct the problem.

Conclusion

The only constant in the world today is that it is an era of continuous change. In this environment, change management strategies are important in order to smooth the transition of change and, importantly, to initiate and manage the change itself for the strategic advantage of the information service and its parent organization.

The catalyst for organizational change occurs in two ways:

- As a result of an organization responding to the need for innovation and revitalization in a changing business environment, being exposure to new leadership practices, ideas and values, having a desire for business growth or the requirement to place the organization in a more financially sustainable position; or
- Due to an unprecedented and sudden significant strategic shock that results in fundamental shifts in the organization's circumstances.

The most desirable situation is for change to be energized from within. However this will not always be the case. Both situations require leadership skills in building and shaping an agile and flexible organization with the mindsets, culture, capacity and commitment to embrace and engage in change, and to develop a commitment to action throughout the organization.

Eaton (2010: 50) shows that outperforming organizations involved in implementing and embedding improvements in performance are those that have:

- Sponsorship – a top level champion that supports and advocates the change;
- Engagement – gaining and maintaining stakeholder engagement;
- Honest and timely communications – 'honest' being the operative word;
- Culture that promotes change – a long-term focus on changing the behaviour of the organization;
- Change agents – individuals with the capacity to lead the actual improvement process;
- Capacity building – continuing investment in building the internal capability of the organization;
- Performance measures – effective measures that are available to, and understood by, everyone;
- Effective structure – an effective and flexible structure for the improvement programme; and
- Incentives – robust financial and non-financial incentives.

In creating and engaging change from within people need to see and understand the big picture. A common purpose needs to be developed with shared meanings and mindsets about the reason for the change and its implications in order to develop a universal understanding and commitment to the new environment. People need to be able to discuss their concerns openly. The right people need to be engaged, especially those who have access to important information, those who can either make an impact or will be significantly impacted, those who have an authority to effect change and make critical decisions in the area of change, those with responsibility for the areas affected, and those who may oppose the change.

Resistance to change is a natural process and will occur at both the organizational and individual levels. Strategies for managing resistance to change include:

- Encouraging participation in decision making, problem solving and planning processes;
- Establishing and maintaining open channels of communication;
- Understanding of all parties' viewpoints and perspectives;
- Providing opportunities for adult learning so that those affected can learn from others' experiences, become skilled at the new work practices, know more about what needs to be done differently and witness firsthand the anticipated benefits;
- Ensuring the changes are compatible with the existing values and experiences of the individuals; and
- Using change agents to facilitate and support individuals through the change.

Change that has the potential to affect the whole organization should be sold and managed quite differently to minor changes affecting one or two people. Radical disruptive change requires strong leadership capable of making quick and far-reaching decisions. In addition to good initial planning, the abilities to demonstrate 'quick wins' and maintain momentum through people acting and making decisions in the new environment are critical to implementing successful continuous change. Finally, in all instances credibility and relationship management needs to be maintained.

Business re-engineering is used in times of radical changing and challenging environments organizations to rethink fundamentally the mindset or way in which they deliver their products and services in line with their business strategy. A subset of business re-engineering is process change. Today this is being driven by the need to be more financially and environmentally sustainable and the always on social media environment and other seamless service delivery initiatives that require instantaneous response and immediate feedback.

References

Axelrod, R.H. 2002. *Terms of Engagement: Changing The Way We Change Organizations*. San Francisco: Berrett-Koehler.

Eaton, M. 2010. How to make change stick. *Training Journal (TJ)*, March, 46–50, available at www.trainingjournal.com.

Hammer, M. 1990. Re-engineering work: Don't automate, obliterate. *Harvard Business Review*, July–August, 104–112.

Reid, J. 2010. Leading in uncertain times. *Ivey Business Journal Online*, March/April, 1.

Further reading

Andriopoulos, C. and Dawson, P. 2009. *Managing Change, Creativity and Innovation*. London: SAGE.

Black, J.S. et al. 2002. *Leading Strategic Change: Breaking Through the Brain Barrier*. Upper Saddle River: Financial Times Prentice Hall.

The Essentials of Managing Change and Transition. 2005. Boston: Harvard Business School.

Galbraith, J.D. et al. 2002. *Designing Dynamic Organizations: A Hands-On Guide for Leaders at All Levels*. New York: AMACOM.

Hollender, J. 2010. *The Responsibility Revolution: How the Next Generation Of Businesses Will Win*. San Francisco: Jossey-Bass.

Kahan, S. 2010. *Getting Change Right: How Leaders Transform Organizations from Inside Out*. San Francisco: Jossey-Bass.

Klein, J.A. 2004. *True Change: How Outsiders on the Inside Get Things Done in Organizations*. San Francisco: Jossey-Bass.

Leading Change: Why Transformational Efforts Fail. 2010. United States: Harvard Business School Press.

Lewis, E. et al. 2010. Successfully managing change during uncertain times. *Strategic HR Review*, 9(2), 12.

Rolfe, J. 2010. Change is a constant requiring a coach. *Library Management*, 31(4/5), 291.

Schulte, A. 2010. Leading bold change. *Leadership Excellence*, April, 4.

Sidorko, P.E. and Yang, T.T. 2009. Refocusing for the future: Meeting user expectations in a digital age. *Library Management*, 30(1/2), 6–24.

Smith, I. 2005. Achieving readiness for organisational change. *Library Management*, 26(6/7), 408–413.

Smith, I. 2005. Managing the people side of organisational change. *Library Management*, 26(3), 152–156.

Smith, I. 2005. Resistance to change – recognition and response. *Library Management*, 26(8/9), 519–523.

12 *Group Dynamics and Team Building*

As a result of the need for greater flexibility and increased interactions in changing environments hierarchical organizational structures are being replaced with groups of individuals who work together in teams. Increasingly people will be working in teams that have been formed across organizations to deliver integrated customer services or in services that have been outsourced or managed as a service. Some of which may be virtual. This warrants a different leadership style as the role of the team builder is not to manage people as individuals, but to facilitate the group's management of its members. The objective is to obtain a higher level outcome than would be provided by the same number of people working individually. This requires an understanding of group behaviour because people act differently when they are members of a team or group. Their behaviours will change according to their role in the team or group.

Types of groups

A group is a collection of people who regularly interact with each other to pursue a common purpose. There are four basic components of a group:

- It needs at least two people to exist;
- The individuals must interact regularly in order to maintain the group;
- All group members must have a common goal or purpose; and
- There should be a stable structure.

Groups can be formal or informal. Formal groups or teams are defined through the organization's hierarchy or centre on a particular task. Informal groups are based upon individual psychological need, activities and interests. Formal groups or teams are created to accomplish a number of tasks within an indefinite or definite timescale. They often relate to the organizational structure. Formal groups are created through formal authority for a purpose, as in Figure 12.1.

FORMAL GROUPS IN ORGANIZATIONS

In most organizations there will be an executive management group or team consisting of senior executives. This team will be responsible for the overall governance of the organization and considers the strategic issues confronting the parent organization.

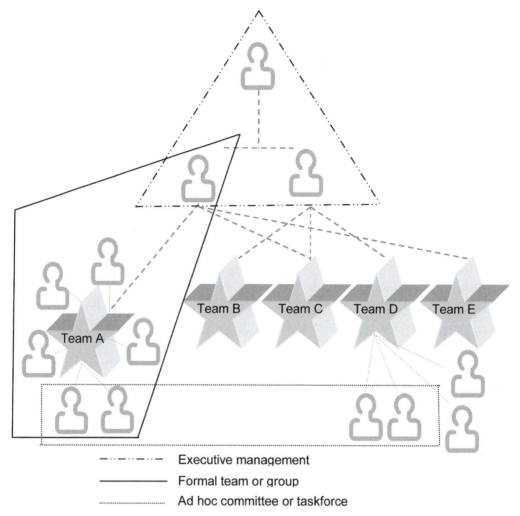

Figure 12.1 The organization as an interlocking network of formal groups

Activities undertaken by the management team include the endorsement of the strategic plan, the ratification of policy and the approval of the overall organizational budget.

The information services manager may be a member of this team as well as being involved in other groups in different capacities: as a supervisor, a chairperson or an ordinary of a team or number of teams. In these capacities they will be the link between the management team and the work teams. In addition to these managers will also be part of an informal group network.

Work teams are the most recognized form of formal groups. They are the functional teams established to achieve corporate objectives and business outcomes. These formal teams usually remain in existence until there is some change in the organizational structure. They have clearly distinguishable line management relationships and are often identified in the formal organization chart as a work team, department or division. The size and level of the work team is scalable according to the size of the parent organization.

In some organizations the information service may be regarded as a work team. In others the research centre, branch libraries, records management section and the ICT services unit will be regarded as individual work teams, with the senior research officer, branch librarian, records manager or information technology manager being formally designated as the leader of the permanent team or work team. Work teams may also reflect the organization's clients or markets. With the rise of integrated service delivery and flexible working conditions, work teams may comprise people who work:

- From home;
- In different organizations and even different countries;
- Virtually, that is only online.

Taskforces are project teams that are created for a particular purpose, usually to accomplish a relatively narrow task within a stated or implied timescale. They are temporary formal teams with a 'sunset clause'. Ad hoc committees also belong in this category.

The team membership is usually specified by management, but may also comprise volunteers. They often have a designated chairperson or a formal leader who is accountable for the results. Like the work team manager, the task or project team leader should review progress at regular intervals and provide performance feedback to members of the team. They must have the appropriate interpersonal skills and be prepared to accept responsibility and accountability.

Taskforces are often used in a matrix style of management. The individuals forming the team have two managers; the work team manager and the taskforce manager. A dual chain of command is established.

INFORMAL GROUPS

Informal groups exist for purposes that may or may not be relevant to the organization. They emerge within organizations without being formally designated by someone in authority for a specific purpose. Each member chooses to participate without being told to do so. As they are formed through a common interest, the activities of the group may or may not match those of the organization.

Informal groups can be a powerful organizational force. The identification of the leaders of the informal groups may provide insight into the politics, power and authority within the information service and its parent organization. Informal groups can coexist with formal groups in an attempt to overcome bureaucratic tendencies or to foster networks of interpersonal relationships that aid workflows in ways that formal lines of authority fail to provide as in Figure 12.2.

The formation of an informal group is often a healthy sign of comradeship and is not necessarily an indication that there is anything wrong within the organization. Social or friendship groups are often formed within organizations across formal work team boundaries for the purpose of sharing a common interest. Informal groups help individuals satisfy shared needs or may be used to provide alternative support to the formal team affiliations within the organization. The choice of informal group may be based on interpersonal attraction, an interest in the group's activities such as sport or chess, generational differences, or an interest in the group's goals such as environmental sustainability.

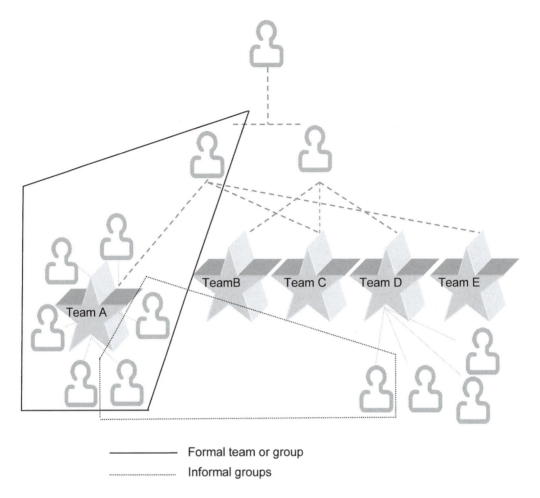

Figure 12.2 Formal and informal groups in organizations

Stages of group development

After a group has been created, either formally by the organization or by group members, it will spend time developing. Group development occurs in four stages: forming, storming, norming and performing. These stages do not occur as discrete steps but are usually quite discernible because of their distinct activities and need for different management techniques as in Figure 12.3. The passage of time between the stages of group development will differ according to the timescale set for the outcome.

THE FORMING STAGE

The forming stage occurs as individual members of the group become acquainted with each other and begin to test which interpersonal behaviours are acceptable and which are not. Group boundaries and group rules are defined. The real task of the group is clarified.

The forming stage usually takes place at the first meeting of the group. Typically, the different members of a group describe their background and personal interests in the group's goals. This serves to define a common purpose and shared values. The members of the group could be drawn from many different work units within the information service, the parent organization or from other organizations. As such, they are often not aware of the role and potential of the other members and where their expertise and values can be shared. Members may act aloof until they become aware of some shared meanings and each other's needs. As they become aware of each other, they achieve higher levels of interaction and mutual identification in pursuit of the common purpose.

The management roles are to clarify tasks and direction for the group, the reasons for its formation and outcomes envisaged, whilst creating a sense of urgency. Communication should be encouraged as members explore the roles, responsibilities, norms and values of different members in the group.

THE STORMING STAGE

The second stage (storming) is usually highly emotional, involving tension among members and periods of hostility and infighting. Each member wishes to retain their individuality and may resist the structure that is emerging. Interpersonal styles are clarified and negotiations take place in an effort to find ways of accomplishing group goals whilst satisfying individual needs. Gradually a group leader emerges. Attention is paid to items that prevent the group's goals from being met. In practice, the storming stage is the stage where problems are confronted, criticism is made and discussion becomes more open.

The management role in this stage is as a facilitator, enabling members to confront, work through and overcome the problems associated change, with the proposed structure and individual roles. In assisting individuals to cope with change and to encourage new ideas, discussion and exploration of new solutions should be encouraged. Purpose and direction should be further clarified to minimize uncertainty and to share the vision or bigger picture.

THE NORMING STAGE

The third stage (norming) begins the integration process. Each person begins to recognize and accept his or her role and those of others. The group becomes more cohesive, adopting group norms that serve to regulate individual behaviour in order to achieve the group's goals. The group begins to be coordinated and teamwork emerges. Harmony is emphasized and minority viewpoints are discouraged.

As group harmony and teamwork develop, the role of the manager is to encourage collective engagement, cooperation and collaboration. Confidence in the group's and individual's contributions may need to be reinforced and direction fine-tuned.

THE PERFORMING STAGE

Performing is the final stage of group development. The group is totally integrated and is able to focus on the situation at hand. It functions well and can deal with complex tasks through the interaction that occurs. The structure is stable and members work as one unit.

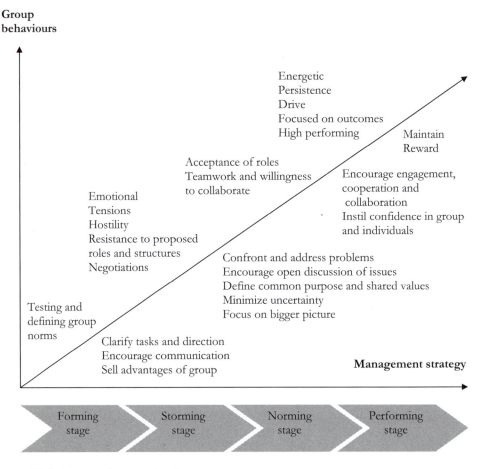

Figure 12.3 Stages of group development

In this stage, the group should be left to perform, with encouragement, support and rewards being openly given.

Group cohesiveness

Group cohesiveness is the extent to which members of the group are attracted to each other and to the team as a whole. Highly cohesive teams occur where members are attracted to each other, accept the team's goals and help work towards meeting them. Cohesion is likely to be higher in teams where members share similar attitudes and needs. Teams based on a particular expertise are usually cohesive because they share common professional values and attitudes. Not all cohesive groups are productive for the organization. Some groups can inflict considerable harm if their goals and values are contrary to those of the parent organization.

Group cohesiveness can be increased through intergroup competition, having supportive management, through personal attraction amongst members of the team, by rewarding the team rather than the individuals, by frequent interaction and by agreement on the team's goals. Group cohesiveness can be decreased by competition within the team, by the domination of one party, by disagreement on the team's goals and by team size.

As the size of the team increases, the number of possible relationships between its members increases. This leads to the need for increased communication and coordination amongst the team members. It also leads to the development of subgroups that may be damaging to the overall team's cohesiveness and its associated productivity. Smaller teams enable members to interact more frequently and increase their cohesiveness. The optimum number for a team is between five and seven people.

Group member roles

A role is a typical behaviour that characterizes a person in a social context. As members of a group, people play different roles. Their behaviours will change according to their role in the social structure of the group. One of the communication tasks in life is to understand the role that a person is playing when they exhibit certain behaviours. David Barry (1991) has identified four leadership roles and behaviours that fall into four broad clusters and which are readily found in teams:

- The envisioning role involves the facilitation of ideas generation and innovation, defining and championing goals, as well as finding conceptual links between systems. Envisioning leaders often have trouble functioning in a group, preferring to invent and create independently. Sometimes they continue to provide new ideas after the group has committed itself to specific actions. The true role of the envisioning leader is to help others to see the vision in order to foster group ownership of the ideas;
- The organizing role brings together the disparate elements that exist within the team and its tasks. This person focuses on details, deadlines, time, efficiency and structure. They often work within a few well-chosen solutions. Whilst it is a necessary role in keeping the group from straying off the task, it can be counter-productive when a completely new and innovative direction is needed;
- The spanning role includes networking, presentation management, developing and maintaining a strong image with outsiders, intelligence gathering, locating and securing critical resources, bargaining, being sensitive to power distributions and being politically astute. Their natural tendency is to circulate outside the group environment. They can also be self-centred. To compensate for this, the spanning leader should provide the group with a constant source of reality checks, ensuring that the outputs of the team are well received with others in the organization;
- The social role focuses on developing and maintaining the team from a social-psychological position. They show concern for individuals and ensure that everyone has their views heard. They are sensitive to the team's energy levels and emotional state. They provide encouragement and reinforcement and are able to mediate conflicts.

There are also several terms that are used to describe the various facets of roles. The expected role is that which the other members of the group expect from an individual. The perceived role is what the individual perceives the role to mean. The enacted role is what the individual actually does in the role. This then further influences the expected role. By rights, these three roles should be congruent. However, this may not always be the case and leads to role dilemmas which occur either through uncertainty, role conflict, role overload or role underload.

ROLE DILEMMAS

Role dilemmas are a normal part of life. However there are limits to which people can cope with role dilemmas. If these limits are reached and left unchecked, they can become sources of internal tension or frustration. They may also result in job disenchantment or dissatisfaction, poor performance and a high staff turnover. The following provide examples where role dilemmas cause individuals to act or exhibit behaviours that are inconsistent with their normal behaviour.

Role ambiguity

Role ambiguity results when there is some uncertainty in the minds of either an individual or members of a group as to precisely what their role is at any given time. If an individual's conception of their role is unclear this can lead to role ambiguity even if it is clear to others. The use of job descriptions can help to overcome role ambiguity in an organizational sense.

Role conflict

Role conflict occurs when the appropriate behaviours for enacting a role may be inconsistent with the appropriate behaviours for enacting either another role or other requirements of the same role. The expectations of each role may be quite clear and the expectations compatible for each role, but the roles themselves may be in conflict.

Role conflict is generally categorized into two types, inter-role and intra-role conflict. Inter-role conflict is found where there are incompatible demands of two or more different roles being played by the same person. The need for the information services manager to act as service provider and policy-maker may cause an inter-role conflict. In intra-role conflict contradictory demands within a single role are perceived by an individual. This might occur where the information services manager may have to cancel the annual leave of a staff member whilst recognizing that they have been overloaded with work and need a break.

Individual-role conflict occurs where a person is asked to fulfil a requirement that is against their own values, attitudes or needs. Such an example may be where the librarian must avoid acting as a censor and so is forced to stock material that is in conflict with some very strong personal beliefs.

Role conflicts may sometimes be eased by reducing the importance of one of the roles, or by compartmentalizing the two roles so that they do not overlap. It is important to take steps to reduce the conflict as role conflict is recognized as a source of stress and poor performance.

Role overload

Role overload occurs when expectations for the role exceed the individual's capabilities. Individuals are required to perform more roles than they originally envisaged or have the capacity for. An example may be where a person is required to be a decision-maker in a complex and changing environment, but they have a low tolerance for uncertainty. Role overload should not be confused with work overload.

Role underload

Role underload occurs when an individual feels that they have the capacity to handle a bigger role or greater set of roles than is assigned to them. Role underload may be overcome by assigning additional roles or by delegating tasks and responsibilities.

Both role overload and role underload can be the outcome of a position being filled by someone who was incorrectly advised about the job at the interview. An unrealistic assessment of a position during the interview situation may lead to role overload or role underload and a person's subsequent dissatisfaction with the job.

Group norms

Group norms are standards of behaviour that the group adopts for its members. These are informal rules that enhance the group's structure and reinforce a certain degree of conformity among group members. Norms differ from organizational rules in that they are not written. They are subtle standards that exist and regulate group behaviour.

Group norms are established during the third stage of group development. They are created through a series of actions by individual members and the others' responses as a group. The ways in which the responses are made provide the basis for the norm. The norms that survive are those that produce the most successful outcomes. The norms are reinforced through their success in positive problem solving and in integration. Gradually it is assumed that if a norm is followed, success will result. As a result, norms are followed unconsciously.

Norms help groups avoid chaos and influence behaviours. They can be:

- Performance related, such as identifying levels of daily work output or appropriate channels of communication;
- Social related, such as how to address senior management in public, or acceptable levels of course language;
- Behaviour related, such as setting standards of integrity, quality of service and professionalism; and
- Appearance related, such as setting standards of dress.

As norms can have either a positive or negative influence on both the group's and the organization's productivity, it is important that positive norms are supported. Positive norms can be supported by rewarding desired behaviours and by monitoring performance and providing feedback regarding the desired and undesired behaviours.

Effective team building

Team building involves all of the leadership and facilitation skills that are required in extending individual performance and applies these to the team. This includes the development of interpersonal relationships within a team so that members share information and experiences so that they can collectively set goals and outcomes to be achieved. The team builder will also need to facilitate mechanisms for managing expertise for the collective good and identifying the roles that each team member will play.

Whilst this sounds straightforward, it may not be easy. Most people value their individuality and independence, taking responsibility for their choice of assignment and their own outcomes within the organizational context. They may be content to work in a group but usually expect to be assessed and rewarded on their individual performance. Teamwork changes this as work and results are shared. The team is assessed on its collective outcome. It can even be promoted in this way. Team members jointly decide upon the choice of assignment, how the task will be accomplished, and their goals and rewards within the context of the overall environment.

With matrix structures the team builder has to get people to communicate, collaborate and work across teams and to align their goals and responsibilities to the service as a whole, rather than to their personal goals or that of a single team. The level of complexity in this task accelerates in the case of virtual teams. Here the team builder will be supporting people who rarely or may never physically work alongside each other but who communicate and collaborate through online collaboration and social media tools.

In the early stage of building teams, the builder has to balance the need to address concerns about individual loss of independence and control whilst building support for team decision making. Multi-skilling and changes to differentiation between professional and non-professional staff are some of the issues to be considered in building teams in information services.

Teamwork builds upon the principles of process re-engineering in that the whole of the activity associated with the provision of the service is managed within the team. Consequently, the team builder has to improve the coordination between team members and have the members of the team work together to deliver outcomes.

In information services, teams can be established to provide specialized services to specific client groups, where all team members are involved in planning, customer relationship management and supplier liaison. These may include self-managing work teams that consist of highly motivated specialists who do not have a formal hierarchy. They bring a variety of skills that they collectively use to deliver end products and services. They value the ability to operate independent of managers, being given a high degree of self-determination in the management of their work.

The success of teams rests on there being very high levels of trust and openness between the team members. Training is also essential to equip all team members with the necessary skills to carry out their cross-functional tasks and to address and manage interpersonal conflicts should they arise. Ensuring this is an important leadership role. Team members should be encouraged to discuss their perception of the situation and what is required of them as a team and in their individual roles.

The team builder needs to be competent at recognizing and resolving conflict. Negativity should not be allowed to grow to the extent where it can weaken the team's cohesiveness. Individual negativity can grow if attention is paid to it, so a judgement call needs to be made as to the reason and whether it is initially best ignored. In this instance, attention should be focused upon the positive energies of the team. If the negativity continues to the extent that it has the potential to be destructive, then the source of the negativity should be openly discussed and dealt with.

Teams also develop a culture of self-discipline. They develop group norms and values and work within these to exercise control over individuals without harming their egos. High performing team members care about the success and growth of others. In this way, teams can be a very supportive mechanism during times of stress and crisis.

In enhancing performance and quality, team communications and team building should encourage employees to review one another's work and suggest alternative ways of doing things. Working properly, teams can be highly creative and innovative in their provision of service and identification of solutions to issues.

Managing virtual teams

The global and virtual business world is resulting in projects and their respective teams being dispersed across geographic locations and spanning different time zones. Such teams also consist of people with different cultural backgrounds, languages spoken and diverse value systems. In addressing this issue, Siebdrat et al. (2009: 64) found that collaboration across distances was more difficult than in a collocated environment. Potential issues include difficulties in communication and coordination, reduced trust, and an increased inability to establish a common ground.

Whilst the regular physical presence of co-workers improves people's feelings of familiarity and fondness, physical distance decreases closeness and affinity, which then leads to a greater potential for conflict. Distance also brings with it other issues, such as team members having to negotiate different time zones and requiring them to reorganize their work days to accommodate others' schedules. On the plus side Siebdrat et al. list the exposure of team members to heterogeneous sources of work experience, feedback and networking opportunities as well as enhanced problem-solving capacities by bringing more vantage points to bear on projects and service delivery.

Managing virtual teams is more effective where processes are put in place that increase levels of mutual support, member effort, work coordination, balance of member contributions and task-related communications. Beyond having task-related processes, Siebdrat et al. found that organizations must also ensure that team members commit to the overall group goals, identify with the team and actively support the team spirit. Social-emotional processes are important in minimizing interpersonal differences that can affect a team's social stability because of the greater difficulty in resolving conflicts across geographic boundaries. Social processes that increase team cohesion, identification and informal communication help to establish and maintain interpersonal bonds that enable a group to better cope with conflicts.

In recruiting team members, those with strong social and teamwork skills should be considered rather than their expertise and availability. Siebdrat et al. also believe that beyond social skills, managers need to ensure that dispersed teams have broad-based leadership capabilities. Members need to be aware of the difficulties of dispersed collaboration and find effective ways to overcome these obstacles on their own. This highlights the need for people to be more self-sufficient in how they manage their own work because the team leader is less in a position to help.

Where possible, periodic face-to face meetings are effective in initiating key social processes. This will encourage informal communication, team identification and cohesion. Finally Siebdrat et al. indicate that having a global mindset, in which people see themselves as part of an international network, helps provide an environment that is conducive to virtual teams. Temporary staff assignments at foreign locations and inter-cultural training can assist the development of this mindset. Practices such as these advance the development of diversity-friendly attitudes and the ability to work in different contexts, which in turn help team members cope with the challenges of distance.

Managing interteam conflict

Interteam conflict occurs when members of a group or team perceive that they are being prevented from achieving their team goals by the actions of another group or team. Most interteam conflict in organizations occurs between work units or departments. This may be linked to differentiation in expertise or cultures. For example, technical support staff may feel that they are prevented from giving a good service to clients because of requirements by the finance or treasury department that all costs and work charge outs are documented in a time-consuming fashion.

Conflict may also occur between hierarchical levels over issues of power, authority and control. Proposed takeovers or mergers of teams or departments will lead to conflict on a hierarchical basis and on a horizontal basis for power and control.

Due to the differences in the technologies, values, work tasks and individuals' attributes in teams within large information services, some interteam conflict or rivalry will be ongoing. Such conflict will be productive by increasing team cohesiveness and output. It is a necessary part of subcultures within organizations. However, when conflicts emerge above the subculture level and become destructive or damaging to performance, managerial action should be taken.

In a major conflict situation, the cohesiveness of each team or department will increase, whilst communication between the conflicting departments will tend to decrease. The group that loses the conflict will find that it will also lose its cohesiveness. It is advantageous with any major conflict involving teams or departments that the issues are resolved quickly and in such a way that each party gains. A win-win situation can be achieved by skilful negotiation and setting a superordinate goal. That is, one that has to be achieved by the cooperation of both groups.

Conclusion

The need to be responsive to changing and complex environments has acted as a catalyst to the widespread utilization of teams or groups to achieve corporate objectives and business outcomes. Formal groups are created through formal authority and usually comprise:

- An executive management team;
- Work teams; and

- Task forces or project teams that perform specific tasks.

Individuals will also join informal groups that serve a personal interest and comprise like-minded people. Informal groups exist for a purpose or common interest and emerge within organizations without being formally designated by someone in authority for a specific purpose. The activities of the informal group may or may not match those of the organization.

As groups develop, they assume certain characteristics of group cohesiveness, group norms and member roles. This occurs through the four stages of group development:

- The forming stage occurs as individual members of the group become acquainted with each other and begin to test which interpersonal behaviours are acceptable and which are not. Group boundaries and group rules are defined;
- The storming is usually highly emotional, involving tension among members as each member wishes to retain their individuality and may resist the structure that is emerging. Interpersonal styles are clarified and negotiations take place in an effort to find ways of accomplishing group goals whilst satisfying individual needs;
- The norming stage begins the integration process. Each person begins to recognize and accept his or her role and those of others. The group becomes more cohesive and adopts group norms in order to achieve the group's goals; and
- The performing stage where the group is totally integrated and is able to focus on the situation at hand. Members accept the team's goals and help work towards meeting them.

Members of a group play different roles and their behaviours will change according to their role in the social structure of the group. Effective team building requires an acknowledgement of these roles and involves all of the leadership and facilitation skills that are required in extending individual performance whilst applying these to the team. The success of team building rests on there being very high levels of trust and openness between the team members and ensuring this is an important leadership role. The team builder also needs to be competent at recognizing and resolving conflict.

Finally interteam conflict also affects the cohesiveness and success of teams. Most interteam conflict in organizations occurs between work units or departments which may be linked to:

- Differentiation in expertise or cultures;
- Issues of power, authority and control; or
- Differences in the technologies, values, work tasks and individuals' attributes in teams.

Interteam conflict can increase competition and group productivity. However, like all forms of conflict it may have an adverse effect upon the performance of individuals and the information service. Therefore it is advantageous with any major conflict involving teams or departments that the issues are resolved quickly and in such a way that each party gains.

References

Barry, D. 1991. Managing the bossless team: Lessons in distributed leadership. *Organisational Dynamics*, summer, 31–47.

Siebdrat, F., Hoegl, M. and Ernst, H. 2009. How to manage virtual teams. *MIT Sloan Management Review*, 50(4), 63–68.

Further Reading

Druskat, V. and Wheeler, J.V. 2004. How to lead a self-managing team. *MIT Sloan Management Review*, summer, 65–71.

Edwards, A. and Wilson, J.R. 2004. *Implementing Virtual Teams: A Guide To Organizational and Human Factors*. Aldershot: Ashgate.

Ghais, S. 2005. *Extreme Facilitation: Guiding Groups Through Controversy and Complexity*. San Francisco: Jossey-Bass.

Kakabadse, A. et al. 2004. *Working in Organisations*. Aldershot: Ashgate.

Katzenbach, J.R. and Smith, D.K. 2005. The discipline of teams. *Harvard Business Review*, July– August, 162, 164–171.

Levi, D. 2010. *Group Dynamics for Teams*, 3rd edn. Thousand Oaks: SAGE.

13 *Effective Negotiation and Conflict Management*

Effective negotiating and conflict management are two necessary leadership skills that are required to sustain the equilibrium of an organization in rapidly changing and complex environments. The ability to negotiate effectively is a critical component in the leadership task of managing change and transforming organizations. For example it is used in:

- Strategically engaging and influencing stakeholders on aspects relating to the future sustainability of the organization e.g. in high level contract management or negotiations with financial institutions to obtain finances for the rapid expansion of the organization;
- Managing and minimizing the effect of change-induced conflict on individuals and within groups;
- Managing relationships between the organization and its customers or other external stakeholders; and
- Implementing decisions brought about by change and transformation.

The need for negotiation as part of conflict and change management is inevitable when:

- People feel threatened or confused either by external forces or internal adjustments;
- There is a disagreement about a course of action;
- There are differences in expectations such as in product quality or service delivery; or
- There is opposition, competition or conflict between individuals or groups, or within an individual or group such as for scarce resources.

Effective negotiation

Negotiation is a process in which two or more parties try to reach an agreement through compromise, persuasion and collaboration on matters where there are both common and conflicting goals. Whilst compromise is the cornerstone to negotiating, effective negotiation uses both compromise and collaboration. Collaboration enables the realization of common interests, whilst finding the middle ground on conflicting interests. Effective negotiating should result in shared meaning between the parties. That is, the convergence of values, views, attitudes, styles, perceptions or beliefs to enable a common view or action.

In using the tools of collaboration and compromise, negotiators have to strike a balance between being steadfast in their desires for certain outcomes whilst allowing concessions and being sufficiently cooperative with the other party to allow negotiations to take place. This is particularly true when personal interests or conflicts are at stake as emotions are prone to be far more volatile in these situations.

Willingness to accept trade-offs between short- and long-term gains is also important in order to effect a workable outcome. This is particularly true when negotiating the implementation of a decision or resolving conflict where it is inherent that the parties will need to continue to work with each other after the event. In some situations, negotiators must be willing to give up more than they would like in order to obtain a preferable long-term outcome. The result may be a less than perfect solution for the conceding party, but in the longer term faces may be saved and important working relationships preserved. A further positive outcome being that the parties understand a good deal more about each other than they may previously have known.

Leigh (2009: 152) identifies four classic negotiation mistakes. They are:

- Not bothering to understand the other side's problem and their interests; addressing and understanding these are ways of solving the issue that is at the centre of the negotiation process;
- Making price dominate everything. Focusing exclusively on price can turn a potentially cooperative process into an adversarial win/lose one;
- Neglecting the best alternative. Sometimes it is better to walk away from the process; and
- Skewing the vision or misreading the situation which may lead to negotiation errors.

Negotiation and conflict management

Conflict has traditionally been viewed as destructive; a state of affairs to be suppressed or eliminated. Managers now realize that conflict is inherent in complex and changing environments and that negotiations should focus on resolving those conflicts that have the potential to affect the equilibrium of the organization. In many instances conflict is a sign of a healthy organization. Conflict of a competitive nature generally leads to improved organizational performance. Throughout history, potentially damaging encounters with natural and physical sources have led to the adaptation of a species, race or community that has been essential for its growth and survival. In a corporate context these encounters and adaptations can be experienced by individuals, teams or the whole organization and result in changes and solutions that are creative or innovative. For instance, budgetary pressures can lead to redesigning services that are new and imaginative.

Conflict is a source of intelligence and feedback to management as it brings issues to the surface. Under stress, individuals are more likely to express their real feelings or problems, which makes it easier to identify and resolve the real issues of concern. As part of the negotiation process in resolving the conflict, issues can be addressed that otherwise may never have surfaced.

Not all situations of conflict require management involvement and negotiation. Some conflict should be left to run its course. Minor conflict can act as a safety valve preventing pressure from building up to the point where it is destructive. For example petty complaints are often examples of tension release. Conflict can serve as a unifying function within a group. Internal differences are often overcome when a group is faced with an external source of conflict. For example, in a financial crisis or if a merger is mooted, people will work more closely together to sustain the organization through the bad times, or in terms of the merger, to be the dominant force in the new organization.

Sources of organizational conflict

Individuals and groups have two drives; to maintain psychological equilibrium and harmony and to actualize their potential. Conflict arises when an individual or group perceives either a threat or opposition to one or both of these drives; when two antagonistic drives or needs have to be satisfied simultaneously; or where there is a tendency to simultaneously accept and reject a course of action.

Conflict is inevitable in changing environments and in situations where there is competition for the use of scarce resources such as in the preparation and finalizing of budgets, industrial relations negotiations, contract management and policy development and implementation. Other sources of conflict include the organizational differentiation, uncertainty about change, organizational growth, role expectations, communication channels, interpersonal relations and behaviours, personal interests of individuals or groups, physical separations and the dependency of one party on another.

ORGANIZATIONAL DIFFERENTIATION

The greater the differentiation between the values and workplace situations of teams or work groups, the greater the likelihood of conflict and the need for mechanisms that will integrate these groups. This is particularly true for individuals working in teams in information services who undertake different kinds of work, often in different locations, and which often require different time horizons, values, goals and management styles. In the case of virtual or transnational teams, some members of the team may never physically meet.

Opportunities for conflict and the misunderstanding of values and personal situations also occur when:

- There is flexibility in the workplace that is not well managed;
- Integrating services such as combining cultural services to deliver one-stop customer services;
- There is an expectation by global organizations that very different groups or work units will integrate their efforts towards accomplishing organizational objectives without having given due regard to understanding of their cultural differences; or
- Groups of people are physically separated by location or shiftwork or have to work rostered hours in order to support customer services.

UNCERTAINTY ABOUT CHANGE

Complexity and continually changing environments bring about uncertainty and repositioning that will inevitably lead to conflict between individuals or groups as each strives for their continued existence and new order in the changed circumstances. The knowledge that new skills will have to be learnt or alternatively may be acquired through external recruitment, together with uncertainty and a concern for their future, will leave some individuals feeling vulnerable.

Where the future is certain, activities are routine and predictable. In the constantly changing environments that are typical of today, the basic rules and regulations are no longer relevant. As a result, conflicting opinions may arise as new problems have to be solved and new systems and policies are established. Conflict can also arise where the new policies, structures, practices and procedures are not in the main interests of some of the parties. This is particularly so where a new structure changes the sphere of influence or removes the decision making or responsibility from one of the parties.

ORGANIZATIONAL GROWTH

For similar reasons to uncertainty brought about by change, conflict can also arise through organizational growth. As information services grow to meet new service needs, new systems and policies evolve that govern tasks and behaviour. Communication and reporting channels may change as additional levels, functions or groups are created. Conflict will arise as individuals and work units vie to assume the higher positions in the hierarchy and either gain or lose their levels of influence as an outcome.

COMPETITION FOR RESOURCES

Resources that are scarce and in demand, particularly in times of constrained finances or determine the interdependence and independence of teams or departments, are another source of conflict. Teams or groups that have to share resources such as motor vehicles or photocopiers may require them simultaneously, resulting in conflict over ownership where one party may seek to impose their systems or requirements on others. To overcome this, units may strive for their independence, thereby creating further tensions and conflict as they demand their own. The perception that teams 'own' their vehicles or equipment, rather than seeing them as a corporate resource, often exacerbates the reluctance to share with others.

PROFESSIONAL TERMINOLOGY

The use of acronyms and specific terminology associated with an area of expertise can lead to distortion and conflict as they are not always recognized or interpreted by others in the same way. Likewise, technical terminology or acronyms that describe events or objects can also threaten people who do not understand their meaning.

Table 13.1 outlines some mechanisms for identifying or bringing any underlying conflict to the attention of the information services manager.

Table 13.1   Mechanisms for identifying conflict in organizations

Conflict identification mechanism	Description
Grievance Procedures	Formal grievance procedures enable dissatisfaction to be communicated to management through official channels. The process assumes that the individual has the courage to complain and to make a formal approach in addition to there being objective and independent people who can be approached. Grievance procedures are most effective when appropriate confidentiality can be assured and where appropriate training in managing grievance processes is provided
Observation	Interpersonal sensitivity, listening and direct observation can often identify interpersonal or intergroup conflicts. Conflicting motives are usually apparent when clashes between individuals or groups occur or work output deteriorates
Internet Grapevines and Suggestion Boxes	Grapevines and suggestion boxes on corporate intranets, social networks, chat or instant messaging can be used as gripe boxes enabling issues to be identified and resolved quickly. Monitoring is important to ensure that individuals are not unduly targeted or defamed; to manage sensitive, private or delicate issues and to respond quickly with objective answers. Anonymous suggestions should also be allowed
Open-door policy	An open-door policy is an effective means of creating an open environment where conflict can be identified and resolved
Exit interviews	Exit interviews provide employees with the opportunity to discuss sensitive matters when they have no further affiliation with the organization. However if unfortunate situations have lead to the resignation of an employee they may not be willing to discuss their dissatisfaction for fear that this may affect a future job reference. The interviewer should be impartial and stress the positive outcomes of the exit interview for resolving future conflicting situations

Sources of personal conflict

At any point in time in organizations there will be individuals who are faced with personal conflict, the source of which may or may not be from within the organization. For example, there may be a conflict of interest between an individual's professional values and organizational demands, or the individual may be dealing with a health matter that interferes with their ability to concentrate on their work. It should be noted that in this chapter the examination of a conflict of interest is of a personal kind rather than as a term used for a situation arising from conflict between the performance of public duty and private or personal interests which could place public confidence in the integrity of an organization at risk. Information on conflict of interest in an ethical setting is found elsewhere in the book.

Conflicts of interest in a non-ethical setting can arise where an individual experiences a dilemma in balancing their time and priorities to meet the needs of the job, to have a home life and care for dependants, to further a professional career, and to pursue personal interests. All of which are important. The conflict may be identified through feelings of guilt or being pressurized to give more attention to one aspect of life than another.

Role conflict also occurs where the information services manager has to compete vigorously for funds with other managers during budget deliberations, yet needs to cooperate at all other times with these as peers.

IDENTIFYING PERSONAL CONFLICT

When faced with conflict an individual's natural instinct (which is common to all living things) is to react through either 'fight' or 'flight'. Either method of conduct is an attempt to adjust to the conflict situation. So to assist individuals to adjust to conflict and substitute acceptable and efficient attitudes and responses, there needs to be an understanding of what lies behind their conduct.

If a reliable staff member suddenly begins to act unpredictably, their actions may be a symptom of conflict. The cause or source of conflict may not be within the information service, but its effect will most certainly be felt there. In such a situation, it is the manager's responsibility to try to help resolve the conflict either by providing advice or by referring the individual to an appropriate source of advice. If the source of the conflict lies within the information service's control the manager must help resolve the issue. If the source is beyond the manager's control, they can choose whether or not to be involved. However, their involvement becomes essential when other staff begin to be affected.

Fight or aggression can be identified by negativism, dominance, displaced anger or hostility. A member of staff may be contentious for no apparent reason or rebellious without cause. Some individuals may become uncharacteristically domineering towards their peers or fellow workers; or instances of anger will be levelled at colleagues rather than management. Others may become sarcastic, or make cutting comments or criticize. All of these are symptoms of an underlying conflict that must be resolved.

Flight can be identified by absenteeism, apathy or hypochondria. A staff member who suddenly begins to arrive late for work or absents themselves from others by being aloof or refusing to become involved is using flight as an escape mechanism from a source of conflict. Other examples of flight are daydreaming and absent-mindedness, an overindulgence in food, substance abuse or continual tiredness.

Occasionally other adjustments to conflict are made. The individual may establish defence mechanisms or perform attention-getting activities in an effort towards self-deception. Compensation tactics may be used in order to reduce the sense of uselessness. The individual may substitute satisfaction in one kind of achievement for the lack of it in another. For example, the person may put more personal energies into sporting activities than their work.

A less well-adjusted form of compensation is used when an individual will bask in the reflected glory of another. Individuals may also push the blame on to someone or something else, such as the boss or personal computer, or attribute to others the faults that really reside in themselves.

Resolving conflict through negotiation

The effective resolution of conflict is critical in ensuring that a potentially damaging situation is turned into a positive outcome for all parties. There are various methods and styles for resolving conflict. Some are more effective than others. In most instances, it depends upon the conflict situation. If the changes in an individual's behaviour are temporary and subtle then the individual should be offered understanding and informal support. However where the individual's or group's actions and behaviours begin to affect the output of others the conflict will need to be formally resolved. It is also important to note that conflict might also become apparent and need to be resolved through communication channels such as in emails and social media.

Most conflict resolution methods involve a process of negotiation. Negotiations are not only needed in a manager and team member situation; they are required in peer-to-peer debates and in resolving differences in opinions and expectations between the organization, customers and other external stakeholders.

THE PROCESS OF NEGOTIATION

The first stage

The initial meeting of the parties establishes the climate that prevails during the ensuing negotiations. The atmosphere created in the first few minutes of the meeting and greeting stage is critical. Tensions need to be relaxed so that commonsense prevails, rather than outright confrontation. Non-verbal clues such as eye contact, posture, gestures and patterns of movement will add to the feeling of the meeting.

The first meeting is usually devoted to establishing the bargaining authority possessed by representatives on both sides. If the parties are unknown to each other, a 'pecking' order will be established and personal interactions developed. The negotiating rules and procedures will also be determined. This stage may be omitted where all parties are known to each other as the negotiating rules and procedures will be well established.

The second stage

The second stage is characterized by each side attempting to consider the opponent's position without revealing its own. Each side will try to avoid disclosing the key important factors in their proposal in order to avoid being forced to pay a higher price than is necessary to have the proposal accepted. Negotiators will also attempt to get greater concessions in return for granting those requests that their opponents want most.

The proposals may be discussed in the order of their appearance on the agenda or in some other sequence. The sequence in which they are discussed may also be a subject for negotiation. If the discussion of the most important issues is deferred until last, this can often serve as leverage for gaining agreement on more minor issues that precede the important ones.

The settlement

A process of haggling, bargaining and settling then begins. The proposals are resolved at a stage when agreement is reached within the limits that each party is willing to concede. The agreement is then ratified. In settling and ratifying the agreement, all the points and concessions of the agreement should be summarized and all actions accounted for. A record should be produced that accurately reports what was achieved. Finally, responsibility should be allocated to individuals or groups for the implementation of the agreement.

CONFLICT RESOLUTION METHODS

Conflicts are often resolved in three ways, win-lose, lose-lose or win-win. The results or outcomes of the first two are not always desirable.

Win-lose methods

In win-lose methods one party inevitably wins and the other inevitably loses. Win-lose methods constitute an authoritarian approach to conflict resolution as legitimate or coercive power is often used to bring about compliance. The dominant party will pursue their own outcomes at the expense of others, and the other party will be forced into submission, often by the use of threats. In organizations, majority rule and the failure of the managers or team leaders to respond to requests for change are also considered to be win-lose methods.

Whilst win-lose methods may prove satisfactory to the winner they can result in resentment and have negative effects on future relationships and the performance of individuals and the organization. Win-lose methods can sometimes lead to grudges or retaliatory action that may cause a further breakdown in the relationship and the associated loss of control will affect work output. Respect for the other party will be diminished.

Lose-lose methods

Lose-lose methods leave no one entirely happy. One such method is the compromise. This is based on the assumption that half a solution is better than none. Another lose-lose strategy involves side payments. One party agrees to a solution in exchange for a favour from the other party. A third strategy is to submit the issue to a neutral third party. The results of this action may be disappointing as arbitrators frequently resolve issues at some middle ground between the positions held by the disputants. Although each gains something, the outcome is rarely satisfying to either side.

Win-win methods

Win-win methods provide a solution that is acceptable to all. Win-win conflict resolution strategies focus upon ends and goals, identifying the sources of conflict and then presenting these as problems to be solved. Superordinate goals (goals that are greater than those of the individual, team or organization) are established. These reflect the objectives or outcomes that all parties must work towards.

The identification of the superordinate goals reminds conflicting parties that even though their particular goals are vitally important, they share a goal that cannot be achieved without cooperation. The win-win approach uses participative management techniques in order to gain consensus and commitment to objectives. The desired solution is one that achieves both individual or work unit goals and the organization's objectives, and which is acceptable to all parties.

Table 13.2 Conflict management resolution model

Style	Avoidance Style	Smoothing Style	Forcing Style	Compromise Style	Collaborative Style
Style Characteristics	Denial that a problem exists or avoidance of the issue. The person may try to remain neutral or withdraw from conflict, e.g. being unavailable, deferring answering an email, not returning phone calls, or refusing to be involved in the conflict	Minimizing or suppression of open recognition of real or perceived differences. Emphasizes common interests. Acts as if the conflict will pass with time. Appeals for cooperation. Reassuring and providing support to the parties in attempt to reduce tensions	Use of coercive or reward power to dominate the other party. Suppresses differences and forces the other party into adopting the lesser position. Results in winners and losers and can create more conflict	Often used when negotiating. Tendency to sacrifice positions when seeking a middle ground for the resolution of conflict. Can compromise exploration of nature of the conflict so real issues surface much later in the negotiating or resolution process	Uses win-win style. Willing to identify underlying causes of conflict, openly share information, and search out alternatives considered to be mutually beneficial. Open evaluation, sharing and assessing reasons for the conflict and alternatives
Circumstances in which style is best used	Where the issue is of minor or passing importance and is not worth the time or energy to confront it. Where bringing attention to the issue will fuel its intensity in a detrimental way. Where the person's power is so low that there is little or no positive outcome by being involved. Where others can more effectively resolve the conflict themselves	Effective in short-term situations when there is a potentially explosive emotional situation that needs to be defused. Where harmonious relationships need to be preserved or where the avoidance of disruption is important. Where the conflicts are of a personal nature between individuals and cannot be dealt with within the organizational context	When there is an extreme urgency and quick action is needed. Where there has been constant deliberation between the parties with no resulting outcome. When an unpopular course of action is necessary for the long-term survival of the information service. As self-protection when a person is being taken advantage of by another party	When both parties recognize that there is a possibility of reaching an agreement that is more advantageous than if no agreement was reached. Where there is a likelihood that more than one agreement could be reached. Where there are conflicting goals	When individuals have common goals. When consensus should lead to the best overall solution to the conflict. Where there is a need to make high-quality decisions on the basis of knowledge and expertise

CONFLICT RESOLUTION STYLES

Accompanying these conflict resolution methods are several different styles that can be used in managing and resolving conflict. Each has its purpose and, if used appropriately, will be successful. Table 13.2 describes each style and the circumstances in which it should be used.

Issues that can affect the success of negotiations and conflict resolution

STRESS

High levels of stress and tension can have a debilitating effect on organizations and negotiations. Stress and tension have the potential to generate greater hostility among those involved in potential conflict situations and impact the conflict management, resolution and negotiation processes. They can result in harder bargaining strategies and less successful outcomes. Increases in tension beyond a certain point may make members of either party less capable of evaluating information and making the fine discriminations necessary in order to achieve a mutually satisfying solution.

It is important that negotiators are aware of their own personal stress levels when undertaking any negotiating procedures. They should monitor their tensions, looking for physical symptoms such as aggression or tension headaches.

CONSERVING THE POSITION

The psychological need to impress others and maintain a reputation of strength is poignant in conflict management, resolution and negotiation. Taken too far, it is likely to lead to rigid and contentious demands that may spoil the conflict resolution and negotiating process. Skilful negotiators like their concessions to be seen as a willingness to deal from a position of strength rather than a weakness. They also like their concessions to be allowed because of their competency and reputation as a good negotiator.

Some people find it tempting to adopt a forcing style, committing themselves to a tough negotiating position when discussions bog down, in an effort to impose such a considerable cost to the adversary that causes them to yield under pressure. This can result in a lose-lose outcome as an entrenched attitude will result either in the perpetrator having to retreat to their former position, losing credibility in the process, or opening the way to subsequent exploitation by the other. Generally, the threat of an impasse being reached when time expires is sufficient in itself for a result to be obtained closer to the time.

COMPLEX SITUATIONS

The complexity of the situation may increase the intricacies in conflict management, resolution and negotiations, with different parties developing different conceptions of the situation or preferring a different structure for handling the situation. These circumstances can also arise if one of the parties is someone who has not previously been involved in the process, or is not sufficiently knowledgeable or obligated to the issue at stake.

An impasse may result from the inability to resolve the differences, and a mediator may be required to alter perceptions or definitions of purpose on behalf of either party. This could delay or jeopardize the implementation of the negotiations. Therefore different negotiating strategies are necessary to suit different environments and different situations.

Similarly, not everyone may want to participate in the conflict resolution or negotiating process; some even may resist. There may also be a multiplicity of emotions that need to be managed as part of the conflict resolution and negotiation process.

PHYSICAL SURROUNDINGS

The physical properties of the meeting arrangements will affect the conflict resolution and negotiating atmosphere. For example the seating arrangements, size of room and shape and size of the table will place participants in a position that is either compromising or contending. Round tables are less threatening than square or oblong ones. Opposing parties will often want to sit opposite each other. This allows them to pick up their opposite members' non-verbal communication signals and places each party in a competitive position. At times when a compromise is to be achieved, opposing parties may sit next to each other. Sitting side by side neutralizes any feelings of competition or animosity between the parties.

AVAILABILITY OF TIME AND INFORMATION

The availability of time and information are critical factors in successful conflict resolution and negotiations. Time can be either a constriction or an advantage. As the deadline approaches, decisions will be made faster, leading to one party losing their demand power. Known time constraints may also result in one party holding their real negotiating process until close to the deadline, in order to place the other party in a more vulnerable or critical position. As the deadline of the other party comes close there may be a shift in power back to the first party.

If a deadlock is threatened there should be a break in the negotiating procedures. This can either be achieved by using a time break such as lunch or morning refreshments, or by talking about some aspect other than that where a deadlock is threatened. A mediator or third party may also be used to help the negotiating process at this stage.

Knowledge and information are critical to the conflict resolution and negotiation. Skilled negotiators quietly and consistently probe the other party for information. They listen rather than talk, asking questions rather than answering them. Sometimes the other party's credibility is tested by asking questions to which the answer is already known. Attentive listening and observation are critical as often unintentional clues can be given out.

Conclusion

Effective negotiation can be used in resolving conflict and implementing decisions, both of which are required in rapidly changing and complex environments. Whilst conflict may be destructive if it is not handled or negotiated correctly, it can be a healthy sign of organizational growth and competition and act as a catalyst for change. In fact, if conflict within an organization ceased, stagnation could set in.

Constructive conflict and competition will often result in the improved performance of individuals and teams. Conflict can also lead to a better understanding of different individuals' or groups' problems. The discussions that take place may find issues that can be resolved to the advantage of both parties, or identify common goals that were previously unknown or overlooked. Conflict also acts as a safety valve.

The sources of conflict and the resulting actions need to be effectively managed to ensure that only positive outcomes arise from conflict. Sources of conflict include the organizational differentiation, uncertainty about change, organizational growth, competition for the use of scarce resources, role expectations, communication channels, interpersonal relations and behaviours, personal interests of individuals or groups, physical separations and the dependency of one party on another. The greater the differentiation between the values and workplace situations of teams or work groups, the greater the likelihood of conflict and the need for mechanisms that will integrate these groups.

Sources of underlying conflict can be detected through having formal grievance procedures in place, through observation, using electronic grapevines and suggestion boxes and through the use of exit interviews.

Conflict can also be found at a personal level such as where an individual experiences a dilemma in balancing their time and priorities to meet the needs of the job, to have a home life and care for dependants, to further a professional career, and to pursue personal interests. If the source of the conflict lies within the information service's control the manager must help resolve the issue. If the source is beyond the manager's control, they can choose whether or not to be involved. However, their involvement becomes essential when other staff begin to be affected.

Effective conflict management, resolution and negotiation are critical in ensuring that a potentially damaging situation is turned into a positive outcome for all parties. There are various methods and styles for negotiating and resolving conflict i.e. through win-lose, lose-lose and win-win methods; each of which can have a place depending on the situation. There are also different styles in negotiating and conflict resolution.

Finally stress, people's attitudes, the complexity of the situation, physical surroundings and availability of time and information can all affect the conflict resolution and negotiating processes.

References

Leigh, A. 2009. *The Secrets of Success in Management: 20 Ways to Survive and Thrive*. Harlow: Pearson.

Further reading

Conflict: From Analysis to Intervention, 2nd edn. 2008. New York: Continuum.

Fells, R.E. 2009. *Effective Negotiation: From Research to Results*. Cambridge: Cambridge University Press.

McConnon, S. and McConnon, M. 2008. *Conflict Management in the Workplace: How to Manage Disagreements and Develop Trust and Understanding*, 3rd edn. Oxford: How To Books.

Malhotra, D. and Bazerman, M.H. 2008. *Negotiation Genius: How to Overcome Obstacles and Achieve Brilliant Results at the Bargaining Table and Beyond*. New York: Bantam.

Mayer, B.S. 2009. *Staying with Conflict: A Strategic Approach to Ongoing Disputes*. San Francisco: Jossey-Bass.

Roberto, M.A. 2005. *Why Great Leaders Don't Take Yes For an Answer: Managing for Conflict and Consensus*. Upper Saddle River: Wharton School.

Tidd, S.T. et al. 2004. The importance of role ambiguity and trust in conflict perception: Unpacking the task conflict to relationship conflict linkage. *International Journal of Conflict*, 15(4), 364–384.

14 *Managing the Political Arena*

Managing the political arena is an important and unavoidable leadership role. This is because political behaviour is a natural process within organizations. It is both an individual and organizational phenomenon, linked to leadership style, power, influence and competition and different values and interests. Even if everyone's interests are catered for, there can be a perception that some individuals, groups or organizational units have been treated more favourably than others. The basis for this is often politics and the personal interpretation of facts. It is inevitable in a competitive environment that people will personally interpret the facts to support their own, or their organizational unit's needs and objectives.

The activity of organizational politics is evident in the competitive behaviour between groups or individuals. Usually this is to ensure that they achieve a higher level of recognition, resource allocation, power or persuasion than their counterparts. To be effective in competitive organizational environments, it is vital that information services managers and their staff identify the political behaviours of others and manage their own. They need also to be aware that, even if their actions are not personally politically motivated, others may assume so.

Most politics and competition are beneficial to organizations as they increase the motivation and output of the various programme units or work groups. Influencing or attempting to influence the distribution of advantages and disadvantages within the organization for the benefit of the information service is part of the role of the manager. However, if unchecked politics or political behaviour are used to further an individual's needs at the expense of others it can be detrimental to all concerned. In considering whether the tactics should be condoned, the deciding feature should be the ethical impact upon the organization and individuals.

Understanding organizational politics

Generally, the higher the individual is in the organization, the more political their position will be. This is because senior managers need to extend their influence beyond and across organizational boundaries to achieve successful outcomes. At this level, the organizational environment is often turbulent and very competitive, with the decisions made at senior management level sometimes being politically influenced.

The political role of the information services manager is to make things happen. This requires them to create a vision and convey this to others meaningfully. For information services managers this is likely to be creating a vision and understanding in the minds of executive management of the benefits and critical importance that information sharing and knowledge management have to the success of the organization. To move the vision forward, they must know how to get things done within the parent organization and use their power constructively to drive the change. This requires them to interpret the political environment correctly, to 'open doors', to identify supporters and sponsors, and to build networks quickly, gaining commitment and support. Noting the importance of political behaviour, Pors and Johannsen (2003: 57) included political actions as part of a study on library leadership:

- The director has to make the library visible in the political system;
- The director's political legitimacy will be very important; and
- The director must create political contacts and networks.

Information services managers who are politically astute know what is going on within the parent organization and have control over the rules of the political game. They manage the boundaries of the information service so that it is viewed in a favourable light by those in positions of authority. Skilled political managers understand what the parent organization wants and position their services to provide creative solutions to the important problems facing the organization. They stay focused and do not let distractions or operational tasks sidetrack them.

In their political role, information services managers must speak the language that is understood and valued by the senior decision-makers. They regard everyone within the parent organization as a customer and pay attention to how they project their personal image and that of the information service. To illustrate this Wilson and Corrall (2008: 474) quote Kent's (2002) perspective of leadership for public library leaders who must be in a position of 'respect and credibility', and seen and valued as equals to other political, cultural and educational leaders in their respective communities and authorities. Kent further comments that the contemporary public library leader must incorporate an ability and willingness to 'sell' the public service while maintaining credibility as a 'non-politicised individual in a politicised environment', balancing commercial expertise, political acumen and a service to the 'public good'.

Political gamesmanship will occur in times of constraint when resources are scarce, when those in control feel threatened such as when integrating services, or where there are competing views, values or agendas. Not all organizations (or groups) are as conspicuous in their political behaviour as others. In some organizations politics are overt and rampant, whilst in others politics are virtually non-existent. Furthermore, some organizations refuse to admit that political behaviour exists, preferring to believe that all is well. Usually this is because they are ill equipped to manage the conflict that is often associated with political behaviour.

The extent and type of political behaviour in organizations is influenced by the internal and external environment. Organizations that operate under pressure, have a role ambiguity or a low level of trust amongst employees are more likely to witness an overt and Machiavellian style of political behaviour than those that have clear and objective performance measures, an open and trusting environment and plenty of resources.

In bureaucratic organizations the politics will emphasize standards of control, rules, policies and procedures. The power of particular individuals to control and enforce adherence to these will lead to internal politics. In organizations that are less traditional, more open and free thinking there will be little emphasis on these aspects. Here the politics will operate within units, work teams or groups, and stress trust and cooperation.

In diverse organizations where there are different objectives, processes and service delivery mechanisms within units or groups, politics and conflict will often arise through misunderstanding and a lack of knowledge of others' tasks and responsibilities. The diverse structures within information services may create an environment where conflict and political rivalry may occur. For example, helpdesk people or reader services librarians who are used to dealing with diverse and immediate demands of customers may view technical service personnel as inflexible, bureaucratic or bogged down with unnecessary standards and rules. Technical service personnel may likewise view customer services personnel with suspicion.

In changing and competitive organizational environments, the competition and uncertainty leads to differences of opinions and values, and conflicts over priorities and goals. This is true regardless of the size of the organizational unit. Whilst there will be no internal competition in a cost centre run by one person, the person would still need to compete for resources. Their power, influence and political persuasion must still be used on an organization-wide basis. Competition also leads to the formation of pressure groups, lobbying, cliques and cabals, rivalry, personality clashes and alliances. All of which are evidence of organization politics.

Politics and competition are beneficial to all organizations as they usually result in increased output between the competing groups or individuals. However, unchecked politics can result in the organization losing its sense of direction, or in its spending too much time resolving the problems at the expense of pursuing its corporate objectives.

Political behaviour that is used to further an individual's own needs may be damaging to others or the organization. An example would be an individual who influences management's perception of a co-worker to the extent that the co-worker was viewed unfavourably for promotion. This is the negative side of political behaviour and should be neutralized.

Political tactics

Politics is unavoidable and a necessary part of life. People have in the past and will continue in the future to engage in political behaviour to further their own ends, to protect themselves from others, to further goals which they believe to be in the organization's best interests, or to acquire and exercise power. Even if an individual perceives politics to be unethical, they cannot help but be occasionally involved in political battles and political networks.

Individuals who regularly engage in political behaviour often exhibit certain traits that characterize their political style. Those who are highly competitive and have excessively high self-actualization and power needs are more likely to be involved in a Machiavellian political behaviour. They look for career shortcuts and quick fixes. Other traits include the willingness to manipulate people or situations, a high need for control and the ability to exploit situations for their own self-interest.

A second type of political behaviour is the collaborative style. People who have a collaborative style get things done through others based on knowledge, rapport and respect. They build networks of important people by serving on and contributing to strategic committees. They keep people informed and build their power based upon knowledge and doing favours for others.

Whilst organization politics may be viewed ambivalently, most people will regard any political tactics that are used by individuals for their personal gain at the expense of others as being unhealthy and unfair. Political tactics can also be genuine, ethical practices that can be beneficial to the organization.

The information services manager should readily be able to identify and use intra-organizational politics for their own benefit and that of the information service. Becoming a 'political animal' takes considerable skill, and necessitates the exercise of

Table 14.1 Ethical and unethical political tactics used in organizations

Clean tactics (ethical)	Dirty tactics (unethical)
Establishing an alliance with others who are willing to support the preferred position or action These may include peers, subordinates and the executive – but it is important that the right allies are chosen. These should be people who have something to contribute and who can be relied upon. Arising out of such an alliance can be the formation of a powerful coalition	Attacking or blaming others Creating a scapegoat by falsely attributing blame for negative outcomes to others is both unethical and unprofessional. A test of leadership is accepting responsibility for: • taking charge of adverse situations • all outcomes – good or bad
Choosing a powerful mentor Having an influential mentor can be beneficial to one's career. Such a relationship can be an effective tactic to acquiring power as others view associates of powerful people as being powerful themselves – part of the aura is passed on. Powerful mentors can assist in the reaching of important goals by 'opening doors' or helping to establish networks. They can also provide protection and guidance when necessary, a valuable asset in tough times	Deliberately misleading others Creating perceptions or holding others responsible for events they did not create
Developing a base support for one's ideas In effect it enhances the individual's personal power base through the use of reverent power. Once a base of support for one's idea is gained, the supporters will want to identify with the individual and the idea	Use of hidden agendas Announcing one agenda for meetings and then following a totally different 'hidden' one. Preventing opponents from being adequately prepared
Creating obligations and basis for reciprocity IOUs can be scattered by doing favours for others, assisting them solve problems or supporting them against their detractors. All these actions will place them in debt. Effective users of these strategies will always gain more than they give. The value of a favour may be worth more to the receiver that the provider, the providers usually find the favours smaller and easy to perform	

caution because, if the tactics are used inappropriately, the exercise will almost certainly backfire. In particular they need to be skilful at identifying and taking action against political tactics that are adversely affecting them or their service.

There are several effective political tactics which are commonly used in organizations. Some of these are ethical, others are not (see Table 14.1).

In deciding which tactics are ethical or unethical, the impact of the political behaviour upon the rights of others should be addressed. If basic human rights are violated, the political tactics are unethical. The principles of equity and fair play should also be considered, both in terms of individuals and the organization. Often political behaviour is judged according to a utilitarian approach, being the greatest good for the greatest number. Where behaviours are viewed as unethical or illegitimate they should be made to cease immediately.

Several steps can be used by the manager or supervisor to minimize the political behaviour of subordinates where it can be seen to be detrimental to their position or that of the information service. These include bringing dispute or disagreements into the open where they can be solved, and providing challenging situations and feedback to all.

Presenting political arguments

Not all dealings with people can be face-to-face where there is the ability to respond to verbal and non-verbal messages to reinforce the political argument. Similarly, the information services manager may not always be present at meetings to respond to questions, reinforce arguments or apply political persuasion. Therefore skills in presenting political arguments in reports are needed.

In presenting arguments, it is important that each item is properly researched and simply portrayed with the appropriate level of detail and content. Often the audience will have little time to read and consider the report. The more explicit and lucid the comment, the more favourably the report is likely to be received.

The contents of the report should anticipate and answer likely questions and be self-explanatory. The argument being presented should be able to stand on its own accord. Reports should include an executive summary that covers the important issues, benefits and recommendations for action. In some situations the executive summary can be the only part of the report that is read, so it should articulate the main points that will lead the decision-makers to a favourable outcome.

The full body of the report should be clearly signposted. It should be broken down into headings and subheadings to make it easy to read and find relevant information. It should include an introductory heading, an introduction, current information on the subject of the report, viable alternative courses of action, and a recommendation(s). The opening paragraph of the main body of the report should summarize any previous history or background and indicate why the report is necessary. The current situation should be described providing up-to-date, relevant information in as precise and brief a form as possible. The alternative courses of action should be identified. These should discuss the relevant advantages, disadvantages, costings and outcomes. A preferred option should be recommended with reasons where applicable.

Sometimes political statements may need to be made or data or information released to prove a point of conjecture or to garner support from a wider community of stakeholders.

Examples include the release of usage figures to support a case for increased funding or to prove a point in the case of imminent funding cuts. How political statements are made should be carefully planned so that they do not backfire or violate the organization's code of behaviour or employment regime. The target audience should be well researched and the statement tailored to appeal to their likely viewpoint. Any data used should be that available in the public domain and not include any information of a personal or commercial-in-confidence nature.

Lobbying and lobby groups

Lobbying is an attempt to influence decisions at the ownership level through persuasion and the provision of information. Occasionally the information services manager may lobby as a political strategy when there are important issues for the information service at stake.

Good communication channels between all levels of the organization will enhance the spread of information. At times, it may be necessary to supply additional information which will further the information service's cause. Lobbying occurs when this is provided to higher levels, either verbally or in writing, in an attempt to influence the decisions. Lobbying is a legitimate practice if used positively and with care and thought.

The information services manager may also be the subject of lobbying from lobby groups or industry. Lobby groups are a form of political group that attempt to impose their view or influence others. They may try to influence the information service on some issues, or see it as a vehicle through which their cause may be further supported.

Lobby groups that result from organized interest groups are features of modern democratic societies. The information services manager should balance the lobby group's concerns with the overall needs of the customers, the community and industry's desires with the requirement for probity. This should be to ensure that no one sector of the community or industry influences the services to the detriment of others.

Lobby groups often regard government as a pervasive and powerful source, influencing every facet of an individual's life. Most information services are also seen to be influential as information is perceived to be power. Lobby groups may attempt to make the information service an avenue through which their point of view is promulgated to the detriment of the opposing point of view.

Lobby or interest groups can constitute the principal potential avenue of influence outside official government interaction. They need to be considered but not allowed to impose their requirements upon the organization. If possible, their energies should be channelled in a direction that can help the information service and its parent organization.

Conclusion

Politics is a natural process within organizations, as individuals and work units compete for recognition and scarce resources. Politics is also about the distribution of advantages and disadvantages and how individuals use their power and influence in this distribution process. Whilst those who lose may perceive politics to be unfair, many are quite ethical.

However, unchecked or unethical politics are unfair. They have the capacity to harm the organization as well as its people and should not be tolerated within the organizational culture.

To be successful in a competitive environment it is important that the information services manager is politically astute and able to engage with key decision-makers in a way that they can understand the issues and opportunities that the information service can present, as well as manage the organizational politics for the benefit of the information service.

References

Pors, N.O. and Johannsen, C.G. 2003. Library directors under cross-pressure between new public management and value-based management. *Library Management*, 24(1/2), 51–60.

Wilson, K. and Corrall, S. 2008. Developing public library managers as leaders: Evaluation of a national leadership development programme. *Library Management*, 29(6/7), 473–488.

Further reading

Bacharach, S.B. 2005. Successful leaders are politically competent. *Leadership Excellence*, June, 6–7.

Kakabadse, A. et al. 2004. *Working in Organisations*. Aldershot: Ashgate.

15 *Policy Making*

Organizations are made up of individuals and groups of people with different values and interests. Policy making is one mechanism to ensure that these individual interests are managed for the greater good, and to ensure that individuals within the organization are moving forward in the same direction. Policy making is also necessary to safeguard individual rights such as in the case of policies on the protection of privacy and commercial confidentiality. Codes of conduct that guide behaviours such as how social networking tools can be used in organizations are also considered policies.

Policy development is an ongoing process that evolves through continuous consultation with internal and external stakeholders. The information service and its parent organization can also be subject to policies and standards that have been established by external parties, such as government bodies or international standard-setting organizations.

Using policies, standards and guidelines

Policy making incorporates the development of policies, standards and guidelines that ensure decisions are in keeping with the organization's philosophies. They can be used to enhance the image of the parent organization as a good corporate citizen. Policies, standards and guidelines are used within organizations to:

- Solve a recurrent problem at the organizational level;
- Provide guidance for individuals in decision making;
- Ensure consistency in approach across the organization;
- Declare an intention or enable a stance to be taken on a contemporary issue;
- Clarify organizational values and intentions;
- Make a commitment; and
- Grant rights or entitlements.

Examples of information service policies include those that determine the type of material eligible to be archived, provide guidance for the personal and professional use of social media in the organization, or how information services and products will be charged to clients. Examples of standards include naming standards for records or data capture and transfer standards.

Policies, standards and guidelines are usually promulgated on the organization's intranet as this is a convenient way of ensuring that everyone has access. Many organizations may also have a set of unwritten rules or policies. Putting policies on the intranet avoids duplication of effort and eliminates the possibility of out-of-date policy material being used in decision making. Making new members of staff aware of the policies and their existence on the intranet is an important part of the induction process.

Policy framework

The policy framework of an information service comprises policies, standards and guidelines. It may also include codes of practice on issues such as social media engagement. Standards differ from policies in that they are usually technical in nature. They define levels of conformity and input, and establish performance outputs. Guidelines supplement policies and standards, providing further background information. They are often used to provide advice regarding the implementation of the policy and standards.

POLICIES

Policies are guides to the decision-making process. Like objectives, policies can either be general or specific. General policies are used throughout the organization, and are usually broad and comprehensive. They affect all work units and levels of staff. General policies address issues such as the use of desktop equipment for home or personal use; or security and risk covering access to systems and the need to protect personal information. In the area of social media, Niall Cook (2008: 129) provides a good example of what needs to be included in such a policy:

- What employees absolutely cannot say – legal and moral obligations extend to comments left on others' blogs, not just company owned ones;
- Who to consult if employees are unsure – perhaps the line manager or HR team aren't the most appropriate people to advise in your organization;
- Guidelines for specific websites – for example, it's against Wikipedia's policies for a company to edit its own entry. Employees need to know this too;
- How to decide whether to engage – there are some arguments the company just won't win, so engagement might be a fruitless exercise;
- Being anonymous – don't be (you generally aren't anyway, even if you think you are);
- Pretending to be someone else – it may sound harmless to pretend to be a customer, but if employees get found out the impact on the company's reputation can be severe; and
- Letting others know about it – harness your employees to be the eyes and ears for interesting online conversations taking place about the company.

Some general policies will be influenced by legislation or policies and standards that have been established by external parties. For example, general policies on the protection and use of software may be influenced by copyright legislation or the parent organization's licence conditions with the software vendor.

Specific policies often relate to operational issues. They have significance for a particular department or work unit and are more relevant to day-to-day issues or specific

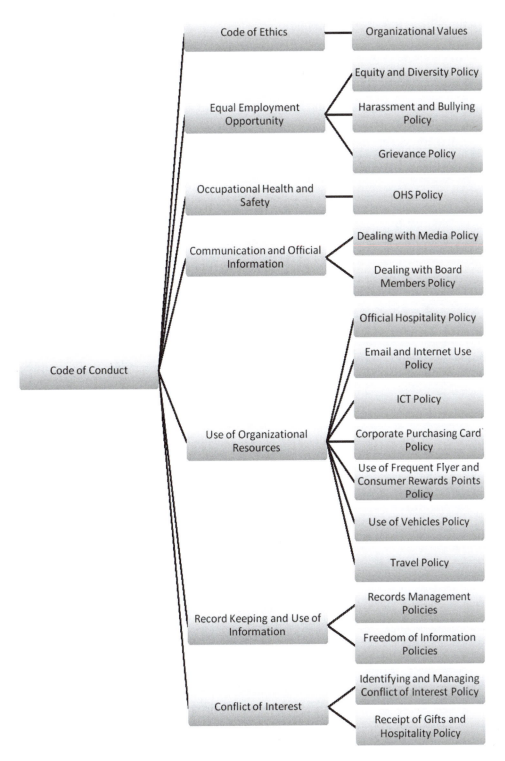

Figure 15.1 A sample policy framework to support a Code of Conduct

activities. Only those individuals who are directly concerned with the activity or work unit will be affected by the policy. A policy that relates to the selection process in a children's collection in a public library is an example of a specific policy.

The policy statement describes the policy. It is usually brief. The policy statement may be supplemented by statements about:

- The policy objective and scope;
- Responsibility for implementation, review and audit;
- Background issues; and
- Implementation strategies.

Figure 15.1 provides an example of a policy framework that may be used to support a code of conduct. It includes guidance on equal opportunity and occupational health and safety, communications and the use of official information, the use of organizational resources, record keeping and managing conflicts of interest.

STANDARDS

Standards provide for consistency in the use of resources. In information services, standards provide rules about the choice and management of information and its supporting technologies. Standards may be set at the international, national and organizational level. They include protocols, data capture and transfer standards, bibliographic descriptions and standards for record keeping. Standards may also determine accommodation requirements and service levels. These will be particularly important in identifying customer service levels or in instances where services are contracted out to third parties.

GUIDELINES

Guidelines provide a more in-depth description about the policies and standards. They are often very practical and address the implementation and operational issues that are associated with the policies and standards.

Policy development

Policy making is a complex activity that requires lots of consultation with individuals and groups from within the information service and parent organization and with other external stakeholders. This is because policies are usually performed by people other than those who design them. Good policies are developed with this in mind, for if they cannot be implemented effectively they will fail.

The policy-making process, including the development of standards and guidelines, should be well planned and thought out in terms of strategic timing, costs, issues at stake, and the values and attitudes of the internal and external stakeholders. The implementation of a policy often implies some form of change, whether at the strategic or operational level. As a result, conflict may arise through the change processes that may in turn jeopardize the policy.

STEP-BY-STEP POLICY DEVELOPMENT

Policy development should be undertaken through a series of steps (see Figure 15.1). The first step is to ensure that all environmental factors that could impact upon the policy are taken into consideration. Those developing the policy should be cognizant of the financial, social and political context of the parent organization and how these could shape the available options and strategies. For example, the financial situation of the parent organization may limit the choice of outcome or scale of the policy or call for a gradual implementation of the policy.

Policy development should not just take into account the current operative environment. It should be future oriented, anticipating new demands or developments,

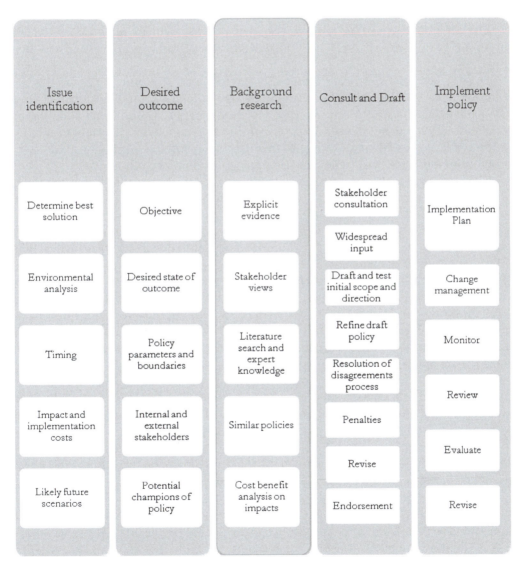

Figure 15.2 The policy development model

whilst ensuring that the end result is workable and able to address the circumstances that are prevalent at the time. The organization's future ability to fund and implement the policy should also be considered. Impractical solutions create frustration and confusion and should be discounted.

The development of the policy should take into consideration all the known stakeholder values and outcomes that stakeholders regard as being possible. 'Success stories' or 'horror stories' from other policy initiatives should be highlighted and this knowledge built upon. Timing is another important consideration in policy development, particularly when the policy may have some political impact for the organization.

The next step is to identify the issue and to determine whether this can be solved through a policy or an alternative mechanism. Not all issues can be solved through policies. Likewise, policies should not be created for aggrandizement or self-importance. Policies are useful to resolve common sources of disagreement or provide guidance on an emerging issue that has been identified through the environmental scanning process.

Once it has been determined that the development of a policy may be the best solution to the problem, the objective and desired outcome should be clearly defined. The parameters and priorities for the policy should be set. The internal and external stakeholders should be identified so that they can be included in the consultation process. It is also useful at this stage to identify any champions who may assist in the promotion of the policy at either the development or implementation stage.

The next stage is the research stage. Evidence used in the preparation of the policy and the development of the policy statement should be explicit. The criteria used for the basis of judgement should be transparent. The sources of information that can be used as evidence to support policy development vary widely. They can range from in-depth interviews with stakeholders to literature searches and consideration of like policies produced by similar organizations. Expert knowledge is essential to policy innovation and experts in the field should be consulted.

A cost-benefit analysis of the policy options and their impacts should be undertaken. Once the background information has been gathered, an impression or judgement of the policy scope and direction can be developed and tested on a number of stakeholders. A draft policy can then be written. This should be further revised after consultation with stakeholders until there is agreement to the policy.

Continuous consultation with both internal and external stakeholders is of particular importance. External stakeholders may include suppliers, the local community, the media, government officials and interest groups. The process of consultation with stakeholders may become a political exercise. The stakeholders may hold vested interests in a particular course of action or in the advancement of their personal power. An objective view should be maintained. Alternative approaches and counter-scenarios should be developed to enable the best possible solution.

The political interests or bias of individual stakeholders cannot be dismissed as the policy will need to be workable for all. The reasons behind the interests must be understood so that these can be considered and accommodated alongside other interests. If these interests are not acknowledged, and the stakeholders are in a position of power such that they can control the activities surrounding the policy, then the result may be that the policy is either ignored or vetoed. Similarly, stakeholders who are known to have opposing interests to the proposed policy should not be ignored. Their views should be canvassed and they should be involved in the decision-making process. When all stakeholders are in agreement to the policy, it should be submitted to senior management for endorsement.

The individual with the task of developing the policy should also ensure that their own values and preferences do not influence the subject matter. The underlying factor is that policy making should be free from bias and all points of view should be considered in the formation of the policy.

The policy development process should take into account how issues may be resolved where there is disagreement about the contents of the policy once it is in place. Where appropriate, a disciplinary process and penalties for failing to act within the policy should be developed. Any disciplinary process should be matched by an appeal process.

The development of the policy is the first part of the policy process. Once developed, the policy needs to be implemented and its performance monitored to ensure the desired policy outcomes. It may need to be refined to take into account changing circumstances. This is because very few policy development processes are fully resourced or provided with sufficient time to investigate and present different options. Often the need for a quick decision limits the level of consultation. There is also the danger that policy development is 'fitted in' to existing workloads and priorities. In these situations, policy solutions can be limited in input, relevant expertise, innovation and strategy.

Conclusion

Effective information service policies solve problems or channel decisions towards achieving the objectives of the service and its parent organization. Once overall policies or standards have been established, they can be effective tools for moving decision-making to the point of service delivery. With an effective policy framework, individuals and groups can take initiatives in making decisions, knowing that the outcomes will still be in line with the ultimate achievement of the organization's objectives.

Policies are also mechanisms for ensuring that individuals are treated fairly and equitably and that individual interests are managed for the greater good. As guides to decision making, policies should be developed through a consultative process with all stakeholders to ensure that different values and interests are considered in decisions.

The following steps can be used in policy making:

- Identify the real issue and determine whether it is best solved through a policy;
- Define the desired outcome;
- Undertake background research;
- Consult with all stakeholders;
- Draft policy and consult;
- Plan and execute the implementation of the policy; and
- Monitor and review to ensure the desired outcomes have been achieved.

Policy making is an ongoing process. It does not start or stop in the form of discrete events. Effective policy making involves continuous modification and adjustment. This continuous improvement process should reflect amendments to the corporate objectives or repositioning of the organization within the changing competitive environment. Where services are integrated the existing policies of the other entities will need to merge with those of the host organization.

References

Cook, N. 2008. *Enterprise 2.0; How Social Software will Change the Future of Work*. Aldershot: Ashgate.

16 *Personal Communication and Networking*

All human interaction is dependent upon interpersonal communication for the exchange of information and the conveyance of ideas. Leadership, influencing and getting things done in the corporate environment require good interpersonal skills that include networking with people and clearly communicating across organizational boundaries and with all levels of people internal and external to the organization. McCallum and O'Connell (2009: 154) quote Balkundi and Kilduff (2006) as saying that an effective leader understands social networking relationships among organizational members and also between members and others beyond the organization boundaries, and is able to leverage individuals' personal networks for the benefit of the organization.

An organization's survival also depends upon individuals and groups maintaining effective and ongoing relationships through communication. Attracting and retaining talented staff who have good connections and networks is one of management's biggest challenges. Whilst the use of the Internet and web applications are now mainstreamed in organizations as effective communications tools, increasingly social software is being used by well connected people for both informal and formal communications inside and out of the working environment and to build and strengthen their networks.

People employed in information services spend most of their day listening, making judgements, evaluating, reasoning, providing advice, networking, expressing emotions, agreeing or disagreeing on opinions and attitudes, sustaining and supporting others, sharing their hopes and ambitions for the future, as well as reassuring and appeasing their bosses, peers, customers and stakeholders. These activities all require highly developed verbal and non-verbal communications skills and take place in a variety of ways, for example in formal and informal meetings, face-to-face, by phone or by email, through formal report writing or casual conversation.

In addition information services managers have to build credibility and strong relationships with key business partners and executive stakeholders in:

- Understanding their business and client needs;
- Selling new ideas, concepts and business applications;
- Being informed about operational issues affecting service delivery within the information service;
- Convincing them of the business value to be exploited from investment in technology; and
- Managing strategic change and challenging circumstances.

The very nature of the activities in information services requires individuals to have highly developed communication skills as well as the ability to assess, select, manage, process and disseminate vehicles of communication in a variety of formats:

- They have to manage and use information in multiple formats to provide information services to their customers;
- They have to understand and provide advice on the business applications of new communications avenues such as social networking;
- They must be expert in recognizing the most appropriate vehicle to communicate information and deliver interactive services to a large number of people; and increasingly
- They also have responsibilities for the sharing, development and brokering of knowledge across organizations.

The information discipline is particularly strong in its use of technical terms and jargon, which can be daunting to those who do not have the same technical background. It is therefore important to be able to communicate technical issues to people without using the technical terminology.

Effective interpersonal communication

The existence of various avenues or media for communicating does not always ensure that communication takes place. The communication process may fail for a number of reasons as no two individuals are alike. Individuals have different perceptions of others and situations that are governed by their past experiences, cultures, values, knowledge, attitudes, expectations and self-image. This can result in an inability to build a two-way communication process because the process is based upon subjective analysis or perception of the other person(s) rather than the objectivity of the message conveyed.

To improve their interpersonal communication, individuals or groups must understand each other better. Strategies for understanding the other person include:

- Seeking clarification or more information about the issue;
- Exploring mutual ideas;
- Emphasizing and sharing an appreciation of feelings; and
- Reflecting upon their own and the other party's position and what is being said.

There are also differences in listening abilities that may be coloured by natural tendencies to judge and evaluate both what is being said and the person saying it. These can lead to differences in the interpretation of the message. Problems may be oversimplified in the message or deliberately generalized, distorted or omitted. Alternatively, the receiver may be insensitive to the problems expressed in the message and so not listen properly to what is being said. There may also be a lack of distinction between information and communication, or a lack of clarity as to who needs the information. Finally, relevant information may not be able to be synthesized due to the overabundance of irrelevant information. Being over-informed is as inhibiting as being under-informed.

Effective interpersonal communication in these instances can be achieved by focusing upon concrete evidence and issues rather than being vague or abstract. Opinions should be formed upon descriptive actions, not judgemental ones or inferences. The emphasis should be upon developing alternatives and the sharing of ideas and information, rather than the giving of advice.

Managers can enhance their interpersonal communication skills by being accessible and by defining each individual's or team's areas of responsibility. Goals should be kept clearly in mind. In situations where a person requires guidance, their actual behaviour should be focused upon rather than their personality. The manager should develop trust between all concerned and be frank with individuals on plans and problems. Above all, effective listening skills should be developed.

It is helpful when communicating with others to appreciate and understand the complexity of interpersonal communication. The interpersonal aspect of communication involves the searching and understanding of the self and others' self-image, needs, values, expectations, standards and norms and perceptions.

Self-image involves the perceptions of an individual about themselves or the group or organization to which they belong. The concept of a group can also be extended to include a nationality or religious group. Self-image takes into account ego, pride, culture, traditions and ambitions. Needs reflect requirements that enable psychological or physiological yearnings to be satisfied. They include love, security, recognition and success. Values reflect subjective ideas held dearly. Expectations are anticipated outcomes, desired or otherwise, which are likely to be the consequence of actions or the lack of actions.

Standards are found in fixed norms that reflect cultural background and experience. Perceptions are preconceived ideas that may or may not distort an individual's views. To this may be added a background of stored information, understanding and knowledge based on the past, and an experience, understanding and knowledge of the present. None of these can be mutually exclusive, and all interact to influence the interpersonal communication process at the time.

Two other issues can also affect the effectiveness of the interpersonal communication. These are stereotyping and the halo effect. Stereotyping involves forming generalized opinions of how certain people appear, think, feel and act. It is an attempt to classify or categorize individuals so that they lose their individuality and are in turn assigned the characteristics of an entire group of people.

Stereotyping affects the interpersonal communication process because it keeps individuals from understanding one another. Stereotyping is 'noise' that prevents one party from hearing the message that the other party is sending. It colours attitudes and creates prejudices.

The halo effect is a tendency to judge an individual favourably, or occasionally unfavourably. In many cases this is on the basis of one strong point on which the other party places a high value. Halo effects can have positive or negative consequences for the other party. It affects the communication process in that anything that they say is consistently interpreted in either a positive or negative fashion.

Effective business communication

In many organizations executive management have little understanding of the value and complexity of information services, yet they are reliant on information services to deliver their business. One reason for this lack of understanding is the fact that many senior executives are of a generation where using desktop and mobile technologies and applications is not a natural instinct as it is with those of later digital native generations who have been born into a digital world. For many senior executives technology is something they have had to learn and they are consequently less comfortable with the technical terms and concepts that form part of everyday conversation. ICT is also regarded as a black hole of spending; the result of people remembering where new technology applications have failed rather than being aware of the positive business impacts that email, the Internet and mobile phones have made in increased organizational efficiencies, communications and service delivery.

Effective business communication requires the information services manager to communicate with senior management and key business partners on their terms, using their language and in their offices, rather them being seen as a backroom technology nerd or keeper of the record. Simplifying messages in explaining concepts, selling new ideas and business applications and establishing business cases; talking in terms of being the financial manager and controller for the information and technology investment portfolio, capital expenditure and revenue opportunities; and explaining proposals in terms of their business benefits and value are three ways of gaining trust and communicating more effectively with senior management.

The role of the information services manager is to work collaboratively with senior management and key business partners in understanding and delivering solutions that meet their business and client needs. To do this the information services manager must take time to discuss and understand their business strategies, agendas and pain points and how the information service can add value to their business and minimize the pain points. At the same time, the information services manager must also gather information about areas for continuous improvement and operational issues that may affect business service delivery.

Convincing senior management and key business partners of the business value to be exploited from investment in new applications such as social media during times of financial constraint and challenging business circumstances also requires a business argument to overcome scepticism. In this instance the business argument is about customer reach and using preferred customer service channels, customer convenience and improving the quality of internal information.

Effective listening

Sustaining the well-being of people in uncertain and challenging times frequently rests on effectively listening to and responding to their concerns. Listening is different to hearing. Effective listening requires the individual to listen to what is being said in terms of what is being meant rather than interpreting the words they hear. Effective listening requires the ability to pick up key words, inferences and prejudices that provide meaningful details and explain underlying thoughts. It is also important to understand the viewpoint of the other party, even though it may contradict or challenge the listener's own ideas and values. Pertinent questions also act as a feedback mechanism to the other party and provide further assurance that what they are conveying is being considered in an objective manner.

Effective listening also includes interpreting non-verbal communication signals such as mood, aggression, nervousness, and incorporating these into the verbal message that is received. Active listening is another valuable technique in that it allows the listener to place themselves in the other party's position and look at things from their point of view. In difficult circumstances the party may need time to be able to sift through their emotions and articulate the underlying cause of their feelings. In these situations the listener needs to be patient, putting the other party at ease and allowing the other party plenty of time.

Using emotional intelligence

Many of the reactions that leaders and managers have to deal with in driving transformational change and managing difficult circumstances and other situations in the workplace are based on emotion. Emotions such as fear, anger, surprise, joy, sadness or disgust are manifested in behaviours such as aggression, distrust, optimism and eagerness. By identifying, using, understanding and managing emotions that may have been uncovered through good interpersonal communication and listening skills, the manager can be more effective in their transformational change role.

Emotional intelligence is one of the 'soft skills' that are increasingly important and legitimate leadership and personal communication tools for recognizing, reasoning and solve problems that involve emotions. Emotional intelligence is the ability to manage yourself and your emotions and relate to other people's emotions. In particular it is well suited to today's workplace and the values of Generations X and Y who look to more people-focused styles of leadership and to the philosophy that it is difficult to separate the impact of events in people's personal lives from those at work.

There are several models that have been developed around emotional intelligence. Salovey's ability based model views emotions as useful sources of information that help one to make sense of and navigate the social environment. In summary it includes four types of abilities:

- Perceiving emotions – the ability to detect and decipher emotions in faces, pictures, voices and artefacts, including the ability to identify one's own emotions. Perceiving emotions represents a basic aspect of emotional intelligence, as it makes all other processing of emotional information possible;
- Using emotions – the ability to harness emotions to facilitate various cognitive activities, such as thinking and problem solving. The emotionally intelligent person can capitalize fully upon his or her changing mood in order to best fit the task at hand;
- Understanding emotions – the ability to comprehend emotion language and to appreciate complicated relationships among emotions. For example, understanding emotions encompasses the ability to be sensitive to slight variations between emotions, and the ability to recognize and describe how emotions evolve over time; and

- Managing emotions – the ability to regulate emotions in both ourselves and in others. Therefore, the emotionally intelligent person can harness emotions, even negative ones, and manage them to achieve intended goals.

Using these abilities, Caruso and Salovey (2004: xv) show how the emotionally intelligent manager can leverage these skills in the workplace, for example in:

- Identifying how all the key participants feel, themselves included;
- Using these feelings to guide the thinking and reasoning of the people involved;
- Understanding how feelings might change and develop as events unfold; and
- Managing to stay open to the data of feelings and integrating them into decisions and actions.

People who are skilful in identifying and managing emotions know what people feel and talk about feelings. They read people accurately and are good at expressing their own feelings. They listen, ask questions and determine how they and the other party are feeling. They examine the causes of the feelings and try to understand what might happen next and the type of emotional encounters that they might encounter whilst also looking at actions that can be taken to alleviate the emotion.

In looking to understand emotions, Caruso and Salovey (2004: 52) have identified that skilful people try to make correct assumptions rather than misunderstand people. They know the right thing to say and have a rich vocabulary, rather than find it hard to explain their feelings. They also understand that a person can feel conflicting emotions towards another or about a situation. In managing emotions, skilful people are open to their feelings and those of others, they connect with people and take steps to manage feelings appropriately by calming people down or encouraging or cheering others up.

Similarly, the model introduced by Daniel Goleman focuses on emotional intelligence as a wide array of competencies and skills that drive leadership performance. Goleman's model outlines four main constructs:

- Self-awareness – the ability to read one's emotions and recognize their impact while using feeling to guide decisions;
- Self-management – involves controlling one's emotions and impulses and adapting to changing circumstances;
- Social awareness – the ability to sense, understand and react to others' emotions while comprehending social networks; and
- Interpersonal relationships – the ability to inspire, influence and develop others while managing conflict.

Each of these models have common themes: the need to accurately recognize and pay attention to one's own and others' moods, emotions and behaviours, especially in stressful and difficult situations. It provides a self-awareness and self-regulating mechanism for understanding and assessing oneself and one's own intentions, responses and behaviour as well as understanding others and their feelings.

Effective networking

In the past, individuals had all the knowledge and information to perform well. However as operations are more dispersed around the world and people advance within organizations, the amount of information necessary to be successful outpaces the knowledge that just one individual can possess (Byham 2010: 67).

Personal networks allow information services managers and their team members to function and communicate effectively. They can be used to seek and impart knowledge and information, for support, and to positively influence outcomes. Increasingly social network services are enabling people to connect online based on shared interests, hobbies and causes both within and outside of the workplace.

Byham (2010: 66) provides six reasons why networking is fundamental to business:

- The level of complexity in the business environment means that a single individual cannot have all the information required to do a job. They must find out who has the necessary information and develop the contacts to get the information when it is needed;
- Business networks facilitate the sharing of information that helps individuals and teams avoid repeating work. It also avoids the situation where processes are developed without benefiting from best practices for similar efforts undertaken elsewhere;
- It is fundamental to coordinating efforts for maximum speed and efficiency;
- Business networks can act as an early warning system that keeps individuals in touch with what is going on in the organization and external environment;
- When making difficult decisions with little information it is useful to have people who can be called on for help and advice; and
- Business networks help people determine the strategic direction of the organization so that personal and unit efforts can be aligned.

Networking is a sharing process where knowledge and information is freely given as well as obtained through formal and informal communication channels. To function effectively, it is important that personal networks are established with relevant people within the organization, various professional bodies that are represented or interact with the information service, and with external stakeholders, such as industry, trade suppliers and politicians. These networks will enable the individual to learn lessons and avoid repeats of past failures, obtain critical information and advice and establish alliances with key stakeholders who are likely to support preferred positions or actions, or supply needed resources or services.

Networks are particularly important for individuals who work in professional isolation. They provide a source of professional knowledge, information and opinions and can be useful in sharing resources. Networks can also comprise a group of trusted people to whom the individual can turn for guidance and personal advice.

Belonging to the right network will 'open doors'. Many legitimate political tactics rely upon networks. In belonging to others' networks valuable information is often obtained that would not otherwise be forthcoming. This will often lead to improved decision making or allow corrective or appropriate action to be taken to avoid undesired outcomes. Networks also provide sponsorship and can influence outcomes. This may be useful at budget time or when major decisions take place about the future role of the information service. To be purposeful, networks rely upon reciprocity. There needs to be a balance of give and take.

Making the first contact is the first and most important stage in networking. It is important to establish good eye contact, introduce yourself and ask open-ended questions. The Six Degrees of Separation is a phenomenon that is based on the premise that you only need six people to be able to reach anyone anywhere in the world; that is you will know someone, who will know someone, who will know someone ... leading to the desired connection to make the inevitable happen.

Belonging to a network is akin to belonging to a group as members within a network:

* Support and advice is freely and positively given;
* Hold sacred certain unchallengeable values and norms; and
* Display common behaviours, certain dress codes and modes of thinking.

Table 16.1 outlines four types of networks that are found in organizations based on a common purpose of power, ideology, people or profession.

Table 16.1   Different types of networks in organizations

Network	Description
Practician-oriented Networks	These networks are formed for a common purpose that benefits those who belong. They may be practician-oriented and comprise individuals who have similar expertise, training or professional interests. They provide true intellectual and professional stimuli for new ideas and innovations. In support of their ideals, they may attempt to influence other employees or organizations
Power Networks	Privilege or power networks comprise people who wield substantial influence or wish to be influential. These culture clubs operate through personal power bases. Introductions to the group are either by invitation or through the 'old school tie network'
Ideological Networks	Ideological networks comprise different types of people who wish to pursue particular ideas. Pressure groups are an example of ideological networks in that they are formed to pursue particular social objectives
People-oriented Networks	The most common networks in organizations are the people-oriented networks that exist for the sake of their members. These networks are important as they are valuable sources of information and support

The entrance to the network is facilitated by identifying a gatekeeper, who is an influential member of the group. Personal sponsorship by a gatekeeper is important as this enables the person entering the network to become quickly acquainted with senior network members and enhance his or her channels of communication and success.

In any new position, individuals should quickly develop their own personal networks inside and outside their organization in order to satisfy their need for information and to establish their power base. This is particularly important in a management role where resources have to be obtained, relationships between organizational units established, and organizational politics managed. The rationale for this is that upon joining any organization, an individual is at first ineffective because they have not established their own internal organizational networks. This situation is often short-lived, but until such networks are established communication and decision-making that takes into account corporate culture and other differences cannot be totally effective in the new environment. For example, the individual will not truly know who they can trust, who to go to for accurate advice or information, or who their allies or supporters are likely to be. Whilst it is likely that they will have brought established external networks with people or organizations from their previous appointments, they will still need support, information and advice from within their new organization in order to deal with everyday internal matters.

Personal networks should be established with thought. Individuals operating in key areas as the executive, finance and personnel sections and who are likely to provide support should be identified and contact made with them. It is often more favourable for the initial contact to be made on a face-to-face basis. This is more personal and polite and enables the person to explain who they are and exchange some of their work ideas and values on a one-to-one basis. In the process of the exchange it will become clear whether common values are held, whether support may or may not be forthcoming and whether the individual may be regarded as a useful ally and member of a network.

Personal contact also allows non-verbal communication channels such as body language to be assessed. The non-verbal communication processes will provide valuable information as to the actual support that may be given. In areas where vital relationships have to be established, and where initial reactions may not be as favourable as had been hoped, it is useful to continue to interact on a person-to-person basis. The positive side of the work relationship should be emphasized until such times as a firm relationship has been established.

Conclusion

Good interpersonal communications skills are critical when leading and managing information services. They are used to:

- Discover underlying concerns and anxieties when sustaining the well-being of individuals in challenging circumstances;
- Influence and get things done in the corporate environment and across organizational boundaries;
- Maintain effective and ongoing relationships with key stakeholders;
- Assess, select, manage and disseminate knowledge and information to meet customer needs;
- Understand business and client needs;
- Sell new ideas, concepts and business applications;
- Identify operational issues affecting service delivery within the information service;

- Convince the executive of the business value to be exploited from investment in technology; and
- Manage strategic change and challenging circumstances.

Emotional intelligence is a legitimate leadership and personal communication tool for recognizing, reasoning and solve problems that involve emotions. In particular it is well suited to the values of Generations X and Y who look to more people-focused styles of leadership and to the philosophy that it is difficult to separate the impact of events in people's personal lives from those at work. It involves:

- Self-awareness – the ability to read one's emotions and recognize their impact while using feeling to guide decision;
- Self-management – involves controlling one's emotions and impulses and adapting to changing circumstances;
- Social awareness – the ability to sense, understand, and react to others' emotions while comprehending social networks; and
- Interpersonal relationships – the ability to inspire, influence and develop others while managing conflict.

Networks are also a vital component of leadership and information service management. There are many business payoffs in networking, including obtaining access to critical information, coordinating work efforts and avoiding repetition, using them as a mechanism of influence to achieve outcomes, as well as providing personal support and advice.

References

Byham, W.C. 2010. Business networking can be taught. *T+D Training and Development*, May, 64–68.

Caruso, D.R. and Salovey, P. 2004. *The Emotionally Intelligent Manager: How to Develop and Use the Four Key Emotional Skills of Leadership*. San Francisco: Jossey-Bass.

McCallum, S. and O'Connell, D. 2009. Social capital and leadership development: Building stronger leadership through enhanced relational skills. *Leadership and Organization Development Journal*, 30(2), 152–166.

Further Reading

Eaton, J. and Johnson, R. 2001. *Communicate with Emotional Intelligence*. Oxford: Communications/How to Books Ltd.

Goleman, D. 1995. *Emotional Intelligence*. New York: Bantam Books.

Goleman, D. 1998. *Working With Emotional Intelligence*. New York: Bantam Books.

Jay, J. 2005. On communicating well. *HR Magazine*, January, 87–90.

Johnson, W.B. and Ridley, C.R. 2004. *The Elements of Mentoring*. New York: Palgrave Macmillan.

Salovey, P. and Grewal, D. 2005. The science of emotional intelligence. *Current Directions in Psychological Science*, 14, 6.

17 *Managing Yourself and Others in Challenging Times*

Managing and sustaining the well-being of individuals who work in the information service is another important function of the leader. It also includes taking the time to manage one's personal well-being as, in a busy and competitive environment, it is sometimes tempting to focus on the demands of the job and overlook personal life needs and those of others.

Career planning, personal development, lifestyle planning and stress management are all important strategies by which the information service can sustain and increase the contributions of individuals and prepare them for their future. By planning their career and lifestyle, knowing themselves better and managing their personal self and image, as well as knowing how best to manage the stressors in their life, individuals can be better equipped to cope and sustain themselves in a complex and changing world.

Personal and professional development strategies should extend individuals' capacities and utilize their maximum capabilities so that there is:

- Improved personal performance and relationships;
- Increased job satisfaction;
- Improved quality of life and work–life balance; and,
- Improved abilities to cope with the stressors of fast-paced changing environments.

These strategies need not be limited to the workplace; everyone has a part to play. As a responsible corporate citizen, the information service can provide lifestyle and stress management techniques and access to counselling services to assist individuals manage and balance their lifestyle and can engender a sense of well-being.

Career planning

With the rapid and ongoing development of new technologies, the library and information services environment is characterized by fast-paced changing landscapes where new and emerging skills are a continued necessity. Training which allows the individual to keep pace with and make the most out of changing technologies and business applications, personal and professional development, and leadership development and career planning is a joint effort involving the organization, management and the individual. The information service can provide the structure, career path opportunities and climate to encourage leadership development, career planning and personal development. The information services manager has a responsibility to ensure appropriate assignments, coaching and counselling to assist individuals in the realistic planning and attainment of their career objectives. They can develop the talents of their people by providing encouragement and support to extend the boundaries of personal growth and development. As part of the appraisal system they can assist individuals choose goals that can stretch them and help identify the means to attain them. From a professional point of view the manager can act as a role model, providing personal and professional qualities that individuals may strive to achieve.

The individual also has to accept responsibility for their growth and development. This includes identifying their long-term career plans and seeking assistance from the organization's personal and professional development programmes. Action plans can be developed to assist in career planning by:

- Identifying critical achievements in their work and personal lifestyle;
- Producing an inventory of their current skills and knowledge together with their anticipated future needs (a 'where am I now?' analysis);
- Identifying the ideal job and lifestyle position ('where do I want to get to?');
- Defining the opportunities, constraints and critical success factors in achieving the ideal position ('how can I get there?'); and
- Determining the strategies, qualifications and skills necessary to achieve the ideal position ('what will I do?').

In addition, individuals will look for evidence of organizational direction and career path opportunities when determining where their own future lies. The motivation for successful career and personal development can be damaged if an individual perceives a lack of progress in their chosen career path, or if there is a lack of challenge in the current position and no foreseeable prospect of change. The lack of a foreseeable career path for a person within any organization is increasingly becoming an issue. Business re-engineering and downsizing has invariably cut into the mid-level management positions that previously created the career opportunities. Likewise, professional associations and their members also have responsibilities for investing in their own future by encouraging individuals to embark on personal and professional development programmes.

Career development is also affected when there is a conflict of interest between personal loyalty, professional loyalty and/or organizational loyalty, since failure to reconcile loyalty dilemmas can cause stress and a feeling of futility or confusion. Problems with immediate supervisors can also lead to a sense of frustration in career progression. Mentors can provide encouragement and support in these cases. Mentors can also help to develop people's talents and often open doors to the future.

Lifestyle planning

Lifestyle planning includes making the most efficient and effective use of personal time at the operational (daily) and strategic (long-term) levels. Operational planning incorporates balancing the competing interests of work, home, family and relationships, travel time, personal fitness and other interests such as hobbies and cultural activities. Strategic planning includes longer-term personal goals, career development and retirement planning. Balance in lifestyle and making efficient use of time may include options such as working part-time, or telecommuting from home.

Self-management of lifestyle begins with the individuals knowing or finding out more about themselves. This is done by critically analysing personal strengths and weaknesses, assets and liabilities. A mind map exercise can help as it allows the participant to identify and map out the important areas of their life as branches out of a central trunk. Each major branch indicates a significant personal development or lifestyle issue that influences their life. This can be further divided into more specific issues. A mix of concrete and abstract issues can be used. For example, concrete issues may be work, home, religion, relationships, travel plans, personal and professional development. Abstract issues may be the future, missing items in the lifestyle, things to avoid. Each of the branches can then be colour coded to identify:

- Areas to develop further;
- Dissatisfiers; and
- Satisfiers.

Mind maps assist in creating a more balanced lifestyle as they identify:

- Those areas that are going well (satisfiers) and those of concern (dissatisfiers);
- Areas to develop; and
- Areas of intense activity and those that are lacking in activity.

Self-management

Managers devote many hours to managing organizations and others to achieve corporate objectives, but rarely is time given to managing themselves and their own personal image. Managing oneself involves:

- Valuing personal time, effort and energy;
- Acting confidently and believing in personal talents and skills to achieve goals;
- Sustaining energy and personal fortitude;
- Determining work–life balance;
- Assessing priorities and saying no at times;
- Deciding on a preferred future and taking ownership and responsibility for the outcomes; and
- Learning from the past rather than regretting it.

Individuals may also review:

- Their successes to reinforce their self-esteem;
- Personal motives to question their true direction;
- Their lifestyle balance to allow time for personal needs such as daily exercise and the enjoyment of simple things; and

- Sources of personal conflict at work, in the home, and elsewhere to create a more positive attitude and reduce tension.

PERSONAL IMAGE

The management of personal image is important if individuals are to be confident and have positive attitudes towards themselves. Image is a communication tool. It conveys an impression and message to others. If team members project an image of being confident, approachable and successful, that image will be reinforced to others.

Individuals should be encouraged to identify and manage the image that they feel most comfortable with. This includes identifying the message that the person wishes to communicate about them and reinforcing this. The image can be likened to a human package. It is communicated through mannerisms, appearance, dress, movement, speech patterns and personality. Facial expressions, posture and eye contact provide important information for others to judge levels of confidence. The sound, quality, intensity, rate and inflection of speech also project a powerful image. The ways in which people stand, sit and move influence others' first impressions.

Increasingly in the virtual environment individuals have to optimize and manage their professional digital presence and image. This includes protection of a person's digital identity integrity, using social networking tools as a strategic career profile and promotion device, as well as being professional in the use of emails and instant messaging.

Stress management

Stress is a response to an environmental force, either real or imagined, that interacts with an individual's tolerance level. It can have a motivational or stimulatory effect, or it can be damaging to the individual. Stress is the response that the human system makes in adjusting to the demands of activating life events. It is not the event itself. The life event is known as the stressor. All individuals are potentially vulnerable to stress: being constantly exposed to life events that are threatening, particularly in complex and changing environments. However, stress tolerances differ between individuals, some being more able to control or manage their responses to stressors than others.

Stress implies a vulnerability to a stressor. Individual vulnerability to specific stressors varies widely. Vulnerability alters with age and is related to phases involving change and failures in the life cycle. Vulnerability also changes according to day-to-day events, moods and individual experiences, roles of individuals in particular settings, perceptions of expectations held of the individual by others, and the ability to control or alter the situation. Stressors produce symptoms only when the context and vulnerability are ripe. The individual must be particularly vulnerable or be in a generally threatening environment to experience the effect of the stressor. Personality has a particular relationship to stress. Certain characteristics predispose individuals to experience more or less stress than their peers.

Stress is also a physiological state. The conditioned body responses, characterized by arousal to meet situational demands and relaxing when the task is accomplished, are natural characteristics of survival in transitory stress-producing situations. If these responses are allowed to accumulate beyond the adaptive capacity of the body they can result in physiological or psychological illnesses. This is because the build-up of physical energy inside the body is inappropriate to the modern life situation. Man is no longer a primitive animal requiring sudden bursts of energy for survival.

Stress is not necessarily unhealthy. Everyone needs a certain amount of stress in order to function well. It is constant or excess stress that produces unpleasant or harmful side-effects. If the stressor's force exceeds the individual's stress tolerance level it will have a debilitating effect upon the individual.

Occupational or status level bears no relationship to the incidence of stress-related disease. However, each stage of life has its particular vulnerability. It is important that these stages are recognized so that managers can assist themselves and their people to manage their stress levels. The stages are:

- Young adult, the stage of transformation from child to adult. This is characterized by growing, maturing and learning;
- The twenties, a stage of establishing a home and career;
- The thirties, this stage provides minor crises of uncertainty concerning career choice;
- Thirty-five to 55, the so-called mid-life crisis stage. This is a potentially stressful stage when most people reach their status in life. It is a time associated with reflection, significant changes in occupation, interpersonal values and commitments, and role conflicts between family and career. The more ambitious a person is, the more they are likely to suffer; and
- The latter work years, this stage may be associated with apprehension of retirement or feelings of competition from younger members of staff.

Stress may be controlled or reduced by management techniques that can be employed at the individual or organizational level.

Managing stress in the workplace

People experience potential stressors in their everyday work situation, especially in changing and challenging environments. Role conflict, role ambiguity, role overload and role underload all have the potential to be stressors depending upon the vulnerability of the individual. However, as Raitano and Kleiner (2004) point out, stress management is as much the responsibility of employees as it is managers. Both must maintain the lines of communication and feedback to determine appropriate means of diagnosis and a suitable mix of primary, secondary and tertiary prevention methods.

In their boundary-spanning role managers will be involved in investigating complaints, troubleshooting and interacting with people and situations, all of which may cause stressful situations. Planning, decision making, negotiating and other management responsibilities can have stress potential. Economic and time pressures, technological change and obsolescence are other environmental factors that are potential stressors.

Potential stressors for any individual in the workplace can be found in job insecurity, lack of work autonomy, unhappy work relationships, group conflict, constant work interruptions, lack of a defined career path, organization demands, promotions and demotions or transfers. Some individuals want to achieve perfectionism in everything that they do and place excessive demands upon themselves. These types of people are their own stressors.

In dynamic environments, people may perceive that changes are imposed solely for the benefit of the organization. Strategies to improve working conditions, increase opportunity, pay or security are interpreted as being intended to meet the goals of management, to increase productivity or reduce costs rather than for the benefit of the individual. This can create a lose-lose situation for management who have often tried very hard to improve the conditions.

The physical work setting, health and safety practices can also be a stress source. Desktop devices, networks, printers and other equipment that continually fail, a lack of natural light and ventilation and poorly designed work areas can inhibit productivity and cause conflict, which in turn become potential stressors for people.

Balancing work and family responsibilities is also a source of stress. People can feel guilty about putting either their work or home responsibilities first; they may worry about the possible impact of promotion or relocation on their family or partner, and they may experience role conflict between their responsibilities for their career and family. However, work can also be a mechanism for coping and a refuge from personal distress, boredom and meaninglessness. It can be the primary means through which people feel useful in society and life and develop a sense of identity.

Burnout is physiological state of stress affecting both managers and their staff. Burnout is most likely to affect the best, the brightest and the most highly motivated. People who are susceptible to burnout are those who set high personal goals and achievements. Burnout can be minimized or avoided through stress management strategies at the organizational and individual level.

Raitano and Kleiner (2004) identify three ways of alleviating stress in the workplace: primary, secondary and tertiary. Primary prevention is the elimination or reduction of factors that promote distress. Although not exclusive, such methods are job design (redesign), participant management and flexible hours. Secondary methods involve moderating the stress response itself; relaxation training and physical exercise are examples. Employer-sponsored aerobic exercise sessions and relaxation sessions can assist. Tertiary prevention is the attempt to minimize or cope with excessive distress from inadequately controlled stressors and inadequately controlled or moderated stress responses. This includes intervention programmes to minimize drug abuse or alcohol abuse.

Understanding stress and personality

Stress that is attributed to pressure is highly related to individual personalities. Certain personality characteristics predispose individuals to experience more or less stress than their peers with the result that some people will handle pressure better than others. The tolerance for stress will also differ according to the stressor.

Introverted people tend to be less sociable and may take longer to form relationships with people. In these instances a promotion may trigger a stress reaction for a period of time if it results in a job that involves working with different people. The additional responsibility is not the problem, just the act of being placed in unknown company.

Extroverts are people who need other people for various reasons. They work well in jobs requiring the establishment of interpersonal relationships. If they are confined to a lonely job they can become stressed.

The rigidly structured individual is security oriented and afraid to take risks. They are stressed by anything that upsets their routine. They are uneasy in implementing new ideas or solutions that have not been tested.

The hard-driving, work-oriented individual is stress prone. They compulsively push activities to capacity and are extremely performance conscious and goal oriented. They seek honour and recognition but rarely achieve self-confidence as they are always looking at acquiring ever-increasing skills. This stress-prone individual's outlook causes continuous work overload.

The stress reducer may be as serious as the stress prone about getting the job done, but will seldom become impatient. They are less competitive and less likely to be driven by the clock. They work without agitation and find time for fun and leisure. Aware of capabilities and confident about themselves, they lead a fuller, less stressful, richer life than their stress-prone counterpart.

Risk avoiders are excessively careful. They are afraid of making decisions as this threatens their security. They experience constant inner tensions through feelings of inadequacy and dependency. Restrictive in innovative thinking, they avoid exploring new ideas. They will also avoid transfers or promotions, clinging to positions that have given them security and success in the past.

Flexible people usually have healthy, mature egos and can adapt to changing situations, whilst tolerating a high degree of stress. Challenges may be seen as stressors, but this will not impede their ability to cope.

Individuals who have a high self-esteem can deal with stress and frustration more easily. Faced with a pressure situation, performance is likely to improve. There is a strong sense of confidence in their ability to conform and optimism in their approach to performance. Individuals with low self-esteem will be overwhelmed and show a sharp decrease in performance if stress is applied. This is particularly true if stress is associated with a new job.

TYPE A AND TYPE B BEHAVIOURS

Type A individuals

Type A individuals have behaviours that are typical of many managers and senior executives. Type A personalities are extremely competitive, constantly struggling with the environment at work, in sport and at social functions. They focus upon gaining power, recognition, money and possessions in a short period of time, and portray excessive strivings for achievement. Sometimes this is accompanied by underlying feelings of hostility towards others, whom they consider to be roadblocks. The hostility may be subtle or undetected until people stand in their way.

Type A individuals are fast-talking, having a sense of urgency concerning time. They thrive on deadlines, create them if they are not set and become impatient if goals and objectives are not achieved. Their work habits and their interpersonal relationships are critical in contributing to the fact that Type A personalities are three times more likely to develop cardiac disease or hypertension than Type B personalities.

Whilst Type A personalities are outwardly confident and self-assured, they can have an underlying insecurity. They may overreact to situations and can be hypercritical both of themselves (to themselves) and of others.

Type A managers or those managing Type A people need to manage their own or others' stress inducing activities and lifestyle actively so as to reduce the risk of illness without sacrificing drive and enthusiasm.

Type B individuals

In contrast, Type B personalities have an easy-going relaxed approach to life. They hold a rational approach to achievement and recognition. They experience positive interpersonal relations and maintain a balance between work and other events. They rarely have desires to become materialistic.

Stress management techniques

Professional and personal relationships are among the most useful weapons of sustaining and supporting people against the distress of work and other people's demands. Effective listening skills, seeking advice, information and feedback and encouraging input from others can make decision making less reactive and crisis oriented. Truth and honesty are important in working relationships as mixed messages or inaccuracies can be stressful to deal with. Supportive working relationships also reduce work stress. The social support offered by the relationships has a buffering effect upon the job demands, providing psychological and emotional support for the individual's well-being.

Personal planning processes can help achievement-oriented individuals. The analysis of an individual's strengths and weaknesses and the periodic reassessment of their vocational, societal and personal goals and aspirations may allow more realistic goal horizons to be set.

Good time-management skills and knowledge of personal body clocks are also a means of reducing the negative impact of stress and increasing an individual's sense of well-being. Where possible the most demanding parts of the job should be handled during the high part of the daily cycle when the individual is most alert, whilst the less important events should be scheduled in the lower part of the cycle.

Preventative stress management strategies can also be employed in the work environment. By altering, modifying or eliminating unnecessary or unreasonable organizational demands, managers can reduce stress in the workplace. Second, coping skills aimed at improving the individual's response to and management of organizational demands should be offered.

Inappropriate work and physical demands can be prevented by job redesign, flexible work schedules and family-friendly work policies, provision for adequate career development and the design of the physical work settings. Role and interpersonal demands can be prevented from being stressors by team-building, providing social support, goal-setting programmes and role analysis techniques.

Individual stressor demands can be controlled by the individual managing their perceptions of stress, and by managing their work environment and lifestyle. Individuals should also have access to physical and emotional outlets such as sporting activities, exercise routines and interpersonal relationships. Counselling and psychotherapy may also be needed. Meditation, corporate opportunities for physical activity and rest, progressive relaxation techniques and moderation in diet and drinking alcohol will also help alleviate stress.

Conclusion

Career planning, professional development and learning involve an investment by the individual and the organization. Development opportunities to learn new skills through conferences and work experience can fill knowledge and skills gaps needed in the knowledge age. A good programme will result in newly acquired knowledge, skills or behaviours. It should also enthuse participants to want to master these new 'tools' and to practise them in the workplace. For the newly acquired knowledge, skills or behaviour to be locked in, they must be applied back on the job. There must be active support and involvement in the workplace for this to happen. The immediate supervisor should be involved in meetings before and after the session with the participant(s) to determine the purpose of the programme, to set individual goals and objectives of the session(s), to look at ways in which the newly acquired behaviour can be reinforced back in the workplace, and to evaluate the outcomes of the programme.

Lifestyle planning acknowledges that work cannot be considered in isolation of other influencing factors. It incorporates balancing the competing interests of work, home, family and relationships, travel time, personal fitness and other interests such as hobbies and cultural activities to create a holistic approach to life.

In concentrating on providing opportunities for the development of others as a significant management task, it is sometimes easy to neglect personal professional and development needs. Self-management is not an act of self-indulgence; it is an important part of self-development. It includes paying attention to self-image, keeping abreast of change in the external environment and career planning.

The ability to manage the well-being of individuals who work in the information service is important from a duty of care perspective as well as from a motivational viewpoint. It is an important management role to ensure that the physical setting, health and safety practices, work relationships and job structures do not create unnecessary stress for individuals. The ability to assist individuals manage their responses to stress and to minimize the stressors in the workplace will also result in a happier and more productive workforce.

References

Raitano, R.E. and Kleiner, B.H. 2004. Stress management: Stressors, diagnosis, and prevention measures. *Management Research*, 27(4/5), 32–39.

Further reading

Ashcroft, L. 2004. Developing competencies, critical analysis and personal transferable skills in future information professionals. *Library Review*, 52(2), 82–88.

Charnock, E. 2010. *E-habits: What You Must Do to Optimize Your Professional Digital Presence*. New York: McGraw-Hill Contemporary.

Leigh, A. 2009. *The Secrets of Success in Management: 20 Ways to Survive and Thrive*. Harlow: Pearson Prentice Hall Business.

Governance and Social Responsibility

The theme for Part IV is effecting high performing organizations through good corporate governance, sustainability and social responsibility. Part IV takes the view that the important features by which organizations are increasingly judged, namely trust in organizations and corporate reputation, is predicated on the organization having good governance, transparency in decision making and social responsibility. This can be achieved by having an integrated approach to transparency and accountability, choice and influence in actions and decision making, realistic risk management strategies, effective security and a focus on sustainability; all of which enhance and support the need to account to stakeholders for the performance of the organization through evaluating benefits and performance.

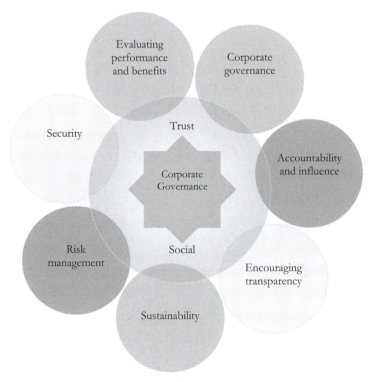

Figure PIV.1 An integrated approach to corporate governance

Along with customer satisfaction and profitability, public and private sector organizations are being judged on the manner in which they encourage sustainable development, demonstrate social leadership and corporate ethics. Chapter 18 explains the concept of good governance and how this can be reinforced through ethical behaviour and codes of conduct. It also considers the need to ensure sustainability in decision-making, programmes and projects as well as the need to manage the many different forms of capital.

Accountability and influence are at the core of governance practices. Chapter 19 explains how accountability, authority and influence can be affected by power and identifies how individuals often acquire power within organizations. The chapter also considers how influence is used to get things done and how power can be institutionalized in authority. Finally the power–authority continuum is extended to the process of delegation, whereby authority can be distributed throughout the information service so that others may share the work and responsibilities.

Transparency is also an important component of good governance. Transparency can be assisted through open decision-making and communications, the theme of Chapter 20. This chapter acknowledges that decisions are influenced by perceptions, emotions and intuition and that the potential for these to provide a biased viewpoint needs to be taken into consideration. Chapter 20 explores the appropriateness of different decision-making styles in ensuring transparency in decisions.

Communication is the vehicle through which decisions and policies that are critical to good governance are made and conveyed within the organization and externally. Chapter 20 includes how governance can be managed through effective communications including reports and meetings as well as a model for a corporate communications plan.

Sustainability is the capacity to endure, which from the perspective of the information service and its parent organization is to survive, grow and prosper in continually changing and challenging circumstances as well as drawing upon, managing and using resources in a sustainable manner. Chapter 21 explains how sustainability can be incorporated into core values and taken into account in ensuring effective governance and decision-making within the information service and, second, the sustainability issues that need to be considered and incorporated into information service delivery.

Chapter 22 identifies major risks that can affect information services. The chapter advocates that a business perspective should be taken for each, including the need to plan according to the event and its impact on the business of the organization.

Chapter 23 focuses on sustaining trust and continued operations in organizations. This includes the issue of security, the objective of which is to preserve the confidentiality, integrity and availability of information, as well as ensuring trust and integrity in online services and transactions through authentication and non-repudiation. Responsibility for security is found at all levels of the organization. The chapter identifies different security threats and how these can be overcome through the appropriate management of people, information, physical environment and the technology. The choice of security level is a business issue. It also addresses access controls and lists other good management practices that maintain the integrity, availability and confidentiality of information. Chapter 23 also considers business continuity issues and treats disaster recovery as a component of business continuity.

An important part of the governance process is to ensure a return on investment and that the organization is performing to expectation. Chapter 24 considers the management issues associated with projects to ensure that they deliver the return on investment for the organization. It also provides details on how the return on investment for information products and services can be enhanced and strategies for charging for information products and services. Chapter 24 also provides strategies for measuring and evaluating performance. It describes the performance evaluation process and how performance can be measured in different work units. This requires consideration of outputs and outcomes, quality and value, cause and effect. Information has specific qualities that make the measurement of its value more difficult. Different mechanisms for measuring its value are explored. The chapter also includes examples of performance indicators that can be used in information services and identifies some criteria for performance.

Management
Influences in a
Changing
Landscape
1. Managing in an
uncertain world
2. Strategic
influences

Strategy and
Planning
3. Strategic
Planning –
positioning for a
sustainable future
4. Attracting and
retaining the best
people in
challenging times
5. Ensuring value
for money and
enabling a cost-
sustainable future
6. Knowledge and
information
management – a
key to survival
7. Strategic
technology and
asset management
– a smarter
approach

Leadership and
Innovation
8. Leadership
9. Utilizing a values
driven culture for
sustainability
10. Innovation and
creativity
11. Engaging
change in
positioning for the
future
12. Group dynamics
and team building
13. Effective
negotiation and
conflict
management
14. Managing the
political arena
15. Policy-making
16. Personal
communications
and networking
17. Managing
yourself and others
in challenging
times

Governance and
Social
Responsibility
18. Ensuring good
corporate
governance
19. Using authority
and influence
20. Encouraging
transparency
21. Managing for
sustainability
22. Managing risk
23. Sustaining trust
and continued
operations
24. Evaluating
benefits and
performance

Customer and
Market Focus
25. Competitive
strategies
26. Corporate
image and
communications
27. Ensuring
service quality

Success and
Sustainability
28. Bringing it all
together

Figure PIV.2 Governance and social responsibility

18 *Ensuring Good Corporate Governance*

Ensuring good corporate governance is far more than complying with a legal and regulatory regime. It is a future-shaping activity, in which directions are set and managed, and decisions made with sustainability, ethics and integrity in mind. Corporate governance is about transparency and accountability, choice and influence in actions and decision-making: choices that can lead to effective and ineffective impacts and consequences, or sustainable and unsustainable futures; as well as using or misusing power to influence outcomes, or doing the right thing versus the wrong thing.

Rapid transformations in science and technology, business and society, and uncertainty about the future and growing domains of inconceivability in the external environment present complex dilemmas in decision making, where the impact of making the wrong judgement can be devastating for employees, the organization or the broader community. Good corporate governance structures can help to ensure the correct and sensitive resolution of such complex problems and proposals to ensure sustainability and value for today and the future. This does not mean that executive management has to be an expert on each and every issue that arises. Rather it is knowing when to seek independent expertise and professional advice to supplement their collective knowledge and expertise.

Effective corporate governance is a value-added activity that is the responsibility of everyone in the organization, including where it exists, the organization's oversight body or governing board. It enhances the increasing importance of corporate reputation and provides a level of confidence for customers and stakeholders in the ability of the organization to:

* Achieve excellence and quality of output;
* Embrace a sustainable future;
* Meet its corporate and legislative responsibilities; and
* Meet the ultimate accountability requirements.

The Chief Executive is ultimately accountable for the organization's reputation, decision-making, compliance, direction and outcomes. This involves establishing a sound foundation through their leadership style and ethical behaviours, instituting and maintaining the right corporate culture, making sure that different forms of capital are identified and managed in a sustainable manner, and ensuring that effective organizational structures, oversight entities and systems are in place to ensure good corporate governance.

Senior management has a responsibility for upholding and reinforcing the desired corporate culture, ensuring the integrity of governance systems, structures, policies, practices and procedures, that staff are aware of and understand the policies and procedures, that value is added when duties are discharged, that rights are recognized and acknowledged, and that adequate procedures and practices are in place to support good governance and responsible decision making. Individuals are accountable for their own ethics and integrity in outlook, practices and decision making, as well as ensuring that they follow the correct procedures and practices.

Corporate governance principles

The Australian Stock Exchange Corporate Governance Council has identified 10 principles for good corporate governance that have been adapted to meet the needs of information services:

- Establishing sound foundations for the management and oversight roles of senior management and other oversight entities that may include boards and committees;
- Structuring to add value, by ensuring that there is an effective composition, size, balance and commitment of skills, experience and independence to discharge adequately responsibilities and duties appropriate to the nature of the operations today and for the future;
- Promoting integrity, ethical and responsible decision making amongst those who can influence strategy and financial performance;
- Safeguarding integrity in financial and other reporting, with independent verification to ensure that there is accountability and transparency in the seeking and use of financial resources;
- Maintaining a corporate culture, practices and procedures so that there is timely, factual, objective and balanced disclosure of all material matters concerning the organization;
- Respecting the rights of all stakeholders, including the community as a whole, and ensuring that these are clearly recognized and upheld;
- Recognizing that every business decision has an element of uncertainty and carries a risk that can be managed through effective oversight and internal control;
- Having formal mechanisms such as a balance of skills, competencies, experience and expertise, and continuing professional development that lead to enhanced management skills and effectiveness in keeping pace with inconceivability in the external environment and other aspects that governance of an information service in challenging times requires;
- Ensuring that the level and composition of remuneration is sufficient and reasonable to attract the skills and expertise necessary to achieve the performance expected, and that the relationship between the remuneration and performance is defined and executed; and
- Recognizing the impact of actions and decisions on the legal obligations and interest of all stakeholders.

Corporate governance document

In order to promote transparency most organizations are required to have a document that outlines the structure upon which it bases its corporate governance. A corporate governance document outlines the necessary contextual and structural framework, division of responsibilities, including the principles, duties and procedures through which governance is enacted and supported within the organization. Text Box 18.1 outlines the suggested content for a corporate governance document and relates this to the corporate governance model.

Text Box 18.1 Sample contents of a corporate governance document

---

Corporate Governance

1.   Mission, values, objectives, aims, principles and accountability

Outlines the strategic context of the direction of the organization (relates to the Strategic Plan component of the Strategic Framework in the Corporate Governance Model):

1.1.   Mission Statement

1.2.   Values of the organization

1.3.   Objectives

2.   Roles, responsibilities and Code of Conduct for Governing Body

Establishes the legal and regulatory framework and governance structure including sources of responsibility, authority and conduct for the Governing Body and defined governance and oversight roles (relates to parts of Accountability and Compliance Framework in the Corporate Governance Model):

2.1.   Constitution of the organization
2.1.1.   Legislation and regulation
2.1.2.   Registration details

2.2.   Constitution of the Governing Body
2.2.1.   Governing Body Charter

2.3.   Summary of activities of the Governing Body

2.4.   Performance measures of Governing Body

2.5.   Role and responsibilities of Chairperson

2.6.   Role and responsibilities of Governing Body

2.7.   Role and responsibilities of individual Board Members

2.8.   Personal liability of Board Members

2.9.   Appointment of Committees and Advisory Groups

2.10.   Board Code of Conduct

2.11.   Management of complaints

2.12.   Audit Committee

2.13.   Details of other committees established by the Board

2.14.   Review of Board effectiveness

2.15.   Role and responsibilities of Chief Executive Officer – including appointment procedures, delegated authority, designated Accounting Officer for organization

2.16.   Delegations – outlines roles and powers reserved for the Board and those that are delegated to the Chief Executive Officer e.g. corporate governance, strategy, audit issues, budget, annual report and accounts, quality, performance management, risk management, human resource management, privacy, communications

3.   Accountability and Compliance

Defines responsible and ethical decision-making processes and other accountability mechanisms (relates to parts of Accountability and Compliance and Strategic Frameworks in the Corporate Governance Model):

3.1.   Aims of the governance arrangements including what is to be achieved

3.2.   Principles that govern the decisions made by the organization and its governance board e.g. observing highest standards of propriety and integrity, strategic priorities, maximizing value for money, accountability regime, openness, internal controls

3.3.   Review mechanisms for governance arrangements

3.4.   Accountability mechanisms e.g. reporting including the annual report, strategic plan, audits, complaint resolution process, disclosure and transparency including declaration of interests

4.   Standing Orders

Provides the procedural framework under which the organization discharges its business (relates to parts of Accountability and Compliance and Integrity Frameworks in the Corporate Governance Model):

4.1.   Place of Business

4.2.   Meetings – calling of meeting, notice of meeting, business transacted, quorum, record of attendance, chairmanship, voting, adjournment, minutes, urgent business, meeting procedure, standards of conduct at meetings

4.3.   Committees, membership of committees and advisory groups

4.4.   Conflicts of Interest – declaration of interests, exemptions, register of interests, gifts and hospitality

4.5.   Information – use of information

4.6.   Appointments – no soliciting for appointment, relatives as candidates

4.7.   Indemnity

4.8.   Use of Common Seal – custody of seal, authority for sealing of documents, register of sealing

4.9.   Appointment of auditors

4.10.   Suspension and amendment of standing orders, including review of standing orders

5.   Statutory Framework

Outlines statutory framework under which the organization operates, (relates to parts of Accountability and Compliance Framework in the Corporate Governance Model) for example:

5.1.   Freedom of Information Act

5.2.   Corporations Act

5.3.   Privacy Act

6.   Financial Framework

Outlines the financial framework of the organization (relates to parts of Structure and Resources Framework in the Corporate Governance Model):

6.1.   Financial policies

6.2.   Capital investment and asset management

6.3.   Treasury management and banking

6.4.   Debt management

6.5.   Procurement

6.6.   Creditor Payments

6.7.   Taxation

6.8.   Budgetary Control

6.9.   Risk Management and insurance

6.10.   Internal controls

6.11.   Audit

6.12.   Accounting systems

6.13.   Claims and litigation

6.14.   Fraud

6.15.   Fees and charging

6.16.   Expenses

7.   Human Resource Framework

Provides the governance context for the management of people in the organization (relates to parts of Structure and Resources Framework in the Corporate Governance Model):

7.1.   Remuneration

7.2.   Appointments

7.3.   Conditions of employment

7.4.   Commitment to workplace diversity

7.5.   Occupational Health and Safety

7.6.   Succession planning

8.   Sustainability and social responsibility

Outlines the roles and responsibilities to enable sustainable outcomes and meet corporate social responsibilities (relates to parts of the Strategic Framework in the Corporate Governance Model):

8.1.   Protection and conservation of the environment

8.2.   Achieving a sustainable future

8.3.   Corporate social responsibility

9.   Communication and disclosure

Outlines how decisions and matters of interest will be communicated (relates to parts of the Integrity Framework in the Corporate Governance Model):

9.1.   Openness and transparency

9.2.   Timely and balanced disclosure

9.3.   Stakeholder engagement and communications

10.   Interpretations

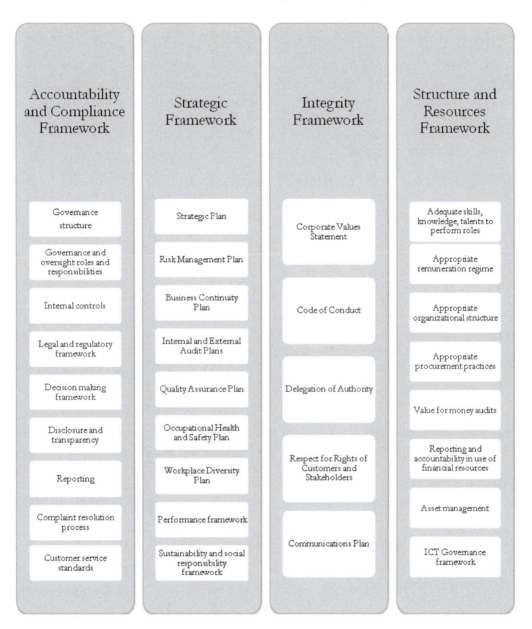

Figure 18.1 Corporate governance model

Corporate governance model

Corporate governance comprises the systems, structures, practices, procedures and corporate culture that organizations have in place to minimize risks and exposures and optimize performance and accountability. Figure 18.1 illustrates how these can be brought together in a corporate governance model to enable the organization to meet its corporate governance obligations. The model provides a framework for corporate governance and outlines the structures, practices and processes that support accountability, transparency and compliance; a strategic framework that addresses the future direction, risks, quality and performance; an integrity framework that sets out values and required conduct; as well as having the correct structures and resources in place to fulfil the organization's responsibilities. To maintain the integrity of these systems, structures, policies, practices and procedures, it is necessary for them to be reviewed for their effectiveness at least annually. Further discussion on many of the topics identified in the frameworks below can be found in other chapters in the book.

ACCOUNTABILITY AND COMPLIANCE FRAMEWORK

The accountability and compliance framework for good corporate governance addresses the roles and responsibilities, systems, structures, processes, legal and regulatory frameworks that support transparency and good governance, responsible and ethical decision making, and disclosures such as declarations of interest and reporting. Board charters and the requirement to account for activities and expenditures such as through the annual report are also included in this framework. The accountability and compliance framework defines service levels and avenues for redress such as a complaints resolution process. It includes the internal controls that organizations use to communicate what is expected of staff, for example making new employees aware of the organization's expectations with regards to accountability through the induction process.

STRATEGIC FRAMEWORK

The strategic framework considers both the future direction of the organization and the critical factors that are necessary for the organization to manage and address risks and to be operationally sustained and survive in challenging environments. It brings together the strategic plan and other specific plans that are in place to ensure that the operations of the organization function correctly. Examples include the risk management plan, business continuity plan, performance frameworks by which individual and organizational performance can be judged, as well as externally facing obligations such as sustainability and social responsibility.

INTEGRITY FRAMEWORK

The integrity framework addresses the ideology, systems, processes and policy frameworks that need to be in place to meet public and social accountability standards and to foster a corporate culture through which honour, reliability and the uprightness of the organization can be instilled and sustained. Included in the integrity framework are corporate values, a code of conduct that outlines the code of ethics, how official information may be used, how records should be kept, guidance on how corporate resources may be used, how conflicts of interest can be identified and managed, and how gifts and hospitality should be declared, accepted and managed. The integrity framework also addresses the rights of customers and stakeholders and outlines plans for how stakeholders are informed and kept abreast of developments, engaged for their support and major events communicated. This is separate to communication of disclosures that is a necessary part of the accountability and compliance framework.

Codes of conduct

Good corporate governance ultimately requires people to act with integrity with today and the future in mind. Whilst societal values, the justice and political systems provide the broad framework within which ethical values operate, ethical behaviour and integrity is also interpreted according to individual values, culture and experience. What may be considered integrity and ethical behaviour to one person could be considered inappropriate to another. A code of conduct sets the boundaries and individual responsibilities for what is considered to be the desired level of integrity and ethical behaviour in situations where personal values systems can be challenged or differ.

A code of conduct recognizes that most people want to do the right thing, but that certain environments present opportunities for temptation and/or material gain. The code is particularly useful in environments where there are financial functions, intense competition, opportunities for insider trading or conflict-of-interest situations to occur. In dealing with issues related to codes of conduct, perception is just as important as reality. Safeguarding corporate reputation and integrity requires the use of the test as to whether it could normally be perceived that an advantage was taken or that a conflict of interest arose out of a situation.

Public and social accountability, which is based on the notions of legitimacy, fairness and ethics, goes further than good governance. As part of the quest for quality management, standards for ethics and integrity are also important in the pursuit of excellence. Ethical standards in the form of codes of conduct define what is right and wrong in terms of the behaviour of individuals towards others, and how those in a position to influence materially the integrity, quality, strategy and operations of the information service can and should operate. Codes of conduct reinforce the roles of executive management and their responsibilities to set standards and demonstrate by example issues such as quality customer service, respect for customers and stakeholders, open communications, honesty, fairness and equity, respect and integrity, and accountability. They enable employees to judge what is right and wrong behaviour.

The nature of the activities of information services means that people are often privy to insider information, other commercial and personal information and financial transactions, either directly or indirectly, that could be used for personal gain. A clearly articulated policy in a code of conduct can assist individuals to deal with confidentiality, ethical problems and conflicts of interest. Ethical policies in the form of a code of ethics that might form part of the code of conduct also guide the necessary behaviour standards and practices to maintain confidence in the integrity of the information service. Ethical policies, code of ethics and in-house ethical committees are useful mechanisms for linking ethical behaviour to the corporate values, providing support in recognizing and dealing with ethical compliance issues, reinforcing personal responsibility for ethical behaviours as well as making ethical conduct easily understood.

Ethics are generally based upon three principles. These are:

- Utilitarian principles, such as the greatest good for the greatest number and responsible care, and accountability in the use of resources;
- Individual rights, or respect and protection of the basic rights of individuals such as the right to privacy, to free speech and to due process; and

- Justice, where fair and impartial rules are imposed and enforced on everyone to ensure the equitable distribution of costs and benefits.

The Australian Stock Exchange Corporate Governance Council identifies several areas for inclusion in a code of conduct that has been adapted as follows to meet the needs of information services:

- Conflicts of interest – managing situations where the interest of a private individual (who may or may not be an employee) or group interferes with or appears to interfere with the interests of the information service or organization as a whole. An example might be where a member of staff has strong religious convictions and attempts to influence the selection policy of a library;
- Corporate opportunities – preventing employees or stakeholders from taking advantage of property, information or position, or opportunities arising from these, for personal gain or to compete within the organization. Examples include where a manager attempts to influence the selection of a candidate who is a close friend for a position, or where a senior executive accepts the offer of hospitality such as a free overseas trip from a supplier;
- Privacy and confidentiality – restricting the use of non-public information except where disclosure is authorized or legally mandated. The right to know principle is appropriate here. Even when there may be no harm intended, or intention of disclosure to a third party or for personal gain, the act of unnecessarily accessing personal information from a system is in breach of confidentiality. For example, unauthorized access to the personnel record of an individual or tracking their choice of websites out of personal interest can constitute a breach;
- Fair dealing – by all employees with the information service's customers, suppliers, competitors and employees. For example the provision of preferential treatment to certain customers at the detriment of others, or favouring one supplier over another because they have the best festive season parties;
- Use of the information service's assets – protecting and ensuring the efficient use of assets such as vehicles and ICT for legitimate business purposes. Acceptable use is appropriate here. For example, the use of corporate time and equipment quickly to undertake electronic banking may be more productive for the information service and individuals than their visiting a bank. However, the continuous use of electronic devices for gaming purposes during work time would not be considered to be a legitimate or efficient use;
- Compliance with laws and regulations – active promotion of compliance. Examples here include compliance with occupational, health and safety regulations, equal employment opportunity awards, consumer protection regulations, corporate taxation and financial reporting requirements, and environmental laws; and
- Encouraging the reporting of unlawful/unethical behaviour – active promotion of ethical behaviour and protection for those who report violations in good faith. Whilst confidentiality may not always be guaranteed, it is important to develop a culture where inappropriate behaviour is not condoned, that appropriate action will be taken when reports are received, that employees are enabled to disclose potential misconduct without fear of retribution, and that exposure is considered an important obligation to maintain an ethical corporate culture.

The presence of a code of conduct does not in itself ensure good corporate governance. An understanding of the contents and what constitutes compliance is necessary for all employees and key stakeholders. The objectives and content of the code of conduct should be readily available on the corporate intranet, visibly promoted on a regular basis and explained to new employees as part of the induction process. Compliance with the code of conduct should be continuously monitored by management, and any departures quickly dealt with.

Managing conflicts of interest

Conflicts of interest need to be considered within an ethical framework that requires employees to act with integrity, impartiality, in good faith, and in the best interests of the organization they serve. The Organisation for Economic Co-operation and Development (OECD) also promotes four core principles for organizations to deal with conflict-of-interest situations, to promote integrity, and for maintaining public confidence:

• Serving the public interest;
• Supporting transparency and scrutiny;
• Promoting individual responsibility and personal example; and
• Engendering an organizational culture which is intolerant of conflicts of interest.

Identifying a conflict of interest is an individual responsibility. The person who has identified that they have a conflict of interest or a potential conflict of interest should immediately declare it to their supervisor or manager in writing. In turn senior management must actively manage or resolve any real or perceived conflicts of interest of which they become aware.

Conflicts of interest may be actual, or be perceived to exist, or potentially exist at some time in the future. Perception of a conflict of interest is important to consider because public confidence in the integrity of an organization is vital. For example a potential conflict of interest may occur where a person has an interest in a matter under consideration by the organization such as undertaking a contract with a company owned by a member of the person's family. An actual conflict arises where the person fails to disclose a potential conflict of interest, and participates in deliberations on the matter, as if the conflict did not exist.

It is not always possible to avoid a conflict of interest, particularly in some specialist industries. A conflict of interest in itself is not necessarily wrong, or unethical. However, a failure to declare a potential or actual conflict of interest is wrong and unethical. Declaring a potential or actual conflict of interest is also an important step in identifying and managing the situation. Some common risk areas where conflicts of interest occur include:

• Managing procurement processes, tenders and contracts;
• Obtaining sponsorship from a third party;
• Allocating grants;
• Accepting gifts, benefits and hospitality;
• Undertaking recruitment, selection and appointment; and
• Undertaking secondary employment.

There is no one 'right' way to identify every situation, however a good starting point is to consider the following six Ps:

- Private interests – do I have personal or private interests that may conflict, or be perceived to conflict, with my employer?
- Potentialities – could there be benefits for me now, or in the future, that could cast doubt on my objectivity?
- Perception – how will my involvement in the decision/action be viewed by others? Are there risks associated for me or my organization?
- Proportionality – does my involvement in the decision appear fair and reasonable in all the circumstances?
- Presence of mind – what are the consequences if I ignore a conflict of interest? What if my involvement was questioned publicly?
- Promises – have I made any promises or commitments in relation to the matter? Do I stand to gain or lose from the proposed action/decision?

Declaring the potential conflict of interest to a supervisor or manager and making a written record of the disclosure in a register is an important first step. Following this an assessment should be made of the situation and a strategy for dealing with the proposed or actual conflict determined. This might including restricting the employee's involvement in the matter, for example, refrain from taking part in debate about a specific issue, abstain from voting on decisions, and/or restrict access to information relating to the conflict of interest. Other options such as relinquishing the personal or private interests that are the source of conflict may need to be considered.

STRUCTURE AND RESOURCES FRAMEWORK

How the structure of an organization and associated organizational assets are resourced and managed also influences the degree to which accountability and answerability can be realized. To be sustainable an organization requires an appropriate structure with the commensurate resourcing and remuneration of skills, talents, knowledge to perform the desired roles, appropriate allocation of budget and accountability in financial and procurement practices, as well as specialized governance mechanisms for the management and deployment of ICT and other assets. The Structures and Resources Framework outlines the desired level of resources and includes reporting and accountability in the use of these resources, including financial accountability.

Conclusion

The capacity to govern effectively is derived from human will and choice, either as an individual or as a group. Corporate governance requires sound management practices that provide effective oversight, promote integrity, enable transparency in decision-making, add value in all processes, manage risk and enable the capacity to make the right decisions. This is sustained through a code of conduct and corporate culture philosophy that is inclusive and upholds ethics and integrity in decision making.

Effective corporate governance comprises structures, practices and processes that support accountability and compliance; a strategic framework that addresses the future direction, risks, quality and performance; an integrity framework that sets out values and required conduct; as well as having the correct structures and resources in place to fulfil the organization's responsibilities. Together these minimize risks and exposures and optimize performance and accountability.

The principles that support good corporate governance include:

- Establishing sound foundations for management and oversight roles;
- Ensuring that there is an effective structure, skills, experience and independence to support the nature of the operations now and in the future;
- Promoting integrity, ethical and responsible decision making;
- Safeguarding integrity, accountability and verification in financial and other reporting;
- Maintaining a corporate culture, practices and procedures that support timely and objective disclosure of all material matters concerning the organization;
- Respecting the rights of all stakeholders;
- Managing business decisions through effective oversight and internal control;
- Having formal mechanisms that lead to enhanced management skills and governance;
- Ensuring that the level and composition of remuneration is sufficient and reasonable to attract the skills and expertise required;
- Recognizing the impact of actions and decisions on the legal obligations and interest of all stakeholders; and
- Responsibly managing different forms of capital for a sustainable future, wealth and to add value.

In order to promote transparency most organizations are required to have a document that outlines the structure upon which it bases its corporate governance. A corporate governance document outlines the necessary contextual and structural framework, division of responsibilities, principles, responsibilities and procedures through which governance is enacted and supported within the organization.

References

Australian Stock Exchange Corporate Governance Council. 2003. *Principles of Good Corporate Governance and Best Practice Recommendations*. Available at www.shareholder.com [accessed: 4 March 2005].

OECD. 2003. *Recommendation of the Council on Guidelines for Managing Conflict of Interest in the Public Service*. Available at www.oecd.org/dataoecd/13/22/2957360.pdf.

Sustainability Reporting Programme. Available at www.sustreport.org/business/report.org/intro_lg.html [accessed: 20 June 2005].

Further reading

Benn, S. and Dunphy, D. 2007. *Corporate Governance and Sustainability: Challenges for Theory and Practice*. London: Routledge.

Das Gupta, A. 2004. *Human Values in Management*. Aldershot: Ashgate.

Davies, A. 2005. *The Practice of Corporate Governance*. Aldershot: Ashgate.

Farrar, J.H. 2008. *Corporate Governance: Theories, Principles and Practice*, 3rd edn. South Melbourne: Oxford University Press.

Fishel, D. 2003. *The Book of the Board: Effective Governance of Non-Profit Organisations*. Leichardt: Federation Press.

Laszlo, C. 2003. *The Sustainable Company: How to Create Lasting Value Through Social and Environmental Performance*. Washington, DC: Island Press.

19 *Using Authority and Influence*

Power and authority are behavioural processes that are manifested in influence and determine the way in which governance is acted out. Power is the ability to influence others. This is an increasingly important ability in order to sustain an organization in challenging times; for example in convincing financial organizations to advance funding to support business growth or in undertaking a merger of services. Power is legitimized in authority. Power may be sought and used by individuals or groups, particularly in times of change. The quest for power can lead to healthy and productive competitive outcomes or it can result in disruptive, selfish or harmful behaviours, where the outcomes are not as beneficial.

Authority is institutionalized power. It is based on position, personal characteristics, expertise and knowledge and the situation. Authority can be delegated by giving responsibility and authority to others to execute a job. However, the manager or persons involved in the act of delegation are still accountable for the outcomes.

Understanding the use of power

Power has a classical double meaning of:

- The ability to influence the activities of individuals, groups, organizations, societies and nations; and
- Determining who gets what, when and how.

This is because power is the capacity or potential of one unit to influence or elicit compliance in another in relation to behaviour or attitude. This may be willing or unwilling, conscious or unconscious compliance. Whilst an individual or group can have the capacity and potential for power, they may never use it.

The use of the word 'power' often has negative connotations. This is the result of many people associating power with its abuse rather than its ethical use. A test of good governance is to avoid the abuse of power. This requires a good understanding of the various power sources and how to use these effectively to persuade and influence ethical outcomes rather than control people and situations for personal gain.

POWER BASES

The acquisition and use of power is a natural process within organizations. French and Raven (1959) have defined five sources of power: three are derived from organizational sources whilst the other two are derived from personal sources. Reward, coercive and legitimate powers are the three power bases that are derived from positions within the organization. Expert and referent power sources are personal power sources.

Reward power

Reward power stems from the ability of an individual to provide tangible rewards in return for certain outcomes. People will comply with the requests of others if this will result in a positive benefit. The power base is contingent on the individual perceiving that:

- The person has sufficient authority to be able to offer rewards; and
- The reward is perceived to be a benefit.

The requests should also be perceived to be feasible, proper and ethical, and the incentive sufficiently attractive and at a level that could not be attained by another less costly course of action. For instance, if an assistant records manager asked a staff member to work late for an hour one night in exchange for two hours off during the following day, the request would be considered in the light of whether:

- The person had the authority to grant the two hours off, or even to ask the person to stay behind in the first place;
- The staff roster situation and personal workload made it feasible to take the two hours off the next day;
- The activities already planned for that night were of more importance; and
- Someone else was available and prepared to work late.

Coercive power

Coercive power is the extent to which a manager can manipulate or control other people. It is a power based upon fear. Coercive power was a factor of traditional management styles where autocracy prevailed. Today it is recognized that coercive power is used in very extreme circumstances and can result in hostility, resentment and aggression as well as erode the manager's referent power. Coercion and punishment are only effective when applied in a small way and in legitimate circumstances.

Legitimate power

Legitimate power is the power based upon position and is found in authority. For example, the request of the finance manager for the information services manager to submit their budget papers by the end of the month. Requests using legitimate power are usually made politely, confidently and clearly, with their underlying reasons explained. From a governance perspective a non-legitimate use of power may be a request to delete certain documents from a file.

Expert power

Expert power is based on the possession of knowledge, experience or judgement that other individuals do not have, but respect or need. Most lecturers demonstrate the possession of expert power over their students. However, possession of expertise is not sufficient for managers or lecturers to influence people. It is also necessary for individuals to recognize the manager's or lecturer's expertise and perceive them to be a credible source of information.

Expert power is demonstrated through the display of certificates or awards on office walls; by acting confidently and decisively in a crisis; by keeping informed and informing others of emerging technology issues, by presenting papers at conferences, and by maintaining personal credibility.

Referent power

Referent power is developed out of a person's admiration for another and their desire to model their behaviour on that person's attributes. Role models and mentors have referent power as they engender a feeling of personal alignment, affection, loyalty and admiration on behalf of the subject. Referent power is often based upon an individual's personal characteristics. An information services manager is likely to build referent power if they are articulate, show consideration for individual needs and feelings, encourage and develop individuals, and if they exhibit ethical behaviour.

ACQUIRING POWER

Individuals often acquire power within organizations through:

- Developing a sense of obligation in others;
- Building a reputation as an 'expert' in certain matters;
- Fostering others' unconscious identification with them or their ideas; and
- Maintaining the belief that others are dependent upon them.

Managers who are ethical in acquiring power are sensitive to what others consider to be legitimate behaviour in acquiring and using power and seek to use it to effect positive outcomes. They recognize that power is an essential management tool. They have a good understanding of the various types of power and its effects on different people. They develop expertise in using different types of power in order that the correct type can be used in the right circumstances to achieve the information service's and the parent organization's objectives. They exercise restraint and self-control to ensure that power is not abused or used impulsively.

COUNTER POWER

Power sources can be neutralized by counter power. Individuals may influence others by exercising a restraint on the use of power. An example of counter power is where employees engage the services of an outside body to negotiate on their behalf their working conditions with management, or where a group of individuals may try to neutralize a negative influence within the organization.

Influence

Influence is the action that creates a behavioural response to the exercise of power. When power sources are activated they are influential in that they get someone to do something in a required way. Influence is important in that it can assist or distort the governance process.

There are many uses of influence within organizations. One of the most common forms of influence is the legitimate request. When an officer in the records management section is asked to check the location of a file, the officer will normally comply. The officer sees the request is made within a work role setting and is legitimate.

Rational persuasion is used to persuade another party that the proposals or decisions are justified and that they will be successful. It incorporates a logical argument in which a party is convinced of the need to change their mind or that the suggested behaviour is the best outcome for all. Rational persuasion is reliant on the party having some knowledge or perception of the issue as the persuader does not have any tangible controls on the outcomes.

Rational faith is based upon expert power, where a person's credibility or expertise is sufficient to influence the other party to take a particular course of action. An example of rational faith is where an employee uses a particular database that has been recommended by the librarian or research officer. The employee may not be aware of the contents of the database, but will use it on the recommendation of the librarian.

Indoctrination establishes certain values and beliefs in people that lead to behaviours that support the organizational objectives. The induction process is a form of indoctrination.

Information distortion influences a person's impression and attitudes as it limits or censors the information that they receive. The target person is influenced without being aware of it. Information distortion takes place when reports are edited or when information is withheld from those who need it. A similar form of distortion occurs in situational engineering, where a physical or social situation is manipulated.

Authority

Authority is institutionalized power. Whilst authority is based upon formal position and legitimacy, its acceptance is governed by the use of factors such as compliance, leadership and expertise. Authority can be gained from position, personal characteristics, expertise and knowledge, and the situation.

POSITION

This is the part of authority that is conferred upon individuals because they occupy a particular position, such as the Chairperson of the Board of Directors or Chief Executive Officer. The position and title are approximately indicative of the relative standing of the position holder's authority compared to other individuals, even though it may not be a specific measure of the exact degree of authority. The true extent of the position holder's authority is measured by the scope and range of their activities within the organization.

PERSONAL CHARACTERISTICS

Personal characteristics such as vision exhibited by leaders in getting others to do things are a part of authority. Domination, physical disposition and certain personality traits are also used to gain authority.

EXPERTISE AND KNOWLEDGE

A person's specialist knowledge and expertise can confer a degree of authority over those not having the same level of knowledge or expertise to make a decision or solve a problem. This is known as authority of knowledge or expertise. It can be independent of level or position, for example a person's knowledge or expertise in a particular information system may provide them with a higher degree of authority over its future management than others who have not been exposed to the system.

SITUATION

Finally, authority can exist in a given context, specific as to time and place and determined by the elements of the situation. As an example, an individual who, upon witnessing a fire in a storage room or taking a bomb threat call, may with their first reactions initiate a course of events that may not occur given a normal situation. The situation therefore provokes leadership behaviour and the acceptance of responsibility on behalf of an individual, who, though not in a position of authority, assumes authority in that particular situation by issuing orders.

Delegation

Delegation is the organizational process by which authority is distributed throughout the information service so that others may share work and responsibilities and contribute to the governance process. The distribution of authority through the delegation process does not occur automatically; it occurs by deliberate design. Delegation is a three-stage process:

- An individual is given responsibility for a task, such as to write a report or to manage a work unit;
- Second, they are given the authority to do the job. They may also be given the necessary position power needed to execute the job; and
- Finally, they are required to be responsible for their actions and outcomes.

Most organizations have formal structures through which delegations are legitimized. However whilst authority may be delegated to an individual to achieve certain outcomes through formal delegation, the Chief Executive Officer or manager is still in possession of their own authority over the situation. They have neither more nor less authority than they did before they delegated it. The same thing is true of responsibility and accountability that is central to good governance. No matter how much authority or responsibility is delegated, the Chief Executive Officer still retains ultimate accountability for the outcomes and results within the information service.

The individual who has been given authority must recognize the fact that they will be judged by their manager on the quality of their performance. They are still responsible and accountable to their manager. By accepting authority, people denote their acceptance of responsibility and accountability.

BENEFITS OF DELEGATION

Delegation improves decision quality and acceptance. It can lessen the load of higher levels of management and allows for quicker responses. Since the delegate is often closer to the point of action and has more specific information than the Chief Executive Officer or manager, it allows for a better decision in less time.

It is also a form of job enrichment and an effective method of managerial development and training, providing for internal promotion and career paths within the information service. Individuals' jobs become more meaningful and challenging, leading to increased levels of motivation. In situations where organizational levels are being flattened and career paths restricted, delegation serves as one way in which team members can be extended and given further responsibility.

Whilst most people will welcome delegation there may also be some resistance. Some individuals do not wish for any more authority or responsibility, or do not wish to increase their already demanding workload. Others may lack self-confidence or have a low personal need for achievement. The amount of delegation that will be acceptable will vary according to the manager, the individual and the situation.

Unfortunately, some managers do not delegate. A failure or reluctance to delegate is caused by a number of reasons. They may feel insecure or do not know what to do. They may lack confidence in individuals being able to perform the task, although it could be argued that this is evidence that their training and staff development programmes are not effective. Their insecurity may be further aggravated by a feeling that their people have the potential to do a better job than themselves. They may also have a desire to maintain absolute control over the operations of the workplace.

Delegation, like other processes, can be learned. The most basic principle to effective delegation is the willingness by managers to give their people real freedom to accomplish their delegated tasks. Managers have to accept that there are several ways of handling a problem and that their own way is not necessarily the one that others would choose.

Individuals may make errors, but they need to be allowed to develop their own solutions and learn from their mistakes. Improved communication and understanding between managers and their people can also overcome barriers to delegation. Knowing the strengths, weaknesses and preferences of their people enables managers to decide which tasks can more realistically be delegated to whom.

The delegation process can be enhanced if the individual completely understands their responsibilities and role expectations, and is given sufficient authority to carry out their tasks. Their responsibilities and limits of discretion should be well defined. Assistance in the forms of psychological support, advice, technical information, should be provided and feedback given at regular intervals. The individual should be willing to accept their responsibilities and be encouraged to act on their own and make use of their newly acquired authority.

Conclusion

Power and authority are inextricably linked and central to the effectiveness of transparency in decisions and good governance. Power is the ability to influence others, which is legitimized in authority. Delegation allows the giving of responsibility and authority to others. Like politics, power can have negative and positive connotations. It can be abused as well as used effectively to persuade and influence outcomes.

References

French, J.R.P. and Raven, B. 1959. The bases of social power, in *Studies in Social Power*, ed. D. Cartwright. Ann Arbor: Institute for Social Research.

Further reading

Kakabadse, A. et al. 2004. *Working in Organisations*. Aldershot: Ashgate.

20 *Encouraging Transparency*

Trust and a good corporate reputation is reliant on having transparency in governance processes, open and participative decision making, as well as having a culture where managers at all levels are approachable and open to suggestions and ideas. Providing clarity on issues and fostering strong communications across the organization and with its stakeholders are other important aspects of having transparency within the organization.

Transparency is an excellent example of 'the chicken and the egg conundrum'. Transparency in processes, communications and decision making generates trust in the organization, yet trust gives people confidence in being candid and open to discuss and resolve issues that may affect performance and the future sustainability of the organization.

Encouraging transparency also involves ensuring that there is no confusion about why and when actions or decisions are being taken, that people are clear about the ramifications of the actions or decision and about the actions or decisions themselves. Openness includes candid and honest discussion leading up to when decisions are taken so that a comprehensive view is formed of the issues being considered, as well as frankness about the decision itself.

Making the right decision

Decisions that are made within information services have multiple impacts: some being strategic and concern transformational change with long-term sustainability implications, others being operational or tactical, affecting and effected by groups or individuals. Certain decisions will be based on simple and well-defined facts whilst others will involve complex and ill-defined situations. Making the right decision and communicating this within the organization and to key stakeholders is an important component of good governance.

PARTICIPATIVE DECISION MAKING

Employees have come to demand and readily expect their employers to engage them in decision-making processes. Likewise enlightened employers acknowledge that higher-quality decisions and greater transparency result from participative decision making. Participative decision making allows people to bring multiple views, aspects and knowledge of the subject area, different abilities, interests and skills, as well as freedom of thought to the decision-making environment. This type of decision making is most successful in open organizations and where individuals possess the knowledge and abilities that enable them to make informed decisions.

Participative decision making is also useful for resolving differences in challenging and changing environments. The sharing of norms and values and the communication processes involved can positively influence the motivation of employees, minimize conflict, clarify issues of concern and result in less resistance to the planned changes. By involving groups rather than individuals in the decision-making process there is likely to be more acceptance of risk with the feeling that there is safety in numbers. Equally, the people directly concerned should be involved as they are immediately affected and have the most practical knowledge of day-to-day operations.

Where tough decisions are needed, participative decision making should not be used as an excuse for stalling the decision or as a substitution for individual action. Likewise the failure to make a decision and indecision are equally ineffective. In these instances it is important that the most sensible and implemental decision is made.

UNDERSTANDING PERCEPTIONS, INTUITION AND EMOTIONS

Many decisions are influenced by perception, intuition and emotion that can skew truth and objectivity. From a management perspective, the need to deal with perceptions is as real as the need to deal with facts. Perceptions are formed from personal experience, knowledge, discussions and conversation that sometimes can be incorrect or misconstrued. Likewise, an individual's perception or interpretation of an issue can be influenced by past experiences that may not be entirely relevant to the case in point, or they may be correctly influenced by variables that are not widely known to others which could lead to their choice of actions being questioned and affect others' evaluation of the outcome of their decision.

Intuition influences decision making in that it involves abstract thoughts that are not associated with concrete evidence but are based on individual instinct or apprehension. Often the words 'sixth sense' or 'gut feeling' are applied to the phenomenon of adding a further dimension to the five conventional senses that are used by individuals.

Decision-making is also an emotional process. What may appear to be a small decision taken at one level may be considered to have significant emotional consequences at another. For example, decisions on eligibility for car parking spaces may be operationally-based but attach considerable emotional importance to those who do not qualify. Feelings of self-worth, biases and experiences also affect the emotional processing of decision-making. Emotions are involved in diagnosing and defining the problem, in selecting acceptable solutions and in the implementation of the solution.

DECISION-MAKING STYLES

Whilst today's environment is fast-paced and actions or decisions need to be made quickly, there is a need to understand that individual styles differ. Some people seem to act quickly, whilst others always appear more hesitant. Much of this has to do with personal decision-making styles which are linked to individual thought systems, people's perceptions of situations, past experience and emotions. It can also be to do with the human brain.

Right and left brain hemispheres

Different personal attributes and decision styles of individuals can be found in the way in which they use the human brain. The human brain can be divided into two halves. Looking down on the top of the exposed brain two hemispheres are present, the left and the right. The left brain controls the right-hand side of the body and the right brain the left side.

The right and left hemispheres have different thinking styles. The left brain in most people is particularly involved in thinking activities that use language, logic, analysis, reason and mathematical ability. It is also associated with awareness of detail, recognition and classification of problems and optimizing results over time. The right hemisphere is more associated with pictorial, image thinking, spatial awareness, creative ability and intuitive thinking. The right, it is argued, is much better at seeing wholes. Problem solving, writing and planning require high-level left side use, whilst the right brain is particularly associated with the ability to make non-logical connections and to see overall patterns or trends. It uses intuition as the basis for decision making.

The knowledge of these two different thinking styles allows individuals to recognize and value the thinking styles involved in the decision-making process.

APPROPRIATENESS OF DIFFERENT DECISION-MAKING STYLES

There are four main decision-making styles: directive, analytical, conceptual and behavioural. Often more than one decision-making style is appropriate, and managers can select the style most appropriate for the situation.

Directive style

According to Rowe (1984: 18) managers with a directive style are efficient and logical yet generally have a low tolerance for ambiguity and a low cognitive complexity. They are autocratic, have a high need for power and maintain tight control. They focus upon technical decisions, preferring a systematic structure. Decisions are made rapidly, with little information, usually obtained verbally, and few alternatives are considered. Only short-range, internal factors are usually considered.

Analytical style

Analytical managers have a greater tolerance for ambiguity than do directive managers, but require control over decision making. As their decisions are based on careful analysis, they require more information and consider more alternatives. They are careful but enjoy variety. They are able to adapt to or cope with new situations. Analytical managers are oriented to problem solving and strive for maximum output.

Conceptual style

Conceptual managers are broad in their outlook, achievements oriented and consider many alternatives. They value commitments and integrity and are creative in finding solutions. They focus on long-range issues, are future oriented and are able to negotiate effectively. They will frequently use participative decision-making techniques.

Behavioural style

The behavioural-style manager is concerned for the organization and development of people. They communicate easily, show empathy and tend to be persuasive. Their focus is short or medium range. They use limited data as their emphasis is on decision making through people.

Organizational communications

Transparency and openness in organizations are dependent on good communications for clarity and comprehensiveness. Communication is the process through which the thoughts, processes, ideals and decisions of management and governance functions are transferred and adopted by others. The extent to which formal and informal channels of communication are used within information services depends upon the complexity and stability of the environment, and the size, nature and corporate culture of the parent organization.

Increasingly, formal and informal communications are conveyed through electronic means. Collaborative information and communications technology (ICT) tools enable individuals and groups to see and hear each other, work on shared documents, and witness changes as they occur. This speeds up not only the process of communication, but also the reaction. Messages are conveyed and received instantaneously so the message that is conveyed needs to be the correct one.

Rapidly changing environments require rapid communication with less time for formalized procedures. In contrast, bureaucratic-type structures create situations where procedures and regulations are followed and communication is much more formal.

FORMAL CHANNELS OF COMMUNICATION

Formal communications are often used by management to inform people of significant corporate issues and to provide answers to routine questions. They convey factual information and explanation without the emotional perspectives often found in informal communication. Intranets and email are often used as vehicles for formal communications. Formal communication can also be oral. Enterprise collaboration tools, meetings, appraisal interviews and formal discussions or conversations are all used to convey important messages. Formal communication should be open and timely in order to engage trust and keep people informed of important events that may affect them.

INFORMAL CHANNELS OF COMMUNICATION

Informal communication occurs as part of the social relationship of people. It is not confined to hierarchies, work relationships or work practices. Informal communication supplements formal communication; in the absence of good official communication, informal communication may supplant it. Informal communication channels distribute information that may not have been communicated officially.

The 'grapevine' and chat groups are widely recognized forms of informal communication. Both are fast, highly selective and discriminating. They provide management with insights into employee attitudes, help spread useful information and act as a safety valve for employee emotions. Both have positive and negative implications. Whilst rumour and/or hostility may psychologically help people by releasing emotions, they can be disturbing to others. They may also spread false rumours. This can be a problem where there is no permanent membership and so cannot be controlled.

STRUCTURED AND UNSTRUCTURED COMMUNICATIONS

Communication within organizations moves along a continuum from unstructured to semi-structured to structured communication. Unstructured communication is difficult to predict in terms of frequency, process and information that is shared. It includes the use of social media, emails, calendaring and scheduling tools, instant messaging and chat groups. Unstructured information does not conform to defined formats or protocols.

Semi-structured information can be based on structured processes but the content or threads of discussion may still be unpredictable. In the case of online forums or shared work spaces there can be distributed authorship. Committee meetings held in person or through video, web or audio conferencing tools are other examples of semi-structured communication environments. Inter-organizational business processes are examples of structured communications where the information and processes are formalized and predictable, usually conforming to defined standards for data interchange.

Niall Cook (2008: 13) relates that the last few years have seen developments in social software that are changing and have the potential to further change the face of organizational communications in four areas:

- Communication platforms that enable people to converse with others, either by text, image, voice, video or a combination of these; for example discussion forums, blogs, instant messaging, social presence and virtual world and their successors;
- Sharing software that enable people to share content with others in structured and unstructured ways;
- Collaboration tools that encourage people to collaborate with each other on particular problems, directly and indirectly in both central and distributed ways, such as wikis;
- Networking technologies that make it possible for people to make connections with and between both content and other people; for example social networking, tagging, syndication and mashups.

Tapping into community expertise

The Internet and social networking tools have evolved to be the primary tools for communicating, information and commerce in the market space. Customers now have their own freedom to connect with each other through the Internet and social networking tools to satisfy their need for information about products and services. Hoffman (2009) advises that rather than pushing messages at consumers, marketers should listen to them and think constantly about ways to engage with them actively.

CROWDSOURCING

Increasingly organizations are using Web 2.0 and beyond technologies to tap into and harness the expertise and collective intelligence that exists in the community and with stakeholders. Often referred to as 'crowdsourcing' it involves obtaining ideas and innovations from external third parties through wikis, blogs and other social networking applications. It is particularly useful in developing user-driven policy, providing creative ideas for new products and services, evaluating new products and ideas and enabling customers to update and contribute to product documentation.

Openness and accountability are fundamental prerequisites for crowdsourcing to be successful. There also needs to be a clear purpose and objectives as well as the ability to respond in real time. Dellarocas (2010: 33) has also identified reputation as being a factor in attracting the right individuals to contribute, to motivate them to act in the right ways and empower them to know and trust others in the network. In doing so Dellarocas (ibid.) made three findings about the successful design of social web platforms:

- Designers have to be driven first by the business objectives of the website;
- There should be four main aims:
  - build trust – encouraging good behaviours and discouraging bad ones in the context of the site,
  - promote quality – recognizing and featuring high-quality contributors as an incentive for contributors to try harder,
  - facilitate member matching – helping members decide how much to trust someone's posting, and
  - sustain loyalty – using reputation as a form of lock-in and as a strategic tool to increase user loyalty and decrease attrition; and
- Design choices can profoundly affect a community's culture, easily turning a good space into an ineffective one.

COMMUNITY ENGAGEMENT

Complementing crowdsourcing is the opportunity to engage the community in discussion about issues affecting them and their community through collaborative tools and approaches offered through Web 2.0 and beyond applications. Community engagement enables organizations to form communities of interest around issues and build up a relationship with their stakeholders that is more accessible and convenient, as well as being the channel of choice for a large proportion of the population. It is a means of making organizations more open, transparent, accountable and responsive, as well as enriching social capital and empowering the wider community.

True online engagement involves many-to-many networks rather than being a one-to-many tool. It requires a shift in mindset, culture and practice. Proper online engagement facilitates discussion within and amongst the community on issues affecting them. It is not a mechanism for pushing agendas or undertaking market research surveys online. Rather it is a means that allows the organization to listen to what its stakeholders are saying amongst themselves and then responding to those messages in terms of improving policy or service delivery.

Social media and online community engagement tools are part of the suite of community engagement methods or channels available for organizations to use. Their strengths lie in the fact that they offer opportunities to get more people involved in discussion on issues affecting them and their community at their own convenience and without leaving their homes and offices. However there will still be those who wish to engage face-to-face. Online engagement tools can be used to complement and promote face-to-face events and continue the discussion afterwards.

Reports

Reports are part of ensuring transparency and the governance process. They formally bring matters to the attention of executive management and stakeholders upon which informed decisions can be made. In order to convey appropriate decision making information or account for their actions, managers write or commission annual reports, monthly or quarterly reports, reports relating to specific issues, submissions and budget papers.

Regular reports provide continuous feedback to senior management. They often contain statistical information, analysis of trends and reports on activities. Issues of concern can be raised through these reports for further action. Regular reports usually follow a specific format that is established by the parent organization.

Regular reports can be supplemented by reports on specific issues. These can include papers for discussion and/or action, requests for the introduction of additional services or changes in service level, requests for changes in policy or reports relating to future planning. Reports such as these are compiled on a less regular basis and vary in length. They begin with a summary of the reasons for the report and contain details of background, progress to date, legal or resource implications and recommendations. Specific reports are either commissioned or written by in-house specialists. They use corporate data and data from external sources. They are written for senior management so that appropriate action can be authorized and taken.

Budgets are a form of report in that they identify the requirement for, and proposed use of, funds. They communicate how funding is to be spent on priority services to senior management, employees and stakeholders.

Meetings

Meetings, whether attended in person, through video, web or audio conferencing tools or online via enterprise collaboration tools, assist the governance process as they bring together a group of people with a common interest to accomplish a goal. Participants in meetings use communication skills to share knowledge and experiences, to plan and make decisions, to solve problems, to negotiate and evaluate, to consult and to disseminate information.

Meetings are important components in ensuring transparency in decision making. Handled effectively and efficiently, a meeting will result in creative thinking, multiple thought input, enhanced group cohesiveness, commitment to the outcome, cooperation and better decision making. Handled ineffectively or inefficiently a meeting can waste time, stifle creativity and foster aggressiveness, or result in attacks on others. This can lead to a breakdown in communications between the participants, which in turn create more problems.

PURPOSES OF MEETINGS

Meetings are a useful tool where decisions require judgement rather than calculations or expertise, or when a pooling of ideas improves the chances of a good decision. They can increase collaboration between work units and be used to ensure that everyone has a shared understanding of issues. Meetings are also helpful where it is necessary to get the participants' acceptance of the decision. Meetings should not be called to solve routine problems, neither are they useful as a vehicle for briefing individuals about issues upon which they have little control or that are unrelated to work. Intranets and electronic collaboration tools can be more efficient mechanisms to use in these circumstances. Figure 20.1 explains some of the purposes and types of meetings that can be held in organizations.

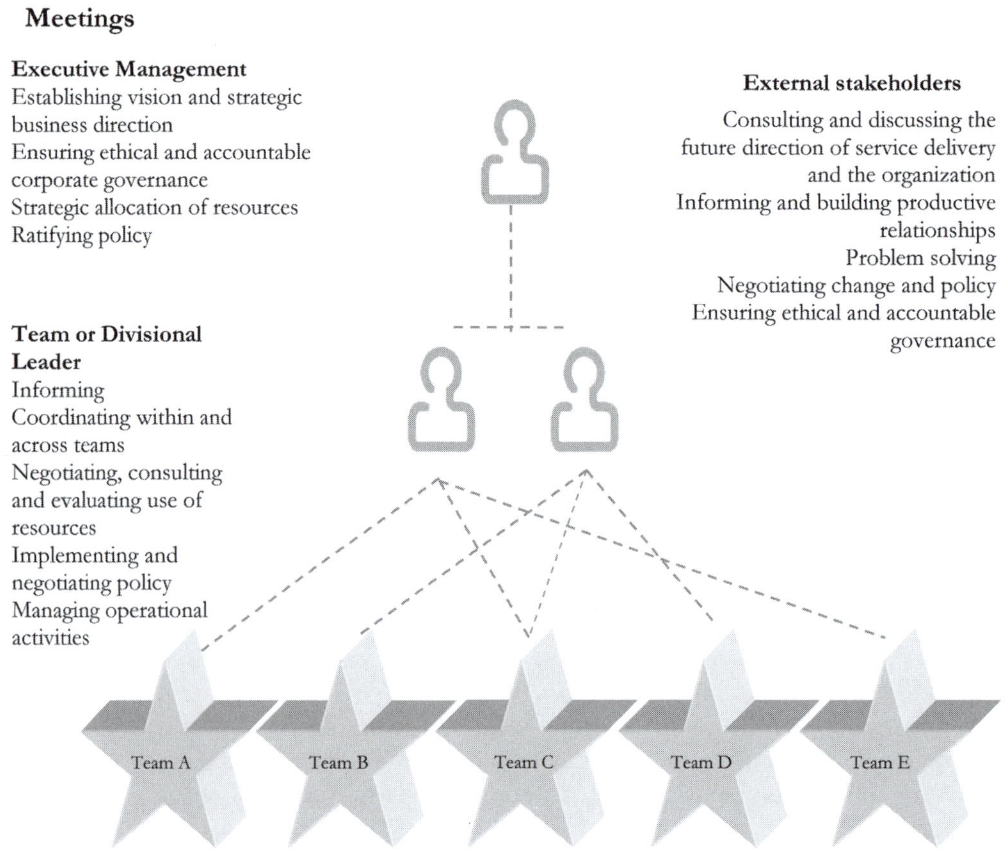

Meetings

Executive Management
Establishing vision and strategic
business direction
Ensuring ethical and accountable
corporate governance
Strategic allocation of resources
Ratifying policy

External stakeholders

Consulting and discussing the
future direction of service delivery
and the organization
Informing and building productive
relationships
Problem solving
Negotiating change and policy
Ensuring ethical and accountable
governance

**Team or Divisional
Leader**
Informing
Coordinating within and
across teams
Negotiating, consulting
and evaluating use of
resources
Implementing and
negotiating policy
Managing operational
activities

Team A   Team B   Team C   Team D   Team E

Figure 20.1 Purposes of meetings

FRAMEWORK FOR EFFECTIVE MEETINGS

Meetings can be scheduled or unscheduled, held in person or through electronic collaborative work tools. They can also be scheduled on a regular or irregular basis. The agenda should communicate a well-defined purpose for the meeting and a sense of direction for the participants. It should prepare participants for the tasks that they need to accomplish during the meeting and afterwards. The agenda should provide details of date, time and place of the meeting. Time refers to both the starting and ending time as open-ended meetings invite time-wasting procedures. A time may also be set for each item on the agenda. It is also useful to label agenda items according to their desired outcome, for example, 'for discussion', 'for endorsement', 'for information'.

The agenda should be circulated to participants in advance to allow time for reading, research and consultation with others. Background material such as reports, statistics and proposals should be distributed with the agenda. To ensure that the meeting is effective and productive, participants should be:

- Stakeholders in the decision-making process;
- Individuals that can contribute through relevant knowledge or appropriate level of expertise; or
- Individuals that can communicate and contribute to the meeting in a positive, creative and open fashion.

The ideal number of participants in a meeting is between four and eight. If too many people attend, or if those who are not directly involved in the agenda issues attend, there is a risk of too much time being spent on explaining the background. Agenda issues may also become sidetracked. Likewise, if the wrong people attend they can stifle creativity and waste their own and others' time.

The role of the chairperson is to keep the pace of the meeting brisk. They should ensure that participants do not waffle or get sidetracked onto issues not relevant to the agenda. The chairperson should facilitate open communication and dissipate potential personality problems to make it easy for all participants to put their point of view forward. Individuals should not be allowed to dominate meetings. The chairperson should have knowledge of group dynamics in order to steer the participants in a creative fashion to the desired outcome. A skilled chairperson is able to persuade participants to think again and get proposals accepted where less experienced colleagues may fail.

The chairperson should ensure that all decisions made at the meeting are recorded, together with details as to who is responsible for follow-up actions, what these actions are and when they should take place.

THE MEETING ENVIRONMENT

It is important that meetings are held in non-threatening environments. If people from different organizations or work units are meeting in person, it is often best that this be on neutral territory. Physical features of the room and seating arrangements can affect the outcome of the meeting. A round or oval table is better for problem solving and group discussion. Participants should be comfortably seated in a business-like manner with room to move and the ability to clearly see all members. People likely to be in conflict or confrontation with each other should not be placed opposite each other. There should be no noise distractions or interruptions, although, in the case of long meetings, breaks should be scheduled with refreshments of non-alcoholic beverages. The size of the room should give the impression of being comfortably full but not crowded. Large premises are threatening and stifle discussion.

Conclusion

Making the right decision is crucial to engendering trust and accountability as well as for ensuring the long-term sustainability of the organization. Transparency in governance processes is achieved through making the right decision, as well as having a culture that is open and accountable. Participative decision making is favoured as a means of encouraging input and transparency to decisions. Generally the additional cost of participative decision making in terms of staff time is offset by the benefits that arise from the commitment to the decision and the greater creativity that arises from a wider range of options arising from the participative process.

Communications in organizations can take many forms: formal and informal, structured and unstructured. All of which serve a purpose in encouraging suggestions and ideas, lessening confusion and providing clarity on issues, and enabling discussion and decision making across the organization and with its stakeholders.

References

Cook, N. 2008. *Enterprise 2.0: How Social Software Will Change The Future*. Aldershot: Gower.

Dellarocas, C. 2010. Online reputation systems: How to design one that does what you need. *MIT Sloan Management Review*, spring, 51(3), 33–38.

Hoffman, D.L. 2009. Managing beyond Web 2.0. *McKinsey & Co.* July.

Rowe, A.J. 1984. *Managerial Decision Making* (Modules in Management). Chicago: Science Research Associates.

Further reading

Allard, S. 2009. Library managers and information in World 2.0. *Library Management*, 30(1/2), 57–68.

Barnes, N.D. and Barnes, F.R. 2009. Equipping your organization for the social networking game. *Information Management*, November–December.

Hammond, J. et al. 1998. The hidden traps in decision making. *Harvard Business Review*, September/October, 47–58.

Quirke, B. 2000. *Making The Connections: Using Internal Communication to Turn Strategy into Action*. Aldershot: Ashgate.

Ruff, P. and Aziz, K. 2004. *Managing Communications in a Crisis*. Aldershot: Ashgate.

21 *Managing for Sustainability*

In keeping with the need for balance and concerns for the future and coexisting with corporate governance and social responsibility principles is the concept of sustainability. The word sustainability is derived from the Latin *sustinere* (*tenere*, to hold; *sus*, up) and is 'the capacity to endure'. In other words it is the ability of the information service and its parent organization to:

- Have the capability to tolerate and survive in continuously changing and challenging circumstances;
- Ensure the long-term maintenance of well-being, which in turn depends on the well-being and support of the natural world and the responsible use of natural resources; and
- Make decisions and manage programmes and projects in a manner that maximizes benefits to the natural environment, humans and their cultures and communities, while maintaining or enhancing financial viability.

In order to achieve the above, sustainability needs to be incorporated into core values, taken into account in ensuring effective governance and decision making within the information service, and considered and incorporated into information service delivery. Protecting the environment isn't the whole story. Organizations must consider their social, economic and cultural impact as well. From a management perspective, sustainability is a holistic process that takes into consideration every dimension of the business environment. It involves incorporating a whole of life approach, balancing short-term needs with society's and the organization's long-term interests, as well as ensuring that resources are used no faster than they are renewed. The latter is known as living within the carrying capacity and can be applied to intangible items such as education and skills development or developing trust and respect in people, as well as the tangible environment of water facilities and ecosystems.

Sustainable organizations and communities invest in and take good care of all their capital assets so that benefits accrue for themselves and others, now and in the future. They look at the entire enterprise, process or acquisition from a 'cradle to the grave' perspective in terms of total cost of ownership, or input, throughput and output to determine inefficiencies or waste. Investments in sustainability practices reap other benefits. For example energy efficient buildings not only consume less energy they have better thermal, visual and acoustic comforts that yield higher labour productivity, attraction and retention rates. With the cost of labour being much higher than energy costs, the bottom line benefits are derived more from people's increased productivity, well-being and commitment and savings in sourcing, recruiting and inducting scarce talent, than just the energy savings.

Sustainability principles include:

- Concern for the well-being of future generations;
- Awareness of the multi-dimensional impacts of any decision (broadly categorized as economic, environmental, social); and
- The need for balance among the different dimensions across sectors (e.g. mining, manufacturing, transportation), themes (climate change, community cohesion, natural resource management) and scale (local, regional, national, international).

The Sustainability Now website presents a holistic view of managing in a way that meets the needs of the present without compromising the ability of future generations to meet their own needs. The principles it espouses include:

- Systems thinking – acknowledging the fact that seemingly discrete projects and activities are in fact a part of many interacting or interdependent social, ecological and economic systems that together form one complex global system;
- Temporal and spatial scales – assessing the environmental, social and economic impacts of our actions over varying scales of space and time;
- Risk, uncertainty and the precautionary principle – identifying and actively managing risk and uncertainty; recognizing the value and limitations of both quantitative risk analyses and subjective risk perception in situations characterized by significant uncertainty;
- Values-focused thinking – developing alternative solutions to problems based on human needs and values and evaluating these options on the basis of those values;
- Engagement and integration – engaging stakeholders and forming integrated design and consultation teams at the onset of appropriate projects to take advantage of a pooled body of knowledge to help define and solve the issues at hand;
- Equity and disparity – ensuring that the equity and disparity of current and future generations have been considered and that a fair and consensus-seeking process is in place to ensure that the benefits and costs are distributed fairly among various stakeholders;
- Efficiency – seeking to maximize the contribution of well-being of humans and ecosystems while minimizing the stress on people and ecosystems, seeking win-win solutions and clarifying irreducible trade-offs; and
- Process and practicality – applying sustainability as a dynamic process rather than a static end point. The scope for living sustainably in the context of changing technology and human values is enormous.

Sustainable business practices

Sustainable business practices integrate ecological concerns with social, cultural and economic ones. In a practical sense this can be achieved through:

- Making workplace adjustments and implementing policies, work practices and processes that reduce energy usage, waste and costs;
- Benchmarking service and process efficiencies against zero waste rather than what competitors are achieving;
- Managing the organization's reputation as a good community citizen by building social capital;
- Respecting and taking care of its employees and families through family-friendly practices;
- Valuing and protecting cultural diversity;
- Embedding a corporate culture, values and mindset of achieving sustainability in all its forms;
- Building a capacity of organizational learning to avoid mistakes and look for innovation; and
- Taking an integrated approach to sustainability, rather than treating each element of sustainability as a discrete item to be managed in isolation.

Reductions in non-renewable resources consumption are also being achieved in the design of the built environment. Green builders are making use of naturally available sunlight, heat, shade and ventilation which have the added advantage of sustaining a healthier work environment. In addition, smart alternatives to transport are also being deployed by wherever possible avoiding unnecessary travel through the use of remote desktop tools to provide user support and video conferencing for meetings.

Berns et al. (2009) observed in a Business of Sustainability Survey that respondents who considered themselves experts in sustainability said their companies had found a compelling business case for sustainability-related investments. These included:

- A stronger brand and greater pricing power;
- Greater operational efficiencies;
- More efficient use of resources;
- Supply chain optimization;
- Lower costs and taxes;
- Enhanced ability to attract, retain and motivate employees;
- Greater employee productivity;
- Improved customer loyalty, lower rate of churn;
- Enhance ability to enter new markets;
- More potential sources of revenue;
- Lower market balance-sheet and operational risks;
- Lower cost of capital; and
- Greater access to capital, financing and insurance.

Sustainable ICT

Environmentally sustainable computing or ICT is also known as 'green computing' or 'green IT'. It incorporates a holistic approach to the design, manufacture, use and disposal of computers, mobile devices, servers and associated subsystems – such as monitors, printers, storage devices, and networking and communications systems – efficiently and effectively with minimal or no impact on the environment. It seeks equipment that comes from a sustainable source (past), is non-toxic (present) and is reusable or recyclable (future). Green IT also strives to achieve economic viability and improved system performance and use, while abiding by corporate social and ethical responsibilities.

Incorporating smart design, procurement and business models into the management of ICT not only reduces the environmental impact it also reduces energy consumption and offers financial benefits by reducing the total cost of ownership. Examples include:

- Sharing ICT services and moving to cloud computing models incorporating pay-for-use principles;
- Redesigning data centres to be more energy efficient and relocating them to non-central business areas reducing costs for energy, space and other requirements;
- Incorporating green criteria for the design, management and disposal of equipment to procurement contracts;
- Extending the replacement programme to a four- to five-year life cycle for desktop equipment through cascading high-end equipment to lower needs end users, consolidating, reducing and recycling equipment;
- Increasing staff awareness of the impact that ICT has on energy and environmental sustainability and the need to switch off and shut down their computers at night, over the weekend and any time when they won't be using it for longer than an hour;
- Utilizing energy saving measures e.g. power management tools, installing networked rather than small desktop printers, setting printers to default duplexing (double sided) and grey scale;
- Digitizing paper images as soon as possible;
- Disposing of or recycling toner cartridges, mobile phones, batteries and used paper appropriately;
- Optimizing utilization by finding the right inventory levels to have as surplus replacement equipment; and
- Introducing green metrics, assessment tools and methodologies.

Most ICT vendors have moved to incorporating aspects of green IT in their design, manufacturing and disposal processes, maximizing energy efficiency and promoting recyclability and biodegradability.

Sustaining different forms of capital

An aspect of sustainability and corporate governance is ensuring that different forms of capital associated with the organization are managed in a responsible and sustainable manner. Capital is a resource that, managed sustainably and effectively, is a source of wealth and value. Managed irresponsibly the viability and reputation of the organization can be brought into question. Traditional management concentrated on managing human and financial resources from an internal perspective of assets and liabilities for the organization. Now it is acknowledged that many different forms of capital exist that need to be managed to add value today and for the future; not just from a governance perspective but with the view that organizations can create worth for themselves and society by better managing these. Increasingly organizational performance is being judged on the way in which it recognizes and takes care of a wide range of capital items, including intellectual, client, social and natural capital.

BUILT CAPITAL

Built capital includes buildings, equipment, vehicles, information and communications technology (ICT) and infrastructure. Managing built assets is akin to good asset management of tangible assets, which includes maximizing the return on investment and reducing future resource requirements by prolonging the asset's life or strengthening its disposal value.

CLIENT CAPITAL

Client capital is the value that results from the relationship that an organization has with its clients. Increasingly organizations are recognizing the importance of customer relationship management in retaining their clients who are in the position of exercising choice in who they deal with. ICT is proving an asset in enabling organizations to add value to the customer and enhance the relationship by providing information on client needs and preferences and then tailoring products and services to meet individual needs anytime, anyplace.

FINANCIAL CAPITAL

Financial capital includes managing the growth, investment and financial value of the organization, maximizing its wealth and the value of its assets in the market place, ensuring its capacity and capability to make a profit, and funding its acquisitions and liabilities.

HUMAN CAPITAL

The many aspects of human capital have been captured by McCallum and O'Connell (2009: 154) in two dimensions:

- Value, represented by contributions made that enhance organizational effectiveness, efficiency and/or competency;
- Uniqueness, exhibited in firm-specific, tacit knowledge or expertise.

Having an appreciation for the importance of people's personal talents, skills and abilities is a significant part of managing human capital. The success of organizations in continuously changing and challenging environments is due to the collective worth of their people's aptitudes, talents, experiences, education, know-how, skills sets, imaginations, thoughts, intelligence and capabilities. How these are encouraged and applied will determine the extent to which they add value and bring innovation and achievement to the organization. Managing human capital also includes concern for the health and well-being of individuals. This includes their physical and mental health; so employing healthy lifestyle programmes or sponsoring lunchtime keep-fit activities help support the well-being of this important capital source.

INTELLECTUAL CAPITAL

Intellectual capital consists of knowledge, intelligence and ideas in an organization and the unique processes and intellectual assets that an organization holds. Its management and protection is increasingly important in preserving the innovative edge that an organization may hold over its competitors. Intellectual capital is reinforced through policies and practices that encourage creativity and innovation. Whilst intellectual capital that resides in people's heads cannot be protected, once it is applied it can be protected through intellectual property rights that include patents, copyright and other forms of legal protection.

NATURAL CAPITAL

In managing natural capital importance is placed on the value of the ecological carrying capacity and sustainability of the natural environment. It includes consideration for the sustainability of natural resources in choosing alternatives for transport and managing water and energy consumption in the workplace. Natural capital consists of:

- Those things that are taken out of nature and used e.g. water, plants and animals, oils, gas, minerals and wood;
- Ecosystems that are the natural processes which communities rely upon such as wetlands that enable water filtration and provide a buffer for flooding, carbon dioxide–oxygen exchanges, and the fertility of soils; and
- Aesthetics or the beauty of nature that contribute to the general quality of life e.g. providing flowers and plants in the workplace, positioning windows to reveal a pleasing view, or providing an outside courtyard where people can relax during a break.

Preventing pollution and managing wastes in an ecologically sound manner are two other examples of investing in natural capital.

SOCIAL CAPITAL

Social capital is the goodwill available to individuals or groups. It is concerned with social awareness and forging commitments, connections and relationships within a community. This might be within an organization, a community of practice or a local community. From a management perspective, this means managing and valuing the interpersonal and institutional relationships and norms that an organization has internally and with the external environment. For example, its abilities to build relationships, goodwill, cooperation and trust, influence and show leadership that adds value to organizational processes and outcomes, or which shapes the quality and quantity of its interactions with society for improved community productivity and well-being. There is also a self-management perspective. Social capital differs from human capital that is based on individual competencies such as skills and abilities. Social capital is about relational competencies and leads to relational wealth that can be used to build competitive advantage and advance organizational performance. It also includes reciprocity and giving feedback.

Developing a social capital programme might include forming relationships with or sponsoring local community groups, supporting an employee volunteer programme, encouraging corporate family days where members of the family can visit on site, or encouraging membership and corporate connections with communities of practice in relevant research fields. McCallum and O'Connell (2009: 164) also point out that social capital also develops as leaders have purposeful conversations and share important stories.

McCallum and O'Connell (2009: 157) outline five positive impacts of social capital on the sustainability of organizations:

- Trust – which leads to the reduced need for monitoring trading partners;
- Improved knowledge creation and sharing due to trust, shared goals and common frames of reference;
- More coherent action that flows from organizational stability and shared understanding;
- Organizational membership is stabilized through reductions in turnover, severance costs, hiring and training expenses; and
- The values of collaboration are maximized increasing the rate of financial return.

Conclusion

Sustainability principles include:

- Concern for the well-being of future generations;
- Awareness of the multi-dimensional impacts of any decision (broadly categorized as economic, environmental, social); and
- The need for balance among the different dimensions across sectors (e.g. mining, manufacturing, transportation), themes (climate change, community cohesion, natural resource management) and scale (local, regional, national, international).

Sustainable organizations and communities invest in and take good care of all their capital assets so that benefits accrue for themselves and others, now and in the future. Sustainability investments in built capital can derive additional benefits for client, financial, human, intellectual, natural and social capital. For example:

- Energy efficient buildings and processes not only consume less energy they have better thermal, visual and acoustic comforts that yield higher levels of labour productivity, increase the well-being and commitment of staff with the added benefits of savings in sourcing, recruiting and inducting scarce talent;
- Incorporating smart design, procurement and business models into the management of ICT. There is not only a reduction in the environmental impact and costs of energy consumption, there are additional financial benefits in a reduced total cost of ownership; and
- In pushing services online and replacing hard copy forms with online forms and authorization work flow the benefits are found in reduced costs of paper usage and

front office staff, savings in trees, reduced waste and emissions in travel and savings in customer time and money.

Redesigning business practices with sustainability in mind often results in several other advantages. It requires a focus on mapping costs of both materials and energy, which in turn identifies waste in the system. As a result of developing a culture of measurement, collaboration, accountability and rewards for minimizing waste and leakages, there are gains in integration and communication, greater employee commitment and productivity, and further savings by turning waste into profit.

References

Berns, M., Townend, A., Khayyat, Z., Balagopal, B., Reeves, M., Hopkins, M.S. and Kruschwitz, N. 2009. Sustainability and competitive advantage. *MIT Sloan Management Review*, 51(1), 20–26.

McCallum, S. and O'Connell, D. 2009. Social capital and leadership development: Building stronger leadership through enhanced relational skills. *Leadership and Organization Development Journal*, 30(2), 152–166.

Sustainability Now. Available at www.sustainability.ca/index/report/intro_lg.html [accessed: 20 June 2005].

Sustainability Reporting Programme. Available at www.sustreport.org/business/report.org/intro_lg.html [accessed: 20 June 2005].

Further reading

Benn, S. and Dunphy, D. 2007. *Corporate Governance and Sustainability: Challenges For Theory and Practice*. London: Routledge.

Hopkins, M.S. 8 reasons sustainability will change management. *MIT Sloan Management Review*, 51(1), 27–30.

Kane, G. 2010. *The Three Secrets of Green Business: Unlocking Competitive Advantage in a Low Carbon Economy*. London: Earthscan.

Markevich, A. 2009. The evolution of sustainability. *MIT Sloan Management Review*, 51(1), 13–14.

22 *Managing Risk*

Managing risk comprises the identification and mitigation of risks that might affect an organization or activity such as its people, financial sustainability, property and assets, reputation and information. Risk management is not an excuse for curtailing freedom, for not being prepared to take a chance, or a reason for not being innovative or risk-taking. In fact the greatest risk is to do nothing and therefore risk nothing. Innovation, progress and opportunities to create the next advantage all involve some elements of risk.

Risks surround us, they are in abundance and there for the taking. Those who do not take risks achieve nothing. The challenge is to identify potential risks and proceed to manage them in a manner that leads to a successful outcome. Awareness of risks through early warning indicators is as important as managing the risks themselves. It is far better to be aware of all possible and probable risks than to progress in ignorance. There is a difference between taking a risk avoidance approach in which everything is slowed down such that progress and initiatives are stifled, or progressing proposals with eyes open, knowing the potential and possible risks to look for.

Risk management specialists may be employed within the organization to identify and monitor possible and potential risks, instigate control and mitigation practices for these risks and ensure regular reporting to executive management on these issues. However, accountability and oversight of risk is an executive management responsibility. This is because risk is tightly coupled with corporate governance, trust and reputation, short- and long-term sustainability and strategic management issues. Executive management should be involved in endorsing strategic risk policy-making, setting the desired levels of risk tolerance, as well as providing oversight of risk management issues within the corporate environment.

Risks can occur from internal and external sources. The complexity of the environment and potential for sudden and serious risks to emerge means that external risks are likely to be more damaging and threaten the reputation and livelihood of the organization than those that are initiated from within, such as through innovation or fraud. The nature of risk is that any member of staff can be in a position to identify the early warning signs of risks, either through observation, through conversations with stakeholders such as suppliers, union representatives, customers, or in coming into contact with other external intelligence sources.

In the world of integrated and global service delivery risk management strategies, risk cannot necessarily be confined to a single organization. Therefore policies and procedures must flow across the organizations collaborating in the venture. The best way to manage this environment is to ensure that systems, practices and processes are in place, communicated and understood by all partners such that they make the identification and management of risk an integral part of the planning and management process and general culture of the organizations involved. These risk policies and processes should clearly describe how risk will be managed across the organization and its collaborative partners and form part of the risk management plan.

Sources of risk

Major risks that can affect information services include:

- Fraud, theft or misappropriation – this can be financially detrimental to the information service and its parent organization and result in a loss of clients and their trust if their relationships with the organization are affected. If the fraudulent person is a member of the information service's staff, this can have an adverse affect on the morale and levels of trust amongst staff members;
- Security violations and computer crime – these can result in the loss of competitive or personal information or severely affect the operations of the organization's systems through the use of logic bombs, computer viruses, etc.;
- Inappropriate use of computer systems – the sending of inappropriate email or text messages or inappropriate access to pornographic or other unsuitable websites can be extremely upsetting and damaging to recipients, expose the organization to litigation and financial liability, as well as tarnishing the reputation of the organization and being a misuse of employer's assets;
- Technology change – that renders practices and processes, products and services obsolete overnight;
- Inefficiency and waste – these lead to high costs, low profitability and low productivity;
- Legal exposure – this includes breaches of contract, statutory breaches or where adverse legal action is financially and organizationally debilitating;
- Loss of public reputation, image or regard for corporate citizenship – the loss of an organization's reputation or image can severely affect stakeholder relationships, as well as the organization's standing in the market including its ability to raise finances;
- Business interruption – circumstances may result in the information service or its parent organization being unable to continue its business activities during times of degraded conditions. Common causes for business interruption include interruption of power supply, electrical surges or spikes that damage equipment, industrial action or denial of service attacks through the Internet;
- Loss of key staff and expertise – this can leave the information service or its parent organization vulnerable in terms of a loss of business knowledge and expertise if there had been poor succession planning. It may also result in an organization's intellectual property being transferred to a competitor;
- Exposure to public liability – especially where inappropriate or incorrect advice or information is provided by inexperienced personnel which can have financial, legal, duty of care and image implications for the information service or its parent organization;

- Property damage – this may inhibit the operations of the information service and its parent organization if access and movement within the organization's building are restricted;
- Unlawful acts, arson, vandalism or terrorism – as well as the potential for property damage, acts of vandalism or terrorism can have a major impact on the safety and psychological well-being of staff;
- Occupational health and safety issues – an unsafe workplace not only exposes staff to health and safety risks, there is an adverse effect on the morale and productivity of staff. Apart from the fact that this can expose the organization to the threat of litigation, there is a duty of care perspective that needs to be taken seriously. The use of information and communications technology (ICT) equipment such as screens and mobile telephones have been identified as possible sources of radiation that may be a health hazard to users over a long period of time;
- Other workplace issues – such as enterprise bargaining disputes, claims of sexual harassment, inappropriate skill mixes, cultural or religious conflicts or language difficulties;
- Equipment breakdown or downtime – especially where there are mission-critical operations that require a 24x7 always on operating environment;
- Poorly maintained or inappropriate equipment or infrastructure – this includes ageing equipment infrastructure that leads to breakdowns or superseded equipment that no longer fits the purpose and needs updating;
- Financial exposures – such as bad debts, exchange rate movements, inadequate costing systems or incorrect budget controls;
- Natural and manmade disasters – these include damage through earthquakes or weather events, fire, exposure to long-term hazards and pollution, or pandemics that affect operational capabilities; and
- Political risks – such as a change of government or board that brings a new political agenda, loss of a significant corporate champion for the information service, or changing community expectations that require the rethinking of funding or service delivery strategies.

Managing risk

Risk management involves having a risk management plan that provides a clear approach to the establishment of the context for risks, identification of risk, analysing the probability of it occurring and the magnitude of the potential risk, evaluating and prioritizing risks, introducing appropriate strategies and responsibilities to treat or manage the risks and monitoring and reviewing risks.

ESTABLISHING THE CONTEXT

Establishing the contextual environment in which risks may occur draws upon much of the information obtained through the strategic planning process; for this identifies the issues in the organization's strategic and operational environment from which risks may arise. Strategic audits, strengths, weaknesses, opportunities and threats (SWOT) analysis, desired future business direction, stakeholder interests, capability profiles, present levels of resources and organizational capability and scenario planning activities can all feed into this activity. It is against this present and future context that risk tolerances and limits are set and possible and probable risks are evaluated. For example, a highly innovative entity where being first to market is of critical importance in a fast-moving environment will have a higher tolerance for risk and evaluate risks accordingly, than a more conservative organization, such as an accounting firm, where corporate reputation and knowledge of the most recent company and taxation regulations and legislation is used as a differentiating factor. Determining the criteria against which risk is to be evaluated is part of the process of establishing the contextual environment in which risk management takes place.

IDENTIFYING RISKS

The second stage in the risk management process is to identify the risks that need to be managed. This requires consideration of all aspects of both the internal and external environments, including the strategic influences identified in the chapter of the same name. As previously identified, unidentified risks pose a major threat to an organization, so it is important to ensure that all sources of risk are identified in the first instance. This is an instance where more is better, leaving the formal risk evaluation and prioritization process to determine which risks are given more attention.

In addition to drawing on the strategic planning process as a source for identifying risks, risks can also be identified through audits, brainstorming, personal experience, focus group discussion and surveys. Communication is extremely important in order to identify risks and to explain risk management strategies to those affected. Different stakeholders will have different perceptions of the likelihood and severity of the risk, so communication with all stakeholders will provide a richer picture of the potential and probable risks than taking a narrower approach.

Once risks have been identified, it is necessary to identify when, why, where and how are the risks likely to occur and who might be involved. The sources, consequences and potential costs of each risk should be calculated. These can be tabulated in a spreadsheet, but if a more serious or comprehensive approach is required, then a commercial risk management product should be used to guide the risk management processes. Accountability mechanisms and control processes should also be incorporated against each risk.

ANALYSING RISKS

Once risks have been identified, the next stage is to analyse the risks according to the likelihood of the event and the magnitude of the associated consequences. Together these provide an indication of the level of risk.

Business Excellence Australia has identified descriptors to assess the likelihood of risk (see Table 22.1). The consequences of risk can be determined by evaluating the potential effect, fallout or outcome of the risk on the organization and its operations. Generally these are considered to be extreme, critical, major, minor or insignificant as per the following (see Table 22.2).

Table 22.1 Likelihood of events

Likelihood	Event occurrence	Event timing
Almost certain	The event will occur in most circumstances	Will occur once a year or more frequently
Likely	The event will probably occur at least once	Will occur once every three years
Possible	The event might occur at some time	Will occur once every 10 years
Unlikely	The event is not expected to occur	Will occur once every 30 years
Rare	The event may only occur in exceptional circumstances	Will occur once every 100 years
Very rare	The event may only occur in highly exceptional circumstances	Will occur once every 300 years
Almost incredible	The probability of this event is highly unlikely	Will occur once every 1,000 years

Source: adapted from Business Excellence Australia, n.d.

Table 22.2 Consequences of events

Consequence	Effect, fallout, outcome
Extreme	An extreme incident that would affect the organization's survival or would result in extensive long-term adverse impacts on the organization, the community and/or its environment
Critical	A significant incident that would compromise the operations of the organization and have a long-term detrimental effect on the organization, the community and/or its environment
Major	A significant incident that would have serious impact on the operations of the organization and require remedial action within the organization, the community and/or its environment
Minor	A localized incident that would have short-term disruption or detrimental impact on the organization, the community and/or its environment
Insignificant	A minor incident with no lasting detrimental effect or impact on the organization, the community and/or its environment

Table 22.3 Level of risk

Risk	Consequence				
Likelihood	Insignificant	Minor	Major	Critical	Extreme
Almost certain	Medium	Serious	High	High	High
Likely	Medium	Medium	Serious	High	High
Possible	Low	Medium	Serious	Serious	High
Unlikely	Low	Low	Medium	Medium	Serious
Rare	Low	Low	Medium	Medium	Serious
Very rare	Low	Low	Medium	Medium	Serious
Almost incredible	Low	Low	Medium	Medium	Serious

The level of risk is determined by plotting the likelihood of the risk against the consequence, as shown in Table 22.3.

EVALUATING AND PRIORITIZING RISKS

Risks are evaluated according to whether they are high, serious, medium or low, following which they are prioritized. Using the identified sources of risks for information services above, Table 22.4 provides an example of how risks can be evaluated and prioritized. In evaluating risks the degree of control over the risk, the cost impact, benefits and opportunities should be considered, against the already established criteria.

Table 22.4 Evaluation and prioritization of risks in information services

Risk source	Likelihood of risk	Consequence of risk	Risk level	Priority
Fraud, theft or misappropriations	Possible	Major	Serious	2
Security violations and computer crime	Likely	Major	Serious	1
Inappropriate use of computer systems	Possible	Major	Serious	2
Technology change	Likely	Major	Serious	2
Inefficiency and waste	Likely	Insignificant	Medium	6
Legal exposures	Possible	Major	Serious	2
Loss of public reputation, image or regard for corporate citizenship	Unlikely	Major	Medium	4
Business interruption	Likely	Minor	Medium	4
Loss of key staff and expertise	Likely	Minor	Medium	4
Exposure to public liability	Unlikely	Major	Medium	5
Property damage	Rare	Major	Medium	5
Unlawful acts, arson, vandalism or terrorism	Very rare	Major	Medium	5
Occupational health and safety issues	Possible	Minor	Medium	4
Other workplace issues	Possible	Minor	Medium	4
Equipment breakdown or downtime	Likely	Minor	Medium	4
Poorly maintained or inappropriate equipment or infrastructure	Possible	Major	Serious	2
Financial exposures	Unlikely	Minor	Low	7
Natural and manmade disasters	Possible	Major	Serious	3
Political risks	Possible	Minor	Medium	6

TREATING AND MANAGING RISKS

After deciding on priorities responsibility for the treatment and management of the risk needs to be assigned and the risks treated within the context of the strategic direction and operations of the organization. Risk treatment strategies can include:

- Avoiding the risk by not proceeding with the activity or choosing alternative paths that have less or more acceptable risks attached;
- Reducing the likelihood of the risk through risk mitigation strategies;
- Transferring the risk, in full or in part, to another party, such as underwriting or taking out insurance on the risk and eventuality of an outcome; or
- Choosing to retain the risk.

MONITORING AND REVIEWING RISKS

Few risks remain static so it is important that risks and the effectiveness of their treatment are monitored and reviewed on a continuous basis. Changing circumstances can affect the likelihood and consequences of the risk. For example, the likelihood of risk of a pandemic or terrorist attack causing significant disruption is significantly higher today than 10 years ago. In addition, the effectiveness, suitability and costs of risk treatment measures can vary and need to be continually assessed.

Conclusion

Taking risks is an ordinary everyday occurrence and is a necessary feature of progressing new ideas, creativity and innovation. Risk management is a process for identifying risks and making informed decisions about courses of action that balance the risks with the outcomes. It comprises:

- Establishing the context of the types of risks in the environment;
- Identifying risks;
- Analysing risks;
- Evaluating and prioritizing risks;
- Treating and managing risks; and
- Monitoring and reviewing risks.

Tolerance for risk will differ across organizations dependent upon their business objectives and the environment in which they operate.

References

Business Excellence Australia. n.d. *Introduction to Risk Management*. Sydney: Standards Australia International Limited.

Further reading

Honey, G. 2009. *A Short Guide to Reputation Risk*. Burlington: Gower.

Wilding, E. 2005. *Information Risk and Security: How to Protect Your Corporate Assets*. Aldershot: Ashgate.

23 *Sustaining Trust and Continued Operations*

Sustaining stakeholder trust and continued operations in organizations is reliant on there being well-established risk identification and management practices in place, embedded security systems and procedures to protect information and transactions, people and physical assets, sound strategies to maintain and quickly recover from incidents through tried and tested business continuity and disaster recovery plans and finally compliance with legal and regulatory frameworks for the protection of intellectual property, personal and commercial information.

Information security has become an integral part of life. It is a business management and governance matter rather than a technical issue, as proper security ultimately results in engendering trust in the organization and minimizing damage to the sustainability of business operations and corporate reputation. As such security issues should be embedded into the corporate risk management processes. Effective security cannot exist just through funding allocations. It must be an adopted state of mind by employees and contractors of the organization, infused into the corporate culture and made a natural way of life.

Organizations today must deal with a multitude of security risks. Terrorist attacks, fires, floods and other disasters can destroy critical information and its associated infrastructure; but in this uncertain world, the physical security, health and safety of staff are increasingly becoming a priority. The other side to this equation is the Butler Group's highlighting that 'with more emphasis being placed on the protection of corporate data and customer information, internal threats posed by employees and business partners must come into the spotlight. Today, information users, and the facilities that organizations make available to them, provide the single largest and least-protected opportunity for data theft and accidental data loss. Poorly managed access controls to corporate systems, lack of regulation over Web usage that allows malicious malware to prosper, and pitifully weak influences over the movement of corporate data between end-user devices, all contribute to operational environments where information assets are being put at risk' (Butler Group 2009: 3–4).

Responsibility for security can be found at all levels. The Chief Executive is ultimately accountable for the confidentiality, integrity and availability of the organization's information resource and systems and for the physical safety of their staff. A position which the Butler Group has determined needs to be 'emphatically supported in order to avoid fines for regulatory or legal non-compliance, keep away from unwanted publicity and the perception that the organization cannot be trusted, and also to address brand-value losses that must remain a high business priority' (Butler Group 2009: 3–4).

Executive management has a responsibility for establishing a security-conscious corporate culture that makes effective security a way of life, for ensuring that there are appropriate standards, policies and procedures on security that reflect the level of risk within the organization, that there is appropriate funding and priority given to security, disaster recovery and business continuity strategies, that staff are aware of and understand the policies and procedures, and that adequate security procedures and practices are in place to manage the risk. Individuals are responsible for ensuring that they follow the correct procedures and practices and maintain a vigilant eye for possible intended or accidental breaches. The information services staff and team leaders are responsible for engendering a security conscious culture and workplace as well as systematic testing of strategies to ensure that all of the correct procedures and practices are in place and followed.

Objectives of information security management

The original objectives of information security management were to ensure confidentiality, integrity and availability of information and resources. The virtual world has since added two other complementary security elements to the original three as a means of ensuring trust and integrity in online services and transactions. These are:

- Authentication – providing assurance that the entities involved in a transaction are who they claim to be; and
- Non-repudiation – meaning that all parties to a transaction can prove that the other took part in the transaction. This can be achieved through technologies such as digital signatures and public key infrastructure.

Ensuring the confidentiality of information includes protecting personal, commercial and competitive information from unauthorized access and use, and ensuring that information is accessible only to those authorized to have use of it for approved purposes. Citizens and businesses need to feel confident that the environments within which their personal and commercial-in-confidence information is stored and electronic interactions occur are secure and do not compromise their information. Organizations also need to be confident that information they transmit and store is protected from any unauthorized access, either internal or external.

Maintaining the integrity of information relies upon the ability to maintain the information and transactions in their intended state through all electronic transfer, storage and retrieval processes and to protect them from any unauthorized manipulation or processing. This includes properly controlling access to sensitive data, safeguarding the accuracy and completeness of information and processing methods, as well as addressing brand-reputation implications of holding and using incorrect business and personal information. Integrity is upheld when the unauthorized creation, alteration or destruction of information, done maliciously or accidentally, is prevented.

The continued availability of information ensures that authorized users have reliable and timely access to information and associated assets when required. This requires mechanisms to ensure that the information is resilient, backed up and that steps are in place to restore and maintain access levels quickly in times of degraded activity. Availability of information also necessitates that ICT systems and networks are designed to provide adequate capacity in order to perform in a predictable manner with an acceptable level of performance. They should be able to recover from disruptions in a secure and quick manner so productivity is not negatively affected. Single points of failure should be avoided, backup measures taken, redundancy mechanisms should be in place when necessary, and the negative effects from environmental components should be prevented. Necessary protection mechanisms must be in place to protect against internal and external threats that could affect the availability and productivity of the network, systems and information. The testing of data recovery should be performed on a periodic basis to confirm that the backup process is effective and that correct and usable information is available.

Authentication is the process of validating the personal identity assertions provided by an individual wanting to access a system or undertake a transaction. Authentication generally involves a one-to-one comparison of an identity assertion against an identity record. A match verifies the user is authorized and they are subsequently allowed access to the system or transaction with a predetermined, fit-for-purpose level of authority. Authentication usually relies on one or more of the following:

- Something that is known to an individual (e.g. PIN, password);
- Something that an individual has (e.g. driver's licence); or
- Something that an individual is (e.g. face, fingerprint).

Repudiation occurs when a party to a transaction denies having carried out that transaction. An example is where the sender of a message denies sending it, or the receiver of a message denies receiving it. The concept of non-repudiation simply means that sufficiently reliable evidence exists so that a party cannot subsequently deny their participation in the exchange. Non-repudiation is an important part of providing a trusted and secure system with which users will be confident to engage for a broad range of transaction activities. Any dispute arbitration over an alleged transaction is considerably simplified when robust non-repudiation protections are in place.

Planning

Security should be planned and managed through a sustainable security strategy that is aligned to agreed critical business objectives, functions and processes, infrastructure and resources, and risks and scenarios. This should be supported by a series of general and application controls that either:

- Prevent threats; or
- Detect and control the effects of damage if it takes place.

The security strategy should encompass human, natural environment and political components, as well as the built environment, hardware and software failures, as the strength of the security chain is determined by its weakest link.

EXECUTIVE COMMITMENT

The first task in undertaking a security strategy is gaining executive management's understanding, support and commitment to the strategy and its degree of specification and adherence to international standards. International standards advocate the world's best practices that are very appropriate for some organizations, but can be too onerous for others. The level of detail and implementation chosen should be commensurate with the business objectives, functions and processes, criticality of infrastructure and resources, and risks and scenarios. This is because:

- Security strategies can be time-consuming and expensive to implement;
- They have considerable impact on the day-to-day operations of the organization; and
- Physical, people, information security issues are one of the biggest risks to organizations today and should not be underestimated.

CHOOSING THE RIGHT SECURITY LEVEL

The choice of security level is a business and risk management issue. It should be sustainable, that is able to be properly resourced, implemented and maintained. In addition, the requirement for an appropriate level of control ought to be balanced against the need to make information easily available for decision making.

Security features can be expensive in terms of the capital costs for the security devices, additional costs for encryption facilities in messaging and telecommunications and labour costs in maintaining security. The level of security should match the level of risk. It is not cost-effective to introduce a higher level of security than is necessary. In fact this could lead to a loss in productivity for the organization.

The level of security should be chosen to be feasible and practical. It ought not to inhibit work or information flows to the extent that it is detrimental to the organization's activities. It must also match the organization's level of expertise and resources. There is little value in information managers or security specialists implementing unrealistic information security levels or increasing onerous network controls if they do not meet operational and practical needs. They need to negotiate to guarantee adequate security of personal and commercial transactions and information whilst ensuring that the business outlets can work within the designed parameters and achieve business outcomes. The level of security should take into account:

- The type of business and its operating environment;
- The level of business risk;
- Ease of use;
- The relative cost;
- Feasibility; and
- Availability of skills and resources.

The everyday use of web-based access and mobile communications provides universal information accessibility. It has enabled cost reductions, increased business efficiency and 24x365 service delivery. However, the growing usage of Web 2.0 and beyond tools and applications, that are the preferred choice of communications for many, has the potential to expose organizations to a range of new threats to the security of its information, corporate reputation and brand value.

The extended communications environment brought about by global collaborative ventures in service delivery, remote and mobile workers is also adding complexity in security. Customers and employees rightly have expectations of data and transactional integrity and confidentiality in their use of mobile and transactional services. They also expect and demand quick and convenient remote access to business systems that results in business applications and corporate data now residing on laptops and mobile devices. At the same time laptops and mobile devices are desirable items and instances of theft/loss of mobile devices are on the rise.

As with the introduction of any new technology or initiative a balance has to be found that optimizes the value and opportunities presented by these applications whilst implementing smart strategies and policies that minimize the risk exposure and threats to the organization. This does not mean more protection technology, rather working more effectively with existing ICT security assets. The starting point is understanding the protection needs of the business: its systems, data, user and usage protection, in addition to its risk profile based on the above, and its end-to-end protection needs in a global 24x365 collaborative business environment.

Risk and vulnerability analysis

An important task in developing a security strategy is to assess the level of risk and potential threats to the organization and its vulnerability to these risks. The level of risk can be calculated according to the amount of damage or loss that could result due to a security exposure, multiplied by the probability (or frequency) that this may occur.

The level of risk is influenced by the type of organization, the external environment, its business and its objectives. An organization that operates in a highly competitive environment, depends upon large-scale information processing and access for its business, or manages a large proportion of personal or commercially sensitive information will have a higher security risk than an organization in a more stable and less sensitive environment. For example, the need for confidentiality, integrity and availability of systems in the banking or airline industry is much higher than in a public library system. In security, a compromise should not be entertained. Best practice should be implemented commensurate with the level of risk.

Threats to security can be found in human error or deliberate human intervention, natural and political disasters, hardware and software failures. Examples of human error include incorrect keying of input data, errors in program development or maintenance, or operator error.

Security can be deliberately violated through:

- Unauthorized access – access to critical information or systems with or without causing damage;
- Damaging information – by damaging, contaminating, destroying, erasing, manipulating or rendering information meaningless; and
- Fraud – manipulating data to obtain a financial or other advantage.

Natural and political disasters include earthquakes, floods, fire, industrial sabotage, terrorism and war. These have the potential to threaten, either partially or totally, access to information and the functioning of the supporting technology. They can also severely degrade the functionality of the organization. Hardware and software failures include power failure, failure of equipment, network failure or systems malfunction. These can lead to loss of information and functionality for the organization.

The most prevalent security vulnerabilities or points of failure can be avoided by adhering to international security standards and having good information and communications technology (ICT) security, people and asset management practices in place. Most common vulnerabilities arise from virus, worm or Trojan infection, insider theft of proprietary or commercial in-confidence information, private information abuse or fraud, degraded performance through external attack, mobile device and laptop theft. Statistics also show that organized crime is much less likely than internal management and employees to pose a threat of theft, fraud and abuse.

Management

Security is achieved through the appropriate management of people, information, physical environment (including buildings), specific library collections and the technology (including networks and systems). The following provides some of the mechanisms used in security management.

PEOPLE MANAGEMENT

People are often a source of security violations. The security risks are found in human error, asset misappropriation and theft, fraud, loss of key staff with in-depth knowledge of competitive information, or the misuse of information and facilities. Apart from deliberate actions, an unfortunate aspect of security violations is that a considerable number are unintended. Security violations often occur through ignorance and negligence of following proper procedures.

Security should be addressed in the recruitment stage and monitored through the individual's life with the organization. Everyone must be made aware of information security threats, the importance of maintaining proper security and backup controls, and be equipped to support the organization's security practices and procedures during their work.

If the parent organization continually deals with sensitive information or operates in a highly competitive environment, all new personnel must be screened before being appointed. All employees and third parties utilizing the organization's information and supporting technical infrastructure ought to sign a confidentiality (non-disclosure) agreement with the organization that extends beyond their employment period. Employees and third parties should be advised in writing of their rights and restrictions of levels of access, the security requirements of the organization, and the appropriate disciplinary action if these security requirements are breached.

Authentication, identity and access management policies and processes should also be in place to determine those who should legitimately be given access and what access rights they should have. Authentication practices enable the users to be positively identified using two or three factor authentication processes that might include a combination of user ID in smart card, biometric or token form, password or other factor known only to the user, and a user ID. Identity management and single sign-on systems provide a centralized view of users and their access across multiple subsystems.

The main fraud mitigation techniques include having codes of conduct and fraud policies in place and ensuring that all staff are familiar with these, maintaining a fraud awareness and incident management programme and having a fraud response plan. All security breaches should be investigated and counter measures taken to ensure that similar breaches do not reoccur.

With all instances of risk through human intervention, a corporate culture that encourages teamwork and collaboration and values ethics and integrity, so that temptation is minimized, is a valuable strategy in avoiding opportunities for security breaches.

INFORMATION SECURITY

Information has varying levels of sensitivity and criticality and is protected through classification schemes for the data and information itself, as well as an identity and access management regime that ensures that 'those who can have access do, and that those who should not have access do not'. Some information may require an additional level of security protection or special handling such as intrusion and change protection devices; examples being some types of personal information or commercially sensitive information. Information classification systems can be used to define an appropriate set of security protection levels and to communicate the need for special handling requirements to users. Information that is classified as high security will require specialized storage and restricted access and circulation provisions.

Information security policies and procedures should relate to information in electronic and hard copy form. Documents, paper records or microfiche are at risk of security breaches as much as information stored in electronic form.

SPECIFIC COLLECTIONS

Libraries, museums, art galleries and archives face particular risks in terms of physical security and wilful or accidental damage to their collections. This risk increases where there is open access to the collection. Damage can occur at both the collection level and the item level through:

- Theft of an item of stock (such as a journal or DVD);
- Wilful damage to an item or part of an item of stock (such as the cutting out of an journal article or picture in a book);
- Accidental damage (such as warping of a CD left out in a hot car, or a pet or small child chewing a book); or
- Fire, storm or other damage.

Many libraries have installed security devices that either scan clients as they exit the premises, or provide videotape footage of movements within the building in order to minimize this type of damage. Libraries that house valuable and unique collections such as national libraries must weigh accessibility and ease of access against the security of the collections. Archives and other institutions that house critical collections in paper or electronic form may require special climatic or security surroundings that physically control humidity or extract oxygen from the air in the event of fire.

PHYSICAL ENVIRONMENT

Critical or sensitive business activities should be housed in secure areas. They can be protected from unauthorized access, damage and interference by a defined security perimeter with appropriate entry and exit controls and security barriers.

Information and communications technology should be physically protected from security threats and environmental hazards. The physical environment that houses the supporting ICT such as file servers, mainframes and network controllers should have hazard detection and suppression controls that minimize risk from damage through explosion, fire, water or other natural disasters. Support facilities such as power supply and cabling infrastructure must also be well protected. A battery-based or independent uninterruptive power supply ought to be installed to provide continuous operations in the case of a total or partial power failure. Equipment (including work stations) should also be protected against power spikes and lightning. Advanced planning should take into account future requirements so as to ensure the availability of adequate capacity and resources.

Physical access to storage locations may be restricted to minimize the risk of disgruntled employees or competitors destroying original and backup copies of information and software programs. A clear-desk policy can be in place to reduce the risk of unauthorized access to information sabotage or damage.

All staff should be aware of the procedures to be undertaken in the case of an earthquake, fire, bomb threat or terrorist attack in the form of chemical or biological agent or hostage situation. The need for evacuation will differ according to circumstance. In the case of an earthquake or bomb threat the safest place may be inside the building, away from windows and protected by a strong structure. Wardens should be appointed and evacuation procedures in the event of fire clearly displayed. In the case of a bomb threat all staff should be issued with a list of questions to ask the caller in order to locate the bomb and assess the situation. Where appropriate, mail should be screened before opening and procedures put in place to deal with any suspected contamination.

INFORMATION AND COMMUNICATIONS TECHNOLOGY

As well as 24-hour physical protection and fault detection, ICT should also be protected against loss, damage and interruption to business activities or wire-tapping. These should be continually reviewed in line with changing security, environmental and operational risks. Firewalls and other network perimeter security devices and procedures should also protect against viruses, spam, intrusion devices and denial of service attacks. Disks should be scanned before being introduced or exported from organizational equipment. Virus and other intrusion detection software ought to be installed on all personal computers, updated at least daily and used as a matter of course. Only authorized software should be used, and the downloading of information or software programs from remote sources should be controlled to minimize the risk of spyware and other adverse types of software being unknowingly installed.

Good asset management should be in place with regular audits performed. Tangible assets should be assigned an asset or inventory number and labelled with the number. The asset register or inventory should maintain a record of all assets, the asset or inventory number and the name of the person to whom they are allocated. This should include all hardware and software, mobile devices, and random checks should be made to ensure that all loaded software is legitimate and where necessary licensed.

GOOD HOUSEKEEPING PRACTICES

In addition to the specific security requirements mentioned above, good housekeeping practices and routines maintain the integrity, availability and confidentiality of information. These include (but are not restricted to):

- Maintaining and periodically revising security plans so that they remain relevant to the level of risk, are complete, and reflect the current business environment;
- A regularly maintained backup copy of critical information and software stored off site;
- A register of security incidents to enable the organization to review regularly all security incidents and identify commonalities to improve the approach to security;
- Controlled access to networks and systems by third parties;
- Instilling norms of ethical behaviour amongst employees;
- Accountability procedures for all assets;
- Protection from the introduction of software containing viruses and other programs that can make unauthorized or unknown modifications to either the software or information; and
- The continuous monitoring of equipment performance.

Access control

Access to information and its supporting technologies should be controlled to prevent unauthorized use or access.

AUTHORIZING USE OF ORGANIZATIONAL-WIDE NETWORKS AND SYSTEMS

There should be formal policies and procedures that control and document the allocation of access, from the initial register and management of new users, management of user privileges and passwords, to the deregistration of users who no longer need access to services. The allocation of privileged access that allows users to override systems controls should be on a very restricted basis. Teleworkers and other remote users will require special considerations for logging, access and control.

NETWORK AND COMPUTER ACCESS CONTROL

To prevent unauthorized network or computer access, technology facilities that service multiple clients must be capable of:

- Identifying and verifying the identity, terminal and location of each user;
- Recording successful and unsuccessful accesses;
- Providing a password management system to allocate, check, maintain and prompt the user to change quality passwords;
- Restricting the access times and connection times of users where appropriate, or when not in use through time-out controls and automatic log offs;
- Providing enhanced user authentication facilities such as dial-back, smart card tokens or key-based encryption; and
- Automatically disabling or disconnecting users when a small number of consecutive incorrect passwords are entered.

Access to network addresses, controls and configuration files must be managed in a secure and controlled manner.

APPLICATION ACCESS CONTROL

Logical access can be used to control access to applications and information residing on computers. These should be protected from any utility software that may be capable of overriding the application, and should not compromise the security of other systems.

Access to systems administration menus and critical system files must be restricted so that only authorized personnel are able to access these to maintain authority and user-level controls. There should be a period review of users' access permissions to ensure that access permissions continue to be valid. Audit trails should be designed to track access and changes to applications and the information in order to confirm that any changes are valid and authorized.

PHYSICAL ACCESS

Access to rooms housing equipment should be strictly controlled. The employees and visitors must be appropriately identified. Proximity devices, badges or other means of identification should be worn at all times, registers (either electronic or manual) need to be kept for when people enter and leave, and closed circuit monitors should be actively monitored by security personnel.

INFORMATION ACCESS AND PRIVACY CONSIDERATIONS

The protection of an individual's personal information is a democratic right. Privacy and data protection can be safeguarded through legislation. Where this is absent, the organization can develop its own code of conduct that:

- Guards against the indiscriminate collection and use of personal information;
- Ensures confidentiality in its information practices;
- Provides individuals with the right to view their personal records, to challenge and have corrected (or noted) any incorrect personal information about themselves; and
- Holds executive management accountable for the security and use of personal information.

Disaster recovery

In the event of a major outage (failure or disaster), disaster recovery and business continuity plans protect critical business processes from their adverse effects. The emphasis for the information services is on protecting and ensuring the continuity of access to information and its supporting technologies. However, other business aspects such as alternative sites for the total business operations must be considered.

Disaster recovery should take a business perspective. It should:

- Highlight preventative actions that may be taken;
- Seek to minimize the impact of the disaster on the information service, the parent organization and its clients; and
- Improve the organization's ability to recover efficiently and effectively.

IMPACT ANALYSIS

Before designing the disaster recovery plan an impact analysis should be undertaken. This describes the types of events that may cause an outage and analyses their impact on the business. The impact analysis links the development of the disaster recovery plan to the business needs of the organization. It also identifies the priorities within the business operations, so that critical processes can be restored first. The business impacts include:

- Loss of business opportunities;
- Likelihood of penalty clauses in contracts that may be affected by the outage, such as penalty fees for delaying the completion of a project or late payment;
- Loss of important material; and
- Impact on staff, customers, stakeholders and executive management.

THE DISASTER RECOVERY PLAN

The disaster recovery plan is part of the business continuity management process. It specifies how an organization will maintain its information services necessary for its business operations in the face of an outage or disaster. The disaster recovery plan has four components:

- Emergency plan – this specifies the type of emergency and the actions to be taken that fit the emergency situation;
- Backup plan – this specifies the facilities required (including data restoration, disks, computing equipment, telecommunications and networks, work stations) as a recovery site and to maintain operations;
- Recovery plan – this specifies how the processing will be restored, including the responsibilities of individuals and a priority list for the retrieval of important material; and
- Test plan – this specifies the frequency and manner in which the components of the disaster recovery plan will be tested.

DISASTER RECOVERY SITE

Arrangements need to be made for alternatives for a recovery site. The alternatives for a recovery site can be:

- Backup facilities that are owned by the parent organization – if the organization operates out of a number of geographic locations, a site (or a number of sites) can act as the backup facility for others;
- Right of access to facilities offered by organizations that specialize in providing disaster recovery sites – the organization may undertake a contract with a specialist organization for the use of a mobile, hot or cold site as a contingency measure. A hot site is a facility that operates equipment compatible with the organization. A cold site is a building that is designed so that it is able to accept equipment at short notice; or
- Facilities at another establishment – a reciprocal agreement may be undertaken with an organization that operates compatible equipment for each to act as recovery sites.

MANAGING THE RECOVERY

The recovery plan should be regularly updated, known and understood. Executive management must know how it will be managed and in what order so that business processes can be restored as quickly as possible. The recovery plan should be maintained in paper as well as electronic form, and copies stored off site, such as in bank vaults, the recovery site and the homes of executive management and key staff members. As the recovery plan will include sensitive and competitive information, it should be secured off site.

A consolidated contact list should be maintained. This should contain the names, addresses, contact numbers and responsibilities of the people required to implement the recovery process. The contact list should be stored alongside the recovery plan.

In addition to the people directly involved in the recovery process, the contact list should also include details of suppliers, vendor contacts, business partners such as electronic trading partners and key customers. One of the first management tasks will be to advise those on the contact list of the event and the actions taken to restore business processes to normality.

Disaster recovery plans assist the organization to restore and recover its business, either on or off site, following an outage or other security incident.

Business continuity

Business continuity differs from disaster recovery in that it is more comprehensive and provides alternatives for all resources and activities so that critical business functions can continue. Disaster recovery only considers the loss of computer-related and network facilities and provides alternatives for data processing at other locations. It does not cover issues such as the requirement for office space or alternative work facilities, emergency telephone systems, operational facilities to support staff that may be disoriented by the changes or the business impact associated with the inability of customers to access services.

Business continuity management counteracts interruptions to business activities and protects critical business processes so that there is an availability of all key resources supporting essential business functions. It requires top level commitment and sponsorship from critical stakeholders, a thorough knowledge and foresight into business impact analysis and the interdependencies on infrastructure, assets, tolerable outages, critical time recovery and process recovery prioritization.

Business continuity involves:

- Prevention through good risk and threat identification, consequences and treatment that are incorporated into a risk management plan, impact analysis, risk 'heat' map. Prevention is also assisted by having an enterprise-wide knowledge and understanding of risks and approaches to identifying, preventing or reducing the possibility of adverse impacts, effects and loss in a significant incident or crisis;
- Preparedness through planning for known events such as the continuity of operations at the end of an outsourcing contract, whilst the service provision is either being transferred to another vendor, or being brought back in house;
- Response such as what to do when the information-related facilities are still working, but employees of the information service or parent organization are denied access to the building because of an incident; and
- Recovery through being able to quickly re-establish the affected services.

Business continuity requires a sound strategy to be developed and maintained to guarantee the availability of processes and resources in order to ensure the continued achievement of critical objectives in the event of an emergency or disaster. This includes having planned arrangements to ensure the continuity of critical services and the speedy restoration of other critical business processes and services in the event of a serious business interruption. The processes will differ according to the event and level of risk. For example, the strategy to maintain business operations in the aftermath of a terrorist bombing of the office building in which the organization operates will differ from the strategy to maintain business operations during a period of industrial unrest that causes the supply of power to be continually interrupted.

Mechanisms that outline how responsive decisions are escalated, made and communicated during and after the event are important components of the response stage. These are usually found in a crisis management plan and a crisis communications plan that includes communications protocols for communicating with those affected and dealing with stakeholders and the media.

MAINTAINING AND TESTING

The efficiency and effectiveness of the business continuity strategy can only be achieved if it is maintained and tested through regular rehearsals, audits, monitoring and critical incidence reproduction. There should also be regular awareness and training programmes for all staff that incorporates human, natural environment and political components, as well as the built environment, hardware and software failures to enable knowledge transfer and understanding of individual responsibilities.

Business continuity is a continuous and ever changing process that needs the support of executive management in order to ensure that the necessary permanent funding and availability of backup infrastructure, recovery strategies, training, testing and revision are in place to cover present day and emerging risk situations. Business continuity tools and processes must also be embedded into the organization so that they are readily understood and automatically followed in times of crisis, rather than having to be learnt during the period of most need.

Legal and regulatory compliance

Finally there will be legal and regulatory compliance issues to be managed. These include privacy protection, adherence to software licensing conditions and other intellectual property rights protection, records and data protection evidence, audit considerations, securing of forensic evidence so that it is admissible in court, and telecommunications interception rights.

Conclusion

In an increasingly uncertain world, security, disaster recovery and business continuity are ever more necessary and complex. Everyone has an important role in ensuring confidentiality, integrity and availability of information, and a duty of care for the physical safety of themselves and others. Sustaining stakeholder trust in the virtual world of online services and transactions is predicated on the five elements of information security management:

- Confidentiality;
- Integrity;
- Availability of information and resources;
- Authentication; and
- Non-repudiation.

The overriding factor in the management of security is that it should be managed in accordance with the level of risk and potential threats to the organization. The requirement for a high level of security should also be balanced against the need to make information available for decision making. Ultimately, the choice is a management rather than a technical issue.

Increasingly people are a source of security violations. Whilst human error is often to blame, security can be deliberately violated through:

- Unauthorized access – access to critical information or systems with or without causing damage;
- Damaging information – by damaging, contaminating, destroying, erasing, manipulating or rendering information meaningless; and
- Fraud – manipulating data to obtain a financial or other advantage.

Security violations often occur through ignorance and negligence of following proper procedures. Security and good housekeeping practices should be addressed in the recruitment stage and monitored through the individual's life with the organization. Everyone must be made aware of information security threats, the importance of maintaining proper security and backup controls on their desktop, and be equipped to support the organization's security practices and procedures during their work such as the wearing of ID tags or use of biometrics to gain access to equipment or sensitive areas.

Physical and virtual access controls should be in place to prevent unauthorized use or access to networks, databases, enterprise systems and applications and storage devices. There should be formal policies and procedures that control and document the allocation of access, from the initial register and management of new users, management of user privileges and passwords, to the deregistration of users who no longer need access to services.

The physical environment that houses the supporting ICT such as file servers, mainframes and network controllers should be fully secured with access strictly controlled. They should have hazard detection and suppression controls that minimize risk from damage through explosion, fire, water or other natural disasters. Support facilities such as power supply and cabling infrastructure must also be well protected.

The disaster recovery plan is part of the business continuity management process. It specifies how an organization will maintain its information services necessary for its business operations in the face of an outage or disaster. The disaster recovery plan has four components:

- Emergency plan;
- Backup plan;
- Recovery plan; and
- Test plan.

Business continuity differs from disaster recovery in that it is more comprehensive and provides alternatives for all resources and activities so that critical business functions can continue. It requires a thorough knowledge and foresight into business impact analysis and the interdependencies on infrastructure, assets, tolerable outages, critical time recovery and process recovery prioritization. Business continuity has four elements:

- Prevention;
- Preparedness;
- Response; and
- Recovery.

Business continuity enables planned arrangements to be understood and able to be put in place to ensure the continuity of critical services and the speedy restoration of other critical business processes and services in the event of a serious business interruption. It identifies different scenarios for which the ensuing processes differ according to the event and level of risk.

Finally stakeholder trust in the organization is sustained and reinforced through compliance with legal and regulatory regimes such as providing for privacy protection, adherence to software licensing conditions and other intellectual property rights protection, and the securing of forensic evidence so that it is admissible in court when things go wrong.

References

Butler Group. 2009. *Information Security: Protecting the Business and its Information: Technology Evaluation and Comparison Report*. Available at www.butlergroup.com [accessed: March 2010].

Further Reading

Callan, J. 2002. *How to Keep Operating in a Crisis: Managing a Business in a Major Catastrophe*. Aldershot: Ashgate.

Matthews, G., Smith, Y. and Knowles, G. 2009. *Disaster Management in Archives, Libraries and Museums*. Farnham: Ashgate.

Saint-Germain, R. 2005. Information security management best practice based on ISO/IEC 17799. *Information Management Journal*, 39(4), July/August, 60–66.

Wilding, E. 2005. *Information Risk and Security: How to Protect Your Corporate Assets*. Aldershot: Ashgate.

24 *Evaluating Benefits and Performance*

A measure of success and long-term sustainability in today's challenging and changing environment is the extent to which an organization is worthwhile and adds value through innovation, inventive systems and processes and the exploitation of knowledge and information. Equally an important component of good governance is in ensuring that the information service is delivering valued and valuable products and services to its customers and stakeholders commensurate to the investment that is being made and that its performance is measured and evaluated. This includes identifying how well the information service is using its resources by relating the outcomes and outputs to the investment in the assets.

There are overlaps between excellence frameworks, quality improvement, standards, accreditation and evaluation. Of the latter, benefits evaluation can be a powerful tool in generating commitment to libraries and information services as it enables the understanding of intangible benefits that are more difficult to measure.

Performance is related to value in that poor performance gives little or no value to the user. However, value is also related to the exchange factor in that often people do not value anything that is free. The provision of information and related services comes at a cost, some of which may be subsidized. Calculating the level of subsidy in prices and costs is quite complex. It involves consideration of issues such as social or cultural value in addition to straightforward economic and financial costing models.

Barton (2004: 140) states that for performance assessment to fulfil its potential as a management tool, it must be embedded within the management culture of the library and its parent organization. She quotes Lakos (2002) as defining a culture of assessment as an organizational environment in which decisions are based on facts, research and analysis, where services are planned and delivered to maximize positive outcomes and impacts for customers and stakeholders, and where staff care to know what results they produce and how those results relate to customers' expectations.

Johannsen (2004) observes that the focus has shifted from an external focus on society to an internal focus on the library itself. There has also been a similar shift from the user as a citizen with rights to the user as a customer with individual preferences and needs that can be observed. Ingrained in this shift are the values of competitiveness, economy, efficiency, enthusiasm, flexibility, honesty, innovation, professionalism, quality, reliability, responsibility, responsiveness, user orientation and work environment.

Benefits evaluation

The need to articulate, evaluate and realize the benefits and costs of information services is becoming increasingly important in gaining political and public support for new and existing initiatives that are competing with other demands in the public and private sectors. Some of this need arises from the unfortunate fact that corporate memories retain recollections of spectacular failures or underperformance with greater clarity than outstanding successes that by their nature are quickly and seamlessly integrated into daily routines, practices and processes. A second reason is that many of the important benefits are intangible or difficult to quantify in a material sense. Yet as Sumsion et al. (2003: 13) point out, knowledge of appropriate cost (and benefit) is an essential ingredient in management's decision making.

Sumsion et al. (2003: 14) identify that economic aspects are only one part of the equation. Values such as learning, education, information, culture, social and community impact, as well as recreation, also contribute a beneficial return on the investment. However, the development of social capital, increased levels of innovative thinking and small incremental efficiency gains are difficult to quantify when compared with tangible outputs such as an increased number of transactions. As organizations move from information provision and interactive services to more high-value transformational outcomes through the exploitation of knowledge and information and information and communications technology (ICT) the span and level of sophistication of benefits evaluation and realization increases (see Figures 24.1 and 24.2).

These benefits arise:

- For the organization in increased organizational performance through efficiencies and productivity gains, more reliable knowledge and information for better decision-making, increased global competitiveness, increased revenue, growth in intellectual capital and renewed investor interest;
- For the customer in quality customer service, convenience and choice through multiple delivery channels, direct cost savings, efficiencies in interactions, more accessible information for better decision making, and personalized, customized and integrated services available anywhere at any time;
- As political benefits which include increased trust and citizen engagement, increased transparency and accountability in elected governments; as well as,
- For society in terms of enhanced quality of life, increased knowledge and skills, greater community cohesiveness and enhanced community development, increased social capital and sustainability.

Sumsion et al. (2003: 14) consider the benefits of public libraries on the basis of 'public' or 'merit goods' and 'private goods'. They explain that the benefits of 'merit goods' extend beyond the individual user to society in general. 'Merit goods' promote causes such as education, culture, informed citizenship, social inclusion and equality of opportunity – which extend beyond leisure use. Positive externalities arise where a better-informed and educated clientele enjoys external benefits that affect others beyond the individual user. The acquisition of a commodity can provide external benefits to others besides the acquirer. We all benefit when ignorance is reduced.

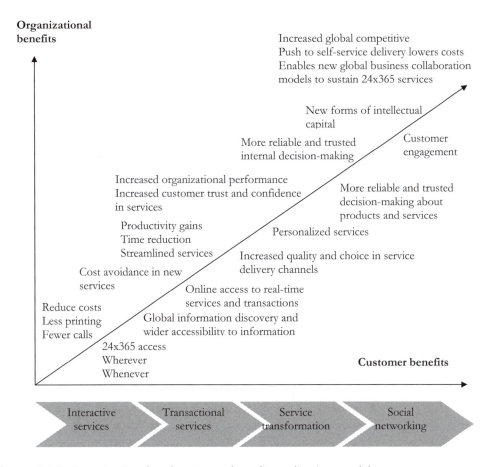

Figure 24.1 Organizational and customer benefits realization model

In support of the 'private goods' argument, they identify that borrowing from a library is an economic alternative to buying and owning as a private person. They provide a formula for the economic value as follows:

Value of benefits = $f(C-L)(N)$
Where
C = cost of commercial alternative;
L = charge made by the library (0 if free); and,
N = number of users (or audiences).

Adding value as a return on investment

The linkages between adding value through the delivery of quality and innovative information products and services and a return on investment are similar to the linkages between corporate governance and decision making. Adding value through knowledge, processes and innovation can lead to an increased return on the investment; whilst at the

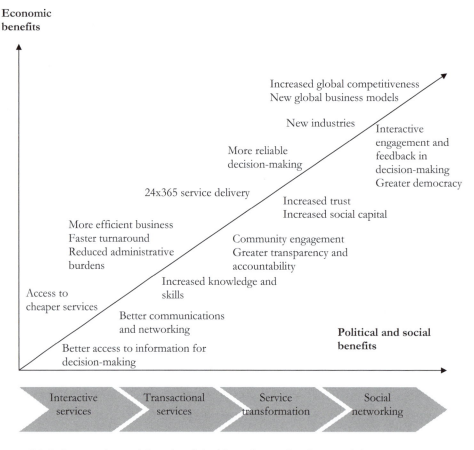

Figure 24.2 Economic, social and political benefits realization model

same time, the need to add value is a fundamental requirement in ensuring that practices and procedures deliver a return on investment as part of good corporate governance.

There are many different ways of valuing and measuring this. The following provides insight into different mechanisms that can be used within information services to determine whether value is being added and if there is a return on the investment.

Performance and value

Information services contribute to organizational performance and transformation, sustainability, and different forms of capital through the following activities:

- Assisting the parent organization increase or sustain its financial capital, competitiveness and market share by adding value to the amount and quality of knowledge and innovation within the organization. For example, in acquiring, organizing and disseminating accurate and timely information to retain its client capital, assist new product development and to make it successful against its competitors;

- Contributing to social capital, democracy and the quality of life. In the virtual world, individual access to and the sharing of ideas, information, skills and knowledge is an important component of lifelong learning, day-to-day living and democracy. Public libraries add value to the quality of life of individuals through the provision of educational, informational, recreational and cultural services;
- Adding value to information as a commodity or resource and subsequently increasing the intellectual capital of the organization. Information utilities and value-added information providers increase the value and create new information products and services by manipulating, merging and redistributing information in a value-added form to meet stakeholder needs. They also create new markets for information to meet prospective customer needs. An example is how spatial information has been incorporated into in-vehicle navigation devices and mobile phones;
- Recognizing that information has different values to different people in different situations and at different times which can affect financial capital. Information has unique economic properties that can affect its value at any one time. It can be stored and used at the same time. It can be reused without diminishing in value, or, in the case of competitive information, its value lies in no one else having access, and more than one client can use it at the same time;
- Assisting the organization to meet its sustainability and natural capital obligations through research and advice on best practice regimes; and
- Developing ICT as a tool for enabling anywhere anytime support and service delivery to mobile devices as well as assisting information services to participate in global information-centric collaboration to deliver 24x365 services.

Within these activities return on investment can be measured by assessing:

- Relative delivered cost – how the information service is increasing its productivity and lowering its costs across all outlays in the value chain;
- Relative performance – how the information service is adding strategic value to the organization and its clients through its ability to offer innovative and valued products and services; and
- Financial savings – how the information service is delivering savings to the organization.

The return on investment for information products and services is also enhanced by:

- Adding other information to the original information;
- Reprocessing and repackaging the information to meet market or customer demands;
- Making information more accessible to customers; and
- Refining the information to meet individual needs.

The above points are regarded as enhancements to the value chain. However, information by itself is not necessarily useful. If it is not used, for example it sits unused within an information system because people do not know of its existence, or it is not useful to clients or the business because it does not meet their needs, then it has no value to the organization. Burk and Horton (1988) have suggested five ways in which the performance and value of information may be measured:

- Quality of the information itself – accuracy, comprehensiveness, credibility and currency;
- Quality of the information holdings – accessibility, adaptability, ease of use, format;
- Impact upon productivity – greater returns, improvement in decision making, more efficient operations;
- Impact on organizational effectiveness – new markets, improved customer satisfaction, meeting goals and objectives; and
- Impact on financial position – cost savings, creation of new assets, improved profits.

They also go on to rank or rate the information resource according to its:

- Effectiveness in supporting the activity it was designed to support;
- Strategic importance of the information resource (or service) to the activities of the parent organization; and
- Strategic importance of the activities being supported to the parent organization.

These generic measurements of performance and value for the information resource may also be applied to measure the value and performance of the individual work units within the information service as well as to the information service as a whole.

PUBLIC VALUE

Public value has been defined by Kelly et al. (2002) as 'the value created by government through services, laws, regulation and other actions'. Concepts of public value developed by Angela Firth (2006) have been further refined by the Office of e-Government (2007) to include:

- Service quality – measured by high take-up, satisfactions levels, degree of accountability and choice, ease of finding information and responsiveness;
- Service efficiency – measured by improved levels of productivity, reduced costs, throughput, transparency, improved procurement and well motivated staff;
- Trust – measured by levels of fairness, reliability, acceptance, security, privacy and citizen participation in decision making; and
- Outcomes – measured by healthier people, skilled and informed people, safer communities, more jobs, economic development and better lifestyles.

The concept of public value is in itself valuable as a benchmark against which valuable outcomes to citizens and business can be measured.

SERVICE QUALITY

In the service era, quality has become an unquestionable value that governs the survival and sustainability of organizations. Balague (2009: 288) describes quality as a multi-dimensional, multi-level and dynamic concept: it is a social construct, always relative and continuously evolving so that what satisfies a customer today, will fail to do so tomorrow. Quality is what customers perceive as a result of the comparison of products and services with others, and through reflecting on their own feelings, previous experiences and expectations, and it is always deeply related to the contextual settings.

Perceived service quality has been defined by Zeithaml (1988) as the customer's assessment of the overall superiority or excellence of the service. Ladhari and Morales (2008) identify three dimensions of service quality as affect of service, information control, and library as place.

Affect of service focuses on the human dimension of service quality, such as how well users are served and treated by library staff. For example, employees:

- Instilling confidence in users;
- Giving users individual attention;
- Are consistently courteous;
- Are always ready to respond to users' questions;
- Have the knowledge to answer users' questions;
- Deal with users in a caring fashion;
- Understand their users' needs;
- Are always willing to help users; and
- Show dependability in handling users' service problems.

Information control is concerned with the ability to navigate the information universe. It considers how well the collections, both print and electronic, support learning, teaching and research; and how easy it is to locate and access the needed materials. For example whether the library's:

- Electronic resources are accessible externally e.g. from my home or office;
- Website enables me to locate information on my own;
- Printed materials meet those required for work;
- Electronic information needs are what I need;
- Modern equipment lets me easily access the information I need;
- Easy-to-use access tools that allow me to find things on my own;
- Information is easily accessible for independent use; and
- Print and electronic journal collections are those required for work.

The third dimension is 'library as place' and focuses on how well a library meets the individual needs of users who look for a place to do research and study. For example, the library has:

- Spaces that inspire study and learning;
- Quiet spaces for individual activities;
- A comfortable and inviting location;
- Facilities to be a gateway for study, learning or research; and
- Community spaces for group learning and group study.

In the physical world libraries are increasingly being seen as spaces for communal discussion, learning and study activities complementing the virtual world that is the provider of universal information. As more services and collections are delivered virtually it will be necessary to consider a fourth dimension; that is 'the library as a virtual place' focusing on how well a library designs, promotes and provides its services in a virtual space to meet the individual needs of users using social media and electronic access to collaborate, study, learn and research in the electronic environment.

SERVICE VALUE

In a world of intense competition, the provision of service value to consumers is increasingly being used as a strategy for success and differentiator of service marketing strategies. The following provide different concepts of service value as referenced by Ladhari and Morales (2008):

- Zeithaml (1988) identified four meanings that consumers associate with value: value is low price; value is whatever the consumer wants in a product; value is the quality that the consumer gets for the price paid; and value is what the consumer gets for what he/she gives;
- Parasuraman and Grewal (2000) have distinguished four value types: acquisition value, transaction value, in-use value, and redemption value. Acquisition value is defined as the benefits buyers think they receive when acquiring the service. Transaction value is the pleasure consumers feel for getting a good deal. In-use value is the utility derived from using the service and redemption value is the residual benefits received at the time of termination;
- Petrick (2002) identified five dimensions of perceived service value. Three of the five dimensions represent what a consumer receives from the purchase: emotional response to the service, quality received from the service, and reputation of the service. The two remaining dimensions are related to what is given and includes monetary and non-monetary price.

BALANCED SCORECARD

Missingham (2005) also includes the balanced scorecard methodology in her research into the value of libraries over the past decade. She notes that this tool, developed by Kaplan and Norton, enables clarification of the organization's vision, defining expected results in terms of financial perspective (including return on capital), customer perspectives, internal business processes and learning and growth of staff. Libraries using this methodology are able to demonstrate value by linking their activities to the organization's value statements.

CONTINGENT VALUATION

Contingent valuation is an economic methodology used to estimate the value that a person places on a good or service. It is based on surveying individuals to establish value. Missingham (2005) explains that it seeks to determine:

- How much individuals would be prepared to pay, willingness to pay (WTP) in order to secure the provision of a public good; and

- How much money they are willing to accept for loss of quality of life, willingness to accept (WTA).

Applied in the information services context, the methodology enables consideration to be given to the cost implications of having or not having an information service.

Missingham (2005) quotes the British Library study of 2004 that was based on contingent valuation and assessed the value enjoyed indirectly and directly by UK citizens. Over 2,000 individuals were surveyed to assess:

- Willingness to pay – asking individuals how much they are willing to pay to continue to access the service and directly measure the demand curve with a budget constraint;
- Willingness to accept – asking individuals how much they are willing to accept in compensation to forgo the service and directly measure the demand curve without a budget constraint;
- Investment in access – estimate of time and cost invested in accessing the service;
- Cost of alternatives – costs incurred if forced to use alternatives; and
- Price elasticity – change in demand with a change in price.

The study showed that the British Library generates value around 4.4 times the level of its public funding.

The ultimate criterion for assessing the quality of a service is its capability for meeting the stakeholder needs it is intending to serve, and the value of a service must ultimately be judged in terms of the beneficial effects accruing from its use as viewed by those who sustain the costs.

Pricing information

The 'user pays' environment and the recognition of the business value of information has created the need to consider the cost of information and how to apply a charge or price to information when it is transferred to another party in the form of an information product or service.

Pricing of information products and services is linked to issues such as financial management and costs of service provision, equity, the opportunity presented to do something with the information, the economic properties of information, value to the customer and willingness to pay. Sometimes avoidance costs are taken into consideration, where the cost of not having the information is factored into the equation. An example is the public utility that offers information under 'Dial before you Dig' programmes where information about water and sewerage pipes, energy pipelines or communications cables are provided free of charge, on the basis of this being more cost-effective than the cost of repairs in the event of accidental severance.

Generally the value of information to an organization can also be assessed as:

- A consumption good – where the organization sells the information as a value-added product;
- A customer service good – where the organization provides information as part of its services; or

- An investment good – where the organization uses it for decision making to achieve competitive advantage.

SUBSIDIZATION

Information products and services are not free. There are costs associated with capturing or purchasing data and equipment, storage, processing, production, distribution and exchange. However, the nature of some information, particularly that which is provided as a customer service good, is that its value and optimum return on investment lies in it being fully subsidized. Subsidization is a policy decision that takes into account social or community service obligations where everyone contributes some or all of the funding of the service so that the service is delivered as:

- Fully subsidized – information products and services are made available at no cost to the user. The total cost being absorbed by the information service or parent organization as part of a community service obligation;
- Partially subsidized – information products and services are made available at nominal cost. The information service or its parent organization exercises partial cost recovery and funds the remainder of the costs of providing the products or services internally; or
- Full cost recovery – information products and services are made available either at market rates (cost and profit) or at the rate required for total cost recovery from the customer.

CONSUMPTION GOODS

Other information products and services have a value to specific customers in that they are designed and offered to fit a specific market need. These fall into the category of a consumption good. An example is where a library may offer specific research services tied to its local history collection to architects who specialize in restoring old houses. These services can be made available on a full cost recovery basis. As a consumption good different charging strategies can be used for information products and services that are influenced by:

- Product or service intensity – information products such as maps that contain very detailed information or services that are provided in depth will often command a higher price than others that have less depth or detail;
- Product life of the information – information that is rare or offers a new perspective will be of greater value. The price can be set much higher than for information that is older. Out-of-date information has no value;
- Supply time – the faster information is made available, the higher the price that can be set;
- Customers' ability to pay and type of customer – organizations that rely on information products and services as a means of creating their next business advantage will recognize that information is a critical resource and will build provisions in their budgets accordingly. Clients requiring information for more personal reasons will be less willing to pay;

- Medium or format – the medium or format influences the cost of dissemination of the information product or service;
- Extent of the value-added processing – information that is tailored to meet specific or individual needs and is highly processed will command a higher price than a more generic information product or service; and
- Intended use of the information – information that is used for commercial purposes may be priced at a higher rate than information that is used as a social good.

Quality management systems

Balague (2009: 288) defines a quality management system as the output of the implementation of a set of structured processes that helps gather, organize and distribute suitable information to suitable people, in optimum conditions of costs and time, to empower them to take the most suitable decisions. Quality management systems develop aspects such as quality policies and quality objectives, establish the functions and responsibilities of staff members, define products and services, identify working processes and the necessary resources to carry them out, and fix mechanisms of supervision, control, prevention, correction and continuous improvement.

Performance evaluation

Performance measurement and evaluation are important management activities. They serve two purposes:

- As an assessment of how effective the information service is in its performance; and
- As an accountability factor to the stakeholders by measuring the appropriateness and efficiencies of services.

Performance evaluation is the process by which the information service determines whether it is on course for the achievement of the parent organization's objectives. The process includes:

- Establishing an appropriate evaluation process;
- Measuring and evaluating the performance; and
- Adopting procedures for acting upon the outcomes and recommendations of the evaluation.

The establishment of the evaluation process requires the development of specific objectives and the establishment of performance indicators to measure progress. The specific objectives define the intended level and quality of the service, the outcomes to be achieved, and the timeframe and resources available to achieve the outcomes.

The timing and format of the evaluation depends upon whether management is evaluating the continuous performance of the information service as a whole, of each of the work units, or a specific project or aspect of the service. In the case of the latter, the performance of the service should be evaluated prior to and at the completion of a specific project. Finally, actions should be initiated in response to any findings or recommendations that arise out of the evaluation.

Tangible evidence of performance for information services operating within profit-making organizations is found in the extent to which they contribute to corporate competitiveness, overall profit growth, sales increase and increased return on investment. The measurements of leadership capabilities of the information services manager could include the information service's ability to:

- Provide an increased level of services to meet customers' needs;
- Improve and extend information systems to match the growth in the corporate demand for information; and
- Maintain the competitiveness of the organization through either doing more with less, obtaining strategic information or applying innovative uses to existing technology.

In non-profit-making organizations effectiveness is usually based upon comparative measures such as benchmarking, or subjective evaluations. Comparative measures are often related to budget expenditures such as cost per unit of output, or on market share ratio such as percentage of senior citizens (clients) who utilize the services of a public library.

APPROPRIATENESS

Appropriateness measures the business fit of the information service with the goals and objectives of the organization and how it meets the needs of key stakeholders. This includes the level of consistency of service with the future business direction of the organization and the extent to which it takes into account risk and other evaluation mechanisms.

OUTPUTS AND OUTCOMES

Outputs and outcomes are two of the most common means of measuring and evaluating the effectiveness and efficiency of an information service's performance. Outputs provide a simple focal point for measuring the cost-effectiveness of the information service. They can be compared with inputs to measure efficiency, and with the corporate objectives to measure effectiveness. They demonstrate value in terms of efficiency in managing human and material resources and in being financially responsible. Examples of output measures include the average number of helpdesk enquiries successfully handled by an individual within a 15-minute response time, or the number of missing files or records located within the organization over a period of time.

Output measures can also be used to determine how processes and services can be made more cost-effective, or to benchmark services and activities against other services.

Services are evaluated or appraised through outcomes. These measure the impact of the outputs on the target market and the environment. They are the intended consequences of the information service's activities and are found in achievements such as changes in circumstances or behaviour, or benefits such as needs that are satisfied.

Impacts are a third means of measuring effectiveness. These measure what differences, positive or negative, have been made.

MEASURING QUALITY AND VALUE

Tangible measures of efficiency are linked to value for money and involve the extent to which productivity is improved or duplication is lessened. Value for money also considers whether there are alternative or more sustainable mechanisms for delivering services for less costs and/or better outcomes.

However, many of the benefits of the information service are intangible. The quality of the service may be recognized by the customers and stakeholders or senior management, but it is often difficult to apply concrete measures that can be directly attributed to the information service. Sometimes an attempt is made to assume some sort of qualitative measures by applying a timescale to the quantitative measures, for example the number of enquiries or advice taking 15 minutes or more. The assumption is that the longer the period of time taken, the more in-depth and valuable the service given. There are two problems with performance measures of this type:

* There is not necessarily a correlation between time and quality; and
* They fail to measure the impact or outcome of the advice and how it was used in the value chain.

For example, the customer may be dissatisfied with the advice but out of politeness and consideration for the staff have made them feel helpful and successful.

The measures of quality (capability) and value (benefit) that arise out of the above example are much more difficult to measure directly. Indirect measures have been used, but as Orr points out (1973: 320), the relationship between capability and utilization is mediated through demand, which is itself a highly complex variable.

There are three measures of performance common to all services. These are efficiency and two other aspects: 'how good is the service?' and 'how much good does it do?'. The latter can be expressed as quality and value or effectiveness and benefit. Orr (1973: 318) states:

> If the work units that comprise the information service collectively supply pertinent and timely information in an efficient manner that enables the organization to take advantage of its competitors, it will be perceived as being a valuable asset by senior management and funded accordingly. Services that are efficient and reflect the needs of the customers are usually well supported. Customers convey positive feedback to senior management and tangible effects are felt upon the parent organization. This support is reflected in the level of funding that the information service receives. In contrast, poorly focused, inefficient information services result in disillusionment for both the staff and customers. This is manifested in a lack of commitment by customers, senior management and other stakeholders. Unless the service is refocused to meet customer needs and the quality of service improved, the information service and its level of funding will invariably decline.

CAUSE AND EFFECT

Orr (1973: 318) has developed four basic propositions:

- That, other things being equal, the capability of the service tends to increase as the resources devoted to it increase, but not necessarily proportionately;
- That, other things being equal, the total uses made of a service (utilization) tend to increase as its capability increases, but not necessarily proportionately;
- That, other things being equal, the beneficial effects realized from a service increase as its utilization increases, but not necessarily proportionately; and
- That, other things being equal, the resources devoted to a service increase as its beneficial effects increase, but not necessarily proportionately.

The cause and effect sequence is useful in that it points out that funds invested in different services or work unit activities may not necessarily have the same impact. There are other important interactions that have just the same, if not more, effect on the services. For example, in competitive, customer-oriented environments it is quality and innovation, not quantity, which distinguishes an information service. The knowledge, creativity and resourcefulness of the staff can have more impact on the quality and value of the service than the funding level. The level of resources and funding still has some bearing upon the output and performance of the information service. Without adequate resources, the services will gradually decline. However, funds alone do not constitute a good service. The effectiveness of the information service's policies and practices, staff competence and morale, and the leadership skills of management also impact the quality of the service.

Performance indicators

A performance indicator is the formula that is used to measure progress, quality and level of service towards achieving the organization's objectives. It is the means of knowing whether a specific objective is being achieved (see Table 24.a). However, even success in producing outputs and achieving outcomes does not call for complacency. The results should be analysed to see if there are better ways of achieving the same results at least cost.

Performance indicators combine the elements of inputs, outputs and outcomes. Generally three types of indicators are used. These are:

- Workload indicators;
- Efficiency indicators; and
- Effectiveness indicators.

Workload indicators are output oriented. They measure the amount of work achieved against set milestones. Efficiency indicators compare resource inputs against resulting outputs.

They quantify the resources used to achieve the intended outputs (services or products) so that the ratio of outputs to inputs can be determined. Effectiveness indicators measure the extent to which services achieve objectives using qualitative and quantitative indicators.

Performance indicators must be relevant to the cause and should clearly relate to the specific objectives of the service. They should be measurable. The information used must be reliable, valid and verifiable. Data collection should be accurate and unbiased,

Table 24.1 Examples of performance indicators in an information service

Type of indicator	Objective	Performance indicator
Workload	To scan 2,500,000 items into a digital image system over a period of three months as part of a project to digitize and preserve an archival collection.	Actual work progress in terms of the number of items accurately scanned at the end of each week of the project.
	To process 10,000 client requests for information per year.	Actual requests for information (reported monthly).
Efficiency	To support an office desktop environment at a maximum cost of $120.00 per person per month.	The actual cost of providing the office desktop environment (based on unit cost).
	e-business application to provide client transactions at a maximum cost of $5.00 per transaction.	The actual cost of client transactions each month (dollar value of resources used divided by the total number of transactions per month).
Effectiveness	Customer satisfaction in level of choice and quality of service.	Levels of customer satisfaction determined by surveys, customer feedback, number of complaints.

interpreted accurately, and collected in time for proper use to be made of it. It is important that the indicators are not subjective. They should be capable of being translated into meaningful information for use by those who require them.

Each indicator should be unique. It should reveal some important aspect of performance that no other indicator does. The value of the information should be weighed against the costs of the collector's and analyst's time, efforts and resources. The degree to which routine operations are impeded in collecting the data, and the acceptance levels of staff time and operating expenses should be balanced against the value of the information provided.

Often mechanisms for evaluating performance through a client or staff survey or client focus group can be reused as part of a quality improvement or external accreditation process, an internal process for meeting service standards and service evaluation.

Taylor (1986: 181–184) has defined several other qualities or attributes that can assist in producing meaningful indicators in information services. For example, the audit should be at a definable point in the process, such as the number of abstracts completed or requests for information processed. The activities should be easy to count and define. For example, enquiries can be classified as taking under one minute, one to three minutes, five to 10 minutes, and so on.

A defined output should also be consistent with existing information systems and, if possible, covered by historical data. Like should be compared with like. The historical context is important as it allows for comparisons over a period of time. The output should have a terminal quality. It should be isolated and counted at the point where it changes function and status. For example, the issue of a library book changes the status of the book from an asset or library resource to a source of information, education, culture or recreation for the customer. By counting issue transaction statistics, public libraries are counting one of the sources of added value to the quality of life in their communities. The outputs are the result of a process in which value is added.

Conclusion

Ensuring the return on investment in the information service is a complex issue that is directly related to planning and managing projects to fit the business needs of the parent organization and the customers' information and service needs. It also requires consideration of how the return on investment can be increased at the different stages of the value chain, and charging strategies for information products and services.

Information services often experience difficulty in designing quantitative and qualitative measures that prove their value as many of the benefits are intangible or linked to other outcomes for which they cannot be directly accountable. Outcomes such as the value of the service in contributing to organizational competitiveness, its social value and contribution to a community, or the creation of value-added information-based products and services can be used to measure performance and value. Other mechanisms through which the performance of the information service (and its information resource) may be valued include accuracy, comprehensiveness, accessibility, adaptability and ease of use, impact on productivity, impact on organizational effectiveness and impact on financial position.

In order to measure performance, information needs to be collected and analysed over time. The information services manager must determine what pieces of information are needed to evaluate or measure the service's performance.

References

Balague, N. 2009. Auditing the library's quality system. *Library Management*, 30(4/5), 286–294.

Barton, J. 2004. Measurement, management and the digital library. *Library Review*, 53(3), 138–141.

Burk, C.F. and Horton, F.W. 1988. *Info Map: A Complete Guide to Discovering Corporate Resources*. New Jersey: Prentice Hall.

Firth, A. 2006. Citizen centric government: Taking it to the next level. *Public Administration Today*, April, 15–19.

Johannsen, C.G. 2004. Managing fee-based public library services: Values and practices. *Library Management*, 25(6/7), 307–315.

Kelly, G., Mulgan, G. and Muers, S. 2002. *Creating Public Value: An Analytical Framework for Public Service Reform*. London: Cabinet Office Strategy Unit.

Ladhari, R. and Morales, M. 2008. Perceived service quality, perceived value and recommendation: A study among Canadian public library users. *Library Management*, 29(45), 352–366.

Lakos, A. 2002. Culture of assessment as a catalyst for organizational change in libraries. Paper to the 4th Northumbria International Conference on Performance Measurement in Libraries and Information Services, Washington, DC, 12–16 August 2001.

Missingham, R. 2005. Libraries and economic value: A review of recent studies. *Performance Measurement and Metrics*, 6(3), 142–158.

Office of e-Government. 2007. *Citizen Centric Government: Electronic Service Delivery Strategy for the Western Australian Public Sector*. Perth: Government of Western Australia, Office of e-Government.

Orr, R.H. 1973. Measuring the goodness of library services: A general framework for considering quantitative measures. *Journal of Documentation*, 29(3), 315–322.

Parasuraman, A. and Grewal, D. 2000. The impact of technology on the quality-value-loyalty chain: A research agenda. *Journal of the Academy of Marketing Science*, 28(1), 168–174.

Sumsion, J. et al. 2003. Estimating the economic value of library benefits. *Performance Measurement and Metrics*, 4(1), 13–27.

Taylor, R.S. 1986. *Value Added Processes in Information Systems*. New Jersey: Ablex.

Zeithaml, V.A. 1988. Consumer perceptions of price, quality and value: A means-end model and synthesis of evidence. *Journal of Marketing*, 52(3), 2–22.

Further reading

British Library. 2004. *Measuring our Value*. London: British Library.

Codling, S. 1998. *Benchmarking*. Aldershot: Gower.

Holt, G. and Elliot, D. 1998. Proving your library's worth: A test case. *Library Journal*, 123(18), 42–44.

Kaplan, R.S. and Norton, D.P. 1996. *The Balanced Scorecard: Translating Strategy into Action*. Boston: Harvard Business School.

Kingma, B.R. 2000. *The Economics of Information: A Guide to Economic and Cost-Benefit Analysis for Information Professionals*, 2nd edn. London: Libraries Unlimited.

Linna, P., Pekkola, S., Ukko, J. and Melkas, H. 2010. Defining and measuring productivity in the public sector: Managerial perceptions. *International Journal of Public Sector Management*, 23(3), 300–320.

McCallum, I. and Quinn, S. 2004. Valuing libraries. *Australian Library Journal*, 53(1), 55–69.

Niven, P.R. 2005. *Balanced Scorecard Diagnostics: Maintaining Maximum Performance*. New Jersey: John Wiley.

Rowley, J. 1997. Principles of price and pricing policy for the information marketplace. *Library Review*, 46(3/4), 179–189.

Sumsion, J. et al. 2002. The economic value of book borrowing from public libraries: An optimisation model. *Journal of Documentation*, 58(6), 662–683.

PART

V Customer and Market Focus

The theme for Part V is positioning the information service to excel in and sustain efficient and effective services that meet the right customer needs. It deals with defining and managing the customer-focused end products and services that result from all of the other activities in the book. It also considers alternative strategies that can be used to deliver products and services. As a reflection of its level of importance, this part could easily be at the beginning of the book. However, it has been located towards the end of the book as it builds upon all the other practices and processes that must be in place within the information service to support service delivery.

Chapter 25 considers strategic marketing strategies to increase and sustain the competitiveness of the information service in both challenging and changing times and where a global context means that services and products can be sourced locally, nationally and internationally. It outlines the process of a strategic marketing exercise and explains the marketing mix, or 'the four Ps' of product, price, place and promotion in the context of information services. The chapter also outlines how markets can be divided into market segment groups of need markets, geographic markets, product markets and demographic markets. Market targeting can be undertaken through three strategies: undifferentiated marketing, differentiated marketing and concentrated marketing. Each strategy is explained drawing upon examples in information services. Customer satisfaction studies also provide an indication as to whether existing information service customers are satisfied with current services.

Underlying the marketing concept is a system of exchange. The theory behind exchange system analysis is explained in the context of information services. A further analysis that can be used in marketing is the competitive portfolio analysis. Chapter 25 explains how the product life cycle and the Boston Consulting Group's portfolio matrix can be used in a competitive portfolio analysis. A specific example of how the competitive portfolio analysis can be used in managing library stock is explained. Today, organizations are making widespread use of customer relationship management systems and tools to understand their customers' needs and behaviours in order to develop stronger relationships with them. Chapter 25 introduces some of the issues for successful customer relationship management. Finally, Chapter 25 describes the rejuvenation strategies that can be used to recover some services' lack of use over time or to stop the decline in the product life cycle.

Positioning the information service to excel requires consideration of how the corporate image is formed, managed and projected. Chapter 26 considers image analysis in the context of determining service provision. Image studies measure the perceptions that people have about the information service. Chapter 26 also looks at strategies for projecting the information service externally through communication. Information on managing the corporate image is included as well as other formal communication mechanisms, such as annual reports and submissions to outside bodies. Chapter 26 also provides a model for a communications plan.

Whilst Chapter 25 focuses on understanding customers, product preferences and the market place, Chapter 27 is concerned with ensuring quality service and service support once the customer has engaged with the information service. Chapter 27 introduces the reader to quality control and choice in service delivery. It makes the point that people have differing perceptions of quality according to how they judge it and their cultural background. The chapter lists the main determinants of quality and identifies five gaps that can cause unsuccessful service delivery. The role of quality in the value chain is covered, as is the need for continuous rather than one-off improvement.

Chapter 27 reflects a customer approach to management. It describes these in terms of 'Rs' that stand for retention, requirements, refined segmentation, etc. The chapter points out that the delivery of the service or product is only the beginning of the relationship between the organization and the customer. Choice of channels and service backup is extremely important to deliver a total quality service. Suggestions for a customer service charter are included. Finally, the chapter describes how technology can be used by organizations to retain their customers.

Management Influences in a Changing Landscape
1. Managing in an uncertain world
2. Strategic influences

Strategy and Planning
3. Strategic Planning – positioning for a sustainable future
4. Attracting and retaining the best people in challenging times
5. Ensuring value for money and enabling a cost-sustainable future
6. Knowledge and information management – a key to survival
7. Strategic technology and asset management – a smarter approach

Leadership and Innovation
8. Leadership
9. Utilizing a values driven culture for sustainability
10. Innovation and creativity
11. Engaging change in positioning for the future
12. Group dynamics and team building
13. Effective negotiation and conflict management
14. Managing the political arena
15. Policy-making
16. Personal communications and networking
17. Managing yourself and others in challenging times

Governance and Social Responsibility
18. Ensuring good corporate governance
19. Using authority and influence
20. Encouraging transparency
21. Managing for sustainability
22. Managing risk
23. Sustaining trust and continued operations
24. Evaluating benefits and performance

Customer and Market Focus
25. Competitive strategies
26. Corporate image and communications
27. Ensuring service quality

Success and Sustainability
28. Bringing it all together

Figure PV.1 Customer and market focus

25 *Competitive Strategies*

Organizations today face many challenges if they are to survive in a continuously changing and highly competitive environment. They must achieve three concurrent goals: customer satisfaction, market domination and increased profitability. They must not only complement existing roles, but also continually embrace opportunities and seek the next new competitive advantage.

Today the information service market is characterized by intense competition. Taking a proactive management approach, developing a marketing-oriented culture and providing consistently higher-quality customer services and new product offerings ahead of competitors are some of the most important means of differentiating services and stimulating customer referral. Originally the argument for this was on a strictly competitive and localized basis. There is now a more pressing reason for providing quality and innovative customer services. The virtual world typified by the World Wide Web and social media is a source of instantaneous and personal customer experiences, reactions and communication. News now spreads instantaneously and globally about positive and negative customer experiences. Customers share their experiences through social networking channels in a candid and forthright manner. As such these media present immediate opportunities and threats to organizations in terms of service delivery and customer retention and relationships.

Strategic marketing is part of the total planning process and assists the organization to remain competitive. Strategic marketing makes use of many of the concepts and functions of strategic planning. Strategic marketing strategies ensure viable market positions and programmes for the sustainability and success of the information service.

Market segments comprise individuals or groups who are actual or potential customers of the information service. Markets can be divided according to need, product, preferred means of contact, demography and geography; each market having its own particular characteristics. Market targeting involves the evaluation, selection and concentration on the desired market segments. There are three strategies for market targeting: undifferentiated marketing, differentiated marketing and concentrated marketing.

Various analyses assist marketing strategies. These are exchange system analysis, image analysis, customer satisfaction studies, competitive portfolio analysis and product life cycles. The exchange system analysis is useful as it enables the information services manager to identify what the customers are prepared to exchange for the services that the information service offers. Its importance lies in the fact that both tangible and intangible items can be identified, including the more esoteric values that the information service community may hold. This may be useful information when planning new services or in justifying existing services in a financially constrained environment. Customer expectations are always increasing and customer satisfaction studies determine whether customer expectations for services are higher or lower than those being provided. Product life cycles and product portfolio matrices help the information service to determine which areas have the potential for growth. Finally, diversification and service rejuvenation can help to instil new growth into ailing services.

Supporting these strategies are customer relationship tools that enable the information service to collect and analyse information about customers' needs and behaviours in order to develop stronger relationships with them.

Strategic marketing

Strategic marketing has been defined by Kotler et al. (1980: 56) as 'a managerial process of analysing market opportunities and choosing market positions, programs and controls that create and support viable businesses that serve the organization's purposes and objectives'. Strategic marketing adds value by creating an understanding of the value that customers seek, which in turn influences organizations to create and communicate that value. It is a business philosophy that puts the customer at the centre of overall activities of the organization.

Ladhari and Morales (2008: 353) quote Snoj and Zdenka (2001) in saying that the intense competition in the information service market is highlighting the importance of marketing knowledge in the management of libraries. Library administrators need to improve their consumer knowledge as well as their performance in providing services as a means to satisfy library users. Consequently it is important for everyone to understand:

- The entire range of existing and potential services;
- Where they will compete and where they will leave areas for the competition;
- The services with which they will compete now and in the future;
- Their competitors' objectives, strengths and weaknesses, performance and strategies;
- Changes in the market place and market space, that includes emerging technology directions;
- Their customers' own business objectives and strategies; and
- How they will best deliver their services into the future.

Strategic marketing is part of the strategic management process of organizations and provides this understanding. Strategies are developed that ensure viable and sustainable market positions and programmes for the survival and success of the information service.

The marketing management process

Kotler (1999: 30) has identified five basic steps in the marketing management process that can be represented as:

$$R \Rightarrow STP \Rightarrow MM \Rightarrow I \Rightarrow C$$

Where:
R = Research (i.e. market research)
STP = Segmentation, targeting and positioning

MM = Marketing mix (popularly known as the four Ps, i.e. product, price, place and promotion)

I = Implementation

C= Control (getting feedback, evaluating results and revising or improving STP strategy and MM tactics).

These five steps are explained as follows.

RESEARCH (R)

The strategic marketing process builds upon the information already obtained through the strategic audit undertaken during the strategic planning process. This includes information about the present and future environment, stakeholders, the external and internal environment, mission, programmes, and performance evaluation and review. Additional information relating to markets, customers and resources is gathered by researching:

- The primary market for the information service;
- The major market segments in this market;
- The needs of each market segment;
- Market awareness and attitude to the information service;
- How potential customers learn about the information service and make decisions to use its services;
- Customer satisfaction levels;
- The major strengths and weaknesses in staff, resources, programmes, facilities, etc.;
- Opportunities to increase resources;
- Key customer groups of the information service;
- Key customer needs to be satisfied;
- The market segments to focus on;
- Major competitors; and
- The competitive benefits that can be offered to the target market through market positioning.

A SWOT analysis can also be used during this process to identify new opportunities that are in line with the objectives of the service. Other analysis tools that can be used to gather information include needs analysis, image analysis and customer satisfaction studies.

Proposed opportunities for information services are then analysed by considering market segmentations, the size and growth rate of the customer base, consumer behaviours, possible exit barriers and some forms of measuring and forecasting the attractiveness and long-term sustainability of the services.

A new service or market opportunity is attractive if:

- It is of good size – that is, if many people would use the service;
- It has the potential for growth;
- It is cost beneficial on both a short-term and long-term basis;
- There are adequate financial and technical resources and a competent and trained staff;
- There are low exit barriers; and

- The service is in line with the information service's mission and objectives.

It may be the case that an opportunity satisfies most of these criteria, but that it has to remain dormant until financial resources or technical solutions can be found or staff trained to provide the service.

The target market, that is the particular group(s) to which the service is aimed, needs to be identified. This is followed by a process of competitive positioning. This involves researching competitors' services and the needs of the target market in order to find a market or market niche. This determines whether the information service is in a strong or weak competitive position, whether the programme is attractive and whether there is high or low alternative coverage.

Once a target market has been defined and the service's competitive position determined, a market strategy is devised. This includes the development of the marketing goals and objectives. Goals may include such aspects as increasing the quality of the information service, its participation level, or its satisfaction level. Funds need to be allocated to the marketing budget. New services that are designed to meet new markets should have the important values explained to staff before commencing the service.

Finally the market strategy is implemented and controls put into place to ensure that the information service's resources, service and objectives are correctly matched to the right markets.

SEGMENTATION, TARGETING AND POSITIONING (STP)

Market segmentation

A market is a set of individuals, groups or institutions that are actual or potential customers for a product or service. Markets can be divided into groups with specific requirements; this is called market segmentation. In information services there are need markets, geographic markets, product markets and demographic markets.

- Need markets – these consist of individuals or groups who have similar or common needs or are seeking similar benefits. By grouping people with similar needs, services can be more effectively planned with some level of individual customization. For example, within a public library the need market for a homebound service would be the frail, the physically impaired, those people who are convalescing at home after surgery or hospitalization, young and old patients with terminal illnesses who are living at home, elderly people who can no longer drive and for whom public transport to the information service is inaccessible, and others who would benefit for some reason to have the library service come to them. Within these needs, as Kotler (1999: 26) indicates, 'there are buyers who seek a low price, others who seek high product quality, and still others who seek excellent service';
- Geographic markets – whilst globalization and the ubiquitous use of information and communications technologies have created a worldwide footprint in the provision of information services, local or geographic markets still need consideration in planning and designing services. Geographic markets can determine the type, size and setting of the information service together with the operating hours and services offered. Using the public library example again, residents living in outer metropolitan areas

and who spend long hours commuting may require the public library to be open at later hours than those operating in the inner city;

- Product markets – are determined by a demand for a particular product or service. A product market may be those people who have a demand for remote access to electronic information services because they work away from the office. This market could be further segmented according to specific scientific or technical information requirements such as spatial information being required by field geologists;
- Demographic markets – this is one of the most popular methods of distinguishing market segments in information services. These market segments have clear market needs, and information relating to these markets is usually readily available. Demographic markets may be identified by age, nationality, or physical needs such as the physically impaired, who may need specialized equipment such as large computer screens or ramp access.

Markets that can be subdivided into identifiable segments or subsets may require individual marketing strategies. The information services manager should be aware of their:

- Market segments' current and potential future size;
- Major customers and potential customers, and their locations;
- Customers' and potential customers' current levels of awareness of the range and levels of existing services;
- Customers' needs and motives for using the services; and
- Customers' concepts of competitive alternatives to the information service.

The strength in the market segmentation approach lies in the fact that it is based upon the customer rather than the product or service. The customer is assured of a service that satisfies as far as possible their individual needs rather than a mass-market offering. This is in line with the societal marketing concept.

Market targeting and positioning

Market targeting involves the evaluation, selection and concentration on specific market segments. There are three strategies for doing this: undifferentiated marketing, differentiated marketing and concentrated marketing.

Undifferentiated marketing – is also called mass marketing and occurs where the information service focuses upon the needs that are common to all people. Services are provided that appeal to the broadest number of customers. In concentrating on these basic services, the information service attempts to achieve excellence. Undifferentiated marketing is often pursued in times of financial constraint, when additional or specialist services are curtailed, and basic services consolidated. Costs associated with providing specialist services can be saved, but whether this is an effective strategy is debatable;

Differentiated marketing – occurs where the information service decides to operate in at least two segments of a market and designs separate services and programmes for each. In a large corporate organization this could mean differentiating services to research and development staff and to team members who work externally to the office environment. A variety of programmes to suit the diverse needs of different customers is provided. The aim of this approach is to provide services catering for specific needs that strengthen the information service's overall identity within the organization and increase its use. However specialist services may also involve additional staff with specialized skills and expertise, administrative and promotional costs;

Concentrated marketing – is also called niche marketing and occurs when the information service concentrates upon a small number of submarkets. Instead of spreading itself thinly, being all things to all people, the information service provides in-depth services in a few areas, serving a smaller percentage of the market place. It purposely determines a small number of target markets and sets out to concentrate on providing quality services to these. As a result, it achieves a strong market position through its detailed knowledge of its market segments' needs and its subsequent reputation.

No one strategy is superior to the others. In adopting a particular target strategy, the information services manager must base their decision upon the type of information service; the financial, technical, human and information resources available; the availability of competitive services; customer and potential customer needs, and the types of services having the potential to be offered. The information services manager must then decide which strategy is the most attractive given the constraints and opportunities of the information service's external environment, and its own strengths and weaknesses.

MARKETING MIX (MM)

A marketing mix is a key part of the marketing strategy. A four-factor classification called 'the four Ps' has been defined by McCarthy (1971: 44). These are product, price, place and promotion.

- Product – refers to the quality, design, features and branding of information services and involves the special features offered, the way they are offered and level of service provision. The driving force is customer value;
- Price – relates to whether a direct fee is attached to the service such as a debit to the cost centre or payment for an online search or a photocopy. There may be price modifiers such as discounts or community service obligation allowances. The driving force is the cost to the customer;
- Place – concerns the logistical provision of the service, coverage and locations of service points in the market place and multi-channel management in the market space. The driving force is customer convenience; and
- Promotion – involves the advertising and publicity campaigns, the message communicated, the media used and the timing of such. Promotional campaigns should be realistic and affordable.

Kotler (1999: 95) suggests the addition of two more Ps that are becoming important, especially in global marketing. They are:

- Politics – political activity such as laws or trade embargos; and
- Public opinion – new moods and attitudes that can affect their interest in certain products and services.

IMPLEMENTATION (I)

Having completed the strategic planning component of marketing, the information service must determine how products and services will be distributed and promoted. This will include choice of delivery channels that are considered in full in Chapter 27.

CONTROL (C)

Getting feedback, evaluating results and revising or improving the STP strategy and MM tactics can be achieved through customer satisfaction studies. These provide an indication as to whether existing information service customers are satisfied with current services. Customer satisfaction studies are a marketing tool as they can be used as an argument to maintain existing funding levels if the results are good, or for increased funding if the results show that customer expectations for services are higher than those provided.

The results of the customer satisfaction study can be plotted onto the matrix graph according to their performance rating and importance (see Figure 25.1). This will determine which services need improved performance and which services should be discontinued. Services falling in quadrant A are important services that are being well provided. Services in quadrant B have possibly too high a performance level for their importance. The information service staff can afford to pay less attention to these services.

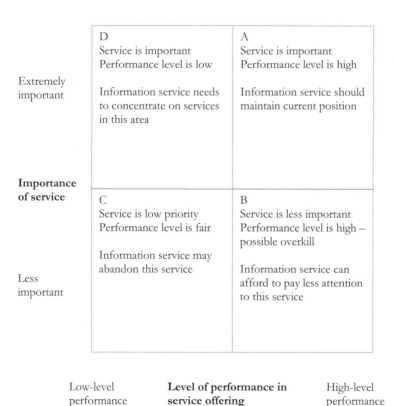

Figure 25.1 Matrix graph to determine services

Services that fall into quadrant C have only a low priority and performance is deemed as low. These services can be the first to be abandoned if resources are scaled back, in order to concentrate on those services in quadrant D. Quadrant D includes those services that are acknowledged to be important, but where the information service is performing badly. This is the area where resources need to be concentrated.

Push and pull marketing

The Internet, Web 2.0 and beyond applications and mobile communications have fundamentally shifted the business model from one of push to pull. Where advertising and other marketing content was once used to make potential customers aware of new products and services and potential employees aware of career opportunities, consumers and potential employees now pull this information themselves off the web and social networking tools.

Hayashi (2010: 16) in a review of Hagel et al.'s The Power of Pull observes the differences in push and pull mindsets. Characteristics of pull are collaboration, flexibility and bottom-up initiatives, with a concern for information flows that leverage internal and external resources to bring new products and services to market. Push, on the other hand, relies on centralized control and the hoarding of customer data.

The pull business model requires rethinking marketing and customer engagement strategies; utilizing crowdsourcing and social media to engage consumers in determining and designing their future product and service needs.

Exchange system analysis

Underlying the marketing concept is a system of exchange. The potential for exchange exists when two or more parties possess something of value that may be exchanged. This may be goods, services, money, a favour or goodwill. The simplest exchange is between two parties, and such an exchange may be seen in a public library where a customer exchanges money for access to a computer. Government departments may provide information services in exchange for monies received from rates and taxes. There is no direct exchange between the customer and the department as the rates or taxes that fund the service are paid to the revenue-collecting agency of the government in power. Information service staff also exchange their knowledge and expertise, time and energy in return for salaries and other fringe benefits from the employing organization.

Multiple-party exchanges occur when three or more parties are involved in exchanging something of value. In the case of the storytelling session example in the public library, the parents require that their children meet others of the same age, engage in a learning process and be happy. They are exchanging their time for social and educational processes for their children. They also require that the library staff are friendly, have security clearance for working with children, and that the library is clean and safe. In this instance they are exchanging monies paid in rates for services and the safety of their children. The children who attend want to have fun, maybe learn something and therefore obtain their parents' approval. They are exchanging their time for their parent's love and acceptance. The public library, in holding the storytelling sessions, wishes to promote the library as a fun place and as a lifelong institution for information and self-education. The storytelling session must meet all of these needs in the exchange process.

Competitive portfolio analysis

The product life cycle and the product portfolio matrix are used to make strategic marketing decisions as part of the competitive portfolio analysis. Whilst they are based upon products rather than services, their general concepts can be used to distinguish which services have potential for growth and which are at the end of their useful life. In addition to ensuring that the information services remain current, knowledge of the growth and decline of services affect tasks and activities, budget allocations, technology use, staff levels and the future direction of the information service.

PRODUCT LIFE CYCLE

The product life cycle is based upon the concept that products or services, like living things, have a finite life span. The basic proposition is that market growth and competitive characteristics change from one stage of the product life cycle to the next. These changes have important implications for marketing and planning strategies.

The introductory stage of an information service is usually marked by slow growth in use, heavy advertising and promotion. Staff must develop the service to suit customer needs, and much enthusiasm is needed. In the growth stage, there is an increase in use of the service that is still promoted quite heavily, and staff may have to fine-tune the service further to suit customer needs. The maturity stage is characterized by such services being seen as standard, a slowdown in growth and the spending of less time and money on advertising. In the decline stage, fewer people use the service, it is often superseded by other more appropriate services or deemed to have a low priority and plans are made to terminate it. Information technology shortens the life cycles of information services with many services quickly becoming obsolete as new applications emerge.

The life cycle concept has some drawbacks. Sometimes the stages in the life cycle cannot be clearly separated and may be difficult to distinguish. For information services, the maturity stage is the dominant stage and most services fall into this category. It is often difficult to predict when the next stage of the life cycle begins or how long it will last. Rejuvenation strategies may be used to stop the decline in the life cycle.

PRODUCT PORTFOLIO MATRIX

Whilst the product-service life cycle focuses upon growth dynamics, the product portfolio matrix emphasizes market growth (attractiveness) and relative competitive position (strength) of products or services. As information services become more competitive the significance of the product (service) portfolio matrix increases.

The most widely used matrix is that developed by the Boston Consulting Group. Known as the BCG portfolio matrix, it classifies each business unit according to its potential for growth and its relative competitive position. In the information service, work units may be substituted for business units. The BCG matrix classifies products, services or markets into four groups and uses circles, with areas proportional to the sales volumes for each, to give a visual image of an organization's current products. In information services, usage rates could be substituted for sales volumes to provide an image of its current services (see Figure 25.2).

According to the BCG matrix, products that have a high market share and high growth (stars) are roughly self-sufficient in terms of cash flow. They have the highest profit margins. These are the important information products or services and should be expanded if possible. Eventually the 'stars' become 'cash cows' as they reach the maturity stage of the product or service.

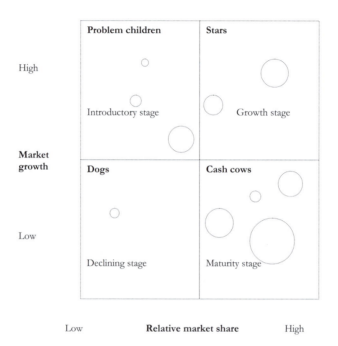

Figure 25.2 The Boston Consulting Group portfolio matrix

'Cash cows' are valuable assets; they have a high share in a low growth market. As products they generate more cash than is necessary to maintain a market position and should be protected at all costs. In information services, 'cash cows' would equate to the established products or services that have a high rate of usage and little competition. 'Cash cow' services maintain the value image of the information service and help to ensure its continued success and survival.

'Dogs' are products with low market share and slow growth. Their outlook for the future is usually bleak. 'Dogs' in information services comprise the information products or services that are declining in use and can often be superseded by new and better services. Alternatively, they are services that have failed to reach their potential.

'Problem children' are products with high growth potential but low market share. They require large net cash outflows if their market share is to be maintained or increased. If successful these products become the new 'stars' that in the future become 'cash cows'. If unsuccessful they become 'dogs'. In information services, 'problem children' usually equate to new services that require fairly large funding allocations for their establishment and promotion. They may also be services that do not perform well. There can be a variety of reasons for their poor performance; they may have been inadequately managed, or have had inappropriate marketing strategies applied to them.

The information service can determine its information products' and services' use and standing by displaying these on the product portfolio matrix. They should also be linked to the product or service life cycle and its associated marketing and planning strategies.

The BCG matrix is useful in that it recognizes that products and services have differential growth rates and emphasizes the relative share of market held by products and services in the same stage of growth.

Diversification and service rejuvenation

There comes a time when it appears that an information service can no longer expand its services in its basic market. Growth has stabilized through the market being saturated and, if growth is to continue, new services or markets must be sought. In addition to radical change associated with business re-engineering, the information service has four other options at this stage:

- To remain in a stable situation and to accept the status quo;
- To look for new markets;
- To diversify into new areas; or
- To provide new services to its existing markets.

Changes in consumer expectations and needs, competitor behaviour, technology or government policies may also influence the information service to adopt one of the above strategies. Rejuvenation strategies can overcome some lack of use of services, or stop the decline in the product life cycle. Lazer et al. (1984: 21–28) have identified four rejuvenation strategies:

- Recapturing strategies – attempts to revive the old market by concentrating on previous and existing customers without modifying the service, for example using promotions that focus attention on existing services;
- Redesigning strategies – marketing a modified version of a service that has been declining or has previously been abandoned. The original reasons for customer rejection may no longer prevail and it may be possible to rekindle interest among present customers, such as releasing a classic film in a new format or digitizing collections for ease of use;
- Recasting strategies – marketing a modified service to new customers, where the object is to capitalize on existing strengths and experience, although some adjustments to the service and market have to take place. For example recasting storytelling sessions in public libraries from being aimed at preschoolers to being used as bibliotherapy with the aged; and
- Refocusing strategies – marketing an abandoned or declining service to new customers. For example marketing an archive or local history collection to a local newspaper for

a series of articles on local identities or places of interest. Such a strategy may result in greater usage of the service by the general public.

The information service's decision to rejuvenate or diversify services should be based upon its resource requirements and capabilities. The potential of the rejuvenated or diversified services to contribute to the profile and value of the information service, the cost involved and predicted extended life span on a cost-benefit basis must also be assessed. In selecting the most appropriate strategy, the extent of service modification and degree of marketing effort needed to stimulate demand need to be evaluated.

Using competitive intelligence

Competitive intelligence supports management's role in managing customers, competition and change in order for the information service and its parent organization to remain competitive in its environment. It:

- Provides an early warning of developments in the external environment, in particular the industry, technology, economic or legislative change, that could adversely affect the business success of the organization;
- Identifies new product, process or collaborative opportunities to create new markets and business opportunities; and
- Creates an early understanding of the competitive environment so that surprises can be eliminated or their impact lessened by allowing a longer time and better opportunity to respond.

Competitive intelligence gathering is not spying or undertaking industrial espionage. Good intelligence gathering is based on information that can be obtained from sources through legal and ethical means. Published sources of competitive information include information on web pages, trade publications (electronic and hard copy), market analysts' reports, aerial photographs, job advertisements, government reports and filings. Other information can be obtained through networking, the continuous monitoring and surveillance of competitor actions for key events or changes, the following of leads, checking of sources and the surfacing of ideas. The art is in knowing what information is relevant, where to find it legally and how to convert it into intelligence for the basis of future management decisions and actions.

Competitive intelligence involves obtaining information about:

- Which competitors are vulnerable;
- Which competitors are likely to make moves that could endanger the organization's position in the market; and
- The requirements of the competitor's customers.

Breeding (2000) identified several problems that users of competitive intelligence (CI) have with the information that they receive from the process. These include shallowness, credibility, timeliness, focus, providers, quantity, and information sharing. Breeding goes on to say that:

if CI providers are consulted late in the decision-making process, shallow and poorly focused information is often the result. If sufficient time is not taken for analysis then the reports are often information-based rather than intelligence-based. In addition, the sheer quantity of information contained within the reports often overwhelms the reader.

Customer relationship management

Customer relationship management (CRM) has been variously described as a corporate philosophy, strategy or tool. The objective is to focus on and learn more about customers' needs and behaviours in order to develop stronger relationships with them. It helps organizations use ICT and people's knowledge to gain insight into the behaviours of customers and the value of those customers, and builds on the marketing strategies previously discussed. CRM brings together information about customers, sales, marketing effectiveness, responsiveness and market trends and enables the information service to:

- Provide a better customer service;
- Enable a better overall customer experience;
- Understand how customers define quality;
- Identify potential problems quickly, and correct service deficiencies before major problems occur;
- Make multi-service channels more efficient;
- Introduce and cross-sell information services and products more effectively;
- Simplify marketing and service processes;
- Discover more customers; and
- Increase customer use of information services and products.

To be beneficial, the CRM strategy needs to be thought through, so that it does not result in a flood of unorganized, ad hoc information. It should be given a business rather than an ICT focus. The information service needs to decide the business objective for needing insight into the behaviours of customers and the value of those customers, what kind of customer information is required, where the data and information are captured and stored, and how they will be used. Business objectives might be to improve customer support, to increase service performance or to improve the marketing effectiveness of the information service. The information service should also learn how to use the information to develop and prioritize tailored customer offerings.

Sources of information will be found in all of the multi-service channels, i.e. mobile, websites, portals, shop fronts, call centres, fax services, and include information collected in:

- Responses to advertising campaigns;
- Transactions data, e.g. multiple-channel analysis of fax, web, face-to-face, kiosk services, letters, phone;
- Account information;
- Customer service and support data, e.g. service requests, complaints, information returns; and
- Demographic data, e.g. usage habits.

It is important that a complete 360-degree picture of the customer or potential customer is built up, with everyone that interfaces with the customer being trained and confident in adding to, analysing and using the CRM data, as well as understanding its value and use as a business intelligence tool.

Conclusion

Marketing is often mistaken for promotion. Marketing includes consideration of promotion strategies but it is more closely aligned to strategic planning. Marketing strategies ensure viable market positions and programmes that meet the objectives of the parent organization, customer information needs and, ultimately, contribute to the success of the information service.

Marketing strategies and customer relationship management tools enable the information service to prioritize and make informed decisions about the continuation of existing services and proposals for new or extended services. These include the marketing management processes of:

- Research;
- Segmentation, targeting and positioning;
- Marketing mix;
- Implementation; and
- Control.

Exchange system analysis and competitive portfolio analysis are other tools that can be used to make informed decisions about service delivery. The bottom line considerations in the marketing decision-making process are the business fit, customer needs and long-term sustainability. Any proposals for new services or extending existing services to new markets must be in line with the information service's objectives. Sufficient expertise, human, technical and financial resources should be available to support such services.

Finally, if the three concurrent goals of marketing: customer satisfaction, market domination and increased profitability are to be achieved there has to be extensive organizational knowledge about competitors and customers. The use of competitive intelligence and customer relationship management software tools are two ways of achieving this.

References

Breeding, B. 2000. CI and KM convergence: A case study at Shell Services International. *Competitive Intelligence Review*, 11(4), 12–24.

Hayashi, A.M. 2010. Are you 'pushing' in a 'pull' world. *MIT Sloan Management Review*, spring, 51(3), 16–18.

Kotler, P. 1999. *Kotler on Marketing: How to Create, Win And Dominate Markets*. London: Simon & Schuster.

Kotler, P., FitzRoy, P. and Shaw, R. 1980. *Australian Marketing Management*. Sydney: Prentice Hall.

Ladhari, R. and Morales, M. 2008. Perceived service quality, perceived value and recommendation: A study among Canadian public library users. *Library Management*, 29(45), 352–366.

Lazer, W., Luqmani, M. and Quraeshi, Z. 1984. Product rejuvenation strategies. *Business Horizons*, November–December, 21–28.

McCarthy, E.J. 1971. *Basic Marketing: a Managerial Approach*, 4th edn. Homewood: Irwin.

Further reading

Adeyoyin, S.O. 2005. Strategic planning for marketing library services. *Library Management*, 26(8/9), 494–508.

Barber, P. and Wallace, L. 2010. *Building a Buzz: Libraries and Word-of-Mouth Marketing*. Chicago: American Library Association.

Calvert, P. and Pope, A. 2005. Telephone survey research for library managers. *Library Management*, 26(3), 139–152.

Cook, S. 2004. *Measuring Customer Service Effectiveness*. Aldershot: Ashgate.

Dowd, N., Evangeliste, M. and Silberman, J. 2010. *Bite-Sized Marketing: Realistic Solutions for The Overworked Librarian*. London: Facet Pub.

Hagel, J. III, Brown, J.S. and Davison, L. 2010. *The Power of Pull: How Small Moves, Smartly Made, Can Set Big Things in Motion*. New York: Basic Books.

Halligan, B. and Shah, D. 2010. *In-Bound Marketing: Get Found Using Google, Social Media, and Blogs*. Hoboken: Wiley.

Helinski, Z. 2008. *A Short-cut to Marketing the Library*. Oxford: Chandos.

McGrath, R.G. and MacMillan, I.C. 2009. How to rethink your business during uncertainty. *MIT Sloan Management Review*, 50(3), 25–30.

Murphy, C. 2005. *Competitive Intelligence: Gathering, Analysing and Putting it to Work*. Aldershot: Ashgate.

Phillips, L.S. 2009. *Cruise to Success: How to Steer Your Way Through the Murky Waters of Marketing Your Library*. Oxford: Chandos.

Singh, R. 2009. Does your library have a marketing culture? Implications for service providers. *Library Management*, 30(3), 117–137.

26 *Corporate Image and Communications*

The management of the information service's corporate image and how it delivers and sells its message about its value and contribution to stakeholders is extremely important. For if the perceptions of the information service differ from reality then:

- The quality and value of the information service may be underestimated;
- The information service may be missing part of its market share; and
- The wrong impression of the service could be projected.

Image analysis is closely related to the marketing issues discussed in the previous chapter. It assists in determining the information service's image to stakeholders such as sponsors, funding and governing bodies, and its customers. It also includes taking account of the image being portrayed in the market place and market space. As a result of the image analysis certain market strategies may need to be undertaken. In addition, the ability to create the right understanding of the value of the information service and manage the communication with the external environment is as important as managing the communication internally. For this is the essential mechanism of projecting and maintaining the importance and benefit of the organization in the eyes of key stakeholders.

Corporate communication is a two-way process. It involves:

- The capacity to understand the environment and market needs in which the information service operates, what is important, and to respond to the different needs and expectations of stakeholders, as well as to gain their input on services through consultation and engagement; and
- The need to promote and celebrate the achievements of the information service, to raise awareness and understanding of the role and responsibilities, implications and benefits of its activities, and to gain key stakeholders' commitment.

A communications plan provides a broad overview and identifies key initiatives for effective communication with stakeholders that include listening to and understanding stakeholder needs.

Stakeholder Analysis

Stakeholder analysis enables the information service to target its two-way communications to the right people. It ensures that the essential people are being listened to and that accurate messages are delivered to the appropriate people as part of the communications plan.

Stakeholders include:

- People who are important for championing the priorities of the information service;
- People important for securing commitment, funding and endorsement for its projects;
- People likely to be directly affected such as suppliers and customers;
- Potential customers and employees;
- Collaborators;
- Internal staff and management of the information service; and
- Other service providers in the sector.

Stakeholders can be further categorized into:

- Partners (with whom active partnering, joint promotion and close cooperation are required);
- Salient external stakeholders such as suppliers;
- Secondary intermediary/influencers such as the media;
- The corporate or local community for whom the information service provides services; and
- Internal stakeholders including staff and governing body.

Communications Plan

A communications plan is used to strategically plan and manage communications with key stakeholders. It has four objectives:

- Increase credibility, awareness and understanding of the roles, responsibilities and activities of the organization;
- Increase awareness and understanding within the organization and its governing body of the different needs and expectations of stakeholders and what is important to them;
- Strengthen consultation and engagement with key stakeholders to ensure that the organization is valued and adds value; and
- Promote and celebrate the achievements of the organization.

Figure 26.1 outlines the objectives in terms of awareness and understanding, consultation and engagement, and promotion and celebration.

The communications plan outlines the stakeholders, key communications messages and desired channel for conveying messages. Table 26.1 provides an extract of a communications plan for a newly integrated public library, local community and cultural centre.

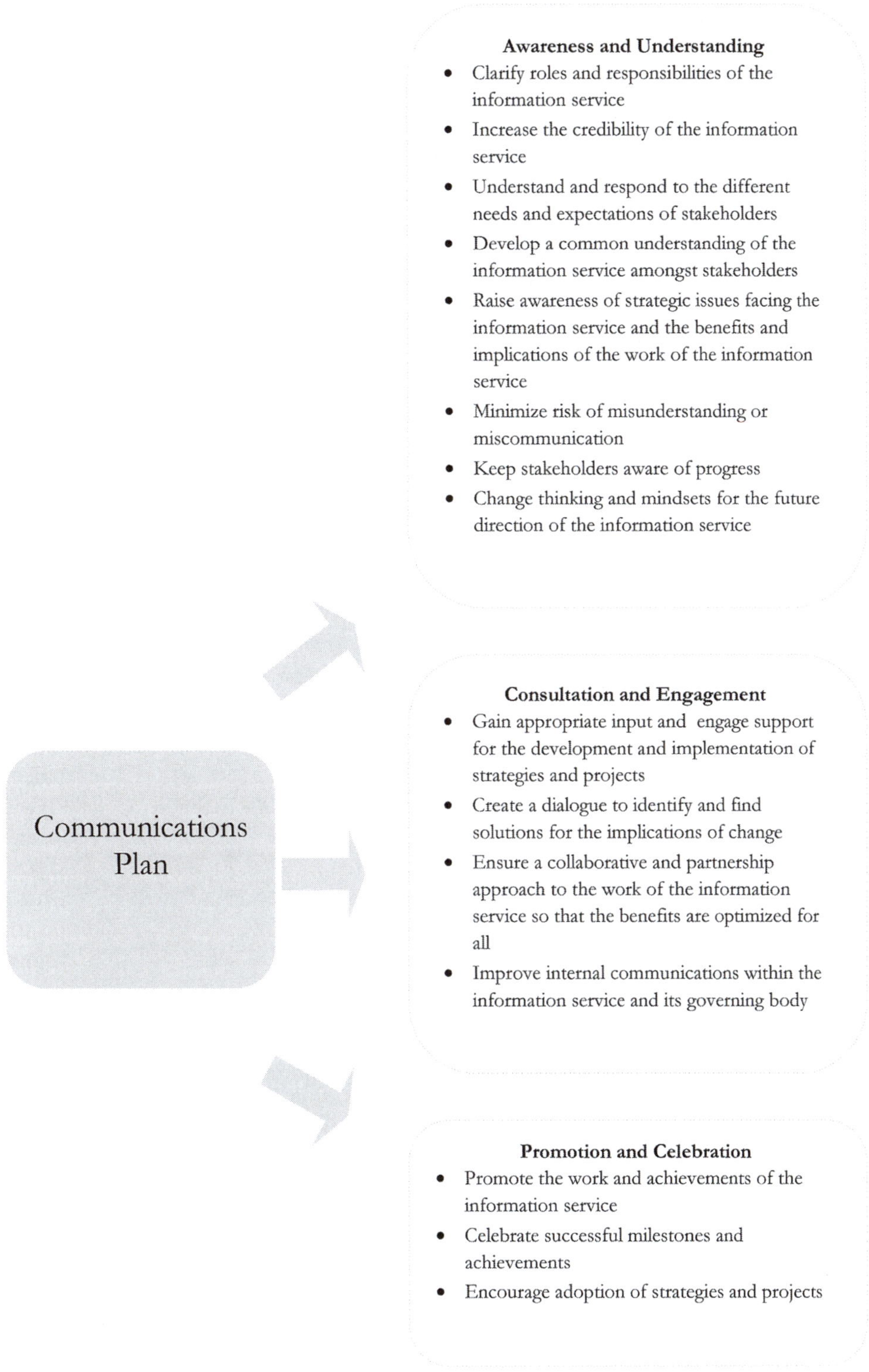

Awareness and Understanding
- Clarify roles and responsibilities of the information service
- Increase the credibility of the information service
- Understand and respond to the different needs and expectations of stakeholders
- Develop a common understanding of the information service amongst stakeholders
- Raise awareness of strategic issues facing the information service and the benefits and implications of the work of the information service
- Minimize risk of misunderstanding or miscommunication
- Keep stakeholders aware of progress
- Change thinking and mindsets for the future direction of the information service

Communications Plan

Consultation and Engagement
- Gain appropriate input and engage support for the development and implementation of strategies and projects
- Create a dialogue to identify and find solutions for the implications of change
- Ensure a collaborative and partnership approach to the work of the information service so that the benefits are optimized for all
- Improve internal communications within the information service and its governing body

Promotion and Celebration
- Promote the work and achievements of the information service
- Celebrate successful milestones and achievements
- Encourage adoption of strategies and projects

Figure 26.1 Objectives of a communications plan

Table 26.1 Extract of a communications plan for a newly integrated public library, local community and cultural centre

Stakeholder	Key communication message	Communication channels and tools
Local community	Raise awareness of the new focus and role of the integrated service centre, its objectives and priorities Manage different community expectations of the integrated service centre and develop a common understanding of its purpose and value Encourage input, buy-in and commitment to the new integrated service centre	Consultation and engagement with community in development of services and initiatives Presentations on the integrated service centre's new focus and role, objectives and priorities One-on-one dialogue between staff and customers Media releases and television coverage e-Newsletter and brochures Static and media displays Web presence, blogs, email and SMS Telephone 'on-hold' messages
Private sector sponsor of services	Raise awareness of the economic and social value of the service Emphasize the value of the sponsorship and synergy of sponsor's aims and objectives with those of the integrated service centre Seek out further opportunities for leveraging the sponsorship and collaboration in projects	Regular briefings and one-on-one meetings with sponsor Web presence Invitations to promotional events
Governing body	Raise awareness of the new focus and role, objectives and priorities. Promote the economic and social value of the new integrated service centre Encourage input, buy-in and commitment to the service Advocate for the strategic issues associated with the service	Regular briefings and one-on-one meetings Conversations with individual members Invitations to promotional events Briefing sheets e-Newsletter
Media	Raise awareness of focus and role, objectives and priorities of the new integrated service Promote the importance of the integrated service to the community Increase the profile and promote the brand image of the integrated service	Targeted articles in local newspapers Targeted messages when contacted by media Regular editorial pieces Media kit including key governing body and staff profiles, images, calendar of initiatives Briefing sheets, media releases e-Newsletter

Corporate identity, image and reputation

CORPORATE REPUTATION

Corporate reputation according to Siano et al. is built on trust and comprises attributes that are assigned to an organization as a result of its past actions. It is a valuable intangible asset to which no value is assigned in accounting standards, but which has immense value to the status, standing and market value of the organization. Siano et al. also state that corporate reputation is the result of a shared judgement socially expressed (degree of respect and credibility) by stakeholders, which is based on the actions of the firm and on its ability to satisfy expectations and create value for stakeholders (customers, investors, employees, suppliers, partners, etc.).

Corporate reputation is difficult to imitate or substitute. Therefore it is a source of competitive advantage and, where protected, can significantly add to the financial and market performance of an organization. Conversely any damage to corporate reputation can severely affect the organization's value, financial and market outcomes.

Corporate reputation is also a significant resource attractor. As well as fostering loyalty and trust by customers, shareholders and investors, it is a significant differentiator in the labour market. Organizations that have good corporate reputations are better able to attract and retain talented and creative people.

Siano et al. (2010: 73) have identified how an organization's unsatisfactory management of reputational risk can cause the loss of stakeholders' trust and loyalty resulting in negative impacts for the organization. These are:

- Customers – loss of market share, sales revenue, and/or customer loyalty (market risk) and the prevention of a premium price;
- Employees – loss of key human resources and the restriction of talent recruitment (human capital risks);
- Suppliers – deterioration of services and invoice conditions (e.g. deferred payments) offered by the supplier (contractual risk);
- Investors – difficulty in securing capital loans, increase in capital costs, reduction of share price (credit/financing risk); and
- Partners – loss of business opportunities and operational process management improvements, due to the opposition to partnerships (agreements and alliances), mergers and acquisitions.

It is therefore important to protect corporate reputation by reducing the probability of events that could be a significant cause of reputational risk and minimizing and potential harm caused to reputation through crisis communications.

IMAGE ANALYSIS

Image studies measure the perceptions that people hold about an information service. They determine what people respond to, which may not necessarily be the same as what the information service really does. All information services need a positive image in order to attract funds, talented people and clients. However, the image differs according to particular groups, their main interests and the way in which they perceive the services offered. Senior management may view an information service according to the strategic benefits to the organization and its return on investment; which may be different to the clients who are the recipients of the services.

The information service's customers and stakeholders can have multiple attitudes, some of which will be positive, whilst others may be negative. There may also be a different image being projected in the traditional market place to that of the market space. Different sectors of the information service's community or target audience should be surveyed in order to determine its image and profile in terms of service provision. This includes surveying stakeholders, clients and non-clients regarding their attitudes and awareness, interest and desires in an effort to ascertain a spectrum of responses within each dimension. This can be done by asking simple questions about familiarity with services and how favourably the services are received. The survey questionnaire should indicate the sector of the target audience to which the respondent belongs so that an analysis can be made of the views of different client groups. The responses can then be plotted on an image matrix.

In the image matrix (Figure 26.2) quadrants B, C and D indicate the need for some development in the information service's image about the services offered. To do this, the information services manager needs to have a mental picture of what the image should be. This should be based on the strategic direction of the information service. This is then compared with the existing image of the information service. The image gap is the difference between the desired and actual images.

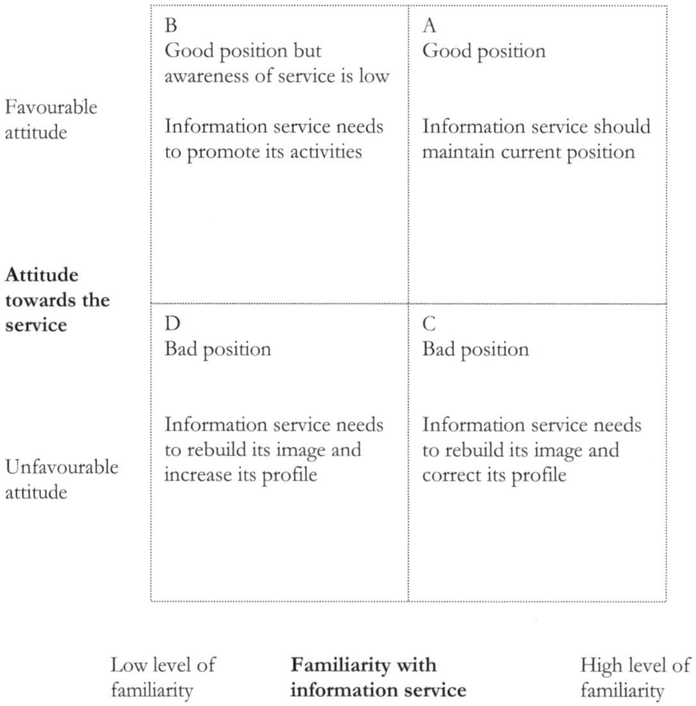

	B Good position but awareness of service is low Information service needs to promote its activities	A Good position Information service should maintain current position
Favourable attitude		
Attitude towards the service	D Bad position Information service needs to rebuild its image and increase its profile	C Bad position Information service needs to rebuild its image and correct its profile
Unfavourable attitude		

Low level of familiarity	**Familiarity with information service**	High level of familiarity

Figure 26.2 Matrix graph of information service's image

It may not be necessary to target all sectors of the target audience in trying to change the information service's image. The matrix graph identifies both those groups most in need of targeting and those groups for whom the information service's current image should be maintained in its present position. Changes in image may be to make the information service appear to be more efficient or relevant to corporate objectives, or more responsive to certain customer sectors. Alternatively, a sector of the client base may have unrealistic expectations of the types of services that should be offered. In which case this sector requires re-educating about the services that can be realistically delivered within the operational and budgetary framework. The reality–expectations gap is the difference between the level of an adequate service and the level of a service to meet real expectations.

PROJECTING THE CORPORATE IMAGE

An important aspect of the boundary-spanning role of the information services manager is to manage and project the corporate image. The corporate image is the set of beliefs, ideas and impressions that individuals have about an organization. Managing and projecting the corporate image comprises the following activities: identifying the target audience, determining the communication objectives, designing the message for both the market place and the market space, selecting the communication channels, allocating the budget, managing the process and measuring the results.

Target audience

The target audience consists of the people or organizations towards which the information service needs to project a favourable image. This is with the objective of building an awareness of the services provided and increasing market share, ensuring the continuation of funds or simply communicating the image of a valued and quality service. The target audience for the information service can include all or any of the following: current and prospective customers, senior management in the parent organization, other information services, suppliers, professional bodies and other stakeholders.

Determining the communication objectives

Having identified the target audience, it is important to establish how familiar the target audience is with all aspects of the information service as well as the value they place on it and the benefits they perceive arising out of it. This provides information for the image gap analysis, that is, the difference between the desired image that the information service wishes to project and the current image that it is projecting. It also identifies the gap between the target audience's awareness of the information services offered and those provided, and their perception of the quality of the information service as compared with that provided.

The next stage is to determine the required audience response in relation to the results of the image gap analysis. This may be to change the customers' attitude to the information service, to alert customers to services that could fill latent needs, to provide a better understanding of the benefits and opportunities presented by the information service, or to engender the understanding and support of senior management and other stakeholders to ensure that the information service continues to receive adequate financial support and conviction.

Designing the message and selecting the communication channels

The aim is to design a positive message about the benefits and service offerings of the information service. There are many different messages and communication channels that can be used, including:

- Web presence, social networking tools and other electronic media such as blogs, television, email or SMS messaging to those who wish to opt in to the service;
- Personal communication, e.g. word of mouth recommendations, personal representation;
- Print, e.g. a brochure or strategy report;
- Oral, e.g. a description of the services that the information service offers being played whilst a person is 'on hold' on the telephone;
- Multimedia or video presentation aimed at a particular audience; or
- Advertisement in the local press or public area.

The choice and mix of the messages and communication channels will depend upon the purpose of the message and the target audience in both the market place and market space. Increasingly the need is towards an integrated approach to delivering the message across all communication channels, rather than planning the use of each communication channel separately. Figure 26.3 provides examples of how different communications messages and channels can be used to support the objectives of the communications plan.

In addition to the above, the physical surroundings of the information service will also create an atmosphere or image. The choice of colours, type of office furniture, wall decorations, floor coverings and spaciousness of the surroundings will communicate an image about the information service.

The house style of the information service's reports, PowerPoint presentations and stationery also communicate a corporate image. The house style should also be continued and included in any multimedia presentations and other information published in electronic form.

Colour and style in the physical surroundings and in the house style are also important. Colour exerts a powerful influence on the mind and emotions. Each colour has a symbology of its own:

- Red – energy and vitality; orange – excitement, creativity, self-confidence;
- Yellow – clarity;
- Green – balance and harmony, wealth; and
- Blue – power.

The way in which information service staff interact with customers and stakeholders will also project an image of the information service. The image conveyed should be friendly, welcoming and helpful, although in some environments a more formal approach may be necessary. Interaction includes the way in which individuals answer the telephone,

		Advocacy/Cooperation
		Joint planning forums
	Support/Involvement	Collaborative decision-making
	One-on-one discussions	Focused dialogue
Awareness/Understanding	Promotion and sponsorship	Active partnering
	Consultation	Word of mouth
Seminars and presentations	Forums	
Static and media displays	Reference groups	
e-Newsletters and brochures	Consultative committees	
Television	Blogs	
Annual Report		
Strategic Plan		
Web presence		
Blogs		
Email and SMS		
Telephone 'on-hold' messages		

Figure 26.3 Examples of communications messages and channels that can be used to support the objectives of the Communications Plan

and the articulation and wording of the greeting on the telephone answering machine. If music (rather than information about the information service) is used for the 'on hold' interval whilst people are waiting on the telephone, the choice of music will influence the person's perception of the information service.

Allocating the budget

Not all of the strategies for managing and promoting the information service's image cost money. A proportion of the image promotion rests with the information services manager and their staff projecting a positive image and 'selling' the service in their interaction with customers, senior management and other stakeholders. Budget allocation for the more formal mechanisms of promoting the information service's image should be based upon the specific objectives, the tasks to be performed to achieve the objectives, and the costs of performing the tasks.

Managing the process

The wide range of communication tools and messages make it imperative that these be coordinated to ensure consistency. Coordination is also required to ensure that the correct message is sent through the correct medium and communication channel to reach the correct target audience.

Measuring results

To measure the results of the promotion, the information services manager will require feedback from the target audience. This will involve talking to or surveying the target audience about how they feel about the service, what level of awareness they have of the information service, and any other information that provides feedback on the communication objective.

Branding

Branding is associated with image building and service recognition, market positioning and creating a value proposition. A strong and well respected brand increases the trust a person has in purchasing a service. Customer satisfaction with the service further builds trust, a key component of a valuable brand, which in turn supports innovation. Innovative offerings further strengthen the brand, which then incites customers to try the new service offerings. Kotler (1999: 55) identifies the main steps in developing a strong brand:

- Develop the value proposition – by choosing a broad positioning, specific positioning, value positioning, or the total value proposition for the product or service; and
- Build the brand – by choosing a brand name, developing rich associations and promises for the brand name, and manage all the customers' brand contacts so that they meet or exceed the customers' expectations associated with the brand.

Kotler (1999: 58) identifies sources for positioning that can be used:

- Attribute positioning – using a special feature such as national library or archive service, or a website dedicated to a specific purpose or campaign;
- Benefits positioning – offering a specific benefit such as extended opening hours;
- Use/application positioning – the product or service is positioned as the best in a certain application such as a national collection of indigenous art, culture, literature, etc.;
- User positioning – the product or service is positioned in terms of a target user group such as a specific information service to scientists or a patient care information system for health professionals;
- Competitor positioning – the product or service suggests its superiority or difference from a competitor's product such as 'service is our strength' or 'the emotionally intelligent organization'; and
- Quality/price positioning – the product or service is positioned at a certain quality and price level such as free lending services in public libraries.

Walton (2008) expands on Kotler's views on developing a brand as per the following steps:

- Establish which customers are to be targeted by the brand and develop an understanding of their needs and values;
- Explore the competition to the service/product and identify what customers value from the competition, monitor competitor's progress and developments;
- Design a compelling brand that encompasses all activities;
- Achieve employees' buy in to the brand and give them the skills, tools and support to deliver the customer experience promised by the brand;
- Measure and monitor how the brand is received and how it is delivered; and
- Show a level of patience, react to competitors and further develop the brand informed by effective evaluation.

In addition to the above Walton (2008) points out that there will have to be 100 per cent commitment to the brand from all library staff if it is to succeed. A real danger exists that if the brand does not touch the entire library it will not achieve what is intended.

In recent years libraries are seeking to rebrand their service in line with changes to service delivery and so that current and potential users have a better understanding of their role and function in the virtual and global world. Rebranding is tied to marketing in that product and service rejuvenation, renewal, reinvention and repositioning are all interlinked. They are concerned with moving an existing service to a new position in the customer's eyes.

Brands are also linked to quality. If a person associates a brand with quality they are more likely to return to the service that the brand represents. In turn, an effective brand will demonstrate the value of the service to a prospective user in the market place or market space.

Brand names carry associations. Kotler (1999: 64) suggests that they should:

- Suggest something about the product or service's benefits;
- Suggest product or service qualities such as action or colour;
- Be easy to pronounce, recognize and remember;
- Be distinctive; and
- Should not carry poor meanings in other countries, languages and cultures.

Kotler (1999: 65) also indicates that brand names should communicate meaning in order to build a rich set of associations for the brand. These can include:

- The ability to trigger in the customer's mind certain attributes or qualities;
- The suggestion of benefits, not just features;
- Connoting values that the organization holds dear;
- Exhibiting personality traits; and
- Suggestions of the kinds of people who may buy or use the brand.

Brands can be strengthened or projected through the use of a symbol, slogan or colour.

Using Web 2.0 tools for effective communications

Web 2.0 tools are increasingly viewed as effective tools for both internal and external communications. Internally these tools are used for purposes of team building, product development and communicating across widely dispersed workgroups. Externally, consumers are readily embracing the Internet and social networking tools to obtain and share their views on product and service experiences online. Deciding whether to pursue an internal or external approach, or a hybrid model, is a business decision based on what best meets the organization's requirements.

With respect to internal use, Barnes and Barnes (2009) have made the following recommendations for social networking sites that are designed internally for an organization's business use:

- Logo – use of the logo on a site signifies an organization's brand and reputation. It is important to develop a policy regarding how logos should be used;
- Disclaimers – each site should carry a disclosure that states that the views of the individuals using the site are not the views of the organization;
- Anonymity – transparency is an effective way of fostering appropriate online behaviour and helps deter abuse. As such a community of creativity, shared knowledge and expertise should be cultivated and anonymity not be encouraged. Misuse of the site by posting inappropriate content should not be tolerated. In circumstances where the site is to be used to address sensitive subjects then a special area for anonymous postings should be established;
- Single sign-on – by using a single sign-on directory infrastructure for employees' site access a unique profile can be created that offers a level of security that can be customized to an individual's position and role in the organization;
- Conditions for use of the site – terms and conditions for the use of the site should be posted on the site, for example the use of a moderator and that personal attacks (cyber bullying), falsehoods and inaccuracies are disallowed;
- Intellectual property and copyright – should be observed;
- Privacy – user privacy should be respected and a privacy policy posted to the site;
- Guide – a guide that incorporates all aspects of the use of the site should be created and posted to the site;
- Training materials – training materials and other opportunities for individuals to educate themselves on the appropriate use of the site should be offered.

The external use of Web 2.0 tools presents both opportunities and potential threats, which managed correctly can be turned to competitive advantage. To help companies make the most out of these tools in their communications with their customers, Hoffman (2009) cites the LEAD (listen, experiment, apply, develop) roadmap that has been developed by the Sloan Centre for Internet Retailing. It encourages organizations to:

- Listen – having formal processes to monitor and analyse what customers are saying about it online and then use this information as an early warning system. Companies should also assume that the digital environment will change rapidly – so they must adapt accordingly. Rather than pushing messages at consumers, marketers should listen to them and think constantly about new ways to engage with them actively;

- Experiment – don't just monitor social media – engage customers using Web 2.0 and beyond tools. By using simple pilots such as creating an organizational profile on social networking sites, greater customer awareness and brand engagement can be achieved;
- Apply – apply the lessons learnt in the simple pilots. Optimize the organization's website so that it connects fluidly with online communities and social media sites. Make it simple for customers to link to you and tag your content, and find ways to make your site more relevant in social networking searches; and
- Develop – Web 2.0 and beyond tools should be a crucial part of an organization's marketing mix. It is critical that these be integrated into marketing programmes and managed as more than just another advertising channel.

Utilizing Web 2.0 and beyond tools for greater competitive advantage requires a different mindset. One that is much more in tune with listening to what customers are saying rather than pushing a marketing message. Leigh (2009: 18) outlines how strategic listening allows the organization to keep in touch with current trends and sudden shifts in the organization's environment:

- What customers say about us;
- Which channels customers use to reach us;
- What our customers are doing today;
- The basis of our competitive advantage;
- The skills or capabilities that make us unique; and
- Decisions or problems that affect your own areas of responsibility.

Crisis management and communications

Changes in communications processes and structures as the result of web and social media are a double-edged sword. On the one hand they have a pivotal role in online monitoring and dissemination of information in times of a crisis, whilst they can also create a crisis by increasing the corporate exposure to the world. When a major crisis hits an organization news of the disaster is communicated instantaneously and globally through the Internet and other social media applications. There is a certain amount of loss of control over communications as details of the crisis, both correct and incorrect, are spread through social networking channels and instant messaging with an immediate effect on the reputation of the organization.

Whilst news in traditional media is usually covered by professional journalists and in most times handled with relative objectivity, this may not be the case with citizen journalism. Mei et al. (2010: 145) outline four major Internet crises that have been developed by Hilse and Hoewner (1998) and which present situations that need to be managed by organizations:

- Reinforcing crisis – the Internet and other social media are used in addition to traditional media as a communications channel to present stakeholder opinions;
- Absurd crisis – this emerges from the Internet's and other social media's uncontrollable and diverse content which can result in absurd theories and opinions circulating online;

- Affecting crisis – this occurs when organizations are critically scrutinized virtually by stakeholders and they become the subject of public discussion with negative impact; and
- Competence crisis – this is characterized by a difference in competencies between the aggressor (stakeholder) and defender (organization). For example online experts that have the capability to damage an organization despite possessing limited resources.

In these situations an immediate response is of the essence and there is little time to produce and manage the required communications strategy. Consequently a tried and tested crisis management plan and a crisis communications plan that includes communications protocols for communicating with those affected and dealing with stakeholders and the media is needed. The crisis communications plan should include responses to a variety of potential circumstances that have been identified by the risk management process.

Forums and online discussions are an important part of the Internet, which bring people together on a common platform and help them exchange information, building social capital along the way. Citizen journalism also offers more choices in determining news sources and individuals now have multiple avenues to air their views. Organizations must now be prepared to harness the new media and be as transparent and accessible as possible on all media channels in order to retain stakeholder confidence and trust. They should also engage in active online news monitoring and environmental scanning.

Other Corporate Communications

ANNUAL REPORTS

At the end of the calendar or financial year, managers are often required to produce an annual report for the information service or provide copy for the parent organization's annual report. Sometimes they need to do both. The annual report serves several purposes. It is used:

- As a governance tool to provide an account of the information service's activities for the year; its achievements and to account for the use of resources;
- To achieve a better understanding of the value, issues, benefits and opportunities presented by the information service;
- As a source of information about the information service. It may contain information about key managerial positions, holders of such positions and their qualifications, an organizational chart, mission statement and corporate objectives;
- As a source of information for benchmarking or comparative purposes, as it often contains statistical data;
- To highlight current and future issues or problems that prevent the information service from carrying out all of its activities;
- To reconcile the use of funds, staff, etc. (inputs) against activities (outputs); and
- To measure the organization's level of performance.

Annual reports are posted to the Internet and therefore available to other related organizations. The format, design and presentation of the report either electronically or as hard copy are powerful mechanisms to project the information service's image. It will send a message about the organization's culture and its willingness to make an impressionable image on stakeholders. For example, some organizations' annual reports are flamboyant or sophisticated and considerable prestige is attached to their contents and format. Others are very formal. Some are very plain as they are only seen as an operational requirement to report on activities once a year.

SUBMISSIONS TO OUTSIDE BODIES

Managers and in-house specialists may also draft submissions to government bodies and other organizations relating to external issues. These submissions can be either reactive to external impacts on their services or functions, or proactive in terms of positioning the information service or its parent organization in the external environment. Examples are a submission on the implications of proposed changes to copyright legislation or a submission that suggests new ways of providing electronic services to the community.

The information services manager, or their staff, will usually draft the submission on behalf of the parent organization. In this case, the submission may need to be ratified by senior management before being forwarded to the appropriate body.

Conclusion

Managing the corporate image of the information service is a vital leadership role, as perceptions of service availability and delivery are as important as reality. The ability to communicate the desired message and obtain information from the external environment is of equal importance to the ability to communicate and obtain information within the organization.

Corporate communication is a two-way process. It involves:

- The capacity to understand the environment and stakeholders' needs, as well as to gain input on services through consultation and engagement; and
- Promotion and celebration of the role, responsibilities and achievements of the information service in order to increase awareness and gain key stakeholders' commitment.

Stakeholder analysis enables the information service to target its two-way communications to the right people. It ensures that the essential people are being listened to and that accurate messages are delivered to the appropriate people as part of the communications plan. The communications plan outlines the stakeholders, key communications messages and desired channel for conveying messages.

Image studies assist in identifying and managing perceptions of stakeholders. They measure the perceptions that people hold about an information service. They determine what people respond to. All information services need a positive image in order to attract funds, talented people and clients. However the truth is that the information service's customers and stakeholders may have both positive and negative images of the service. The reality–expectations gap is the difference between the level of an adequate service and the level of a service to meet real expectations.

The corporate image is the set of beliefs, ideas and impressions that individuals have about an organization. Managing and projecting the corporate image comprises the following activities: identifying the target audience, determining the communication objectives, designing the message for both the market place and the market space, selecting the communication channels, allocating the budget, managing the process and measuring the results.

Branding is associated with image building, market positioning and creating a value proposition. As brand images create association brand names should communicate meaning in order to build a rich set of associations for the brand.

References

Barnes, N.D. and Barnes, F.R. 2009. Equipping your organization for the social networking game. *Information Management*, November–December.

Hoffman, D.L. 2009. Managing beyond Web 2.0. *McKinsey & Co.*, July.

Kotler, P. 1999. *Kotler on Marketing: How to Create, Win and Dominate Markets*. London: Simon & Schuster.

Leigh, A. 2009. *The Secrets of Success in Management: 20 Ways to Survive and Thrive*. Harlow: Pearson.

Mei, J.S.A., Bansal, N. and Pang, A. 2010. New media: A new medium in escalating crises? *Corporate Communications: An International Journal*, 15(2), 143–155.

Siano, A., Kitchen, P.J. and Confetto, M.G. 2010. Financial resources and corporate reputation: Toward common management principles for managing corporate reputation. *Corporate Communications: An International Journal*, 15(1), 68–82.

Walton, G. 2008. Theory, research, and practice in library management 5: Branding. *Library Management*, 29(8/9), 770.

Further Reading

Carter-Silk, A. 2005. *Brand Protection: Understanding and Managing Threats to Your Brand*. Aldershot: Ashgate.

Charnock, E. 2010. *E-Habits: What You Must Do To Optimize Your Professional Digital Presence*. United States: McGraw-Hill Contemporary.

Cornelissen, J. 2008. *Corporate Communications: A Guide to Theory and Practice*. London: SAGE.

Hannington, T. 2004. *How to Measure and Manage Your Corporate Reputation*. Aldershot: Ashgate.

Hatch, M.J. and Schultz, M. 2008. *Taking Brand Initiative: How Companies Can Align Strategy, Culture and Identity Through Corporate Branding*. San Francisco: Jossey-Bass.

Honey, G. 2009. *A Short Guide to Reputation Risk*. Burlington: Gower.

Mulvey, P. 2008. *Reputation Really Matters: How to Guard Your Corporate Image, Featuring Insights from Leading Australian Chairmen and Senior Executives*. Carlton North: Monterey Press.

Thompson, M. and Whates, P. 2005. *Communicating Corporate Social Responsibility*. Aldershot: Ashgate.

27 *Ensuring Service Quality*

Service quality in the design and delivery of the service or product is an excellent way to differentiate an organization's offerings, sustain its long-term longevity and competitively position it as a leader in both the market place and market space. However, design and delivery are only part of the equation. Ensuring that the service support programmes encourage the continual use of the service or product is of equal importance, particularly in relation to customer retention. Maintaining market position is also essential and the information service should consistently offer high-quality, customer-focused services or products that meet current and emerging needs as well as presenting choices in the delivery of these services or products through a multi-channel approach. The emphasis in all of the above being on the customer, rather than on the products or services.

Information services are in the business of delivering services to customers who are already exposed to retail and business experiences that offer seamless, ongoing and personalized interactions in an always on, anywhere, anytime world. These retail and business experiences increase the expectations of what can be delivered. The World Wide Web and its successors in Web 2.0 and beyond have extended the market place to the market space where products and services are instantaneously and globally sourced and marketed, information sought and obtained and corporate reputations enhanced and destroyed.

In this connected world, information and communications technology (ICT) can be used to enhance the relationship between the information service and the customer. It can be used to deliver the multi-channel approach and new business advantages that enhance customer relationships through the use of value-added services.

An important component of quality is to get the steps in the value chain right first time, every time. If any part of the process falls down, then the remaining processes in the value chain will build upon an inferior product or service. Differentiation at the end of the value chain can be what distinguishes one product or service from another in terms of quality.

Customer expectations and perceptions of quality often vary as this is based upon an individual judgement, so the manager must understand both their customers' needs and perceptions of quality. There are also cultural and generation differences in customer expectations and perceptions of quality, which impact on the service delivery. Gaps in service delivery can influence the perception of the level of quality offered in products or services. Customers also judge quality according to certain determinants of service quality.

The bottom line of the customer-focused approach is valuing the customer. This service philosophy is reinforced through management fostering a culture that is service driven and oriented to customer needs. It is incumbent on senior management demonstrating a commitment to quality by making it a self-sustaining way of life within the organization.

Meeting customer expectations and perceptions

To be in tune with customer needs and what they value in terms of choice and type of service requires the ability to listen to customers, to identify their requirements, and to suggest improvements for current information products and services. Increasingly organizations are using social media to listen to their customer feedback.

It is also important to maintain a total service focus in meeting the needs of the customer as this can be important in creating a win-win situation. The total service focus makes it easier and more efficient for the customer as they have to deal with fewer organizations; it also lessens the interface between competitive entities and the customer, resulting in a significant business advantage to the service provider.

MEETING EXPECTATIONS OF QUALITY

Customer expectations and perceptions of quality often vary as this is based upon an individual judgement. Quality control is an internal process management issue, being an important part of the value chain. However, it is judged externally by customers and stakeholders who only see the outputs or outcomes of the internal processes. In information services service quality is often measured by high take-up, satisfaction levels, degree of accountability and choice, ease of finding information and responsiveness. From the perspective of the customer quality can be judged in terms of:

- Responsiveness and timeliness of service delivery – in responding to requests for information, files, helpdesk queries or the ordering and supply of new equipment;
- A well-designed product or service – that fits the purpose for use and is superior to others in the market place and market space;
- A product that does not break down or a service that is not suspended and which is easy to use;
- Convenience and accessibility of services;
- The customer's experience in relation to the physical or virtual environment;
- Pricing and value for money; and
- Courteous, knowledgeable and accurate staff who know their products and services.

Expectations and perceptions of quality can also differ from a cultural viewpoint. For example in:

- Germany, the dominant element of quality is an acceptance of standards;
- Japan, quality is measured through the pursuit of perfection;
- France, quality is viewed as luxury;
- The United States of America, quality means 'it works'; and
- Australia, quality is found in the relationship between the customer and the provider of the product or service.

As a consequence, the delivery of information services may subtly differ between countries in the quest for a quality service or information product.

Parasuraman et al. (1985) have developed a service-quality model that highlights the main requirements for delivering the expected service quality. The model identifies five gaps that cause unsuccessful service delivery:

- The gap between customer expectation and management perception. Management does not always perceive correctly what customers want or how customers judge the service components;
- The gap between management perception and service quality specification. Management might not set quality standards or very clear ones. They might be clear but unrealistic, or they might be clear and realistic but management might not be fully committed to enforcing this quality level;
- The gap between service quality specifications and service delivery. This includes factors such as poorly trained or under-resourced staff, low morale, equipment breakdown or drives for efficiency at the expense of customer satisfaction;
- The gap between service delivery and external communications. Through advertising or promotions, customer expectations may be driven to a higher level of service delivery than can actually be delivered; and
- The gap between the perceived service and expected service. This gap results when one or more of the previous gaps occurs.

Parasuraman et al. (1985) have also developed a list of the main determinants of service quality. These include:

- Access – the service is easy to obtain in convenient locations at convenient times with little waiting;
- Communication – the service is described accurately in the customer's language;
- Competence – the employees possess the required skill and knowledge;
- Courtesy – the employees are friendly, respectful and considerate;
- Credibility – the organization and employees are trustworthy and have the customer's best interests at heart;
- Reliability – the service is performed with consistency and accuracy;
- Responsiveness – the employees respond quickly and creatively to customers' requests and problems;
- Security – the service is free from danger, risk or doubt;
- Tangibles – the service tangibles correctly project the service quality; and
- Understanding or knowing the customer – the employees make an effort to understand the customer's needs and provide individual attention.

Whilst these determinants are fundamental to good service delivery, ICT has increased customer expectations for customized and seamless service delivery. Table 27.1 illustrates the differences in customer orientation and service delivery between traditional thinking organizations and organizations that successful embrace a customer-focused approach to meet a highly competitive environment.

Table 27.1 Differences in service delivery focus between traditional organizations and customer-focused organizations

Service delivery focus	Traditional organizations	Customer-focused organizations
Customer	Invisible	Core
Organization	Silo	Networked
Prioritization	Arm's length	Interdependent
Services	Silo, specific	Seamless, customer focused
Channels	Discrete	Optimized
Technologies	Interdependent	Inter-operable
Access experience	Channel specific	Consistent across channels
Service delivery collaboration	Silo and independent	Global, networked and ubiquitous

MEETING EXPECTATIONS OF CHOICE

Customers of information services vary, which is why having choices in service delivery is important. For example, the customers of a public library will be a cross-section of people who vary in age, interests, lifestyle and take-up of electronic media. They may include local business entities, schoolchildren and tertiary students, the aged and those whose primary language is not English. The staff and elected members of the local authority may also be customers of the library. To meet these divergent interests, multiple services and choices in delivery channels will be necessary.

The primary customers of an information service in a small entrepreneurial organization will be the management and employees of the organization. The information service will manage the information systems, keep the corporate records and deliver research services in such a manner so as to assist the management and employees maintain the parent organization's competitiveness. Increasingly in support of flexible working conditions there will be a demand for remote access to these services. A secondary role may be to disseminate information about the organization's products to the external customers of the entrepreneurial organization. Immediacy and creativity in service delivery will be important for the service to be responsive to the young and innovative corporate environment.

Ensuring service quality based on expectations of choice requires considerations of customer:

- Reach – numbers of people to be served and location, geographic distribution, reliability and ease of access to technology, e.g. broadband and the Internet;
- Demographics – language and cultural differences, stage of life that may influence the design and numbers of service channels offered;
- Frequency of interactions – average size and duration of interaction;
- Expectations – convenience and speed, customer habits, preferred mode of interaction; and
- Skills and capabilities – familiarity with services, ability to learn new ways of accessing services, need for personal support and advice.

MEETING EXPECTATIONS OF NEED

Within the market place and market space there are at least five generations of customers with distinct preferences and approaches to learning, acquiring and using information. Libraries and information services must tailor services and service delivery channels to appeal to the needs of each generation. This means designing a range of services that offer flexibility and choice. To do so requires a knowledge of how people with different needs communicate and use different channels, with the view to designing the channels to meet the preferred means of communication.

Designing a multi-channel service

In acknowledgment of the diversity of customer demographics, expectations and needs, organizations are embracing a multi-channel approach to service delivery. ICT offers opportunities to offer quality and customized services to customers through a channel of their choice, e.g. over the counter, over the phone (mobile or fixed), through websites. However, whilst potential savings in operational costs in the introduction of computer-generated solutions are appealing, these need to be countered with the reality that demand for these services and customer expectations of response times and ability to solve the problem is also increasing. Table 27.2 explains how different needs and activities can be met through various channel types.

Table 27.2   Meeting needs and activities through different channel types

Need	Activity	Channel type
I just want to do it	Transactions, order, renew, access information and opinions	Web services, mobile, email, social networking applications, SMS, key pad/touch phone transactions
How do I do it	Immediate assistance, quick answers	Social networking applications, call centres, frequently asked questions (FAQs), web services
Relate to me	In-depth discussion, knowledgeable advice	Over the counter service, phone calls

Most of the Generation X and Y population now use Web 2.0 and beyond social media applications delivered through mobile devices as their preferred or only means of communication. This always on, instantaneous, anywhere, anytime environment has implications for not just designing services to meet the small screen environment, but also in terms of responsiveness to enquiries and other peoples' opinions. For example, whilst email conventions consider a 24-hour response time as acceptable practice, short messaging service (SMS) conventions have expectations of an immediate response. Social media further moves this shortened timeframe into an even more complex environment as it invites universal and unsolicited comments and opinions on quality of services and customer expectations in a virtual environment.

Designing and implementing a multi-channel strategy is quite complex, so it is essential to have an effective change management plan to engage stakeholders and drive long-term behavioural changes. The costs and benefits of a multi-channel approach can be difficult to calculate, especially if there is seen to be duplication of services. The key is to design the strategy around well-defined customer groups and transaction volume and complexity, rather than the products or services. This means having a well-defined customer value proposition for each channel. For example, transactions that are high in complexity but low in volume often fall into the 'relate to me' category and should be designed in a manner where human judgement and professional expertise can be provided, i.e. utilizing on-call and on-site services. High-volume transactions with little complexity fall into the 'I just want to do it' category and can be delivered utilizing on-mobile and online services.

To maximize efficiencies and ensure consistency of a 'brand' it is essential to have a common channel management framework across functional groups. Different channel types offer different features and qualities and will attract different users, but it is important that there be a common experience across each channel. This includes common terminology, consistency in service offerings, and a common look and feel. It is also essential that back-end processes support front-end customer requirements, and that careful attention is paid to the integration points with internal systems.

Table 27.3 Channel types and their attributes

Channel service types	Attributes
On the move – Web 2.0 and beyond applications, SMS, MMS delivering video and graphics to mobile phones, PDAs, other portable devices	Anytime, anywhere, instantaneous, convenience, reach, two-way communications, habit
Online – websites, portals, virtual communities, email, social networking	Speed, 24x365, self-service, convenience, reach, cost efficiency, record keeping
On site – shopfronts, meetings	Security, high touch, habit, identification
On paper – letters, brochures, books, journals, facsimile	Convenience, record keeping, reach, tradition
On call – call centres, IVR, voice recognition	Convenience, two-way communication, reliability, cost, speed, self-service, habit
On air – radio, television, pay to view services	Speed, 24x365, reach

Customer Retention

An important strategy to achieve a high customer focus and retention rate is to concentrate on the 'Rs':

- Retention – the information service must develop services and strategies that keep the right customers from defecting to competitive services, or from ceasing to use services. This is sometimes known as 'stickiness'. Customers are retained through adding value and quality to standard products and services;
- Requirements – different customers have different requirements and the important part of service delivery is to tailor services to meet customer requirements;
- Refined segmentation – all information services have limited resources. By understanding customer preferences, a more refined segmentation can be achieved. This allows each segment to be serviced in a cost-effective manner that is valued by the customer;
- Reach – different customers need to be reached in different ways. These may be reflected by offering different channels for the delivery or dissemination of information;
- Response – customers will also respond differently to different messages about services and products. Messages should be tailored and disseminated in a manner that communicates the right message to the right customer group;
- Relationship – the relationship between the customer and the organization delivering the service is very important. Value can be added through having knowledgeable staff who make an effort to understand their customers' needs and provide individual attention;
- Receptiveness – to build a true commitment to customer service, the information service must be receptive to feedback from customers and stakeholders about its services and product. A culture should be fostered that regards complaints as valuable information about systems failures rather than as an annoyance. Formal suggestions and complaint procedures should be in place. The information service should also act on the feedback to improve quality or overcome shortfalls;
- Regular consultation – consultation with customers to establish their service and product requirements can be achieved through focus groups, surveys, interviews and forums; and
- Review – the customer approach to management requires a formal planning cycle of review, design, implementation and improvement of systems. Complaints and service difficulties should be regularly analysed to identify recurrent problems.

Maintaining service quality

Quality control should be a regular item on the agenda of executive management meetings. This serves two purposes. Commitment to service quality and the value that the organization places on quality goods and services is an important corporate governance and long-term sustainability issue. It also allows executive management to review progress and evaluate performance. The agenda items should cover customer and stakeholder relationships, a review of quality initiatives and programmes, identification of service delivery gaps and the strategies to close these, and a general evaluation of the current levels of service delivery.

In a continuously changing and challenging environment, the information services manager needs to set realistic expectations of the choice of channels and services at levels that can be achieved. In the drive for efficiency, there is often the temptation to put choices and quality specifications in second place. This is false economy.

Service quality is a driving force of sustainability as well as having a strong human dimension, such as how well users are served and treated by information staff. Therefore all employees should be given responsibility for quality and be made accountable for the quality of their individual output. They should be aware of the products, services and channels offered by the information service and its parent organization, and make an effort to understand their customers' needs. Individuals should be given training and skills development opportunities in quality management, measuring customer satisfaction and in any additional areas that may be needed to improve the service they deliver.

QUALITY AND THE VALUE CHAIN

An important component of quality is to get the steps in the product or service development process, the value chain, right first time every time. The value chain is the chain of activities through which the organization transforms its input resources such as raw data or incoming correspondence into products and services that it delivers to customers. Each of the activities in the chain should build upon the value of the previous activity and contribute to the value of the final product. If any part of the process falls down, then the remaining processes in the value chain will build upon an inferior product or service. This is wasteful of resources and time. It is the quality of the total service that matters: the end product or service, and the process that creates it.

The value chain not only leads to process improvement, it can also differentiate the product by offering an additional service. For example, raw data can be identified, captured and merged or manipulated in a series of steps to create a value-added information product. The product is marketed and can be further differentiated by offering it in either a value-added form, for example a choice of formats, or by providing consultancy expertise to assist the customer to make the most out of the value-added information product for their purposes. The area of differentiation can be what distinguishes the product from another in terms of quality of service.

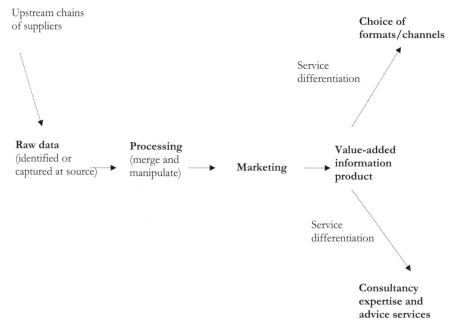

Figure 27.1 The value chain for a value-added information product

BUILDING CONTINUOUS IMPROVEMENT

Continuous improvement, 'kaizen' in Japanese, is a crucial part of both quality-based and time-based competitive strategies. The idea is that organizations can continuously improve the cost, quality and timeliness of their output by making small, incremental process improvements to achieve total service quality.

The important feature is that the improvement is built into the organization as a continuous process to which all staff have a sense of ownership and pride in improvements, rather than it being subject to a one-off improvement strategy that is initiated through a consultant.

CUSTOMER SERVICE CHARTERS

Customer service charters articulate the organization's commitment to the customer. They contain statements on:

- Who the customers are;
- The value that the organization places on the customer – 'the customer is the most important person to the information service';
- The relationship between the customer and the information service and how they may be expected to be treated – 'we will respect our customers' requirements of confidentiality and privacy';
- The level of service that can be expected – 'we will respond to enquiries within 10 minutes of receipt of the enquiry'; and
- The value placed on employees and their roles in customer service – 'we respect our employees and encourage them to make creative suggestions that will further improve our service'.

Understanding customer value is important in increasing service quality. In thinking insightfully about what customers are really worth, resources can be focused on attracting and keeping the right customers. Customer value can be based on the:

- Total value of their relationship with the information service;
- Potential value of their relationship;
- Profitability of their relationship;
- Insights they can provide to the information service; and
- Influence they wield over other customers.

Service quality feedback

Barwise and Meehan (2010: 65) observed that 'although many organizations make an effort to track customer satisfaction, in most cases the idea is to increase positive satisfaction as opposed to understanding and addressing the sources of customer dissatisfaction'. User surveys are useful in ascertaining customer perceptions and experiences on service quality and areas of customer dissatisfaction during times of change. They measure these perceptions and expectations over time, map their shifting priorities and preferences, and subsequently inform policy review and service development. At the same time, they provide valuable supporting evidence when making a case for increased resourcing, or communicating the rationale for changes in library services to users (Self and Hiller 2002).

Hiller (2002) cites the approach used by the University of Washington where, similar to other libraries and information services, changing patterns in usage and user expectations have led to an increased emphasis on providing electronic access to full-text resources. In this instance, survey data not only informed this change in policy, but also helped to make the case for associated changes in resource allocation and to communicate the implications of the change in policy to users.

Customer service support and relationship management

ACTING ON FEEDBACK

The delivery of a service or product to the customer is only the beginning of sustaining the relationship between the information service and the customer. What is of equal importance is the customer relationship management, service experience and service support that encourages the continual use of the service or product. Barwise and Meehan (2010) also observed that 'customer dissatisfaction is rarely caused by the actions of a single department; directly or indirectly, many parts of the business play a role ... The challenge is to ensure that the company somehow hears the message and communicates it to those with the power to act – and that those managers then uncover and act on the cause of the problem ... To make it happen, managers need unfiltered and unfettered information about the actual customer experience – both positive and negative – and ideas about how to improve the offering and the company's internal processes. The acid test is to probe whether front-line employees – those with day-to-day contact with customers – are comfortable presenting the CEO and other top managers with candid suggestions for improvements or other "inconvenient truths"'.

SERVICE SUPPORT

The customers' level of satisfaction or dissatisfaction with the quality and efficiency of the service experience and support will influence their perception of the product or service and either sustain or end their use of the service. Service support can be found in:

- Delivery or installation – services and products should be delivered or installed at the customer's convenience. The delivery should be fast, on time and efficiently handled. For example, the opening hours for libraries and information services should be decided with customer convenience in mind, requests for paper records files to be brought up should be executed promptly, and an upgrade of software should be installed quickly out of hours or at a time when there is not an urgent deadline being met by the operator of the personal computer;
- After-sales service – follow-up should be made with the customer regarding the service or product. After-sales service should be efficient and attentive. For example, public library staff may enquire about the success of material selected for a school project

when the child returns the material, special library staff may follow up on a request for information to ensure that no additional information is required, or the helpdesk may ring a customer to ensure that no more trouble is being experience with a laptop or other portable access device;

- Complaints handling – complaints should be acted upon immediately and managed in a positive manner. Complaints should also be logged so that trends can be identified and rectified before there is an adverse effect on the product or service. This is particularly important when dealing with software;
- Warranty repairs – repairs under warranty should be efficiently handled; and
- Account management – the invoicing of accounts should be efficient and accurate. Account payment processes should be designed to be convenient for the customer. The account management aspect of service delivery is potentially the highest risk area in customer service. Inaccurate accounting systems that result in goods or services not being charged, undercharged or payments outstanding have a negative impact upon the cash flow and profitability of the organization. Conversely, the continued overcharging for products or services will sour customer relationships with the organization.

Conclusion

The customer approach to management is service driven, quality oriented and centred on the customer rather than the product or service. It gives high priority to the efficiency and effectiveness of product and service delivery to the customers and aims to retain their custom through excellence in customer service support and in meeting emerging needs. Service quality in the design and delivery of the service or product is an excellent way to differentiate an organization's offerings, sustain its long-term longevity and competitively position it as a leader in both the market place and market space.

Meeting customer expectations can be categorized into three areas that can be used to distinguish the information service from its competitors:

- Service quality which is often measured by high take-up, satisfaction levels, degree of accountability and choice, ease of finding information and responsiveness;
- Offering choices in service delivery that requires considerations of customer reach, demographics, frequency of interactions, expectations and skills and capabilities;
- Knowing how people with different needs communicate and use different channels.

A high customer focus and retention rate can be achieved through:

- Concentrating on retaining customers;
- Tailoring services to meet customer requirements;
- Understanding customer preferences;
- Offering different channels for the delivery or dissemination of information;
- Tailoring and disseminating messages in a manner that communicates the right message to the right customer group;
- Having knowledgeable staff who make an effort to understand their customers' needs and provide individual attention;

- Being receptive to feedback from customers and stakeholders about the information service's services and product;
- Undertaking regular consultation with customers to establish their service and product requirements; and
- Having a formal planning cycle of review, design, implementation and improvement of systems.

The delivery of a service or product to the customer is only the beginning of sustaining the relationship between the information service and the customer. What is of equal importance is the customer relationship management, service experience and service support that encourages the continual use of the service or product. It is also important to get the steps right first time, building continuous improvement and quickly rectifying the situation when things occasionally do go wrong.

References

Barwise, P. and Meehan, S. 2010. Is your company as customer-focused as you think? *MT Sloan Management Review*, spring, 63–68.

Hiller, S. 2002. Listening to our library users: 2001 survey results. *Library Directions*, winter, 2–4.

Parasuraman, A., Zeithaml, V.A. and Berry, L.L. 1985. A conceptual model of service quality and its implications for future research. *Journal of Marketing*, fall, 41–50.

Self, I. and Hiller, S. 2002. A decade of users surveys: Utilizing and assessing a standard assessment tool to measure library performance at the University Of Virginia and University Of Washington. Paper to 4th Northumbria International Conference on Performance Measurement in Libraries and Information Services, Washington, DC, 12–16 August 2001.

Further reading

Calvert, P. and Pope, A. 2005. Telephone survey research for library managers. *Library Management*, 26(3), 139–152.

Cook, S. 2004. *Measuring Customer Service Effectiveness*. Aldershot: Ashgate.

Gower Handbook of Quality Management. 2003. 2nd edn. Aldershot: Gower.

Hernon, P. and Altman, E. 1996. *Service Quality in Academic Libraries*. Norwood: Ablex.

Hill, N. and Alexander, J. 2000. *Handbook of Customer Satisfaction and Loyalty Measurement*, 2nd edn. Aldershot: Gower.

Johannsen, C.G. 2004. Managing fee-based public library services: Values and practices. *Library Management*, 25(6/7), 307–315.

Robinson, M. 2008. Digital nature and digital nurture: Libraries, learning and the digital native. *Library Management*, 29(1/2), 67–76.

Rowley, J. 2005. Making sense of the quality maze: Perspectives for public and academic libraries. *Library Management*, 26(8/9), 508–519.

Singh, R. 2009. Does your library have a marketing culture? Implications for service providers. *Library Management*, 30(3), 117–137.

PART VI

Success and Sustainability

Figure PVI.1 Success and sustainability

Management Influences in a Changing Landscape
1. Managing in an uncertain world
2. Strategic influences

Strategy and Planning
3. Strategic Planning – positioning for a sustainable future
4. Attracting and retaining the best people in challenging times
5. Ensuring value for money and enabling a cost-sustainable future
6. Knowledge and information management – a key to survival
7. Strategic technology and asset management – a smarter approach

Leadership and Innovation
8. Leadership
9. Utilizing a values driven culture for sustainability
10. Innovation and creativity
11. Engaging change in positioning for the future
12. Group dynamics and team building
13. Effective negotiation and conflict management
14. Managing the political arena
15. Policy-making
16. Personal communications and networking
17. Managing yourself and others in challenging times

Governance and Social Responsibility
18. Ensuring good corporate governance
19. Using authority and influence
20. Encouraging transparency
21. Managing for sustainability
22. Managing risk
23. Sustaining trust and continued operations
24. Evaluating benefits and performance

Customer and Market Focus
25. Competitive strategies
26. Corporate image and communications
27. Ensuring service quality

Success and Sustainability
28. Bringing it all together

28 *Bringing it all Together*

This chapter is the sixth and final part of the book. It brings together all of the leadership skills and expertise that have been described in the previous five parts. That is, those which are the very essence of management and leadership to make things happen and sustain organizations in an unpredictable, challenging and changing world. It summarizes critical content that is included within each part of the book which is based on a framework of excellence that delivers a smarter and more sustainable approach to the future. The following outlines the framework which forms the structure of the first five parts of the book as well as illustrating the five critical success factors for success and sustainability in challenging and complex times:

- Understanding and managing the influences in the changing landscape;
- Strategy and planning;
- Leadership and innovation;
- Governance and social responsibility; and
- Customer and market focus.

Management influences in a changing landscape

Dynamic environments that are indicative of uncertainty, complexity and change call for strong leadership and excellent strategy to withstand these challenging circumstances. For example globalization presents both threats and opportunities. The Global Financial Crisis illustrated how an economic crisis in one country can rapidly affect the general economic health of another country and the sector in which information services operate. Conversely, technology opens up a new world of collaboration, enabling organizations to deliver 24x365 services by forming global networks or alliances with like-minded organizations. However the will to make this happen, be successful and sustain the required energy to effect change is dependent on strong leadership, passion and vision to:

- Drive organizational and personal renewal, including the capacity to think differently;
- Build the organizational capacity to create and embrace change;
- Take a global perspective and understand different cultures;
- Look for new and innovative ways of exploiting technology for business outcomes in an always on, anywhere, anytime environment;
- Identify, value and enable people who share their talents, intelligence and knowledge;

- Create creative environments that support and actively encourage people to bring their creative ideas to work;
- Instil a culture that is based on ethics and integrity;
- Have the foresight and capacity to endure and confront financial, environmental, technological and workforce challenges; and
- Build productive relationships with stakeholders, listening to other viewpoints as well as understanding and meeting their needs.

Strategy and planning

Positioning an organization for a sustainable future and to achieve its vision is built upon developing and implementing strategy, rigorous planning and consideration of alternatives; especially those that are conceivable (may be likely), possible (likely) and probable (most likely). It is undertaken with the view that organizations will need the capacity and capability to endure challenges and that external influences will also shape decisions about the future. However, the putting of energy and resources into the initial stages of the planning process is likely to reap significant dividends in the future, over leaving the future to chance or reacting to situations as they arise. In doing so, the information services manager should choose strategies and initiate new activities and services such that they meet their strategic business needs and achieve the right outcomes and the right approach.

Acknowledging the interrelationships between assets that impinge on the information service and strategic planning, the information services manager assumes an integrated approach to planning human, financial, knowledge and information, technology and strategic assets. They advise on how each of these assets can be leveraged to embrace the future through the strategic and effective use of information and ICT, how they can capitalize on other business environment changes, and offer added value and excellence in integrating services. As an enabler of business change, the manager needs to have flexibility and agility in order to respond to changing market and environmental conditions.

Planning for resources and implementing strategies that lead to the most desirable future should be undertaken with the objectives of:

- Attracting and retaining the best people in challenging times;
- Ensuring value for money and enabling a cost-sustainable future;
- Maximizing the use of information and knowledge within the organization; and
- Being smarter about the use of assets as strategic business tools to create the advantageous edge.

This is with the view to:

- Maintaining or enhancing financial viability and maximizing the return on investment for the organization;
- Developing business capacity and capability as well as supporting strategic alliances;
- Enhancing the organization's competitiveness and improving customer relationships and service delivery;

- Making decisions and managing programmes and projects in a manner that maximizes benefits to the natural environment, humans, their cultures and communities;
- Delivering positive, tangible results and outcomes;
- Providing a point of differentiation in the market place or market space; and
- Reducing future resource requirements by prolonging assets' lives or strengthening their disposal value.

To achieve all of the above the information services manager must be a visionary, providing leadership in the use of information and ICT to enhance and add value to the business of the organization. Their role includes:

- Developing their people to maximize their talents;
- Shifting mindsets as to what is possible in the future;
- Extracting the best value for money out of their resources;
- Providing new frameworks that use knowledge and information to rethink service strategies;
- Blending information and ICT strategy with the business strategy; and
- Creating strategic changes at a competitive pace.

Through appropriate strategies the information services manager is in a position to deliver internal efficiencies by driving down their own costs, increasing the quality and personalization of customer quality services, and helping to achieve costs savings elsewhere. A key role is to develop and implement strategies for the management of knowledge, information and data in many different formats and media to support a variety of business needs, within the organization and externally to clients and other stakeholders. Highly developed communication and interpersonal skills are needed in order to make judgements, listen, evaluate, reason, reassure, appease and provide advice to peers, customers, their bosses and stakeholders in this environment.

Leadership and innovation

The digitally connected and intelligent world requires a far-sighted leadership approach that creates a sense of passion, energy and excitement on the information service's future role in a virtual world. It requires the information services manager to understand and share this understanding about the rapidly changing environment, as well as to lead and enable shifts in thinking about how services might be delivered. For this reason change, innovation and leadership are inextricably linked.

Strong leadership, interpersonal and change management skills and an understanding of a values-driven culture are critical in developing innovative mindsets to envisage future scenarios and surviving changing and challenging environments. These skills come to the forefront when:

- Repositioning information services in the global and digital economy, especially in negotiating and implementing 24x365 services that are supported through global collaboration;

- Sustaining the impetus of organizations in times of global financial constraint as well as managing the impact of other sudden and strategic changes that emanate from the external environment;
- Providing the required amount of flexibility and innovation in managing multiple generational needs in the workplace; and
- Understanding and leading across different cultures and subcultures during the process of integrating services.

Creating a values-driven culture is an essential leadership role in times when attracting and sustaining talented people are critical to the success of the information service. It underpins trust and confidence that can sustain the reputation of the information service as an employer of choice, a quality service provider and corporate entity demonstrating ethics, good governance, accountability and social responsibility in challenging times.

Leadership and innovation are also significant change agents that can be used to future-proof information services so that they can be flexible and embrace an organizational philosophy and culture in keeping with the demands of the digital and virtual world as well as reposition information services in the global and digital economy and society.

In addition to the above-mentioned skills, there is a strong correlation between the other leadership roles of understanding and managing group dynamics and building teams, effectively negotiating conflict, managing the political arena, ensuring effective policy making, communications and networking, and managing and sustaining the well-being of individuals who work in the information service. This is particularly evident when:

- Employing people from different backgrounds for multinational collaborative service delivery;
- Bringing together and reconciling the functions, cultures and professional expertise of differing services;
- Ensuring the correct cultural fit when implementing more customer self-service programmes; and
- Adopting new ways of collaboration and communication using social media tools to enhance the organization's competitive advantage and sharing of knowledge and information.

Leaders both create and make sense of change by engaging people to accept that change is the norm. In addition, they must also make sense of the environment that is changing around them including emerging customer needs, making connections and applying intuition. In growing the skills and competencies of their people, they:

- Demonstrate high expectations for others and drive people to do their best through the implementation of a values-driven culture;
- Give people important activities and sufficient autonomy to exercise their own judgement in undertaking the tasks;
- Manage diversity and understand differences in values that arise from different generational work styles, backgrounds and people with specialist skills and expertise;
- Understand individual drivers to succeed and motivate accordingly;

- Enable and empower people to share knowledge and information which are considered key roles in creating and innovative environment; and,
- Monitor their results and provide continuous feedback on how they perceive their performance and if they have met their needs and expectations.

As a service organization, the information service's culture needs to espouse values of excellence and quality services leading to high levels of customer satisfaction. Collaboration and teamwork are important in excelling in service delivery, so values of belonging, openness, learning, trust, pride, respect for others' ideas and mutual support are also important. Likewise, integrity and ethical behaviour should also be included as values, particularly where the information service is dealing with commercially sensitive or personal information. Creating a sense of usefulness, belonging and achievement is also important in building corporate rapport and commitment. Strategies that can be put in place at the organizational level and at the individual level to increase motivation include having an atmosphere that welcomes and embraces challenges and is open and sharing of good and bad news, and encouraging an environment of respect for each other.

In a busy and competitive environment it is sometimes tempting to focus on the demands of the job and overlook personal life needs and those of others. Managing and sustaining the well-being of people is also important from a duty of care perspective as well as being strongly connected to motivation and productivity factors. This also includes managing one's personal well-being and career.

With an increased focus on building stakeholder relationships, information services managers need to be politically active and engage in business issues inside their organization and with external stakeholders. This includes being politically astute, championing relationships and being able to recognize, control and manage organizational politics for the benefit of the information service. Political behaviour can also drive change and move forward items on the corporate agenda. The information services manager must understand what the parent organization wants and position the information service to provide creative solutions to important problems.

In the policy-making role, the information services manager ensures that the policies are well planned and thought out in terms of strategic timing, costs, the issues at stake, the values and attitudes within the organization, and those of their clients and stakeholders. Their policies are future oriented and anticipate new demands and developments.

Finally personal communications, networking, effective negotiating and conflict management are four necessary interpersonal skills that are important for leadership and which are required to sustain the equilibrium of an organization in rapidly changing and complex environments. For example these skills are used in:

- Discovering underlying concerns and anxieties when sustaining the well-being of individuals in challenging circumstances;
- Selling new ideas, concepts and business applications and clearly communicating important corporate messages across organizational boundaries and with all levels of people internal and external to the organization;
- Strategically engaging and influencing stakeholders in high level contract management or negotiations on aspects relating to the future sustainability of the organization;

- Managing and minimizing the effect of change-induced conflict on individuals and within groups; and
- Implementing decisions brought about by change and transformation.

Governance and social responsibility

Increased public scrutiny and the increasing involvement of the private sector in public sector service delivery are two matters driving the governance agenda. A third and important factor is that of trust in an organization; a factor that is either enhanced or damaged by its corporate reputation. In turn, trust is predicated on the organization having good governance, transparency in decision making, accountability for actions and performance, effective security for its information and people, and a focus on sustainability and social responsibility.

Good governance practices and structures are also beneficial in changing environments where there are far-reaching consequences in actions, and where ensuring ethics and integrity, making the right choices and correctly attending to and dealing with dilemmas are paramount in decision making. Good corporate governance structures can help to ensure the correct and sensitive resolution of such complex problems and proposals to ensure sustainability and value for today and the future.

In terms of trust and good governance, the important features by which stakeholders judge organizations include:

- Good corporate citizenship and achievement of excellence;
- The manner in which they encourage sustainable development, demonstrate social leadership and corporate ethics;
- Having high-quality practices and processes in place not just for today, but for the future;
- Having a visible code of conduct;
- Utilizing independent audit practices;
- Maintaining a sound system for risk oversight and management;
- Managing for sustainability and for different forms of capital; and
- Regularly reviewing the effectiveness of their systems, structures, policies, practices and procedures.

A further test of good governance is to avoid the abuse of power in organizations. This requires a good understanding of the various power sources and how to use these effectively to persuade and influence ethical outcomes rather than to control people and situations for personal gain.

Trust and a good corporate reputation are reliant on having transparency in decision-making which is assisted by open and participative decision making, as well as having a culture where managers at all levels are approachable and open to suggestions and ideas. Openness and participation in decision making are also important in resolving differences in changing environments. Openness includes encouraging candid and honest discussion leading up to when decisions are taken so that a comprehensive view is formed of the issues being considered, as well as frankness about the decision itself. Participative decision making also allows people to bring multiple views, aspects and knowledge of the subject area, as well as different abilities, interests and skills that will result in better decisions.

In keeping with the need for balance and concerns for the future and coexisting with corporate governance and social responsibility principles is the concept of sustainability. Sustainability is important in order to:

- Tolerate and survive in continuously changing and challenging circumstances;
- Support and ensure the long-term maintenance of well-being of the organization and the natural world; and
- Maintain or enhance an organization's financial viability whilst maximizing benefits to the natural environment, humans and their cultures and communities.

In addition to sustaining the tangible environment of water facilities and ecosystems, sustainability can also be applied to intangible items such as education and skills development or developing and sustaining trust and respect in people. Sustainability needs to be incorporated into core values, taken into account in ensuring effective governance and decision making within the information service, and considered and incorporated into information service delivery. Sustainability is contingent on there being a whole-of-life approach, balancing short-term needs with society's and the organization's long-term interests, as well as ensuring that resources are used no faster than they are renewed.

Planning for adversity is the key to overcoming adversity. Risk management strategies identify the potential for adversity and put appropriate actions in place to manage the event or situation according to the probability of it occurring. In turbulent and changing environments, a major role of the manager is to anticipate, assess, manage and minimize risk. Information services have traditionally considered information security to be one of the foundation elements of risk management. Whilst information security is still a major risk management issue, there are other risk issues that should also be managed. These include theft of intellectual property rights, personal safety and occupational health and safety risks, loss of public reputation, image or regard for corporate citizenship, and loss of key staff and expertise; all of which require other risk management strategies.

Sustaining stakeholder trust and corporate reputation as well as continued operations in organizations is reliant on there being well-established risk identification and management practices in place, embedded security systems and procedures to protect information and transactions, people and physical assets, sound strategies to maintain and quickly recover from incidents through tried and tested business continuity and disaster recovery plans and finally compliance with legal and regulatory frameworks for the protection of intellectual property, personal and commercial information.

Good governance also includes ensuring that the information service is delivering valuable and valued products and services to its customers and stakeholders commensurate with the investment that is being made and that its performance is measured and evaluated. Value is linked to both performance and the exchange factor and can be illustrated in many different ways:

- Public value concepts that include service quality, service efficiency, trust and outcomes;

- Service value exemplified by low price, whatever the consumer wants in a product, the quality that the consumer gets for the price paid, and what the consumer gets for what he/she gives;
- Acquisition value received in acquiring the service, transaction value that relates to pleasure felt in getting a good deal, in-use value derived from using the service, and redemption value which is the residual benefits received at the time of termination; and
- Perceived service value represented by emotional response to the service, quality received from the service, reputation of the service, what is given as well as monetary and non-monetary price.

Customer and market focus

Having:

- Identified and managed the challenges and strategic influences in the changing landscape;
- Shaped the right corporate environment through leadership such that it values creativity, supports innovation and positively engages in transformational change; and
- Ensured that proper governance is in place and that sustainability and other social responsibilities are met;

the information services manager has one further challenge: how to sustain a customer and market focus in order to excel in service delivery.

The bottom line for this is in meeting customer needs. It involves ensuring that the correct competitive strategies are in place to identify needs, that the correct image is projected to attract and continue to attract and retain potential and existing customers, and to ensure that service quality prevails at the initial point of contact and in all subsequent dealings.

There are many ways in which strategic marketing and competitive strategies can be used to identify the right path in transforming the organization to harness the unpredictable world ahead, to meet the challenges of the increasingly sophisticated needs of clients and to excel in service delivery. The challenge is to choose and meld the different strategies to get the right mix, to optimize competitive intelligence to advantage, to know when to diversify or rejuvenate services, and to learn more about customers' needs and behaviours.

The management of the organization's image and messages to the external environment is as important as managing the internal communications. In their boundary-spanning role, the information services manager needs to ensure that the impressions and beliefs that individuals have about the information service are the correct ones. The image of the information service is conveyed electronically in its web presence and use of social media, orally through personal communication, physically through its built environment including the physical design and colours used, and by other communication mechanisms such as reports that may be in electronic or hard copy form.

The design and delivery of the service or product to the customer is only the beginning of the relationship between the organization and the customer. Loyalty and customer retention are also key components to the service's competitive edge. Trust, choice of service channel, complaints handling, accounts management and service backup that supports the continual use of the product or service and commitment to the customer must be of equal quality.

Conclusion

The focus for leading and sustaining information services in an unpredictable, challenging and changing world is to create a vision, plan strategies and inspire others to work towards the achievement of that vision. Along the way, challenges will be encountered, often on a daily basis that will require creative thinking and innovation to resolve them. This thinking will also be needed to continually invent the next advantage and ensure financial, environmental and physical sustainability. It will involve using bright ideas, information, knowledge, creativity and innovation to do so. In addition the leader must build individual and organizational capability to create, engage and sustain change and protect their corporate reputation in the global media environment.

Governance, benefits realization, social responsibility and having an outcomes focus are high on today's list of stakeholder expectations for a sustainable future offering social and economic value and return on investment. Information services exist to add value to the business of the organization, whether this is to ensure survival and success through continuously inventing new advantages in a global environment or to build social capital in a local community. The bottom line in adding value is transparency, sustainability, relevance and quality such that the service excels in the mind of the customer.

Index